Debt Restructuring: an alternative to insolvency proceedings

Jurisdictional comparisons **2015**

Founding Editor:
Jacques Henrot, De Pardieu Brocas Maffei

General Editors:
Ole Borch & Lars Lindencrone Petersen, Bech-Bruun
Alessandro Varrenti, CBA Studio Legale e Tributario

THOMSON REUTERS

Founding Editor
Jacques Henrot, De Pardieu Brocas Maffei

General Editors
Ole Borch & Lars Lindencrone Petersen, Bech-Bruun
Alessandro Varrenti, CBA Studio Legale e Tributario

Commercial Director
Katie Burrington

Commissioning Editor
Emily Kyriacou

Publishing Assistant
Nicola Pender

Design and Production
Dawn McGovern

Editing and Typesetting
Forewords

Published in December 2014 by European Lawyer Reference Series,
Friars House, 160 Blackfriars Road, London SE1 8EZ
part of Thomson Reuters (Professional) UK Limited
(Registered in England & Wales, Company No 1679046.
Registered Office and address for service:
Aldgate House, 33 Aldgate High Street, London EC3N 1DL)

A CIP catalogue record for this book is available from the British Library.

ISBN: 9780414028623

Contents

Foreword Alessandro Varrenti, CBA Studio Legale e Tributario
Lars Lindencrone Petersen & Ole Borch, Bech-Bruun v

Obituary: Jacques Henrot, 1952–2014 Antoine Maffei
De Pardieu Brocas Maffei vii

Belgium Glenn Hansen, LAGA 1

Canada Justin R Fogarty, Jason Dutrizac & Pavle Masic, Justin R Fogarty Professional Corporation 19

Denmark Ole Borch & Lars Lindencrone Petersen, Bech-Bruun 41

Finland Pekka Jaatinen, Salla Suominen & Anna-Kaisa Remes
Castrén & Snellman Attorneys Ltd 53

France Joanna Gumpelson, De Pardieu Brocas Maffei 71

Germany Florian Gantenberg, LADM Liesegang Aymans Decker Mittelstaedt & Partner Rechtsanwälte Wirtschaftsprüfer Steuerberater 91

Hong Kong Philip Gilligan, Richard Hudson & Tiffany Cheung, Deacons 109

Italy Alessandro Varrenti & Daniela Sorgato, CBA Studio Legale e Tributario 123

Malta Nicolai Vella Falzon, Fenech & Fenech Advocates 143

The Netherlands Lucas Kortmann & Niels Pannevis, RESOR N.V. 159

Norway Jon Skjørshammer, Advokatfirmaet Selmer DA 177

Poland Marcin Olechowski & Borys D Sawicki, Sołtysiński Kawecki & Szlęzak 191

Portugal Mafalda Barreto & Carlos Soares, Gómez-Acebo & Pombo (Portugal) 209

Romania Bogdan Bibicu, Kinstellar 231

Singapore Sim Kwan Kiat, Rajah & Tann Singapore LLP 251

Spain Fermín Garbayo & Julio Pernas Ramírez
Gómez-Acebo & Pombo Abogados 263

Sweden Odd Swarting, Mathias Winge & Nina Baecklund, Setterwalls 299

Turkey Gokben Erdem Dirican & Erdem Atilla, Pekin & Pekin 315

UK Jatinder Bains, Paul Keddie & Simon Beale, Macfarlanes 327

United States J William Boone, Michael A Dunn & Doroteya N Wozniak
James-Bates-Brannan-Groover-LLP 343

Contact details 365

Foreword

Alessandro Varrenti, CBA Studio Legale e Tributario
Lars Lindencrone Petersen & Ole Borch, Bech-Bruun

The financial crisis that started quite dramatically with the bankruptcy of Lehman Brothers in 2008 has been historic. Several other financial crises have been confined to a certain area and have been quite short lived, but the one that started in 2008 has affected all parts of the world to varying degrees and is not fully over more than eight years later. It has not only stress-tested undertakings and banks; it has also tested countries and the entire way of perceiving the financial structure.

At the outset of the financial crisis, quick fixes were desperately needed. During this phase, countries had to ensure that their banking sectors did not collapse. At the same time, undertakings in crisis had to be handled, and in this process an adjustment of the set of rules available to such situations has taken place. These sets of rules could be said to have many similarities, but if you look at the finer details quite a few differences become apparent. As an experienced specialist in the law of your own country, you have not been able to rely on your experience and judgement to figure out how a specific situation would be handled in another country.

With this in mind, Thomson Reuters asked one of the grand old men of the world of insolvency, Jacques Henrot of De Pardieu Brocas Maffei, to lead a project in which Jacques and we – Alessandro Varrenti of CBA Studio Legale e Tributario (Milan), and Lars Lindencrone Petersen and Ole Borch of Bech-Bruun (Copenhagen) – were to work together to prepare an easily accessible yet detailed presentation of the sets of rules applicable to restructuring and distressed undertakings in a number of countries.

Jacques undertook the task and was a driving force during the start-up phase, and this in spite of the fact that Jacques was quite seriously ill. Sadly, Jacques passed away in the summer of 2014 and thus before the book was ready for publication. We are dedicating this book to Jacques in honour of his huge effort with the book and a number of similar projects in the past.

We hope that the readers of the book will share our enthusiasm about the finished project and that the book may contribute to understanding and decision-making in cross-border situations where there is a need to understand at least the fundamental principles of the rules of other countries.

We would like to extend our thanks to all the contributors for their efforts on the project. The dialogues we have had with the contributors from the various countries in the course of the project have confirmed the great expertise involved as well as the high level of enthusiasm for the project. We would also like to take this opportunity to express our respect – which is perhaps done too rarely – for the legislators of the many countries. Restructuring legislation is quite difficult to draft as it requires decisions according to which some parties are to relinquish rights to the advantage of other parties for the sake of the bigger picture. It is the quality of such legislation which determines the possibilities of obtaining successful restructuring – and this applies to both in-court and out-of-court restructuring. Out-of-court restructuring will typically reflect the possibilities of the in-court options, as the rights holders will hardly be willing to contribute to an out-of-court solution providing them with a poorer result than an in-court process. At the same time, in-court restructuring is presumably still the very last thing you want. Professor Lawrence P King was quoted as saying that the American rules on restructuring, Chapter 11, may well be effective, but for him they are the equivalent of using a hammer to put out the fire in your hair. We believe that this book will demonstrate that it is not quite that bad, either in the US or in other countries.

1 November 2014

Jacques Henrot

1952–2014

As mentioned in the foreword, this book has been dedicated to our partner, Jacques Henrot. No better tribute could be paid to Jacques, who, until the very end of his long fight to overcome his terminal illness, remained strongly committed to ensuring the publication of what he considered to be a significant contribution to the merging into a single instrument an analysis and description of the complexities of a wide variety of policy and legal issues in the work-out and restructuring areas across many countries.

Our partner and friend Jacques passed away late this summer. Above all, Jacques was a very talented lawyer, dedicated to the long tradition of the practice of law rooted in the old cultural values of a general practitioner and combining those values with a remarkable understanding of the diversity of legal cultures and conceptual diversities between the continental legal tradition and the common law approach. Often those skills turned out to be material in bridging the gap between the different cultures prevailing in those different environments, paving the way to consensual approaches to resolving difficulties in complex matters.

He combined unequalled expertise in the property area with a unique practice in the insolvency sector and a strong understanding of the needs of the financial services industry. Moral integrity and compliance with the highest ethical standards were among his key attributes.

Jacques had a great sense of human relationships, and was most sensitive to the needs and aspirations of our younger professionals. He was a great team builder, dedicated to training his assistants and colleagues towards excellence and achievement of the highest standards in the practice of law.

In the pursuit of that goal, he has paved the way to the emergence of a younger generation to develop a practice based on those values.

Before leaving us, Jacques has passed the torch on to that new generation sharing those values to continue to develop a practice rooted in the high standards he advocated.

For those accomplishments he will be forever remembered.

Antoine Maffei
De Pardieu Brocas Maffei

Belgium

LAGA Glenn Hansen

1. WHAT COURT-MONITORED RESTRUCTURING PRE-INSOLVENCY PROCEEDINGS OR SCHEMES HAVE BEEN DEVISED BY THE LAW OF YOUR COUNTRY TO LIMIT VALUE DESTRUCTION FOR FAILING BUSINESS ENTITIES?

In 2009, Belgium passed the law on the continuity of enterprises (LCE). This law provides several non-court and court-monitored proceedings to ensure that enterprises are not lost but can be saved in case of (financial) difficulties.

The non-court monitored proceedings consist of the appointment of an out-of-court mediator, a court trustee or an out-of-court settlement with at least two creditors. As these proceedings are not court-monitored, they will not be treated further in this chapter.

The court-monitored proceedings are called gateways and consist of

1. the judicial reorganisation through settlement;
2. the judicial reorganisation through collective agreement with all creditors; and
3. the judicial reorganisation through transfer of the enterprise.

1.1 What is the objective of the proceedings?

The objective of the law, and thus of all proceedings, is to make sure that enterprises in distress can be saved as much as possible. Special attention is given to saving as many jobs as possible.

The judicial reorganisation through settlement tries to achieve this objective by giving the enterprise the opportunity to make a settlement with at least two creditors. This has to ensure that the enterprise can deal with certain important difficulties first.

The judicial reorganisation through collective agreement tries to save the business by proposing a reorganisation plan to all creditors. Such plan will provide the measures to be taken, potential haircuts for the creditors, etc.

The judicial reorganisation through transfer of the enterprise tries to save the business and the employment by enabling the enterprise to sell all or some of its assets or activities.

1.2 Do all kinds of businesses qualify?

Article 3 of the LCE states that the law is applicable to all businesses that are merchants as mentioned in Article 1 of the Belgian Commercial Code, agriculturalists, agriculture and civil companies with a commercial form as identified in the Belgian Company Code.

However, certain businesses are explicitly excluded. Article 4 of the LCE sets out that the law is not applicable to civil companies with a commercial form exercising a liberal profession (eg law offices, architects, doctors).

Furthermore, the law does not apply to financial institutions, insurance companies, management companies for collective investments and similar institutions, financial holdings and mixed financial holdings.

1.3 What are the necessary approvals?

It is recommended that the board of directors takes an official decision to go into an LCE court-monitored procedure.

1.4 What is the procedure?

Any of the three possible gateways of judicial reorganisation has to be initiated with a petition that must be deposited at the registry of the Commercial Court of the jurisdiction where the corporate seat is situated. The petition must, under penalty of inadmissibility, contain the following information and be accompanied by the following documents:

- an explanation of the events on which the request for initiating an LCE procedure is based, which shows that the continuity of the company is immediately or eventually threatened;
- an indication of the goal(s) for which the LCE procedure is requested;
- an electronic address at which the enterprise can be reached for as long as the procedure is in effect and from which the enterprise can communicate the receipt of the received messages/communications (these first three requirements can be incorporated into the petition);
- the two most recent (deposited) financial statements and the financial statement of the last accounting year that has not yet been deposited;
- bookkeeping documents (eg balance sheet) clearly showing the assets and liabilities and the profit-and-loss account, which may not be older than three months and which must be drafted under the supervision of an auditor, an external accountant, an external certified bookkeeper or an external certified tax specialist;
- an estimate of the income and expenses for at least the duration of the requested period of suspension, drafted with the assistance of an external accountant; an external certified bookkeeper or an auditor;
- a complete list of the allowed or alleged creditors in suspension, mentioning the name, address, amount of claim and capacity of extraordinary creditor, if applicable;
- proof that the employees or their representation have been duly informed or consulted;
- a list of measures and propositions to restore the solvency, to possibly start a social plan and to meet the claims of the creditors; and
- any other document that is deemed to strengthen the petition.

The petition must be signed either by the enterprise itself or by a lawyer representing it.

Immediately after the filing of the petition, the court will appoint a delegated judge, who will report on the admissibility and the merits of the petition.

As long as the court has not rendered a judgment on the petition, the enterprise cannot be declared bankrupt, nor can it be wound up. In addition, the creditors cannot proceed with the realisation/execution of their claims.

The only criterion to open the procedure is whether the continuity of the enterprise is threatened, immediately or over time. The fact that the company meets the criteria for bankruptcy does not exclude the company from the LCE procedure.

In case it concerns a legal entity, the criterion of threatened continuity is assumed to be met when the losses have reduced the net assets to less than half of the registered capital.

In principle, the court will treat the petition within 14 days after filing. The company will then be heard in the consultation room (*Raadkamer*). This means that the hearing is private, and no other parties are allowed (except for parties that would already intervene in the procedure).

The court has to decide on the opening of the procedure within eight days after the hearing. When the criterion seems to be met, the court will open the judicial reorganisation procedure and determine the period of suspension (this is the period during which creditors cannot execute their rights on the goods of the enterprise and the enterprise cannot be declared bankrupt or be wound up).

The judgment that opens the procedure is publicly announced within five days in the Belgian Official Gazette. The enterprise has to notify its creditors individually of this judgment within 14 days of the judgment. Proof of such notification has to be added to the court file.

How the procedure continues depends on the chosen gateway.

In a judicial reorganisation through amicable agreement, the enterprise has to try to negotiate an agreement with at least two of its creditors under the supervision of the delegated judge and, if necessary, with the assistance of a court's trustee (*gerechtsmandataris*). When an agreement is reached, the court confirms the agreement and closes the LCE proceedings. The agreement is published in the Official Gazette.

If the enterprise chooses the gateway of judicial reorganisation through collective agreement, the procedure is more extensive.

Within 14 days after the opening judgment, the enterprise has to communicate to each creditor the amount of the claim that is outstanding and has to mention any privileges or mortgages.

If the creditor does not agree with the communicated amount, he can challenge it in front of the court that has opened the LCE procedure. It is the creditor's responsibility to be vigilant about this. If he does not challenge an error concerning his claim no later than 15 days before the hearing on which the collective agreement is voted upon, he will only be able to vote for the amount that is in the books of the enterprise.

During the procedure, the enterprise will draft a reorganisation plan, which it will present to the creditors to be voted upon.

A reorganisation plan contains the measures that the enterprise will undertake in order to enhance its financial position/solvency so that the continuity is again guaranteed. Such plan consists of two parts. The first (descriptive) part describes the current state of the enterprise, explaining the reasons why the continuity of the company is threatened and why the LCE procedure is needed. The second (decisive) part specifies the actions the enterprise will take to meet the claims of its creditors. This part contains the repayment terms, the decrease/abatement of the claims in suspension, of the capital and of the interests due that are agreed upon. However, a payment proposal must not be less than 15 per cent of the amount of the claim.

The content of this plan is not limited to those measures. Other measures to enhance the solvency position of the debtor can be included as well (eg sale of assets or reduction of employees).

The reorganisation plan also has to take into account specific rights of specific groups of creditors. The LCE makes a distinction between extraordinary creditors and ordinary creditors (see question 1.11 for more information).

The execution duration of the plan cannot take longer than five years as of the date of homologation of the plan.

As soon as the reorganisation plan is final, it has to be deposited at the court's registry. The creditors will then receive a notification that they can consult the reorganisation plan. The court will also set the date for the voting.

For the plan to be approved, the majority of creditors that attend the voting hearing and which represent at least half of the claims have to vote in favour of the plan. Extraordinary creditors will have to agree explicitly if their claim is affected by the reorganisation plan.

After such voting, the court has to homologate the reorganisation plan. Homologation can only be refused when the enterprise did not comply with the formalities of the procedure or when the public order is violated.

If the plan is homologated, the court will close the procedure and will publish the judgment in the Belgian Official Gazette.

Homologation makes the plan binding on all creditors involved.

As previously explained, the enterprise can also choose for the gateway of judicial reorganisation through transfer.

Although the procedure to open this gateway is the same as for the two other gateways, the main difference is that this gateway can also be forced upon the enterprise.

The opening of the procedure can also be granted upon writ of summons by the public prosecutor (*procureur des konings*), by a creditor or by anyone else who has an interest in acquiring the whole or a part of the concerned enterprise, but only in the following situations:

- the debtor is in state of bankruptcy without having requested an LCE procedure;
- the court refuses the opening of a procedure of judicial reorganisation because one of the conditions is not fulfilled, the court orders the early

termination of the procedure or the court repeals the reorganisation plan under the collective agreement;
- the creditors collectively do not approve the proposed reorganisation plan; or
- the court refuses the homologation of the reorganisation plan.

The court appoints a court's trustee, who has to organise and realise the sale/transfer for and on behalf of the enterprise. Either the court itself decides whether the company has to be transferred as a whole or only partially, or it decides that the court's trustee must take that decision.

The court's decision will be published in the Belgian Official Gazette. The advantage of such publication is that it might attract more candidate-buyers.

The court's trustee investigates which (useful) assets the enterprise has, he looks for interesting offers from candidate-buyers and he collects those offers. He chooses whether he organises a private sale (*verkoop uit de hand*) or a public sale through auction (*openbare verkoop*), and determines the procedure to be followed by the candidate-buyers to make an offer and the time limits to be respected.

An offer can only be taken into consideration if the price offered is at least as much as the value of the forced realisation of the assets in case of bankruptcy or liquidation.

Since all candidate-buyers must be treated equally, the court's trustee prefers the offer of the highest bidder. If there are similar offers regarding price, the court's trustee chooses the offer that guarantees employment through a social agreement with the employees.

The advantage of this procedure over a normal sale of an activity is that certain rules related to the rights of employees do not apply. This makes it possible for candidate-buyers to 'cherry-pick' the employees that they need without taking over other personnel.

If there is real estate up for sale, the court's trustee has to appoint a public notary, who will be responsible for the sale of that real estate.

When the court's trustee accepts an offer, he drafts a sales contract, which must be submitted to the court for final consent. If the court accepts this sales contract, it will grant the court's trustee permission to continue the sale within the boundaries of the approved contract.

Through the sale, the rights of creditors automatically transfer to the sales price. The court's trustee will distribute the available funds from the sale of moveable goods to the creditors, while the public notary does the same with the proceeds from the sale of real estate.

If the court's trustee judges that all useful activities have been transferred, he will ask the court to release him from his task and to close the procedure.

The decision to close the procedure will also release the buyers from any other obligation towards the enterprise than the ones stipulated in the sales contract.

The rest of the company will then go bankrupt or into liquidation.

1.5 Is there recourse against the opening judgment?

Only appeal is possible against the opening judgment; opposition is not allowed.

The appeal has to be lodged by petition within 8 days after notification of the judgment. Only if the judgment denies the procedure does the appeal have a suspending effect.

1.6 What are the substantive tests/definitions?

As explained, the only test to be allowed to open an LCE procedure is whether or not the continuity of the enterprise is threatened.

1.7 What is the role of a court-appointed agent?

In every LCE procedure a delegated judge (*gedelegeerd rechter*) will be appointed. This delegated judge is the main point of contact at the court. He will investigate the company and advise on the admissibility and progress of the procedure.

As already pointed out, in gateway 3 (judicial reorganisation through transfer of the activity of the enterprise) a court's trustee is appointed to organise and realise the transfer of the activity/assets.

1.8 What protection is there from creditors?

The opening of an LCE procedure creates a period of suspension (*periode van opschorting*). The duration of the suspension depends on the chosen gateway/is determined case-by-case by the court. In the first instance, a maximum period of six months can be requested. However, this term can be prolonged in certain circumstances. During the term of suspension, the creditors cannot execute their (payable) claims: no realisation of movable or immovable assets can be done or continued, and seizure is not possible. Neither can the debtor be declared bankrupt or be wound up during the term of suspension.

1.9 What is the usual duration of the restructuring process?

As already explained, the opening of an LCE procedure creates a period of suspension. The duration of that period depends on the chosen gateway or is determined case-by-case by the court. In the first instance, a maximum period of six months can be requested.

The enterprise can ask the court for a prolongation. Such prolongation can be for a maximum period of six months.

In extraordinary circumstances, and when it is in the interest of the creditors, the period of suspension can be prolonged by yet another six months. Extraordinary circumstances are the size of the enterprise, the complexity of the file or the preservation of employment.

This means that an LCE procedure can take a maximum period of 18 months.

1.10 Who prepares the restructuring agreement and what are the available tools?

Only in gateway 2 does the enterprise have to prepare a reorganisation plan that is presented to the creditors. To be approved, the majority of creditors that attend the voting hearing and which represent at least half of the claims have to vote in favour of the plan. Extraordinary creditors will have to agree explicitly if their claim is affected by the reorganisation plan.

1.11 Are subordination agreements necessarily given full effect?

When drafting the reorganisation plan, the enterprise has to take into account that creditors are divided into two groups: extraordinary and ordinary creditors.

Extraordinary creditors are creditors whose claim is covered by a special privilege (eg pledge), a mortgage or a proprietorship claim. Ordinary creditors are creditors whose claim is not covered by any privilege.

In order to suspend the execution of the rights of the extraordinary creditors in the reorganisation plan, certain conditions have to be met. First of all, the enterprise has to continue to pay interest. Secondly, the execution can only be for a period of 24 months after deposition of the petition to open the procedure. This term can be prolonged by 12 months, but only if the enterprise can prove that the revenues and financial condition of the enterprise make it possible to fully reimburse these creditors.

For any other measures, the extraordinary creditors have to agree individually.

Ordinary creditors can also be divided in separate categories and can be treated differently if an objective justification is provided. For instance, the reorganisation plan can foresee that strategic suppliers can be repaid for 85 per cent while non-strategic suppliers can only be given 15 per cent (which is the minimum).

If creditors with a general privilege (eg tax authorities, social security agency) are involved, these have to be in the most favoured category. In our example of strategic and non-strategic suppliers, this would mean that such creditors would be categorised in the strategic suppliers category, with an 85 per cent repayment.

1.12 How is exit managed?

In any of the gateways, the procedure is closed with a judgment. In gateway 2, the court will indeed homologate the reorganisation plan (see section 1.5 above).

There is, however, also the possibility of changing gateways. This can be requested by the enterprise at any time during a procedure. However, there are some restrictions. For example, an enterprise can go from gateway 1 to gateway 2 or 3, or from gateway 2 to gateway 3, but no other options are possible.

The procedure can also be closed prematurely.

The enterprise can request this at any time during the procedure under the condition that it will honour the agreements already made with the creditors.

If the enterprise is no longer able to ensure the continuity of the whole or part of the enterprise, or when the information provided to the delegated judge, the court or the creditors is incorrect, the court can end the procedure.

This can take place upon request by the creditor or on writ of summons by the public prosecutor or any interested third party. In such a case, it is possible for the court to immediately declare the enterprise bankrupt.

The suspension period ends at the moment of the judgment that orders the closing of the procedure, and all creditors can execute their rights again. This also happens when the period of suspension ends and the procedure was not officially closed.

1.13 Who are the necessary parties?

In an LCE procedure, the enterprise remains in the driver's seat. This means that the enterprise is the most important party.

In a gateway 1 scenario, the enterprise has to find an agreement with two or more creditors, so those creditors play an important role.

In a gateway 2 scenario, all creditors have to vote on the reorganisation plan.

In a gateway 3 scenario, a court's trustee will play an important role as it is his task to sell the activity or assets of the company.

In all gateways, a delegated judge is appointed. This delegated judge is the first point of contact at the court and he reports regularly to the court about the progress of the procedure.

Furthermore, the enterprise or interested third parties can also request that a court's trustee is appointed to assist the enterprise during the procedure. The court can do this itself if the enterprise or one of its decision-making bodies has committed a gross shortcoming.

If it concerns a gross error, a judicial administrator can be appointed on request of any interested third party or the public prosecutor.

2. POST-INSOLVENCY PROCEEDINGS

2.1 What is the objective of the proceedings?

A post-insolvency proceedings would typically mean a bankruptcy proceedings. Such proceedings is regulated by the bankruptcy law of 8 August 1997 (the Bankruptcy Law).

Unlike an LCE procedure, the objective of a bankruptcy procedure is not to save the continuity of the enterprise; rather, the main purpose of a bankruptcy procedure in Belgium is to liquidate the company by selling its assets, and using the sales proceeds to repay the creditors, taking into account the various privileges established by law.

A court's liquidator could decide to sell the company as a going concern. In practice, however, this only happens if the court's liquidator believes that the company can be revived and if he receives reasonable offers shortly after the company has been declared bankrupt.

2.2 Do all kinds of business entities qualify?

The only criterion to qualify for bankruptcy is that a commercial activity is carried out. This means that private persons who carry out a commercial or craftsman's activity and legal entities which, according to their by-laws, serve a commercial purpose (the actual activity does not matter) can go bankrupt.

A non-profit legal entity cannot go bankrupt since it has no commercial activity in the by-laws except in two cases:

1. falsely qualified non-profit legal entities: by-laws are in conflict with the goals of the non-profit legal entity law; and
2. falsely used non-profit legal entities: the legal entity is used to make profit contrary to the by-laws.

In these cases the Bankruptcy Law will apply nevertheless.

2.3 What are the necessary approvals?

The court will in principle ask that a formal decision from the board of directors be submitted when the enterprise files for bankruptcy itself.

Other parties can also initiate a bankruptcy procedure. The creditors, the public prosecutor, any temporary receiver who is appointed by the court and the bankruptcy trustee of the main bankruptcy procedure in another EU country can demand bankruptcy by writ of summons.

2.4 Is it valid and binding to agree that such proceedings be a default/termination event?

In Belgium, it is quite common for contracts to provide that the filing of a bankruptcy declaration constitutes a termination event. This is called an explicit termination clause (*uitdrukkelijk ontbindend beding*).

If a party wants to use such a clause, it will have to notify the other contract party. Of course, it is never guaranteed that the notified party will not challenge the termination in front of court. However, in a bankruptcy scenario, it is likely that the termination will be accepted, as a court's liquidator will mostly not continue the existing agreements.

2.5 What is the procedure?

In Belgium, an enterprise can be declared bankrupt if two objective criteria are met: (i) the enterprise must have permanently ceased paying its debts; and (ii) the enterprise must have an unstable credit supply.

Most bankruptcy claims are dealt with at the introductory hearing of the Court of Commerce (the Court), where all parties involved can set out their arguments related to the two objective criteria. The case will always be heard within a short delay after the writ of summons has been served or after the voluntary filing.

After the hearing, the Court will render a judgment. This judgment will grant or reject the claim for bankruptcy.

If the claim is granted, the bankruptcy judgment must be served upon the enterprise, which will then have 15 days to lodge an appeal. The judgment will also be published in the Belgian Official Gazette within five days after rendering the judgment to inform the creditors of the bankruptcy. The creditors will not be informed individually.

Appeal or third party opposition proceedings will also be dealt with within the shortest possible delay.

In its judgment, the Court will appoint a court's liquidator, who will be in charge of the further liquidation of the company and of the payment of the creditors. The parties involved have no influence on the choice of the court's liquidator.

Throughout the process, the court's liquidator will be supervised by a magistrate of the Court of Commerce, the official receiver (*rechter-commissaris*). The court's liquidator is also liable if he does not respect his obligations.

Within a set period (usually 30 days as of the bankruptcy judgment), all creditors (including the privileged creditors) must file their claim at the court's registry. They must do so in writing, and indicate whether they have priority and, if so, what the legal basis for such priority is. Any creditors that do not file their claim will not be taken into account when the available funds are distributed.

After the declarations of claim have been filed, the court's liquidator will draft a report of verification of the claims. In most cases, the closing of this report is scheduled somewhere between day 5 and 30 after the last possible date for the declarations of claim. In the following 16 months, the court's liquidator will update this report every four months.

The court's liquidator will verify all claims in the presence of the responsible director of the enterprise.

The court's liquidator will then have to decide which claims he will contest and which claims he will propose be accepted by the Court of Commerce. The court will in principle follow the recommendation of the liquidator.

Both the enterprise and the separate creditors can contest the report of verification within one month after its deposition. For this, a writ of summons must be served upon the court's liquidator.

Claims contested by the court's liquidator will become subject to separate proceedings before the Court of Commerce.

If court proceedings were already initiated before bankruptcy, the court's liquidator will have to decide whether or not to continue those proceedings. If there are no valid grounds to further contest a claim, the court's liquidator will immediately cease the pending proceedings and have the claim accepted by the Court of Commerce.

The court's liquidator will sell all assets. The enterprise will be consulted on the best ways to proceed with such sale.

When all assets have been sold off, the trustee will draft an overview of the costs of the liquidation and the distribution of the available funds amongst the creditors according to their priority rank.

The creditors will be invited to a hearing on these documents. There is no voting, only a discussion.

If the court has settled all disputes regarding the distribution list and, if necessary, corrected it, the Court will close the bankruptcy procedure after hearing the delegated judge and the enterprise.

The decision to close the procedure will automatically result in the dissolution of the company and the closing of the liquidation.

The decision is published in the Belgian Official Gazette.

2.6 Please provide information about voluntary filings

An enterprise can file for bankruptcy by filing a bankruptcy declaration at the Court's registry. Moreover, Article 9 of the Bankruptcy Law imposes an obligation to file for bankruptcy within one month after the cessation of payments. The following documents have to be attached to the declaration:

- a balance sheet, which contains an overview of the assets and liabilities, the annual account, an estimation of all moveable goods and real estate, and an overview of profit and loss. The enterprise has to state that these data are correct and sign it;
- the accounting books of the enterprise;
- the register of personnel, contact data of the social office, the identity of the union members and the access code to the electronic register of personnel;
- a list with the names and addresses of the customers and suppliers; and
- the names and addresses of natural persons who acted as guarantor.

The creditors will not be invited by the Court to the initial hearing. In principle, the creditors will only gain knowledge of the bankruptcy after the judgment has been published. The procedure is the same as described in section 2.5 above.

2.7 How are creditors' representatives chosen?

The court will appoint a court's liquidator who, at the same time, represents the enterprise and acts in the interest of the creditors. Neither the creditors nor the enterprise has a say in who will be appointed; the Court decides.

The court's liquidator will take over the decision power and will eventually sell all assets and repay the creditors.

2.8 Is there recourse against the opening judgment?

All normal recourse actions are open against the opening judgment. This means that either the enterprise or the creditors can lodge an appeal, opposition or third party opposition against the judgment.

These proceedings have to take place without any delay. On the request of the most interested party, the case will be given a date for the oral hearing, which has to take place within one month after the request for such date has been filed.

2.9 What are the roles and powers of committees?

N/A.

2.10 What are the consequences of opening judgments for creditors?

When the enterprise is declared bankrupt, the execution measures of creditors are automatically stayed.

For non-privileged creditors, there are no means to start or reactivate any execution measures. All attachments of goods by non-privileged creditors and creditors with a general privilege (this is a privilege on all movable goods) are automatically stopped.

A distinction must be made for privileged creditors (mortgage holders, pledgee creditors and holders of a specific privilege).

Mortgage holders maintain a special position during the bankruptcy procedure.

The rights of a mortgage holder to enforce the mortgage will automatically be suspended until the closing of the first report of verification of the claims. As for all other creditors, the mortgage holder will have to declare its claim.

After the closing of the first report of verification, the mortgage holder can in principle proceed with the enforcement of the mortgage. However, the court's liquidator can, in the interest of the bankrupt estate and provided that one may expect a sale of movable assets which does not prejudice the priority creditors, request from the Court of Commerce an extension of the suspension for a maximum period of one year.

This exception is only valid for the mortgage holder in first rank; no other mortgage holder can benefit from this exception.

A similar arrangement is applicable to pledgee creditors and creditors with a specific privilege on movable goods.

In the case of a pledge, the court's liquidator can reclaim the pledged good by repaying the debt to the pledgee. If the pledgee sells the pledged good for a price that exceeds his claim, the surplus must be transferred to the court's liquidator.

Concerning interest, there is also a distinction between non-privileged and privileged creditors. For non- privileged creditors, the interest stops accruing as from the judgment that opens the procedure. For privileged creditors, the interest continues to accrue, but the interest can only be paid out of the proceeds of the goods related to the privilege.

The opening of a bankruptcy procedure also has as a consequence that all undue claims become immediately due. In this respect ,it is also common that agreements stipulate that the agreements are terminated in case of bankruptcy and that all claims become due. This is a valid provision.

2.11 What is the duration of the restructuring process?

The duration depends on the circumstances. In most cases, the proceedings linger on for several years.

If litigation proceedings are pending, these proceedings must be brought to an end in order to (be able to) close the bankruptcy. However, if it seems that the assets of the enterprise are insufficient to even cover the costs of the bankruptcy procedure, the court's liquidator or even the court itself can close the bankruptcy procedure. All parties involved (enterprise, creditors, etc) will be notified and heard.

Such decision can only be taken if the court determines that the court's liquidator has done everything he could to pay the employees/provide them with the necessary documents.

The judgment is published in the Belgian Official Gazette.

2.12 How do creditors vote?

Creditors do not have the right to vote. There is only the possibility to comment on the distribution proposed by the court's trustee. If a creditor does not agree, he has to initiate a legal procedure.

2.13 What are the rules on clawback/voidability?

According to Belgian bankruptcy law, there is a suspect period just before the opening of the bankruptcy procedure. The suspect period is the period between the date of the bankruptcy judgment and the date of the cessation of payment (*staking van betaling*) (as determined by the court). Pursuant to the Belgian bankruptcy law, such date in principle concurs with the date of the bankruptcy judgment, but it may be fixed up to a maximum of six months prior to the bankruptcy judgment. In certain circumstances, the court is even entitled to determine that the date of cessation of payment occurred earlier than six months prior to the bankruptcy judgment.

The bankruptcy law provides that certain actions do not have to be taken into account when they were performed since the date of the cessation of payment.

It concerns:

- actions where assets are transferred for free or against a price that is far below the value of such goods (Article 17,1°);
- payments by the enterprise for amounts that are not due can be held unenforceable against the liquidator of the bankruptcy estate (Article 17,2°); and
- granting mortgages and/or pledges on the goods of the enterprise for claims that already existed before the cessation of payments (Article 17,3°).

Furthermore, any payment for due debts and all transactions effected under consideration between the date of cessation of payment and the date of the bankruptcy judgment can be declared unenforceable if the counterparty that received something from the bankrupt enterprise knew of the cessation of payment (Article 18).

In any event, fraudulent transactions or payments with the intent to harm the creditors are not enforceable, whenever they are committed.

2.14 What are the rules on set-off/netting?

Legal set-off takes place when parties have mutual claims in cash or other replaceable goods which are due and which can be set-off immediately.

Such set-off is no longer possible after the opening of a bankruptcy procedure. If the conditions for set-off are met after bankruptcy or because of the bankruptcy, such set-off is not enforceable.

There is, however, an exception. If the mutual claims are closely connected, set-off remains possible after bankruptcy (Cass. 7 December 1961, *Pas*. 1962, I, 440).

Netting agreements have the important advantage that they can be enforced during a bankruptcy procedure. The following conditions have to be met:

- the netting agreement has to be concluded before the bankruptcy; and
- the claims exist at the moment of bankruptcy.

Also, during the suspected period the clawback provisions of Articles 17,2° and 18 of the Bankruptcy Law are not applicable to netting agreements.

2.15 How is exit managed?

Typically, the bankruptcy procedure ends with the distribution of the available funds to the creditors if all disputes are settled and all assets are sold off. The court will close the bankruptcy procedure after hearing the delegated judge and the enterprise. The decision to close the procedure will automatically result in the dissolution of the company and the closing of the liquidation.

If the available assets are insufficient to cover the costs of the bankruptcy procedure, the court can close the procedure. The enterprise, court's liquidator and public prosecutor will be heard by the court.

If the debtor is a natural person, he will be declared excusable. This means that creditors cannot continue to execute their claim after closing of the bankruptcy procedure. This will happen automatically if the natural person acted in good faith and the bankruptcy was due to misfortune.

An enterprise cannot be declared excusable, as it will typically be wound up.

2.16 Are 'prepackaged' plans, arrangements or agreements permissible?

N/A.

2.17 Is a public authority involved?

In Belgium, typically no public authority is involved.

The court's liquidator, usually a lawyer, will be appointed to organise the bankruptcy procedure on behalf of the Belgian state.

As already explained, the court's liquidator will take over the decision power. He will take all necessary decisions on behalf of the bankrupt enterprise.

In addition, he will make an inventory of all assets and liabilities, and will sell all assets.

He will also take the first decision on the admissibility of the claims of the creditors. If the creditors do not agree with the court's liquidator, they have to initiate proceedings against him.

He will also make a first assessment on possible director liability and further actions against those directors.

2.18 What is the treatment of claims arising after filing/ admission?

To govern the assets of the bankrupt enterprise, it is always necessary to make additional costs. These claims are called claims *of* the bankrupt estate, while normal claims are called claims *in* the bankrupt estate. For creditors/ suppliers to be willing to work with the court's liquidator, and also for the costs of the court's liquidator, there is a special arrangement for claims made after the opening of the bankruptcy procedure (claims of the bankrupt estate).

Basically, those claims will be paid out before the claims of other creditors. However, privileged creditors do not have to contribute to these costs as it is assumed that the costs of the bankruptcy are not to the benefit of those creditors. They have their own goods out of which they are paid back.

Nevertheless, if the costs made by the court's liquidator are in the interest of those creditors, they will have to participate in the costs. If it concerns a cost that is made exclusively to the benefit of the privileged creditor (eg cost to preserve the specific good), these costs cannot be seen as costs of the bankrupt estate, and will have to be paid by the specific creditor (Bergen 15 December 1992, *T.B.H.* 1994, 935).

It is also assumed that the court costs and the fee of the court's liquidator are deemed to be claims of the bankrupt estate.

2.19 Are there ongoing contracts?

The law does not provide an automatic termination of contracts. The court's liquidator has the authority to decide what will happen with ongoing contracts. In most cases, however, he will decide to terminate them (in order to avoid personal liabilities).

Another party to the agreement can urge the court's liquidator to take a decision within 15 days. If no extension was agreed or if the court's liquidator did not take a decision, it is assumed that the contract was terminated by the court's liquidator. A possible claim for damages will be included in the overview of claims against the enterprise.

If the court's liquidator decides to continue to execute the agreement, the other party has the right to be compensated before all other creditors, but only for those services rendered after the bankruptcy.

The court's trustee can also terminate the agreements with the employees without following the normal procedures. It is also possible to fire the employees and to rehire them at new conditions.

With the consent of the official receiver, the court's trustee can grant the employees an advance on their claim for unpaid wages. This advance can be up to a maximum of EUR 12,000.

2.20 Are consolidated proceedings for members of a corporate family/group possible?

Belgium does not recognise groups of enterprises. All legal entities have to file for bankruptcy separately.

2.21 What are the charges, fees and other costs?

The most important charges and fees related to bankruptcy are the costs of the procedure and the fee of the court's liquidator.

Examples of costs of the procedure are the costs to publish the opening judgment and the costs to serve the judgment upon the bankrupt enterprise.

In addition, the court's liquidator is entitled to a fee. This fee will be determined based on the importance and complexity of their assignment. The fee cannot exclusively be determined as a percentage of the proceeds of the sale of assets.

The fees of the bankruptcy trustee are determined in the Royal Decree concerning the rules and scales for the determination of the costs and fees of bankruptcy trustees of 10 August 1998.

Although the fee cannot exclusively exist out of a percentage of the proceeds, the ordinary fee of the court's liquidator is a proportionate remuneration based on the amounts received from selling assets or collecting debts. The Royal Decree gives the remuneration per bracket.

Article 6 determines additional remuneration from the mortgage holders or preferred creditors if the court's trustee has to sell real estate on which such mortgages or privileges are granted.

The court's trustee receives an extraordinary fee for activities which are not part of a normal liquidation if those activities contributed to or had to contribute to the preservation of the assets of the bankruptcy estate, for example, the continuation of the activity of the bankrupt company. This fee is specified by the Court.

As indicated in section 2.18, these fees are claims of the bankrupt estate. The court's liquidator will be paid before the other creditors.

3. LIABILITY ISSUES

3.1 What is the liability of managers/directors *vis-à-vis* creditors?

Personal liability for the directors will mainly be looked at in a bankruptcy scenario. During an LCE procedure, the directors, in principle, do everything they can to avoid bankruptcy and thus avoid possible liability.

Article 530 of the Belgian Company Code provides for a specific liability regime in case of bankruptcy. In case of bankruptcy, a director (real directors) may be held liable for shortage of assets if he has committed a serious and specific misconduct which has contributed to the bankruptcy of the enterprise. The law gives as an example of such serious and specific misconduct any fiscal fraud, whether or not it was intentionally set up.

The court will have full discretion to assess whether or not there is a serious and specific misconduct.

Such liability may be prosecuted by the liquidator of the bankrupt estate (the curator) or by any creditor of the company (but subject to prior notification to the liquidator of the bankrupt estate). Of course, the creditor has to have an interest in initiating this procedure. In such case, if the court grants such claim initiated by a creditor, the compensation is limited to the actual damage of that creditor.

In addition, the social security office or the liquidator can initiate a liability claim against a legal, factual or past director for all or part of the social security debt if the serious misconduct of that director caused the bankruptcy. Besides the example already given (see above), the law stipulates that such serious misconduct is where the director was involved in two previous bankruptcies in which there was a debt towards the social security office.

As indicated above, and pursuant to Article 9 of the Bankruptcy Law, the directors of an enterprise must file a declaration of bankruptcy with the court's registry of the competent commercial court within one month after the cessation of payment.

There are criminal sanctions in case of failure to timely file such declaration (Article 489 of the Belgian Criminal Code). However, these are not within the scope of this contribution, so will not be discussed further.

Besides such criminal liability, the directors may also be held liable for the aggravation of the losses of the company should they have not complied with the provisions of Article 9 of the Bankruptcy Law.

3.2 What is the liability of the lender?

Pursuant to the Articles 1382–83 of the Belgian Civil Code, a lender has a duty to act as a normal and prudent lender.

More specifically, the maintaining of credit to an enterprise which is in financial distress may inflict liability for the lender. The lender has to judge as a normal and careful lender whether the maintaining of credit is still justified. The lender could be held liable towards (new) creditors/counterparties of its borrower for damage that might be caused to these third parties by the appearance of solvency (*schijn van solvabiliteit*) which is created by the unjustified maintenance of the credit.

Case law states that, by continued support to a company, by maintaining the credit lines while monitoring the worsening of the financial situation of the company, a financial institution may keep an enterprise alive in an artificial way. In this manner, the financial institutions could be held liable for the creation of the appearance of solvency towards third parties (Kort. Ged. Kh. Nijvel 22 januari 1997).

In order to file a liability claim against a lender, the creditors must establish that:

- the maintaining of the credit constitutes a fault at the level of the lender (ie that another prudent lender, in the same circumstances, would have accelerated the loans); and
- this fault has caused them damage.

If there are no third parties/creditors/suppliers which trust, on an appearance of solvency, to conclude new agreements with the enterprise, there is no risk of incurring such a (civil) liability.

Canada

Justin R Fogarty Professional Corporation
Justin R Fogarty, Jason Dutrizac & Pavle Masic

1. WHAT COURT-MONITORED RESTRUCTURING PRE-INSOLVENCY PROCEEDINGS OR SCHEMES HAVE BEEN DEVISED BY THE LAW OF YOUR COUNTRY TO LIMIT VALUE DESTRUCTION FOR FAILING BUSINESS ENTITIES?

There are two primary statutory regimes designed for the restructuring of Canadian companies: the Bankruptcy and Insolvency Act, RSC 1985, c B-3 (BIA) and the Companies' Creditors Arrangement Act, RSC 1985, c C-36 (CCAA). While one may argue that there are other legislative tools available to effect restructurings in specialised situations, such as the Winding-up and Restructuring Act, RSC 1985, c W-11 and certain provisions of the Canada Business Corporations Act, RSC 1985, c C-44 and its provincial counterparts, the BIA and CCAA are the only primary statutes specifically dedicated to the restructuring of companies and will be the focus of this chapter.

This review is in response to specific questions; it is not exhaustive. The authors have tried to provide a flavour of the legislation and practice. For more detailed analysis pertaining to specific problems, it will be essential to consult with a Canadian insolvency practitioner.

1.1 What is the objective of the proceedings?

The objective of both the BIA and the CCAA is to provide for an orderly restructuring of companies under court supervision. The BIA is driven by an administrative process while the CCAA is a more flexible process driven by court order and direction of the court. The BIA provides a rules-based approach to resolving insolvencies, which rules must be strictly adhered to. By contrast, the CCAA conveys wide discretionary powers to the court to make any order its sees fit under the circumstances in furtherance of resolving the insolvency (CCAA, section 11).

1.2 Do all kinds of businesses qualify?

BIA

The BIA applies to any company, no matter how large or small, regardless of size of secured or unsecured debt. The BIA has often been utilised in major restructurings because of the manner in which proceedings can be commenced and the short process that can be provided as compared with proceedings under the CCAA.

The court-appointed agent in BIA proceedings is called the proposal trustee. The proposal trustee is an independent party, typically an accountant, and is normally chosen by the debtor but can be chosen by a major secured or unsecured creditor with the consent of the debtor. Once proceedings have been commenced under the BIA, the creditors of the debtor corporation may, by special resolution at any meeting of creditors, appoint or substitute another licensed trustee as the named proposal trustee (BIA, section 14).

Once appointed by the court, the role of the proposal trustee shifts somewhat. The proposal trustee remains an agent to assist the company in restructuring efforts, but also becomes responsible for reporting to the company's creditors and to the court on progress in the restructuring, or lack thereof, for the protection of all stakeholders (BIA, section 27). Given its responsibilities to both the debtor and the creditors, the proposal trustee must act impartially.

CCAA

The CCAA is restricted to larger corporations. In order for the CCAA to apply, a company must be at least CAD $5 million in debt (CCAA, section 3). Under the CCAA, the court-appointed agent is called the monitor. As with a proposal trustee, a monitor is typically chosen by the debtor and, once appointed, assumes a reporting role to the court, with concordant responsibility to all stakeholders in the restructuring. A monitor is obligated to act impartially (the duties of a monitor are listed in section 23 of the CCAA).

1.3 What are the necessary approvals?

In order for proceedings to commence under either the BIA or the CCAA, a special resolution of directors is required, authorising a member of management to sign the necessary paperwork to file under the BIA or to commence court proceedings under the CCAA.

1.4 What is the procedure?

BIA

Under the BIA, the process is initiated administratively by filing a notice of intention to make a proposal (an NOI) with the Office of the Superintendent of Bankruptcy (OSB). In support of the NOI, a listing of all creditors owed CAD $250.00 or more is included (BIA, section 50.4(1)). The creditors must be given notice of the filing, which is administrative in nature, within five days after the filing (BIA, section 50.4(6)). Upon filing of the NOI, a stay of creditors' proceedings takes effect and remains in effect until either the proposal trustee is discharged or a bankruptcy occurs (BIA, section 69).

Within 10 days of the initial filing of the NOI, the debtor must file a cash-flow statement with the OSB to demonstrate that it can meet its post-filing debts as they come due, as well as a report on the reasonableness of the cash-flow statement signed by the proposal trustee (BIA, section 50.4(2)). The debtor then must, within 30 days of the initial filing, either file a restructuring plan (in BIA terms, a proposal) to its creditors or return to court on notice to all creditors (BIA, section 50.4(8)). At that hearing, creditors may make various motions as to why they should not be caught by the stay or why the proceeding should not continue. The debtor at this hearing will ask the court for an extension of time and must meet a number of threshold tests in order to be granted such an extension, which will be discussed in greater detail further on.

All documents that are filed during this process are public in nature and are not subject to confidentiality. There are no provisions against disclosure of court documents and the current prevailing practice is that the relevant public court documents are posted on the website of the proposal trustee for easy access to creditors.

CCAA

Under the CCAA, an application is made to the court with supporting affidavit material to demonstrate that the company meets the threshold test to invoke the provisions of the CCAA and that the restructuring would be for the benefit of the company and the creditors. If the debtor company is seeking the protection of a judicial stay of proceedings, it must satisfy the court that it is acting in good faith (CCAA, 11.02(3)). The application must include a cash-flow statement, a report containing representations of the debtor company regarding the cash-flow statement and copies of all financial statements prepared during the year before the application (CCAA, section 10(2)).

Though the statute provides for the initial application to be made without notice, in practice this application is always initially on notice to the major secured creditors, as many typical features of the initial order, such as a security or charge over the property of the debtor to pay the costs of the CCAA process, require notice to secured creditors (CCAA, section 11.52).

If the court is satisfied that the circumstances warrant granting the application, the court will appoint a monitor and has the authority to issue an order giving the company 30 days of protection from its creditors to allow for the preparation of its restructuring plan (in CCAA terms, the plan of compromise or arrangement, or plan; CCAA, 11.02(1)). On the assumption that the court grants the initial order, standard procedure provides that the court will fix another date as a return date, at which point in time all creditors will be given notice and have an opportunity to address their concerns with the court.

The court may make an order prohibiting the release to the public of any cash-flow statement, or any part of a cash-flow statement, if it is satisfied that the release of this information would unduly prejudice the debtor company and the making of the order would not unduly prejudice the company's creditors (CCAA, section 10(3)). Like proposal trustees, court-appointed monitors typically post court documents on their websites to facilitate access to information for all affected parties.

1.5 Is there recourse against the opening judgment?

Under both the BIA and the CCAA, any creditor has standing to make an argument that the process should not continue.

BIA

As indicated above, if a debtor company is unable to file a proposal within 30 days of filing an NOI, it must apply to the court for an extension of time within which to do so. For the court to give an order to continue the proceedings, the debtor must satisfy the court that:

(i) it is acting in good faith and due diligence;

(ii) it would likely be able to make a viable proposal if the extension applied for were granted; and

(iii) no creditor would be materially prejudiced if the extension being applied for were granted (BIA, section 50.4(8)).

At any point after the initial NOI filing, any creditor can apply to the court for an order terminating the time for a debtor to make a proposal to its creditors. The test for granting such an application is essentially the converse of the test for a debtor seeking an extension of time (BIA, section 50.4(11)).

Creditors will typically either object to an extension or seek an order terminating the proposal period based on the grounds that the debtor will be unable to make a viable proposal to its creditors. Where the court is of the view that the company is not in fact insolvent (in cases, for example, of fraud or an out and out liquidation) or cannot make a viable proposal to its creditors, the court can put the company into formal receivership.

CCAA

Under the CCAA, after the initial order is granted, a debtor may move to extend the judicial stay protecting it from its creditors. The court may grant an extension of the stay to any time period it considers necessary (CCAA, 11.02(3)). In order to obtain such relief, the debtor must satisfy the court that circumstances exist that make the order appropriate, and that it is acting in good faith and with due diligence (CCAA, 11.02(3)). A creditor can resist on various grounds. For example, it may allege that the debtor is acting fraudulently.

1.6 What are the substantive tests/definitions?

BIA

An insolvent person is defined in the BIA as *'a person who is not bankrupt and who resides, carries on business or has property in Canada, whose liabilities to creditors provable as claims under this Act amount to one thousand dollars, and*

(a) who is for any reason unable to meet his obligations as they generally become due,

(b) who has ceased paying his current obligations in the ordinary course of business as they generally become due, or

(c) the aggregate of whose property is not, at a fair valuation, sufficient, or, if disposed of at a fairly conducted sale under legal process, would not be sufficient to enable payment of all his obligations, due and accruing due.' (BIA, section 2)

Interpreting the definition of 'insolvent' is an area of controversy in Canadian law. The question is complicated by the fact that the above test is essentially twofold: it tests assets as measured against liabilities as well as cash flow. It is not uncommon that a company can meet one area of this test but seemingly fail another. If, for example, a company may be able to meet its current debts because it has cash, but will eventually run out of cash at a certain point in time if it continues on its current trajectory due to its ratio of assets to liabilities, the insolvency test would be met.

There have been numerous court cases where companies have filed for protection under either the BIA or CCAA and solvency was the central question (see eg *Stelco Inc. (Re)*, 2004 CanLII 24933 (ON SC)).

CCAA

The CCAA defines a 'debtor company' as a company that is bankrupt or insolvent; has committed an act of bankruptcy within the meaning of the BIA; or is deemed insolvent within the meaning of the Winding-up and Restructuring Act, whether or not proceedings in respect of the company have been taken under either of those acts.

The word 'insolvent' is not defined in the CCAA. When a company files for protection under the CCAA regime and its solvency is questioned, the same twofold test is used by the courts as under the BIA to determine whether the company is insolvent.

1.7 What is the role of a court-appointed agent?

BIA

The proposal trustee provides assistance to the debtor during the restructuring process and also acts as the eyes and ears of the court. The proposal trustee observes the development and implementation of the restructuring process and provides reports to the court, which reports set out the various stages of progress or lack of progress in the restructuring. This reporting is used, among other things, to assist in selling off assets with the approval of the court. The proposal trustee is also charged with collecting in all the claims of creditors, both secured and unsecured, and to vet those claims.

Perhaps the most important powers of the proposal trustee are the power to approve or deny any claim advanced by a creditor, and the power to run a vote on the proposal during the process.

CCAA

As mentioned above, the powers of the monitor are listed under section 23 of the CCAA. These powers can also be (and usually are) augmented by extra powers granted by the court. Though their powers are somewhat different, given the nature of the two regimes, the role of a monitor is very similar to that of the proposal trustee as described above.

1.8 What protection is there from creditors?

BIA

As indicated above, filing an NOI triggers a stay of proceedings against the debtor. The initial stay is for 30 days but can last, with periodic extensions from the court, for up to six months. Each extension of the stay is for a maximum of 45 days (see BIA, section 50.4(9)).

After an NOI has been filed, secured or unsecured creditors must file a proof of claim with the proposal trustee. The proposal trustee is obligated to review each proof of claim submitted to it (BIA, section 135(2)). If the proposal trustee declines to interfere in a dispute regarding a claim, either the debtor or creditor may apply to the court to have the claim expunged or reduced (BIA, section 135(5)).

If the proposal trustee denies the claim, the creditor has 30 days to appeal the disallowance to a judge of the Superior Court of Justice (BIA, section 135(4)). There is divided opinion in the case law as to whether this hearing is treated as an appeal as opposed to a trial *de novo*. Thus, creditors would be wise to diligent in filing the proof of claim, as the court is unlikely to allow them to put forward additional evidence in the appeal.

CCAA

Under the CCAA, there is no time limit for the lifting of the stay. Generally, if a claim is disallowed, it will be put through a claims process, which is usually set out in the appointment order. We have seen cases where a retired judge or other party is appointed to deal with specific claims and has, in effect, conducted a mini-trial or hearing to determine their validity. Such a process is typically defined in the appointment order and designed to promote efficiency and timely resolution of disputes. If a claim is disallowed, it is normally appealable to either the Ontario Divisional Court or the Ontario Court of Appeal, depending on the process defined in the appointment order itself.

1.9 What is the usual duration of the restructuring process?

As detailed in section 1.5 above, proceedings under the BIA typically last between 30 days and six months, whereas proceedings under the CCAA last as long as the judge deems appropriate under the circumstances.

1.10 Who prepares the restructuring agreement and what are the available tools?

BIA

The company, with the assistance of the proposal trustee, will prepare the proposal to the creditors. The proposal may be made to the creditors as a mass or separated into classes of creditors, which classes can be defined in the proposal (BIA, section 50 (1.2)). Upon application, the court may determine the appropriate classes to be included in a proposal (BIA, section 50 (1.5)). The proposal is put to the creditors for a vote and is deemed to be accepted by the creditors if all classes of unsecured creditors vote for the acceptance of the proposal by a majority in number and two-thirds in value of the unsecured creditors of each class voting (BIA, section 54).

In the case of a partial restructuring and sale of assets, the company will choose the broker or investment bank tasked with selling portions of the company's assets or selling an active business, but any such retainer must be approved by the court. At the hearing seeking such approval, a creditor can argue against the choice of broker.

CCAA

The company, with the assistance of the monitor, will prepare and present a formal plan of compromise or arrangement to its creditors. There are no statutory restrictions on the content or structure of the plan. As with a proposal under the BIA, once a plan has been tabled, it is voted on by the creditors and requires approval by a majority in number representing two-thirds in value of the creditors voting. If approved by the creditors, the plan may be sanctioned by the court and, if so sanctioned, is binding (CCAA, section 6).

1.11 Are subordination agreements necessarily given full effect?

Subordination agreements in effect prior to the restructuring will be given full effect under both statutes. In a vote, under either statute, tactics are usually employed to try and group or lump together creditors in classes that will likely result in a positive vote in favour of a restructuring plan. Creditors must be vigilant in determining whether they are appropriately placed in a class to avoid having their vote undermined.

Early bird fee/preferential treatment is not possible under either regime, with the exception of supply of goods or suppliers deemed critical to the ongoing viability of the process. In certain circumstances, the court can agree that some pre-filing amounts can be paid in order to ensure the supply of critical goods or services continues during the restructuring (CCAA, section 11.4).

1.12 How is exit managed?

In the case of either a plan of compromise or arrangement under the CCAA or a proposal under the BIA, the court has an obligation to review any plan or proposal and determine whether it is appropriate, and must exercise its jurisdiction.

BIA

The proposal trustee must apply to the court for an appointment for a hearing of the application for the court's approval of the proposal within five days of its acceptance of by the creditors (BIA, section 58). Notice of the hearing of the application must be sent, at least 15 days before the date of the hearing, to the debtor, to every creditor who has proved a claim, whether secured or unsecured, to the person making the proposal and to the official receiver. Any of these parties has standing to contest approval of the proposal (BIA, section 59). At least two days before the date of the hearing, the trustee must file a report on the proposal with the court.

The court may refuse to approve the proposal where it is of the opinion that the terms of the proposal are not reasonable or are not calculated to benefit the general body of creditors.

CCAA

A plan does not become binding on the creditors or trustee until it is sanctioned by the court (CCAA, section 6(1)). The CCAA includes a number of prescriptions that may act as a bar to approval of a plan. For example, the court cannot sanction a plan that does not provide for payment in full of amounts owing to the Crown under the deemed trust provisions of the Income Tax Act, unless the Crown orders otherwise (CCAA, section 6(3) and Income Tax Act, RSC 1985, c 1 (5th Supp), s 224(1.2)). Similarly, the court cannot sanction a plan that does not provide for payment to employees of an amount at least equal to what they would be entitled to in a bankruptcy under the BIA (CCAA, section 6(5) and BIA, sections 81.1 and 81.2). Any plan submitted to the court for approval must be seen by the court as fair and reasonable, and must meet these and other statutory requirements.

1.13 Who are the necessary parties?

See section 1.4 above.

2. POST-INSOLVENCY PROCEEDINGS

In Canada, there is no distinction between pre- and post-insolvency proceedings. Once a company is unable to meet its obligations generally as they become due or its liabilities exceed the value of its assets, it is insolvent and insolvency proceedings will generally be commenced. When a company is bankrupt, it loses the legal capacity to deal with its assets and a trustee in bankruptcy is appointed over those assets with a mandate to, among other things, liquidate the assets and distribute the proceeds of sale to creditors. Additionally (or alternatively), the assets of a business may be liquidated or sold on a going-concern basis in creditor-initiated proceedings such as the appointment of a receiver and manager of the business.

As noted above, there are two primary statutory regimes designed for the restructuring of Canadian companies: the BIA and the CCAA. In the event that a restructuring proposal fails under the BIA, the company is deemed by statute to have made an assignment in bankruptcy and or proceedings are commenced for a receivership order. If a restructuring plan fails under the CCAA, the company is placed into receivership.

2.1 What is the objective of the proceedings?

See section 1.1 above. Restructurings and reorganisations are generally negotiated within the statutory framework of the BIA and the CCAA, and Canadian courts allow insolvent debtors a limited period of time within which to develop a plan or proposal to its creditors to be accepted or rejected.

2.2 Do all kinds of business entities qualify?

See section 1.2 above.

2.3 What are the necessary approvals?

See section 1.3 above. A bankruptcy can be initiated by means of any of the following:

- an insolvent debtor may file a voluntary assignment to place itself in bankruptcy;
- creditors of an insolvent debtor may apply to court to have the debtor declared bankrupt, which proceedings may be disputed by the debtor at a hearing; and
- the insolvent debtor may try to restructure under the BIA's proposal provisions and, if that proposal is rejected, the debtor is deemed to have assigned itself into bankruptcy.

Receiverships can be initiated privately or by court appointment. In a private receivership, a secured creditor can engage a receiver or receiver-manager pursuant to rights under its security and/or provincial statutes governing personal property and security. There is no stay of proceedings that prevent others from commencing or continuing proceedings against the debtor during a private receivership, and private receivers do not operate with the protection of the court.

2.4 Is it valid and binding to agree that such proceedings be a default/termination event?

By operation of the BIA, the 'date of the initial bankruptcy event' in respect of a company is the earliest day on which any one of the following is made, filed or commenced, as the case may be::

(i) an assignment by or in respect of the company;
(ii) a proposal by or in respect of the company;
(iii) a notice of intention by the company;
(iv) the first application for a bankruptcy order against the person; or
(v) proceedings under the CCAA (BIA, section 2).

2.5 What is the procedure?

See section 1.4 above.

2.6 Please provide information about voluntary filings

See section 1.4 above.

2.7 How are creditors' representatives chosen?

The appointing creditor or senior secured creditors can choose a court-appointed receiver. A petitioning creditor can choose the trustee in bankruptcy.

The roles and powers of a trustee and monitor are discussed in section 1.7 above. The powers and authority of a court-appointed receiver are derived from the appointment order. The court-appointed receiver is an officer of the court and is accountable to the court and all stakeholders of the debtor company. The receiver will shut down the business and liquidate the assets, and/or operate the business in an effort to generate monies and liquidate assets.

Other creditor representatives may be appointed by the court or committees may be formed to represent the interests of creditors at large. In the context of the BIA and bankruptcy proceedings, creditors may elect inspectors.

Creditors' committees are rare in CCAA proceedings. The more common practice is that creditors' committees may be formed on an *ad hoc* basis and, if necessary, given standing by the court.

2.8 Is there recourse against the opening judgment?

See section 1.5 above.

2.9 What are the roles and powers of committees?

In the context of bankruptcy proceedings under the BIA, creditors with proven claims must confirm the trustee's appointment and elect a board of inspectors. The inspectors act in a supervisory role and instruct the trustee. There are certain actions that a trustee cannot engage in without inspector approval, such as carrying on the business of the bankrupt or the sale or other disposition of any property of the bankrupt. Inspectors stand in a fiduciary relation to the general body of creditors, and should be disinterested (*Re Cynar Dry Co.*, [2005] O.J. No. 47 (O.S.C.J.) at paragraphs 29–31) and perform their duties impartially in the interests of the creditors who appoint them (*Higginson v Bryant, Isard and Co. (Trustee of)*, [1923] O.J. No. 693 (Ont. H.C.) at paragraph 24).

In the general context of reorganisation proceedings, shareholder interests are subordinate to those of creditors, thus expressly denying shareholders any right to vote on the restructuring plans proposed by the debtor company (or the trustee, as the case may be). In principle, the interests of the shareholder must give way to preserving all of the creditors' interests. The exception is when it can be shown that shareholder interest is not without value and must be considered in the restructuring plan. In such a case, jurisprudence holds that it would be unjust and inequitable to not consider shareholder interests in a restructuring plan (*In the Matter of the Companies' Creditors Arrangement Act, R.C.S. 1985, c. C-36, as amended & In the Matter of a proposed plan of compromise or arrangement with respect to Stelco Inc. and the Other Applicants listed in Schedule 'A'*, O.S.C.J. (commercial list), Justice James Farley, decision rendered on January 20, 2006 (04-CL-5306)).

In most situations, there are senior secured creditors who hold comprehensive security against the debtor's assets. A shareholder (among other parties including secured creditors and other affected stakeholders, or secondary market lenders) may consider making a debtor-in-possession (DIP) loan to the debtor company. DIP financing is now codified under section 50.6 of the BIA and is adopted by the courts in CCAA proceedings. A DIP lender will have to determine, on the best available evidence, whether there is sufficient equity in the debtor's assets, after taking into account existing secured loans, to support the DIP financing. Where it can be demonstrated that the debtor company has insufficient equity to support the DIP financing, the lender will look to the courts for an order granting the DIP lender priority over existing lenders (for a list of the factors the court will consider in determining whether or not to approve a DIP loan and any priority, see section 50.6(5) of the BIA). A DIP loan will affect priorities in the distribution scheme, but will not change or alter the voting status of the shareholder.

2.10 What are the consequences of opening judgments for creditors?

BIA

The court appointment of a receiver is typically accompanied by a comprehensive stay of proceedings restraining creditor action against the debtor and providing a more stable platform for the realisation to occur. The receivership order invariably includes a stay of proceedings restricting creditors from exercising any rights or remedies without first obtaining permission from the court. This stay will be much broader than the statutory stay of proceedings that occurs when a company simply becomes bankrupt, and is generally analogous to the comprehensive stay of proceedings found in CCAA proceedings.

Once a receiver has realised on the assets of the debtor, it will seek to distribute proceeds to creditors in accordance with their entitlements and priority, following court approval. If the only recovery is to secured creditors, there may be no need for a claims process. If there are any surplus funds after satisfying all secured claims, the receiver may run a court-sanctioned claims process or seek the court's approval to assign the debtor into bankruptcy and have unsecured claims dealt with through bankruptcy.

Generally speaking, when a company becomes bankrupt, the debtor ceases to have the legal capacity to dispose of its assets or otherwise deal with its property, which vests in a trustee in bankruptcy. Such appointment is expressly subject to the rights of secured creditors. Within the context of the commencement of bankruptcy proceedings, unsecured creditors are stayed from exercising any remedy against the bankrupt or the bankrupt's property, and may not commence or continue any action or proceeding for the recovery of a claim (unless the creditor is granted special permission by the court).

Secured creditors, on the other hand, are not subject to this stay of proceedings. The rights of a trustee in bankruptcy are expressly subject to the rights of secured creditors. Generally, a bankruptcy does not affect the rights of secured creditors except to the extent necessary to allow the trustee to realise on any value in the collateral subject to the security, above and beyond what is owed to the secured creditor. For example, the trustee can demand that the secured creditor prove its security; cause the secured creditor to value its security; inspect the collateral subject to the security (generally for the purpose of valuing it); and redeem the collateral subject to the security by paying the secured creditor the amount of the assessed value of the security. On redemption, the collateral subject to the security becomes an asset of the bankruptcy estate.

To the extent that the amount of a secured creditor's debt exceeds the value of the collateral subject to its security, a secured creditor may participate in the bankruptcy process and file a proof of claim in respect of the unsecured deficiency portion of its claim.

All unsecured creditors must complete a statutory proof of claim form in order to prove their claim. Although there is no predetermined bar date, a creditor is not entitled to vote at a meeting of creditors to approve the proposal, or participate in distributions provided for under the proposal, if they have not submitted a proof of claim by the meeting time or prior to distributions.

The trustee is required to review each proof of claim and either allow or disallow each claim with supporting written reasons. A proof of claim must be filed with the trustee prior to the completion of the administration of the bankrupt estate and the trustee's application for discharge.

CCAA

In CCAA proceedings, there is no mandatory time-frame in which affected creditors must prove their claim. However, the court will generally establish a claims process. An important part of the court-appointed monitor's role is to inform the creditors about the claims process and provide proof of claim forms, together with instructions on how to complete and file the proofs of claim. All creditors are responsible for and required to prove their respective claims. To be able to vote at a creditor's meeting, a creditor must file a completed proof of claim and supporting documents before the start of the first meeting.

In some cases, there may be a deadline for filing the proof of claim ('claims bar' date). If a creditor does not file a proof of claim before the claims bar date, the creditor's rights could be severely and irreversibly affected.

2.11 What is the duration of the restructuring process?

There is no statutory maximum for the administration of receiverships and or bankruptcies under the BIA or the CCAA. Receiverships are generally governed by the terms of the initial receivership order, which will usually include a comeback date on notice to all stakeholders and set out the various powers of the court-appointed receiver. The duration of the court-supervised restructuring process will depend upon the complexity of the issues that the receiver will face in the administration of the debtor company and the realisation of its assets.

2.12 How do creditors vote?

BIA

In the context of a bankruptcy, a creditor is not entitled to vote at the first meeting of creditors unless it has proved a claim in bankruptcy, and the proof of claim has been lodged with the trustee before the time appointed for the meeting.

A secured creditor that does not surrender its security can only vote if the creditor files a proof of claim showing the particulars of the security, the date when the security was given and the value at which the creditor assesses its security. The secured creditor is entitled to vote only in respect of the balance due to it, after deducting the value of the security as shown in the proof of claim.

Creditors are divided into classes based on the nature of their respective claims (secured, unsecured, landlords etc). Every class is entitled to express its views and wishes separately from any other class. The trustee may vote as a proxy holder for a creditor at a creditor meeting.

CCAA

As described in section 1.10 above, after the debtor files a plan with the court, creditors are separated into classes based on the nature of their claims against the debtor. Creditors will then vote on the plan. Approval of the plan is achieved by a double majority (two-thirds in dollar amount and a majority in number) on a class-by-class basis. If the creditors approve the plan, the debtor must seek approval of the court before implementation.

2.13 What are the rules on clawback/voidability?

Under the BIA, the trustee is responsible for scrutinising the actions of the bankrupt before the bankruptcy and for reporting to creditors on transactions that may be impugned as preferences, fraudulent conveyances, transfers at undervalue or on other grounds and, where appropriate, commencing proceedings to challenge such transactions. If a challenge is successful, depending on the remedy, either the transaction is voided and property transferred by the debtor prior to the bankruptcy must be returned to the bankrupt estate or, in the case of a 'transfer at undervalue', the difference in value between the actual consideration given by the debtor (if any) and the fair market value as determined by the court must be paid to the bankrupt estate.

The BIA creates a complete framework for challenging transactions that may have diminished the value of the estate of a debtor company. A trustee or receiver, as the case may be, can challenge these transactions between the debtor company and a creditor that occur:

- within three months of the initial bankruptcy event if it appears that a certain creditor was paid at the expense of other creditors or a creditor received a transfer of property at undervalue; or
- within 12 months of the initial bankruptcy event if it appears that a creditor was paid at the expense of other creditors or a creditor received a transfer of property at undervalue and is a creditor not dealing at arm's length (BIA, section 95(1)(a) and (b)).

There are additional provincial statutory regimes that are available to trustees, receivers and creditors in Canada to attack payments and conveyances and transfers of property made to certain creditors. These provincial statutes generally operate in conjunction with the BIA and the CCAA.

The CCAA provides a right to review transactions, including preferences and 'transfers at undervalue' by importing into the CCAA avoidance concepts from the BIA that were previously only available in bankruptcies. The monitor in CCAA proceedings may challenge preferential payments or dispositions of property by the debtor for conspicuously less consideration than fair market value, unless a plan of arrangement provides otherwise.

2.14 What are the rules on set-off/netting?

Creditors are not precluded from exercising their set-off and/or netting rights.

The law of set-off and compensation continues to apply in bankruptcy/restructuring to the same extent and in the same manner outside of bankruptcy/restructuring ,and there is no stay on set-off claims. However, under the CCAA, there are cases where set-off rights can be temporarily stayed. Stay of set-off claims is not customary in receivership proceedings, but may be ordered in appropriate circumstances. Preservation of set-off claims in BIA and CCAA includes both legal and equitable set-off.

2.15 How is exit managed?

In the CCAA context, there is no concept of 'cram-down' in Canada. Each class of creditors to which the plan is proposed must approve the plan by the requisite majorities.

Courts have approved the purchase of assets from an insolvent business by way of a credit bid under the CCAA. A proposed sale by way of a credit bid will be scrutinised carefully as a sale involving a credit bid by one of the debtor's secured creditors will normally disadvantage all subordinate creditors (*Montrose Mortgage Corp. v Kingsway Arms Ottawa Inc.*, 2013 ONSC 6905 (Ont. S.C.J.)).

In the context of the BIA, the powers to sell, encumber and dispose of certain assets of the debtor company are contained in the original appointment order. In some instances, a receiver may be at liberty to dispose of or sell assets of the debtor company without court approval if the value of the asset does not exceed a certain monetary value referred to in the appointment order. On all large dispositions of assets, the receiver requires court approval. The purpose of the sale approval motion is to consider the best interests of the parties with a direct interest in the proceeds of the sale, primarily the creditors. Dissatisfied creditors, unsuccessful bidders and/or owners of the insolvent business may oppose approval of the sale. A court should consider the following issues in examining a proposed sale of asserts by a receiver:

- whether the receiver has made a sufficient effort to get the best price and has not acted improvidently;
- the interests of all parties;
- the efficacy and integrity of the proceed by which offers are obtained; and
- whether there has been unfairness in the working out of the process (*Royal Bank v Soundair Corp.*, (1991), 7 C.B.R. (3d) 1 (Ont. C.A.)).

2.16 Are 'prepackaged' plans, arrangements or agreements permissible?

Yes. 'Prepackaged' plans are arrangements under which the sale of all or part of a company's business or assets is negotiated with a purchaser, prior to the appointment of a proposal trustee, CCAA monitor or receiver. On appointment, a court application is made to approve the transaction and the sale is closed shortly thereafter. In order to obtain court approval, a satisfactory sales process leading to the agreement is usually required.

2.17 Is a public authority involved?

BIA

At the outset of receivership proceedings, the appointing creditor will seek a receivership order and the court will be required to rule on the eligibility of the company for court protection, and approve or opine upon the feasibility/sustainability of, for example, an asset sale or distribution scheme. In the context of bankruptcy proceedings, the court may be required to rule on whether or not a debtor is bankrupt on a contested application for a bankruptcy order and make rulings on certain dispositions of assets of the trustee. Trustees are licensed by the OSB, which supervises the administration of bankruptcies and proposals under the BIA. The OSB is not involved in the approval process.

CCAA

The court establishes the claims process. Within days of the vote accepting a plan, the debtor company must apply to the court for the plan to be sanctioned. In sanctioning a plan, the court must determine that the plan is fair and reasonable, that it complies with all statutory requirements and that it respects the previous orders of the court.

2.18 What is the treatment of claims arising after filing/admission?

See section 2.10 above. Under both the BIA and the CCAA, creditors will be permitted to file a proof of claim up to a claims bar date, which is established in conjunction with a proposed distribution scheme (under the BIA) and or the implementation of an approved plan (under the CCAA).

2.19 Are there ongoing contracts?

BIA

If an NOI has been filed, no person can terminate or amend any agreement, including a security agreement with the insolvent person (BIA, section 65.1). Similarly, no person can terminate or amend any agreement with a bankrupt (BIA, section 84.2). By contrast, the debtor can terminate most types of agreements if and only if the trustee approves of the termination (BIA, section 65.11). Financing agreements where the debtor is the borrower are among the types of agreements that cannot be terminated by the debtor (*ibid.*). Though the credit agreement between debtor and creditor cannot be cancelled by either party, it is difficult to conceive of a credit agreement that would allow the borrower to draw on credit post-filing.

CCAA

The CCAA contains nearly identical termination provisions as the BIA in this respect.

2.20 Are consolidated proceedings for members of a corporate family/group possible?

There are no specific provisions concerning substantive consolidation in the BIA or CCAA. In proceedings under the CCAA and BIA where the benefits of consolidation outweigh the prejudice, the courts have exercised their inherent authority to permit consolidation. There is no definitive case outlining what criteria are to be considered. Therefore, it is fair to state that Canadian courts take a more contextual approach to issues of substantive consolidation. Canadian courts have a history of interfering as little as possible with stakeholder rights.

In determining whether to order consolidation, the courts will consider all relevant factors, with particular emphasis on the difficulty in segregating the identifying ownership of individual assets and liabilities, the actual level of commingling of assets and business functions, and the similarity of interests and ownership between the various corporate entities. The courts also consider the level of integration and interdependence of the financing arrangements of the affiliated entities and the behaviour of the debtor prior to filing, such as whether there has been a transfer of assets without corporate formalities, under unreasonable commercial terms or with intent to prejudice creditors.

Consolidation can be sought as part of the initial proceedings or by way of application or motion during the course of a proceeding under the BIA or CCAA. The motion or application could be brought by any interested party and on notice to all stakeholders. In theory, the court could permit partial consolidation if circumstances were such that it was demonstrably just and equitable for the stakeholders in general. The factors that the court considers typically do not focus on the creditworthiness of the debtors or the asset allocation between debtor companies with a family of companies *per se*. The court will take into account all relevant factors, including the interests of secured creditors and lien holders, in determining whether to permit consolidation (for a detailed discussion on substantive consolidation in the Canadian context, see *Atlantic Yarns Inc. (Re)*, [2008] N.B.J. No. 150).

2.21 What are the charges, fees and other costs?

It is a well-established practice for court-appointed receivers in Canada to be granted a first ranking administrative charge over a debtor's property to secure the receiver's fees and disbursements. However, it is not a given that a receiver will automatically be granted a priming administrative charge in all cases. Under the BIA, receivers must serve notice on principal secured creditors whose security interests the receiver seeks to have primed by a court-ordered administrative charge (see BIA, sections 47.2 and 243(6)). Receivers should also disclose in court reports any intention to apply proceeds or realisations against their fees and disbursements.

The BIA provides that a trustee in bankruptcy becomes a creditor of a bankrupt estate upon its appointment, is entitled to receive funds from the debtor company and is named as a preferred creditor for services performed after the date of bankruptcy (BIA, section 136).

Notwithstanding a court-ordered administrative charge or the provisions of the BIA that protect the fees and disbursements of a trustee in bankruptcy, all professional fees and disbursements of a court-appointed receiver and or a trustee are subject to taxation of the court as required under the provisions of the BIA and CCAA, as the case may be.

3. LIABILITY ISSUES

3.1 What is the liability of managers/directors *vis-à-vis* creditors?

Can management/directors (*de jure* or shadow) be held personally liable?

The ability of various stakeholders to take action against directors or officers for breach of their duties is limited in an insolvency context. Once a corporation files an NOI under the BIA or obtains a stay from the court under the CCAA, claims against directors and officers will automatically be stayed and can only be lifted with leave of the court (BIA, section 69.13; CCAA, section 11.03). Further, a resolution or settlement of claims and/or lawsuits against directors and officers will usually be subsumed into the plan of arrangement or proposal. Most proposals under the CCAA or BIA will include a release of claims against officers and directors, although these releases may carve out claims for fraud (section 13 of the BIA and section 5.1 of the CCAA authorise the inclusion of such releases).

As a result, these types of cases are rare, and will usually only proceed if the proposal or plan of compromise and arrangement is unsuccessful. Generally, these sorts of lawsuits fall into one of two categories:

- instances where the company did not file in a timely manner; and
- instances where there has been fraud.

In a bankruptcy scenario, the stay will expire and directors and officers can be held personally liable in certain circumstances. First, in both BIA and CCAA proceedings, directors and officers may be liable for preferences and transfers at undervalue; on application by the trustee, the court may make an order that a party to the transfer pay to the estate an amount equal to the difference between the value of the consideration received by the insolvent company and the fair market value of the assets (BIA, section 2.69; CCAA, section 36.1).

Secondly, the BIA provides that if a corporation commits an offence listed in part XIII of the statute, any officer or director of the corporation who authorised or participated in the commission of the offence is a party to and guilty of the offence, regardless of whether the corporation has been prosecuted (BIA, section 204). Where a person has been convicted of an offence under the BIA and any other person has suffered loss or damage because of the commission of the offence, the court may make an order as to compensation for loss of or damage to property suffered as a result of the commission of the offence (BIA, section 204.3). Such offences include, but are not limited to:

- any fraudulent disposition of property;
- knowingly making a material omission in accounting records;
- obtaining false credit; or
- fraudulently concealing property of the debtor.

For a full listing of offences under the BIA, see sections 198–208 of the statute.

Directors may also attract liability for many other acts prohibited under federal and provincial law in Canada which will not be reviewed in detail here. For example, directors may be liable for the declaration of dividends if the corporation was insolvent, or nearly insolvent (BIA, section 101(2)). Certain conduct may also breach directors' and officers' duties and responsibilities under securities, employment, tax and environmental law. Whether or not such liability could extend from directors and officers to creditors would depend on the specific nature of the offence and the remedy provided for under the applicable legislation.

Finally, creditors may resort to launching an application for relief pursuant to section 241 of the Canada Business Corporations Act, RSC 1985, c C-44 (CBCA) and equivalent provisions in provincial business corporation statues, commonly referred to as an 'oppression remedy'. Though it is less common, creditors may also bring a derivative action on behalf of the corporation pursuant to CBCA, section 239.

The oppression remedy is a broad remedy that provides creditors and other stakeholders with a cause of action against directors and officers for a significant range of unfair conduct. Canadian courts will grant the remedy where a corporation enters into a transaction that breaches creditors' reasonable expectations in a manner that is oppressive, unfairly prejudicial to or unfairly disregards the interests of a creditor.

The remedies available under CBCA, section 241 are broad and flexible, and the court has the power to make any order it sees fit. Common remedies include:

- an order restraining the conduct complained of;
- appointing a receiver;
- compensating the aggrieved person;
- liquidating the corporation; or
- replacing the directors.

A derivative action is an administrative proceeding whereby an application is made to court seeking leave to bring an action in the name of the corporation. Unlike a claim based on oppression, which is personal in nature, the derivative action focuses on harm done to the company. The remedies available in a derivative action are limited to the standard remedies available in a court action.

Prerequisites?

If a creditor wishes to initiate an action or application against an officer or director during a formal restructuring, it would first have to obtain an order from the court lifting the stay of proceedings. Under the BIA, a creditor who is affected by the operation of the stay may apply to the court for a declaration that the stay does not operate in relation to it, which application will be granted if the court is satisfied that the creditor or person is likely to be materially prejudiced by the continued operation of the stay, or that it is equitable on other grounds to make such a declaration (BIA, section 69.4). The CCAA provides no guidance as to when a motion to lift the stay will be successful, and regard must be paid to case law as to the test to be applied by the court on such a motion. In *Re Canwest Global Communications Corp*, 2009, 61 CBR (5th) 200, the Ontario Superior Court of Justice enumerated nine situations in which the stay may be lifted, including situations when the plan is likely to fail or when the applicant can demonstrate hardship caused by the stay itself.

If the court has lifted the stay against a director or the restructuring has failed, then a creditor may commence an application seeking an oppression remedy or leave to bring a derivative action.

In order to bring a derivative action, the creditor must satisfy the court that:

- it is acting in good faith;
- the relief sought is in the best interests of the corporation; and
- the creditor has given notice to the directors of the corporation or its intention to apply to the court.

There are no such prerequisites to bringing an application for an oppression remedy.

Who has standing to sue? Can creditors force the court agent to introduce an action? How?

A creditor cannot force a court agent to sue, but, in the event of a bankruptcy, can request that the trustee initiate an action on behalf of the estate of the bankrupt. A trustee can only initiate court action with the permission of the inspectors appointed to oversee administration of the estate (BIA, section 30(d)). If the trustee fails, refuses or neglects to take a proceeding, a creditor may obtain from the court an order authorising it to take the proceeding in its own name and at its own expense and risk, on notice being given to the other creditors of the contemplated proceeding, and on such other terms and conditions as the court may direct (BIA, section 38).

Can creditors join in the court agent's action? Under what conditions? Is there a need to prove specific loss (different from the one suffered by the creditors)?

Under the BIA, actions can only be initiated by the trustee, unless court approval is granted under section 38 for a creditor or creditors to pursue a matter directly. The CCAA offers no specific guidance in this regard.

3.2 What is the liability of the lender?

If recognised, is it by statute? By case law?

Lender's liability is not recognised by statute in Canada. Actions based in lender's liability are rare in Canada and, to the extent that they are recognised, are founded in case law under the doctrine of fiduciary duty or in tort. The contract is considered paramount in commercial lending relationships and, as such, if a remedy for lenders' liability is not provided for in the contract, it is very difficult for a borrower to establish a claim against a lender for lender's liability.

Prerequisites?

Assuming the contract between the debtor and creditor does not provide for an action grounded in lender's liability, the two main bases of lender's liability claims are founded in cases where the lender is alleged to owe a fiduciary duty to the borrower, or otherwise in tort.

In a claim of breach of fiduciary duty, the main threshold will be establishing that a duty was owed by the lender to the borrower. Such a duty will only be recognised in extraordinary circumstances where there exists a special relationship between the lender and the borrower. In deciding this question, the court will consider whether one party could reasonably have expected that the other party would relinquish its own self-interest and act in the former's best interests, and will look to factors such as discretion, influence, vulnerability and trust to make its determination (for a detailed discussion of the law of fiduciary duty in the context of lenders' liability, see *J.R. Investments Ltd v Moncton Flying Club Estate*, [2011] N.B.J. No. 303 and *Bank of Montreal v Witkin*, [2005] O.J. No. 3221). If the borrower is able to discharge its onus of establishing that a fiduciary duty exists, it must then prove that the lender breached this duty and such breach was not permitted by the contract between the parties.

Lenders' liability claims in Canada have been attempted in tort, under theories of negligence and unlawful interference with economic relations. In a claim of negligence, as in a claim of fiduciary duty, the borrower would once again have to establish that a 'special relationship' exists between the parties in order to establish the threshold question of whether the lender owed it a duty of care. A finding of unlawful interference with economic relations requires that three elements be satisfied:

(i) the defendant intended to injure the plaintiff;
(ii) the defendant interfered with the business or livelihood of the plaintiff by illegal or unlawful means; and
(iii) as a result of the interference, the plaintiff suffered economic loss.

The requirement of an unlawful act makes such claims difficult to prove.

Who has standing to sue?

Any party to the commercial relationship at issue and or a court-appointed agent, if applicable.

Ground? The laws of torts? Other?
See above.

For further reading on the concept of lender's liability in Canada, readers are referred to Lee Cassey and Lily Coodin, 'Assessing "Lender's Liability" in Workouts' (2013) 30:1 Nat. Insolv. Rev.

Denmark

Bech-Bruun Ole Borch & Lars Lindencrone Petersen

1. WHAT COURT-MONITORED RESTRUCTURING PRE-INSOLVENCY PROCEEDINGS OR SCHEMES HAVE BEEN DEVISED BY THE LAW OF YOUR COUNTRY TO LIMIT VALUE DESTRUCTION FOR FAILING BUSINESS ENTITIES?

Danish law does not have any rules on the processing of failing business entities that are not insolvent. The Danish Companies Act (Consolidated Act No. 322 of 11 April 2011) contains rules on the solvent liquidation of limited liability companies. In order to be able to apply these rules, the company must be solvent, and the reason for the solvent liquidation is usually either that the company was created for a fixed period, which has expired, or with a restricted object, which has been realised, or that the owners have decided for some other reason to dissolve the company by way of solvent liquidation.

1.1 What is the objective of the proceedings?

N/A.

1.2 Do all kinds of businesses qualify?

N/A.

1.3 What are the necessary approvals?

N/A.

1.4 What is the procedure?

N/A.

1.5 Is there recourse against the opening judgment?

N/A.

1.6 What are the substantive tests/definitions?

N/A.

1.7 What is the role of a court-appointed agent?

N/A.

1.8 What protection is there from creditors?

N/A.

1.9 What is the usual duration of the restructuring process?
N/A.

1.10 Who prepares the restructuring agreement and what are the available tools?
N/A.

1.11 Are subordination agreements necessarily given full effect?
N/A.

1.12 How is exit managed?
N/A.

1.13 Who are the necessary parties?
N/A.

2. POST-INSOLVENCY PROCEEDINGS

2.1 What is the objective of the proceedings?
Since 1 April 2011, the Danish Bankruptcy Act (Consolidated Act No. 11 of 6 January 2014; DBA) has contained rules on restructuring proceedings (see sections 10–15b). This is a one-string set of rules, which may result in the restructuring of the debtor by way of compulsory composition – such that the undertaking continues with the same ownership – or in a restructuring of the undertaking by way of a sale thereof – such that bankruptcy proceedings are commenced against the former owner.

The object of the rules is to improve the possibility that an undertaking that is viable, but temporarily insolvent, is not discontinued through bankruptcy proceedings, but is restructured.

Restructuring proceedings are not a mandatory preliminary stage preceding bankruptcy.

2.2 Do all kinds of business entities qualify?
The rules apply to all insolvent debtors – both natural and legal persons. Associations in which one or more participants is/are personally liable, eg general partnerships and limited partnerships, can only be subjected to restructuring proceedings if proceedings are also commenced against the party/parties with personal liability. There is no requirement in respect of the size of the undertaking or the degree of insolvency.

2.3 What are the necessary approvals?
A petition for restructuring proceedings can be filed by a creditor or the debtor (see section 11(1) of the DBA). If the debtor is an association, the petition must be filed by the supreme governing body (board of directors/ management board). Creditors whose claims rank subordinate by way of agreement (capital base) are not entitled to file a petition. Employees in the debtor's undertaking may file a petition, but only if they have a claim for wages due for payment.

Generally, it is a condition that a creditable interest exists in the commencement of restructuring proceedings. A creditor, for instance, who must be assumed to have adequate security for his claims in the assets belonging to the debtor cannot file a petition.

In the case of financial undertakings, petition for restructuring proceedings may be filed by the Danish Financial Supervisory Authority.

Petitions for restructuring proceedings must be filed with the bankruptcy court situated in the district where the debtor engages in commercial activity (see section 3 of the DBA). The restructuring proceedings must be handled by a restructuring administrator and a restructuring accountant and the petition must contain the debtor's proposal for who is to be appointed (see section 11(2) of the DBA), but the bankruptcy court making the appointment is not bound by the debtor's proposal. No formal requirements exist in respect of these persons, though, in practice, the restructuring administrator is a lawyer and the restructuring accountant is an auditor.

If the petition is filed by the debtor or if the petition from a creditor is consented to by the debtor, the petition will be processed on the basis of documents. A petition from a creditor which has not been consented to by the debtor will be served on the debtor and a court meeting will subsequently be held. If a debtor who is a natural person objects to the petition, the petition will be processed as a petition for bankruptcy (see section 11(5) of the DBA). If the management of a debtor who is a legal person objects, the bankruptcy court may remove the management and let the restructuring administrator take over the management and control in connection with allowing the petition (see sections 12a–b of the DBA).

No creditors (except for the creditor having filed the petition) are convened to the meeting.

If the petition is filed by the debtor, any creditor who has an individual and substantial interest may receive information in this respect (see section 9(2) of the DBA). Access to information that creditor has filed a petition is not granted until the petition is allowed.

2.4 Is it valid and binding to agree that such proceedings be a default/termination event?

As a consequence of the rules described in section 2.19 below, a condition in a bilateral agreement according to which it constitutes breach entitling the non-breaching party to termination that restructuring proceedings are commenced for a party is as a general rule without legal effect. Such condition only has legal effect if, due to the nature of the legal relationship, the contract could not be continued during the restructuring proceedings (see section 12n of the DBA). It may, for example, be agreed with legal effect that the fact that restructuring proceedings are commenced against a partner does entitle the other partners to force the partner in question to leave the general partnership.

2.5 What is the procedure?

It is a condition for allowing a petition for restructuring proceedings that the debtor is insolvent (see section 11(1) of the DBA). This means that the debtor is incapable of meeting its obligations as they fall due and that this inability is not merely temporary (see sections 11(1) and 17(2) of the DBA). This is thus an illiquidity criterion, and it is in principle of no importance whether or not the debtor has positive equity.

The bankruptcy court does not examine whether there are prospects of successful restructuring proceedings, but only ensures that the formal requirements for the contents of the petition for restructuring proceedings have been met.

If the petition for restructuring proceedings has been filed by the debtor, the debtor will only participate in the court hearing at which the bankruptcy order is made. If the petition has been filed by a creditor, this creditor will also be convened to the court hearing; the other creditors, however, are not convened.

If the petition is allowed, this will be announced in the Danish Official Gazette (see section 11a(2) of the DBA) and the restructuring administrator will immediately notify any holders of company charges and receivables charges (see section 11b(3) of the DBA).

2.6 Please provide information about voluntary filings

According to Danish law, a debtor is never under an obligation to file a petition for restructuring proceedings (or bankruptcy). A number of restructurings of undertakings are therefore conducted out of court.

Danish law does not stipulate any special rules on voluntary creditor arrangements, with regard to either the process or the contents thereof. Such arrangements are therefore governed only by the general rules of contract law. The rules of the Bankruptcy Act on set-off, bilateral agreements and avoidance as well as the rules of the Securities Trading Act (Consolidated Act No. 831 of 12 June 2014) on netting therefore only apply in a voluntary arrangement with creditors if this has been specifically agreed.

2.7 How are creditors' representatives chosen?

The rules on restructuring proceedings do not stipulate that a creditors' committee has to be set down. The restructuring process is managed by the restructuring administrator. The restructuring administrator is not under an obligation to consult with the creditors prior to entering into transactions. The creditors exert their influence through the voting procedures in respect of the restructuring plan and the restructuring proposal. The restructuring accountant must ensure the validity of the financial information forming the basis of the creditors' voting.

2.8 Is there recourse against the opening judgment?

The decision of the bankruptcy court may, irrespective of whether the decision is to allow or deny the commencement of restructuring proceedings, be appealed to the High Court by the debtor or creditor seeking a reversal of the decision (see section 248(2) of the DBA). The decision of the High Court will generally be obtained within one to two months, but there is no fixed time limit for when the appeal has to be determined.

The issue of insolvency or legal interest in the restructuring proceedings may be grounds for appeal; however, the lack of any prospects of success in completing a restructuring is not. Creditors who believe the latter to be the case are advised to voting against the restructuring plan presented to the creditors.

2.9 What are the roles and powers of committees?

N/A – see section 2.7 above.

2.10 What are the consequences of opening judgments for creditors?

The restructuring administrator will immediately notify the holders of company charges and receivables charges upon the commencement of restructuring proceedings (see section 11b(3) of the DBA). Other known creditors must be notified within one week of the commencement of proceedings (see section 11b(1) of the DBA). Notification must be given to both unsecured and secured creditors. No special rules apply to non-Danish creditors.

The debtor will maintain his right to enter into transactions in the course of the restructuring proceedings, but may not enter into transactions of material significance without the consent of the restructuring administrator (see section 12(1) of the DBA). Payment of debt must only be effected in accordance with the rules of the order of priority of payment of debtors or if a payment is necessary in order to avoid a loss. The debtor will thus in practice be prevented from making use of any credit facilities granted without the consent of the restructuring administrator.

The restructuring administrator may set up a framework by which the debtor is allowed to continue its operation of the undertaking. This means that the debtor may subsequently enter on its own into transactions which fall within the usual operation of the undertaking.

If the debtor is a limited liability company, the bankruptcy court may decide that the restructuring administrator is to take over management and control of the company (see section 12a of the DBA). This requires that the restructuring administrator or creditors representing at least 25 per cent of the voting amount (see section 2.12 below) make a request to that effect. If the bankruptcy court determines that the restructuring administrator is to take over the management and control of the undertaking, the restructuring administrator will be recorded as the management in the public registers and may subsequently exert the powers awarded to the board of directors and the management board in the Danish company legislation.

During the restructuring proceedings, the debtor may not be subjected to the levying of attachment or execution (see section 12c(1) of the DBA). This prohibition applies to both unsecured and secured claims. Where a claim is secured by a charge and is not voidable, the debtor must pay the regular payments for the time from commencement of the restructuring proceedings, to the extent that it must be assumed that the claim will be covered by way of sale of the asset charged. Where the debtor fails to pay, execution may be levied, but only against the asset charged (see section 12c(5) of the DBA).

Any dispute as to the extent to which a claim is voidable and/or actually covered by a charge will be decided by the bankruptcy court. The decision of the bankruptcy court is only of relevance to the question of individual proceedings in the restructuring proceedings and does not have a prejudicial effect during subsequent examination of the claim.

The right to satisfaction of claims secured by proprietary rights (retention of title, leasing rights) or pledge (eg receivables charge) is not affected by restructuring proceedings (see section 12c(4) of the DBA).

In connection with compulsory composition, the claims are included with their amounts as at the date of commencement of the restructuring proceedings, which means that claims for interest for the time after this lapse (see section 10a(3)(ii) of the DBA). Where the debtor is declared bankrupt after the restructuring proceedings, the claims are included with their amounts as at the time of commencement of the bankruptcy proceedings.

A claim not filed is not precluded, but a compulsory composition will also have effect for such claim (see section 14(2) of the DBA).

A compulsory composition will not affect creditors' rights *vis-à-vis* guarantors and others who are liable together with the debtor (see section 14(3) of the DBA).

The creditors must be treated equally unless they consent to less favourable treatment (see section 10c of the DBA). Claims with preferential rights in the event of bankruptcy are not covered by a compulsory composition (see section 10a(2)(iii) of the DBA). Loans which rank subordinate by way of agreement will lapse in the event of a compulsory composition, unless otherwise provided for in the agreement (see section 10a(3)(v) of the DBA).

A chargee must accept to receive only dividend for the part of the claim exceeding the value of the asset on which he holds a charge. This value is determined by the bankruptcy court on the basis of the valuation conducted by the restructuring accountant (see section 12e of the DBA). A claim secured by way of a mortgage on real estate, a vessel or aircraft, however, cannot be restricted.

2.11 What is the duration of the restructuring process?

The duration of the restructuring proceedings is laid down in the Bankruptcy Act. The restructuring plan must be presented within four weeks of commencement of the restructuring proceedings (section 11a(2) of the DBA) and the restructuring proposal must be discussed at a meeting to be held no later than six months after this date (section 13(1) of the DBA). As a general rule, the maximum duration of restructuring proceedings will thus be approx. seven months. However, subject to the consent of the creditors the deadlines for both the plan and the proposal may be extended such that the proceedings may last a total of approximately 12 months (sections 11e(5) and section 13a(1) of the DBA). In practice, extensions of these deadlines are rarely needed. See also section 2.16 below.

2.12 How do creditors vote?

The restructuring administrator will prepare and present both the restructuring plan and the final restructuring proposal. The plan and the proposal will be adopted unless a majority of the creditors vote against them. Rejection of the restructuring plan is also subject to the majority rejecting the plan constituting at least 25 per cent of the total claims entitled to vote.

When calculating the outcome of a voting procedure, only the amounts of the claims are used, whereas the number of creditors is not of importance (see section 13d(2) of the DBA). Creditors not voting are not included in the calculation. Claims belonging to the debtor's connections do not carry voting rights (see section 13d(3) of the DBA). Claims which will receive full or no coverage irrespective of the outcome of the voting do not entitle the holder to voting rights. As a general rule, contested claims are not part of the voting. Where it turns out that these claims would be decisive to the outcome of the voting, the bankruptcy court will determine which of the claims entitle the holder to vote and for which amounts (see section 13d(2) of the DBA). It is not possible to vote in classes. Claims entitle the holder to vote to the extent that they are not covered by a charge or any other security provided by the debtor.

Disputes as to the extent of the voting rights are settled by the bankruptcy court. Decisions in this respect cannot be brought before a higher instance (see section 249(1) of the DBA).

Claims which rank subordinate by way of agreement only have voting rights if it has been agreed that they are to be given equal ranking in the event of restructuring proceedings.

Claims deriving from the holding of shares do not entitle the holder to voting rights.

2.13 What are the rules on clawback/voidability?

The rules on avoidance of the Bankruptcy Act also apply to restructuring proceedings (see section 12i of the DBA).

The objective rules on avoidance of the Bankruptcy Act relate to both transactions defrauding creditors and creditor preferences. Transactions defrauding creditors – gifts (section 64 of the DBA), disclaimer of inheritance (section 65 of the DBA) and unreasonably large wages to the debtor's connections (section 66 of the DBA) – may be avoided if the transaction has been effected less than six months prior to the reference date. Creditor preferences – payment by unusual means, before the standard due date or with amounts which have substantially impaired the debtor's ability to pay its debts (section 67 of the DBA), charge created for old debt (section 70 of the DBA), increase of company charge (section 70a of the DBA) and legal enforcement (section 71 of the DBA) – may be avoided if the transaction has been effected less than three months prior to the reference date.

In all the rules, if the preferred party is one of the debtor's connections, the transaction may be avoided if it has taken place less than two years prior to the reference date.

The legal effect of avoidance according to an objective rule is that the preferred party must renounce such preferential payment, though not in excess of the loss of the estate (see section 75 of the DBA).

Furthermore, avoidance may be obtained according to the general provision of section 74 of the DBA. This may in principle be applied irrespective of the length of time between the transaction and the reference date, but it is conditional that the debtor was or became insolvent by way of the transaction, that the preferred party knew or ought to have known this, and that the transaction was fraudulent.

With respect to transactions effected after the reference date, the general rule is that they are avoided. This rule does not apply if a payment has been effected according to the rules of the order of priority of creditors or has been necessary in order to avoid loss, or if another transaction has been necessary in order to maintain the debtor's business or to reasonably safeguard the creditors' common interests (see section 72(1) and (2) of the DBA). In practice, however, the importance of these rules is limited, as they do not apply if the restructuring administrator has approved the transaction (see section 72(3) of the DBA).

The legal effect of avoidance being effected according to section 72 or 74 of the DBA is that the preferred party must pay the loss of the estate (see section 76 of the DBA).

The rules on avoidance also apply to any third party whose guarantee or security in respect of the debtor's debt has been released as a consequence of the transaction or legal enforcement which is avoidable (see section 80 of the DBA).

Any creditor entitled to vote has the right to propose that avoidance proceedings be commenced. The proposal must be made at the latest at the meeting at which the creditors vote on the restructuring proposal. The potential respondent does not have a right to vote (see section 12k(1) of the DBA). If the proposal is adopted, the bankruptcy court will appoint a lawyer to handle the case. Where the proposal is not adopted, any creditor may, at its own initiative, after having given notice thereof to the bankruptcy court, commence avoidance proceedings (see section 12k(4) of the DBA). Avoidance proceedings must be commenced no later than four weeks after termination of the restructuring proceedings (see section 12k(5) of the DBA).

2.14 What are the rules on set-off/netting?

The rights of set-off and netting are not restricted by the commencement of restructuring proceedings for the debtor (see sections 12g and 42 of the DBA).

2.15 How is exit managed?

Ordinarily, termination of the restructuring proceedings takes place by the creditors adopting the restructuring proposal, which contains either a compulsory composition for the debtor or a business transfer, which, according to the Bankruptcy Act, is combined with bankruptcy proceedings being commenced against the debtor's estate.

Irrespective of the contents of the restructuring proposal, including the size of the dividend entailed in the compulsory composition, the proposal is adopted unless a majority of the creditors vote against it (see section 13d(1) of the DBA). With respect to the calculation of the majority requirement, see section 2.12 above. Where the restructuring proposal is adopted, it is also binding on the creditors who have voted against it or who have failed to react in the restructuring proceedings (see section 14(2) of the DBA).

The adopted proposal must be ratified by the bankruptcy court in order to be valid (see section 13e(1) of the DBA). The bankruptcy court will not carry out a substantive examination of the proposal but must ensure that the rules of the act on equal treatment of the creditors and on the completion of the proceedings are observed. Furthermore, the bankruptcy court may deny ratification of an adopted proposal for compulsory composition if the dividend is lower than the expected dividend in the event of bankruptcy.

The restructuring proceedings will also terminate if the time limits laid down in the act for filing of the restructuring plan or the restructuring proposal and for the holding of meetings with the creditors are not met, or if the creditors reject the restructuring plan or the restructuring proposal. In these cases, the effect will be that bankruptcy proceedings are commenced against the debtor (see section 15 of the DBA).

The restructuring proceedings will terminate with final effect if it is established that the debtor is solvent.

The restructuring will be implemented once the restructuring proposal has been adopted and ratified. This applies irrespective of whether the restructuring entails composition for the debtor or a business transfer.

2.16 Are 'prepackaged' plans, arrangements or agreements permissible?

In principle, there is nothing to prevent an out-of-court agreement being concluded on the transfer of the debtor's business, subject to the creditors in the restructuring proceedings accepting this, typically in combination with a compulsory composition for the debtor. Alternatively, the business transfer can be agreed during the in-court restructuring proceedings, so that the meetings to adopt the restructuring plan and to vote on the restructuring proposal are held one after the other.

2.17 Is a public authority involved?

The restructuring proceedings take place under the auspices of the bankruptcy court. The bankruptcy court will thus appoint the restructuring administrator and the restructuring accountant, and the mandatory meetings to vote on the restructuring plan and the restructuring proposal are held in the bankruptcy court.

The control of the bankruptcy court is primarily of a formal nature; it is the creditors who decide on the content of the restructuring by way of voting. The bankruptcy court thus cannot deny ratification of a restructuring proposal adopted by the creditors on the grounds that the debtor has mismanaged the business, or that it does not believe that the debtor will be able to meet the conditions of the composition. The bankruptcy court must, however, (mandatorily) deny ratification of an adopted restructuring proposal if:

- errors in the process or the incompleteness of the information provided are considered to be of material importance to the result of the voting (see section 13e(3)(i) of the DBA);
- the restructuring proposal contains a provision on compulsory composition which is not compatible with section 10a of the DBA or is contrary to the Act in some other manner (see section 13e(3)(ii) of the DBA); or
- the debtor or a third party has, in order to influence the voting, granted advantages to any creditor outside the restructuring (see section 13e(3)(iii) of the DBA).

Finally, the bankruptcy court may (discretionarily) deny ratification of the adopted proposal if it is disproportionate to the debtor's financial position – in particular, if the composition dividend is lower than the dividend that would be expected in the event of bankruptcy (see section 13e(5) of the DBA).

2.18 What is the treatment of claims arising after filing/admission?

Claims arising after commencement of the restructuring proceedings will typically have arisen with the consent of the restructuring administrator. Such claims will have preferential rights if the debtor is declared bankrupt, either because the restructuring attempt fails or because a business transfer is completed, and the assets do not cover the claims in question. Where the restructuring proposal is successful, such claims will therefore not be covered by the restructuring, but must be met according to their contents (see section 10a(2)(iii) of the DBA).

Claims created by the debtor at its own initiative during the restructuring proceedings will not have a preferential right in a bankruptcy, if any, and will therefore be covered by the restructuring.

Claims created after the bankruptcy court has received a restructuring proposal containing a provision on compulsory composition are not covered by the restructuring (see section 10a(2)(i) of the DBA).

2.19 Are there ongoing contracts?

With the consent of the restructuring administrator, the debtor is entitled to continue bilateral agreements (see section 12o(1), first sentence of the DBA). If this happens, the debtor's contracting party is prevented from invoking the restructuring proceedings as breach entitling him to terminate the agreement for cause. Agreements which the contracting party has already terminated due to the debtor's non-payment can also be continued (see section 120(1), second sentence of the DBA). Such continuation is subject to notice being provided to the contracting party no later than four weeks after termination of the agreement and, prior to this, to the contracting party not having entered into transactions as a consequence of the termination, eg by letting premises which the debtor has had in its possession. If the bilateral agreement is part of a business transfer, the contracting party is under an obligation to accept the buyer as its new contracting party.

2.20 Are consolidated proceedings for members of a corporate family/group possible?

Under Danish insolvency law, consolidated companies are treated as independent units. Intra-group accounts between such companies are in principle treated equally to all other claims. Intra-group claims do not entitle the holder to vote (see section 13d(3) of the DBA).

2.21 What are the charges, fees and other costs?

A court fee of DKK 1,500 (EUR 200) is payable for filing a petition for restructuring proceedings. No fees are payable to public authorities for the actual restructuring proceedings.

The fees payable to the restructuring administrator and the restructuring accountant are determined by the bankruptcy court on the basis of a recommendation from the persons in question. In this assessment, particular regard is attached to the scope of the work and the nature of the undertaking, the responsibility associated with the work and the result achieved under the circumstances in question (see section 239(1) and (2) of the DBA).

3. LIABILITY ISSUES

3.1 What is the liability of managers/directors *vis-à-vis* creditors?

The management of a limited liability company may incur liability *vis-à-vis* the company's creditors if they suffer a loss in connection with the financial collapse of the company. Such liability is subject to the existence of a basis of liability. In order for such basis of liability to exist, the management member must be guilty of errors or neglect, ie a fault liability standard. This concerns the individual liability of each member of the management. The rules in this respect may be found in sections 361–65 of the Danish Companies Act.

Furthermore, it is a condition that the loss suffered must have been caused by the actionable behaviour.

The documentation material which must accompany the restructuring proposal must contain information about any actionable matters on the part of the debtor (see section 13b(1)(iii)d of the DBA).

There is no case law on the liability of management in connection with restructuring proceedings, but in connection with bankruptcy the general rule is that a claim is raised by the trustee on behalf of the bankruptcy estate. The creditor who has suffered an individual loss based on a factual basis other than that the management had continued operating beyond the time at which bankruptcy appeared an obvious possibility will be able to pursue his claim separately.

3.2 What is the liability of the lender?

No statutory provision or case law exists determining lender liability.

Finland

Castrén & Snellman Attorneys Ltd
Pekka Jaatinen, Salla Suominen & Anna-Kaisa Remes

1. WHAT COURT-MONITORED RESTRUCTURING PRE-INSOLVENCY PROCEEDINGS OR SCHEMES HAVE BEEN DEVISED BY THE LAW OF YOUR COUNTRY TO LIMIT VALUE DESTRUCTION FOR FAILING BUSINESS ENTITIES?

The Finnish system does not recognise court-monitored pre-insolvency proceedings as such. However, court-monitored official restructuring proceedings exist, and they are governed by the Restructuring of Enterprises Act (47/1993; the Restructuring Act). A prerequisite for initiating the restructuring proceedings is that the debtor faces imminent insolvency or is insolvent. However, restructuring proceedings must not be commenced if it is likely that the restructuring programme will not remedy the insolvency or prevent its recurrence otherwise than for a short period.

It should be noted that voluntary (ie out-of-court) restructuring proceedings are also common in Finland. However, the Restructuring Act does not cover unofficial voluntary restructuring.

1.1 What is the objective of the proceedings?

Restructuring proceedings are undertaken in order to rehabilitate a distressed debtor's viable business, to ensure its continued viability and to achieve debt arrangements. Throughout the process, the debtor remains a going concern. Restructuring proceedings aim to enable the continuation of the operations of the debtor company.

1.2 Do all kinds of businesses qualify?

A private entrepreneur, a general partnership, a limited partnership, a limited company, a co-operative, a housing company or an association engaged in economic activity may be the subject of restructuring proceedings.

In contrast, a partnership, corporation or co-operative in liquidation, a credit institution, an insurance company or a pension institution cannot be the subject of restructuring proceedings. Under special circumstances, however, a deposit bank may be a subject of restructuring proceedings.

The main prerequisite for court-monitored restructuring proceedings is that the entity is insolvent or faces imminent insolvency, but the restructuring programme will probably remedy the insolvency.

1.3 What are the necessary approvals?

According to the Restructuring Act, an application for restructuring proceedings may be filed by:

- the debtor;
- a creditor or several creditors together, but not a creditor with a claim contested as to its basis, a claim essentially contested as to its amount or a claim otherwise unclear; or
- a party for whom the insolvency of the debtor would probably cause financial loss on a claim, on grounds other than partnership or shareholding (probable creditor).

Typically, the debtor company's board of directors will decide on the filing. However, a shareholders' meeting should approve the filing in order for the court to continue to examine the application. The final decision concerning the commencement of the proceedings is made by the court.

1.4 What is the procedure?

A restructuring application must be filed with a district court along with the supporting documents, such as extracts from the Trade Register, copies of the articles of association and of financial statements, and a list of creditors. It is common practice for the application to also include a draft of a preliminary plan to facilitate the forthcoming restructuring process.

The court will grant major creditors the right to give statements regarding the debtor company's application. The creditors may claim that there are barriers to the commencement of the proceedings, which the court should consider before its decision. The creditors may also suggest candidates to be appointed by the court as an administrator.

Restructuring proceedings may be commenced if:

- at least two creditors whose total claims represent at least one-fifth of the debtor's known debts and who are not related to the debtor file a joint application with the debtor or declare that they support the debtor's application;
- the debtor faces imminent insolvency; or
- the debtor is insolvent and it is probable that the restructuring programme will remedy the insolvency or prevent its recurrence for more than a short period.

In general, all matters pending with the court are public unless specifically provided otherwise. However, a debtor may request that the application or other documentation should be declared confidential due to business secrets not to be disclosed.

1.5 Is there recourse against the opening judgment?

The opening judgment is subject to appeal by both the debtor and the creditor, unless appeal has been separately prohibited or unless the judgment in question concerns only a procedural issue. Typically, the debtor appeals to a rejecting decision of the court. The appeal shall be considered as a matter of urgency.

1.6 What are the substantive tests/definitions?

No particular tests are required. Insolvency means other than temporary inability of the debtor to repay its debts when they become due. The main prerequisite for the commencement of the restructuring proceedings is that the entity must be insolvent or face imminent insolvency, but the restructuring programme will probably remedy the insolvency.

1.7 What is the role of a court-appointed agent?

The court appoints an administrator at the commencement of the proceedings. It is also possible to appoint more than one administrator. Typically, the candidate suggested by the major creditors is appointed. The administrator should have sufficient independence from both the creditors and the debtor.

The administrator is entitled to participate in meetings of organs of a debtor business and to be heard there. Notices of such meetings shall be sent to the administrator. The administrator is also entitled to retain expert advisors.

In order to perform his or her duties, the administrator is entitled to enter the business premises in the possession of the debtor and to examine the debtor's books, business correspondence, other business documents and data files. Notwithstanding any provisions on secrecy, the administrator is entitled in the same way as the debtor to obtain information on the debtor's bank accounts, financial transactions, financial agreements and undertakings, assets, taxation and other factors relating to the financial position or the activities of the debtor.

It should be noted that the debtor's day-to-day administration and management remains with the board of directors and the managing director of the company, and the debtor remains in possession of its property unless specifically provided otherwise. However, the board and the management of the debtor shall co-operate with the administrator so that the administrator can perform his or her duties appropriately and so that the restructuring proceedings can be brought appropriately to a conclusion. On the request of the administrator or a creditor, the authority of the debtor may be restricted if there is a risk of the debtor acting in a way that harms or compromises the interests of a creditor.

Also, the debtor shall continue to be entitled to exercise its right of action in pending court proceedings or in other corresponding proceedings where it is a party, unless the administrator decides to undertake to exercise the debtor's right of action.

While the creditors do not legally have control over the debtor, in practice, the debtor is restrained by the creditors. Their sufficient support is essential for the success of the restructuring proceedings.

The competent court appoints a committee of creditors as the joint representative of the creditors, unless this is deemed to be unnecessary. The committee is an advisory body assisting the administrator in the performance of his or her duties and monitoring the activities of the administrator on the behalf of the creditors.

1.8 What protection is there from creditors?

The commencement of the proceedings brings the restructuring debts to an immediate standstill. Once the proceedings have commenced, the debtor shall not repay restructuring debts or provide security for such debts (interdiction of repayment). Nevertheless, a secured creditor is entitled, in accordance with the terms of the debt, to receive payments of interest and other costs of credit that have become due after the filing of the application. The creditor shall not invoke a term of the debt concerning the payment of costs of credit before they become due.

After the commencement of the proceedings, no measures shall be directed at the debtor in order to collect on a restructuring debt subject to the interdiction of repayment or in order to enforce its payment (interdiction of debt collection). Measures that have already been initiated shall not be continued. Moreover, no sanctions for default shall be directed at the debtor in respect of such a debt.

The following measures, among others, fall within the sphere of the interdiction of debt collection:

- the exercise of rights of liquidation or recovery based on real security rights and the other utilisation of security in order to obtain payment;
- the termination of a debt and the termination or cancellation of the contract underlying the debt owing to a default, with the exception of the termination or cancellation of a book credit facility or another revolving credit contract in order to refuse new credit;
- set-off by a credit institution against funds that the debtor has on a cheque deposit account at the institution when the interdiction of collection takes effect or thereafter, or funds that are at the credit institution at that time for transfer into the debtor's account, where the account can according to its terms be used for payments (note that set-off would otherwise be permissible as explained below);and
- the issue of an administrative decision detrimental to the debtor on the basis of a restructuring debt being in default.

The commencement of the proceedings interrupts the accrual of overdue interest on restructuring debts. The same provision applies to other consequences of delayed payment that are dependent on the length of the delay.

Moreover, after the commencement of the proceedings, precautionary measures based on official decisions shall not generally be directed against the debtor (interdiction of precautionary measures). A precautionary measure taken before the commencement of the proceedings shall lapse at that time.

Subject to certain exceptions, contracts of the debtor remain in force regardless of the commencement of restructuring proceedings. To enable successful restructuring process, the creditors' and claimants' rights to terminate their contracts with the debtor are limited.

1.9 What is the usual duration of the restructuring process?

There is no statutory maximum duration for the restructuring process. Usually, restructuring processes last approximately one year. However, the Restructuring Act provides a fast track (summary) approval of the restructuring programme, which may shorten the process by several months.

Restructuring proceedings terminate once the court confirms the restructuring programme. The implementation of the restructuring programme usually takes 5–10 years.

1.10 Who prepares the restructuring agreement and what are the available tools?

The administrator shall prepare a draft restructuring programme and submit it to the court within a period set by the court. Such period shall not exceed four months without a special reason.

When preparing the draft, the administrator shall negotiate with the debtor and the committee of creditors and, if necessary, with creditors.

The restructuring programme shall include an account on the financial status of the debtor and on other circumstances affecting the restructuring, as well as the provisions on measures and arrangements that pertain to the status of the debtor and the creditors, and shall aim for the continuation, alteration or termination of activities. The programme shall indicate the division of the creditors into groups and the possible absence of a right to vote.

The following debt arrangements may be applied to restructuring debts under the restructuring programme:

- a change of the payment schedule of a debt;
- an order that payments made by the debtor shall first be considered as payments against the balance of the debt and only later as payments against credit costs;
- a reduction in the obligation to pay credit costs relating to the remaining credit period; or
- a reduction in the balance of the unpaid debt.

The debt arrangement may also incorporate the full or partial refinancing of the debt as a one-off payment with new debt taken for this purpose, or with substitute performance that is reasonable in view of the creditor's field of activities and status.

The Restructuring Act does not provide for debt-for-equity swaps. However, a restructuring programme may include a provision requiring the debtor company to perform separate company law decisions, such as debt-for-equity swaps or sales of certain business areas.

1.11 Are subordination agreements necessarily given full effect?

As a principal rule, the creditors with the same priority position should be treated equally in the arrangements of debts outlined in the restructuring programme. For instance, a creditor with a secured debt is in a privileged position, since the balance of a secured debt cannot be reduced.

Subordinated debts, including both subordination by law and subordination by contract, will be treated as debts of lowest priority. Typically, lowest priority debts will not receive any payments. On the other hand, the administrator often decides to pay minor debts in full to simplify the process.

1.12 How is exit managed?

The restructuring programme shall be approved by the court. The restructuring programme may be approved if all of the known creditors or a majority in each of the groups of creditors accepts it.

In addition, the restructuring programme may be approved if a sufficient majority has voted for the approval of the programme in at least one group of creditors, and the claims of all of the creditors who have voted for approval represent at least one-fifth of all the known claims.

However, the programme shall not be approved if, for instance, the contents of the programme violate the right or justified interest of the debtor, a partner or shareholder in the debtor company or a third party, or are unreasonable in respect of such a person, or if adequate evidence has not been presented of the chance that the implementation of the programme will succeed.

1.13 Who are the necessary parties?

Court order in a matter connected with restructuring programme is subject to appeal, unless appeal has been separately prohibited or unless the order in question concerns a procedural issue. The restructuring programme shall be complied with regardless of appeal, unless the appellate court orders otherwise.

2. POST-INSOLVENCY PROCEEDINGS

The bankruptcy proceedings are the only court-monitored post-insolvency proceedings. The bankruptcy proceedings are governed by the Bankruptcy Act (120/2004).

2.1 What is the objective of the proceedings?

The bankruptcy is a form of insolvency proceedings covering all the liabilities of the debtor, where the assets of the debtor are liquidated and used in payment of the claims.

In the beginning of bankruptcy, the assets of the debtor shall become subject to the authority of the creditors. An estate administrator appointed by the court shall handle and liquidate the assets of the debtor and distribute the proceeds to the creditors.

2.2 Do all kinds of business entities qualify?

The principal rule is that the debtor must be insolvent to be declared bankrupt. Insolvency means that the debtor is other than temporarily unable to repay its debts as they fall due.

A private individual, a corporation, a foundation and another legal person may be declared bankrupt. A legal person may be declared bankrupt even if it has been removed from the relevant register or dissolved. A decedent's estate and a bankruptcy estate may also be declared bankrupt.

A creditor may file for debtor's bankruptcy if its claim against the debtor is clear and indisputable, such as a claim based on a res judicata judgment or a commitment signed by the debtor. However, a creditor's petition for bankruptcy shall be ruled inadmissible if the claim is insignificant and an order of bankruptcy would be obviously inappropriate in view of the costs and benefits of bankruptcy proceedings or clearly contrary to proper debt collection practice.

2.3 What are the necessary approvals?

Bankruptcy proceedings can be initiated by the debtor itself (voluntary) or by its creditor or creditors (involuntary) with a written petition. If the debtor itself files for bankruptcy, insolvency assumption will apply. This means that the debtor shall be deemed insolvent if the debtor declares its insolvency and there are no special reasons for not accepting this declaration. If the debtor itself applies for bankruptcy, the board of directors usually decides on the filing.

If bankruptcy application is filed by a creditor or creditors, they shall demonstrate that the debtor is insolvent. The debtor shall be deemed insolvent especially if:

- the debtor has discontinued payments;
- it has been determined in enforcement proceedings during the six months preceding the filing of the petition for bankruptcy that the debtor cannot repay the claim in full; or
- a debtor who is, or who during the year preceding the filing of the petition for bankruptcy has been, under the obligation to keep accounts has not repaid the clear and due claim of the creditor within a week of the receipt of a reminder.

2.4 Is it valid and binding to agree that such proceedings be a default/termination event?

Based on specific provisions under the Bankruptcy Act, contract clauses linking certain effects to the bankruptcy, such as the immediate termination of contracts, are considered null and void.

2.5 What is the procedure?

As a part of the 'first phase' of the bankruptcy proceedings, the estate administrator shall prepare an estate inventory and a description of the debtor. Based on such documents, the estate administrator shall present to the court and the major creditors his view on whether the bankruptcy has sufficient funds to continue to the 'second phase'.

If the bankruptcy continues, the estate administrator must set a lodgement date without delay. The creditors must lodge their claims by the lodgement date.

Based on the lodgements, the estate administrator draws up a draft disbursement list and delivers it to the creditors for statements. After having heard the creditors and the debtor, the estate administrator shall draw up a disbursement list and submit it for certification by the court. Disbursements to the creditors in bankruptcy shall be paid out in accordance with the certified disbursement list. A special audit is always conducted as a part of the bankruptcy proceedings.

2.6 Please provide information about voluntary filings

As a rule, the court always accepts a petition filed by the debtor and declares the debtor bankrupt. The court will also appoint one or more estate administrators. Before the appointment, the court shall reserve the main creditors and, at its discretion, the other creditors an opportunity to be heard. Usually, the administrator proposed by the main creditors is appointed.

Minutes of the board meeting where the board decided to apply for bankruptcy must be attached to the petition. In addition, the debtor must attach to the petition an account of its assets and the value thereof, information on the total amount of debtor's outstanding debts and the list of main creditors.

When deciding on an order of bankruptcy, the court shall organise the publication of an announcement of the beginning of bankruptcy. The announcement shall be published in the Official Gazette without delay. The court may also order the estate administrator to publish the announcement in one or several daily newspapers. If there is a special reason, the court may also order the estate administrator to publish the announcement abroad in a suitable manner.

The announcement shall state that a separate notice will be given on lodgements of claim, unless the examination of lodgements is unnecessary owing to insufficient funds or some other reason.

2.7 How are creditors' representatives chosen?

The authority in the bankruptcy estate shall be exercised by the creditors insofar as the matter by law is not to be decided or dealt with by the estate administrator. The estate administrator shall represent the bankruptcy estate. The estate administrator shall discharge his or her duties to the common interest of all creditors and comply with the instructions and orders issued by the creditors on matters within their authority.

The creditors shall exercise their authority primarily in the creditors' meeting. Alternative decision-making procedures are also admissible.

In addition, the creditors may establish a creditors' committee. The court may issue such instructions as it deems necessary on the composition, duties and term of the creditors' committee. The creditors' committee shall have a composition where the main creditor groups are represented. The committee shall have at least three members and it shall elect a chairperson from among its members. The estate administrator or a chairperson shall convene the committee. Decisions of the committee shall be made by simple majority voting.

If no creditors' committee has been established for an extensive bankruptcy estate, the court may establish one at the request of the estate administrator or a creditor. The court shall reserve the main creditors and, at its own discretion, any other creditors an opportunity to be heard so as to take due note of the opinions of the various creditor groups.

2.8 Is there recourse against the opening judgment?

Bankruptcy may be ordered to be reversed on the joint petition of the debtor and the creditor who filed the bankruptcy petition or, if the debtor has been declared bankrupt on his or her own petition, on the petition of the debtor. It shall be a prerequisite for a reversal that the petition has been filed within eight days of the order of bankruptcy and that a valid reason is supplied for the reversal. The court shall reserve the estate administrator and, at its own discretion, the creditors opportunity to be heard.

A court order of bankruptcy shall also be open to appeal by a creditor or the debtor. The court that has decided a matter pertaining to an order of bankruptcy shall forward any letters of appeal to the appellate court without delay. The appeal shall be heard as a matter of urgency. The legal effects of the beginning of bankruptcy remain valid even if an appeal is filed against the order of bankruptcy.

The bankruptcy may be ordered to lapse if, after the preparation of the estate inventory, it is evident that the funds of the bankruptcy estate are insufficient for the costs of the bankruptcy proceedings and none of the creditors assumes liability for the costs, or if the disbursement to the creditors out of the funds of the estate would be so insignificant that the continuation of the bankruptcy would not for that reason be expedient.

2.9 What are the roles and powers of committees?

The creditors shall exercise their authority primarily in the creditors' meeting. The decisions are made by voting using the one-vote-per-euro principle.

The creditors' committee is an advisory body that assists the estate administrator, supervises his or her activities and discharges the duties assigned to it by the creditors' meeting. The creditors' committee does not have any decision-making powers.

In order to discharge their duties, the creditors' committee and its members have the right to receive any necessary information from the estate administrator.

2.10 What are the consequences of opening judgments for creditors?

Stay?

A claim in bankruptcy that has not fallen due shall in the bankruptcy be considered due as between the creditor and the debtor.

The contracts entered into by a debtor will not automatically terminate, as the bankruptcy estate has the right to commit to contracts.

Forbidden payments?

In the beginning of bankruptcy, the debtor shall lose his or her authority over the assets to the bankruptcy estate. This means that a representative of the company may no longer make any payments or otherwise use these assets. All debts will be handled as part of the bankruptcy proceedings. Thus, no separate payments for the creditors are made.

Should interest accrued during the period be paid at contractual payment dates? Deferred and paid after plan is adopted? Capitalised? Is the rate necessarily the contract rate?

The debtor may lodge the interest accrued on bankruptcy debts both before and after the commencement of the bankruptcy. However, interests accrued on bankruptcy debts after the commencement of the bankruptcy are regarded as lowest priority debts and may only be settled after all other debts of the bankruptcy estate have been paid.

Is the opening judgment a valid draw stop (for undrawn facilities)?

The opening judgment is a valid draw stop (especially for undrawn facilities), and creditors should prevent the debtor from making any withdrawal or taking out any new loan. Only the bankruptcy estate shall have authority over the possible assets in the debtor's accounts.

Is it necessary to file proof of claim? Are all creditors required to file proof of claim? Are secured creditors necessarily notified? Are there any time limits? Are non-resident creditors treated differently? What are the consequences if a creditor is time-barred? Is the debtor discharged?

In order to be entitled to a disbursement, a creditor shall lodge a claim in bankruptcy in writing (letter of lodgement) by delivering it to the estate administrator no later than on the lodgement date, unless the claim is to be taken into account without lodgement.

A claim lodged to the court no later than on the lodgement date shall be deemed to have been lodged on time. A claim lodged by the creditor after the lodgement date (retroactive lodgement) can be taken into account only if the creditor pays to the bankruptcy estate a charge amounting to one per cent of the amount of the lodged claim. However, the charge shall not be less than EUR 600 or more than EUR 6,000. If the creditor has not been notified of the lodgements or there has been a valid excuse for not lodging the claim, or if the creditor is a private individual and the collection of the charge would be unreasonable in view of the creditor's circumstances, the charge shall not be collected. Retroactive lodgements shall no longer be taken into account when the disbursement list has been certified.

A creditor who wants payment out of collateral given by the debtor shall provide the estate administrator with the information on the claim and the collateral.

Does such proceedings entail any limitation on enforcement of contractually created security?

The assets subject to collateral may be liquidated by the creditor holding the security notwithstanding the ongoing bankruptcy proceedings (separatist rights). However, the bankruptcy estate has the right to prohibit the liquidation for at most two months in order to examine the rights of a creditor protected by collateral or to safeguard the interests of the estate. The prohibition may be issued only once. In practice, the creditor protected by collateral often agrees with the estate administrator that the administrator will handle the liquidation of collateral on behalf of the creditor.

The proceeds of collateral accruing during the bankruptcy shall come to the benefit of the creditor secured by the collateral. However, the bankruptcy estate shall be entitled to compensation for the costs of management and sale of collateral.

2.11 What is the duration of the restructuring process?

There is no statutory maximum duration for the bankruptcy process. Usually a full-length bankruptcy will take from two to five years, but it may be protracted due to legal disputes or if the bankruptcy estate is extensive.

2.12 How do creditors vote?

The creditors shall exercise their authority in the creditors' meeting. Each creditor shall have a voting strength equal to his or her current claim in the bankruptcy. The lowest priority debt shall confer no votes if it is evident that no disbursement towards such claim will be made. A conditional, disputed or otherwise unclear claim shall be assessed at its probable amount. A conditional claim in recovery shall, however, confer a vote if the creditor does not exercise a vote based on the same claim.

In the event of disagreement, the estate administrator or, if the matter is discussed in the creditors' meeting, the chairperson shall decide the voting strength conferred by a claim.

2.13 What are the rules on clawback/voidability?

In accordance with the Finnish Act on the Recovery to the Bankruptcy Estate (758/1991; the Recovery Act), a transaction concluded prior to the commencement of the bankruptcy proceedings may be recovered to the bankruptcy estate. In addition to bankruptcy proceedings, the provisions of the Recovery Act also apply to restructuring proceedings.

According to the general grounds for recovery, a transaction shall be revoked if the transaction, individually or together with other measures, unduly favours a particular creditor to the detriment of another creditor or transfers property out of the reach of the creditors or increases the debts of the debtor to the detriment of the creditors. A prerequisite for recovery is that the debtor was insolvent at the time of the transaction or the transaction contributed to the debtor's insolvency, and that the other party knew or should have known about the insolvency or of the excessive indebtedness.

Furthermore, a debt paid less than three months before the cut-off date (the day when the petition for bankruptcy has been filed) shall be reversed if the debt has been paid using an unusual means of payment or prematurely, or if the amount of the payment is deemed significant in relation to the assets of the bankruptcy estate. However, the payment shall not be reversed if it can be deemed as customary under the circumstances.

Also, collateral assigned or other security lodged by the debtor against his or her debts less than three months before the cut-off date shall be reversed if such security had not been agreed at the time the debt arose or if measures required by the establishment of a right to the security had not been performed without undue delay.

If the payment or security has been allocated to a related person of the debtor more than three months but less than two years before the cut-off date, the payment or security shall also be reversed, unless it is shown that the debtor was not insolvent or did not become insolvent as a result of the payment or security arrangements.

Since the purpose of the Act is to ensure equality among creditors and prevent the debtor from privileging one of the creditors at the expense of the others, any kind of proceedings, arrangements or measures taken may be recovered if the conditions set out in the Recovery Act are met. Both restructuring and bankruptcy administrators, as well as creditors, may seek to recover assets of the debtor on the basis of recovery legislation.

2.14 What are the rules on set-off/netting?

The creditor has the right to use a claim in bankruptcy for set-off against a debt owed to the debtor at the beginning of bankruptcy. However, the right of set-off is not available when the claim does not entitle the creditor to a payment out of the bankruptcy estate, or when the claim is based on debt with lowest priority.

Moreover, a claim that has been acquired from a third party later than three months before the cut-off date referred to in the Recovery Act cannot be used for set-off against a debt owed by the creditor to the debtor at the time of the acquisition. Also, a creditor who has committed to a payment of a debt to the debtor under circumstances where the arrangement is comparable to a payment made by the debtor has no right to set-off insofar as the payment would have been recoverable to the bankruptcy estate.

Furthermore, a credit institution shall not set a claim off against funds that the debtor has on deposit in an account with the institution at the beginning of bankruptcy.

2.15 How is exit managed?

Once the bankruptcy estate has been wound up, the assets belonging to the estate liquidated and the proceeds distributed to the creditors, the estate administrator shall draw up a final settlement of accounts. The final settlement of accounts shall be approved by the creditors' meeting, and the bankruptcy shall end by this approval.

The final settlement of accounts may be drawn up even if, for instance, the estate is not partially wound up because collateral, or other assets of little value, have not been sold.

In the case of debt conversion(s), what approvals are necessary? Is it possible to force shareholders' consent?

Debt conversion is not applicable in bankruptcy proceedings as the equity is lost in bankruptcy.

In the sale of the business as a going concern to an entrepreneur, do creditors have the right to make their own proposal? Is credit-bidding possible? Automatic release/survival of existing pledges and charges?

The estate administrator may decide to continue the business of the debtor if it is likely that the business can be sold as a going concern. The creditors may make their own proposals for buying the business of the debtor. The creditor making a proposal to buy the assets is, however, disqualified from voting in the creditors' meeting on the decisions of the business transaction in question. In order to oversee the best interest of all the creditors, the estate administrator shall ensure that a fair market value is used.

The disbursement of the funds

Creditors with similar priority principally have equal rights to disbursement from the bankruptcy estate in proportion to the amount of their claims. The order in which the debtor's debts are settled is determined by the Finnish Act on the Ranking of Claims (1578/1992).

Prior to any disbursements to unsecured creditors, the following creditors are to receive disbursement: (i) secured creditors and holders of retention rights, who have priority to the proceeds from the respective asset; (ii) creditors of expenses and administrative costs of the bankruptcy estate, creditors with claims based on contracts that the bankruptcy estate has entered into or become party of, and creditors of liabilities for which the bankruptcy estate is responsible for by the of law; and (iii) creditors with claims that are secured by a business mortgage; the disbursement has been limited to 50 per cent of the value of the encumbered business assets.

Certain debts – such as interest accrued on bankruptcy debts after the commencement of the bankruptcy, capital loans or bonds issued with a lower priority in relation to other indebtedness by the debtor – are regarded as lowest priority debts and may only be settled after all other debts of the bankruptcy estate have been paid.

2.16 Are 'prepackaged' plans, arrangements or agreements permissible?

Prepackaging arrangements are not forbidden by law in Finland. However, the estate administrator should not be involved in the planning and the arrangements of the transaction, in order to prevent him or her having a conflict of interest in acting as an estate administrator. Even in prepackaged arrangements, certain mandatory stages in bankruptcy process must be met.

2.17 Is a public authority involved?

Powers?

A court's role in bankruptcy proceedings is that of an approving body. The court shall, for instance, appoint the estate administrator, make the order of bankruptcy and certify the disbursement list.

Also, in some cases, the estate administrator may use the help of an execution officer, if necessary. A special authority, the Office of Bankruptcy Ombudsman, oversees the work of the estate administration.

Does it have to rule on the debtor's eligibility to court protection?

The court shall consider whether the debtor is insolvent and, based on that decision, make the order of bankruptcy.

Does it have to approve/opine upon the feasibility/sustainability of the plan?

The court shall verify that the estate administrator's disbursement list meets all the requirements and that the procedural provisions relating to the draft disbursement list have been observed. The court shall also make a decision on any disputed claim, unless the dispute is to be resolved separately.

If the estate administrator's disbursement list meets all the requirements, the court shall certify the disbursement list and make an order as to which claims shall receive disbursements (certified disbursement list).

Does the debtor receive any kind of protection?

The debtor does not have any protection in the bankruptcy proceedings. According to the Bankruptcy Act, the debtor shall, however, be treated with respect and his or her interests shall be taken appropriately into account in the winding up and administration of the estate.

The debtor shall also have the same right as a creditor to receive information from the estate administrator on the estate and its administration, as well as on the matters to be dealt with in a creditors' meeting or in an alternative decision-making procedure.

2.18 What is the treatment of claims arising after filing/admission?

The bankruptcy estate shall be liable for the debts arising during the bankruptcy proceedings or based on a contract or commitment entered into by the estate, as well as for the debts for which the estate is liable under the law (administrative expenses).

2.19 Are there ongoing contracts?

If, at the beginning of bankruptcy, the debtor has not performed a contract to which he or she is a party, the other contracting party shall request a declaration of whether the bankruptcy estate commits to the contract. If the estate declares, within a reasonable time, that it commits to the contract and posts acceptable security for the performance of the contract, the contract cannot be terminated for cause.

However, the other contracting party may terminate the contract if the contract is of a personal nature or there is another special reason for which it cannot be required that the other party stay under contract with the bankruptcy estate.

Credit agreements are handled in a similar way as other agreements of the debtor company. Thus, the bankruptcy estate should post an acceptable security for the credit institution in order to be able to continue to draw post-admission. Filing as such does not alter the contractual relationships of the debtor company.

The bankruptcy estate shall be liable for the debts arising from the bankruptcy proceedings or based on a contract or commitment entered into by the estate, as well as for the debts for which the estate is liable under law (administrative expenses, the payment to the estate administrator).

2.20 Are consolidated proceedings for members of a corporate family/group possible?

Generally, consolidated proceedings are not applicable in Finland. In practice, however, the bankruptcy of an operative part of a business group may cause severe difficulties to other group companies as well, thereby leading to the bankruptcy of another group company or the whole corporate group. Each of the group companies will, however, be handled as a separate bankruptcy estate.

2.21 What are the charges, fees and other costs?

The court charges a fixed mandatory fee for issuing a decision.

3. LIABILITY ISSUES

3.1 What is the liability of managers/directors *vis-à-vis* creditors?

Board members and the managing director shall be personally liable for damages for the loss that they have caused deliberately or negligently to the company (i) by violating the duty of care or (ii) by violating the provisions of the Companies Act or the articles of association of the company. Furthermore, they may also be liable to a shareholder or a third party for a violation of the provisions of the Companies Act or the articles of association of the company.

According to the Companies Act, the duty of care means that the management of the company shall act with due care and promote the interests of the company. This provision also contains a certain duty of loyalty of the management towards the company. A breach of the general duty of care can, as such, result in board members' or managing director's liability to the company. This means that a board member and the managing director shall be liable for damages for the loss that he or she has deliberately or negligently caused to the company in office. Liability for damages does not require a breach of any specific provision of the Companies Act or the articles of association as a breach of the general duty of care alone can create liability.

According to the so-called business judgment rule, the management has not acted against its duty of care when:

- they perform their duties in good faith and in a manner they reasonably believe to be in the best interest of the company;
- they make logical decisions based on reasonable preparatory work;
- the actions and decisions taken are not affected by their own personal interests; and
- the risk management of the company is properly managed.

A board member and the managing director shall be liable for damages caused not only to the company but also to a shareholder or a third party. In accordance with the Companies Act, liability for damages shall not occur unless the damage is caused by a breach of the Companies Act or the articles of association. This means that a third party cannot successfully demand compensation only on the grounds of a breach of the duty of care; the third party must always be able to point out a specific provision of either the Companies Act or the articles of association that has been violated by the action of a board member or the managing director. Thus, a breach of provisions of other laws and regulations cannot result in a board member or the managing director being liable for damages to a third party.

The general grounds for consideration of liability of the board of directors and the managing director are similar, but are considered based on the respective duties of the board of directors and the managing director. Actions of the board members and the managing director are considered both objectively, ie how a careful person would have acted in the same situation, and subjectively, with respect to his or her experience, education and expertise.

The debtor has a duty of co-operation and disclosure. However, it should be noted that the debtor has a privilege against self-incrimination. This means that a debtor who is a suspect in a preliminary investigation or has been charged with a crime is not under an obligation to provide the estate administrator with information the he would otherwise have to provide under the debtor's duty of co-operation and disclosure insofar as this information serves as the basis for the investigation or charge.

In addition, the board members and the managing director can be criminally liable for a breach of the Companies Act or acts criminalised under the Penal Code. Under the Penal Code, the management of the company can be sentenced to fines or imprisonment for, for example, dishonesty by a debtor, fraud by a debtor or favouring a creditor.

3.2 What is the liability of the lender?

In general, the lenders are not liable for the damage caused to the debtor company or other creditors.

According to the Finnish Credit Institutions Act (121/2007), a credit institution must monitor its risks and may not, in the course of its operations, incur a risk that fundamentally endangers its solvency or liquidity. Also, a credit institution must monitor and control the exposures to customers. However, there are no sanctions indicated for breaching these duties.

France

De Pardieu Brocas Maffei Joanna Gumpelson

1. WHAT COURT-MONITORED RESTRUCTURING PRE-INSOLVENCY PROCEEDINGS OR SCHEMES HAVE BEEN DEVISED BY THE LAW OF YOUR COUNTRY TO LIMIT VALUE DESTRUCTION FOR FAILING BUSINESS ENTITIES?

The French Insolvency Code provides for three different restructuring proceedings available to solvent companies facing difficulties:

- two out-of-court proceedings: *ad hoc* proceedings (*mandat ad hoc*) and conciliation proceedings (*conciliation*); and
- one court-monitored proceedings: safeguard proceedings (*procédure de sauvegarde*).

1.1 What is the objective of the proceedings?

Out-of-court proceedings

Ad hoc and conciliation proceedings are flexible, voluntary and to a certain extent confidential processes in which the president of the court appoints an agent to monitor discussions between the company and its major creditors. Those proceedings aims at reaching a workout agreement which sets out terms and conditions for the restructuring of the existing debt (waiver, rescheduling, conversion of debt into equity, etc) and, if any, new loans extended by creditors or shareholders.

Safeguard

The primary objective of safeguard is to encourage reorganisation at a preventive stage. Safeguard proceedings allow companies that, though still solvent, face difficulties that they cannot overcome to be restructured at a preventive stage under the court's supervision and with an automatic stay on quasi-all enforcement actions in order to preserve the business as a going concern.

1.2 Do all kinds of businesses qualify?

Ad hoc proceedings apply to all private (as opposed to state) businesses.

Conciliation and safeguard proceedings apply to all private businesses and to individuals acting as merchants, craftsmen or independent professionals, such as lawyers.

1.3 What are the necessary approvals?

All types of pre-insolvency proceedings can only be initiated at the request of the debtor (ie the legal representative in the case of a company).

The board of directors does not need to approve the petition unless the company's articles of association state otherwise.

Before filing a petition for safeguard, the management must inform and consult with the employees' representatives, but these representatives do not need to approve the filing.

In all types of pre-insolvency proceedings, the debtor may suggest, in its petition, the name of a court-appointed agent or administrator, but the court does not have to follow such suggestion.

1.4 What is the procedure?

Out-of-court proceedings

Only the debtor can file a petition to the president of the court.

In *ad hoc* proceedings, the request is filed with any document deemed appropriate to evidence the difficulties faced by the company. In conciliation, certain documents (such as a certificate of incorporation, the list of claims and liabilities, the list of secured assets and annual accounts) must be attached to the request.

The procedure is *ex parte* and creditors are not informed of the filing made by the debtor and the court order opening proceedings is not public, nor is it notified to creditors.

In practice, major creditors are invited to participate to the negotiations by the court agent (usually by way of a letter).

Safeguard

Only the debtor can file a petition to the court (and not merely to the president of the court, as in out-of-court proceedings). The French Insolvency Code provides for a list of certain documents that must be attached to the filing (such as a certificate of incorporation, the list of secured assets and cash-flow projections).

The procedure is *ex parte* and creditors are not invited to participate to the hearing.

The judgment opening safeguard is, however, public and a notice in relation thereto must be published by the clerk office of the court in the legal gazette.

1.5 Is there recourse against the opening judgment?

No recourse is available against the order of the president of the court opening *ad hoc* or conciliation proceedings.

In safeguard, the opening judgment may be appealed by:

- the debtor; or
- the public prosecutor.

The opening judgment is immediately enforceable and the public prosecutor's appeal is the only one which stays the proceedings.

A third party recourse (*tierce opposition*) can be filed against opening judgments, with no stay effect.

Should the recourse filed be declared admissible and well grounded by the court, safeguard would terminate immediately. Assuming that the recourse be rejected by the court, the third party would have 10 days from the notification of the decision to file an appeal. Proceedings in front of the Court of Appeals should last approximately between six months and one year.

1.6 What are the substantive tests/definitions?

The French insolvency test is a pure cash-flow test (in contrast to a balance sheet test): a company is deemed insolvent (*en état de cessation des paiements*) when it is unable to meet its current debts out of its current assets (those in the form of cash or those that can be quickly turned into cash), taking into account undrawn committed facilities and other credit reserves and moratoriums/standstills accepted by creditors.

Ad hoc proceedings and safeguard proceedings are available to solvent debtors only. In safeguard, the debtor must also show that it is facing legal, economic or financial difficulties (whether actual or foreseeable) that cannot be overcome.

By contrast, conciliation is available to solvent or insolvent debtors (provided they have been insolvent for less than 45 days before the petition is filed).

1.7 What is the role of a court-appointed agent?

In out-of-proceedings (*ad hoc* and conciliation), the agent is appointed by the president of the court to organise and supervise discussions between the company and its major creditors. The court agent does not have any management responsibilities or any coercive powers.

In safeguard, the court-appointed administrator is in charge of monitoring or, as the case may be, assisting the management to assess the company's financial situation and prepare a restructuring plan.

1.8 What protection is there from creditors?

Automatic stay

The opening of *ad hoc* or conciliation proceedings does not trigger any automatic stay. The management can apply for a moratorium (two years maximum) if creditors attempt to enforce their rights while proceedings are pending. In conciliation, this can be requested during both the negotiation phase and the implementation phase (that is, after the workout agreement has been approved by the court).

The opening of safeguard proceedings triggers an automatic stay of enforcement actions against the company and individuals acting as guarantors and joint debtors. All pre-filing creditors are barred from enforcing their rights to seek payment from the debtor, subject to a few exceptions, such as:

- claims secured by a security interest conferring a retention right. During the observation period, at the request of the administrator, the insolvency judge may, in exceptional circumstances, authorise the payment of a pre-filing creditor to obtain from that secured creditor the

surrender of the retained pledged asset to the estate. The pledged asset must be necessary to the debtor's pursuit of its business activity;
- claims assigned by way of Dailly assignment of receivables. The creditor to which the debtor's receivables have been assigned by way of Dailly assignment can directly seek payment of those assigned receivables despite any filing. This was held by the Paris Commercial Court in the *Coeur Défense* matter (Paris Commercial Court, 19 October 2009), and confirmed by the Versailles Appeal Court on 28 February 2013;
- claims secured by a trust (*fiducie*) agreement. The creditor can enforce its rights over the assets transferred to the trust except where the creditor initially agreed, at the time the trust (*fiducie*) agreement was executed, that those assets would remain in the debtor's possession; and
- set-off and close-out netting of financial obligations. These are provided for by the French Monetary and Financial Code.

In both out-of-court proceedings and safeguard proceedings, *ipso facto* provisions are deemed null and void: creditors are therefore prohibited from accelerating a loan or terminating an ongoing contract based solely on the opening of proceedings (or of any filing for that purpose). More generally, any contractual provision increasing the debtor's obligations (or reducing its rights) by that sole same reason is also null and void.

Proof of claim

In *ad hoc* or conciliation proceedings, no proof of claim is required.

In safeguard, creditors other than employees must file proof of claim within two months of the publication of the opening judgment (or four months in the case of foreign creditors).

If such proof of claim is challenged by the creditors' representative, the dispute is submitted to the bankruptcy judge.

1.9 What is the usual duration of the restructuring process?

In *ad hoc* or conciliation proceedings, it usually takes a few days to obtain a court order appointing an agent.

Conciliation proceedings shall not last more than five months in total, whereas no time limitation applies to negotiations in the course of *ad hoc* proceedings. The process usually lasts from one month to a year.

Safeguard proceedings begin with an observation period of up to six months to assess the company's financial position. This period can be extended once for six months and, in exceptional circumstances, can be extended further at the public prosecutor's request for an additional six months. If a safeguard plan is approved by the court, the duration of the plan cannot exceed 10 years (unless otherwise agreed upon by creditor classes).

1.10 Who prepares the restructuring agreement and what are the available tools?

In *ad hoc* and conciliation proceedings, the management must co-operate with the court-appointed agent and the creditors to negotiate a solution to the company's difficulties. The major creditors are invited to consider debt rescheduling and/or cancellation. In addition, shareholders can be invited to negotiate and potentially recapitalise the company. A debt-rescheduling plan accepted by some creditors cannot be imposed on other dissenting creditors. The process is purely consensual and no cram-down can be imposed. In practice, majority rules provided for in the existing loan/bond documentation will apply. Any conversion of debt into equity shall require prior shareholder approval (at a two-thirds majority). If there is no solution to the company's difficulties and it later becomes insolvent, the only option is to initiate insolvency proceedings.

In safeguard proceedings, creditors are invited to vote on the debt restructuring proposals made by the company or, as the case may be, by any creditor within creditor classes. For companies of a certain size (that is, companies with more than 150 employees or with an annual turnover of more than EUR 20 million), three classes of creditors must be set up, comprising:

- financial institutions (the bank class);
- major trade creditors (that is, trade creditors with more than 3 per cent of the total trade claims) (the trade class); and
- bondholders (gathered into one single class, regardless of the currency or applicable law of the various bond indentures).

These classes of creditors can also be organised for small companies, subject to court approval. Creditors with claims that were initially held by a financial institution or by a major trade creditor are invited to participate and vote within the class of financial institutions. However, creditors benefiting from a trust agreement (*fiducie*) do not vote within the classes of creditors. There have been cases where a shareholder that granted shareholder loan(s) was invited to vote in the class of financial institutions.

Any member of the bank class or of the trade class (but not bondholders) can submit an alternative safeguard plan competing with the plan prepared by the debtor.

The plan is deemed approved by the classes if the required percentage in each class votes in favour of the plan, ie a minimum two-thirds majority.

If the plan provides for a debt–equity swap (or any other operation requiring shareholder approval), shareholders must also be consulted and vote in favour of the plan at a two-thirds majority (no cram-down of shareholders is possible in safeguard). However, the majority applicable to shareholder meetings convened at first notice can be reduced by court order to a simple majority of the shareholders present or represented provided they represent at least 50 per cent of the voting shares.

If the classes of creditors are not set up or if one of the classes has rejected the proposals, the plan must be negotiated on a one-to-one basis with each creditor.

If the creditors consulted individually refuse to approve the proposals made by the company, the court can impose a 10 year maximum term-out to dissenting creditors (subject, of course, to any longer maturity date agreed upon in the original loan agreement). The court cannot impose any debt write-off of principal or interest in a term-out scenario. Consenting creditors benefit from the shorter maturity date (if any) that they would have negotiated.

The yearly instalments under the term-out plan must not, after year three following court approval of the plan, be less that 5 per cent of the total admitted pre-filing liabilities.

Since the 2014 reform of French bankruptcy law, this 10 year maximum term-out cannot be imposed on lenders that provided new money financings in the framework of a court-approved agreement in conciliation unless they agree otherwise.

Interest continues to accrue if it results from a loan or a contract with deferred payment having an initial term of more than one year. Interest cannot, however, be compounded.

Interest accrued during the observation period of safeguard proceedings is not paid in cash but added to the amount to be restructured under the plan.

1.11 Are subordination agreements necessarily given full effect?

In *ad hoc* and conciliation proceedings, the process is purely consensual and no cram-down or discrimination between categories of creditors is possible.

In safeguard, subordination agreements and voting agreements entered into before the opening of the proceedings, if any, have to be taken into account in the process.

When classes of creditors are set up, each relevant member of the classes must inform the administrator of the existence of any

- subordination agreement;
- agreement restricting or conditioning its vote; or
- agreement allowing for third party payment of the debt.

The administrator must then submit to the relevant class member a proposal for the computation of its voting rights. If there is disagreement, the concerned class member can petition the president of the court through motion proceedings.

1.12 How is exit managed?

Ad hoc proceedings

If an agreement is reached between a company and its major creditors, the agent's duties end and there is no specific court approval process. If there is no solution to the company's difficulties and it later becomes insolvent, the only option is to initiate insolvency proceedings.

Conciliation proceedings

When an agreement is reached between the company and its major creditors, the company has two options:

- it can request a formal court approval of the workout agreement. This is to encourage creditors to extend new credit facilities. Indeed, new money facilities granted in the framework of a court-approved workout benefit from a statutory priority of payment should the company subsequently file for insolvency. Except where fraud has taken place, a court-approved workout agreement is also protected from the risk of future voidance. However, this court approval must be recorded in a full judgment accessible to the public and therefore subject to challenge by a third party (*tierce opposition*) or appeal; or

- it can obtain a simple stamping from the president of the court. This option does not involve publicity, but implies that creditors waive their right to priority of payment for new money facilities and to protection against the risk of future voidance.

If no solution can be found to the company's financial difficulties and the court agent reports that the company is insolvent, the court must open insolvency proceedings.

Safeguard proceedings

Once approved by the court, the safeguard plan is enforceable against all creditors, including the dissenting minority within creditor classes. The judgment approving the plan appoints an agent to supervise its implementation (*commissaire à l' exécution du plan*). If the company fails to meet its obligations under the plan and becomes insolvent, the court must order the plan to be terminated and initiate rehabilitation proceedings or, if the rescue of the company appears to be obviously impossible, liquidation proceedings.

If no plan has been presented or if the plan is rejected by the court, the safeguard proceedings end.

1.13 Who are the necessary parties?

Not applicable in *ad hoc* proceedings, the procedure is strictly confidential and is not subject to appeal.

In conciliation proceedings, when an agreement is reached between the company and its major creditors, it can receive either:

- a simple stamping from the president of the court. This option does not involve publicity and the agreement is not subject to appeal; or
- a formal court approval of the workout agreement. The court approval must be recorded in a full judgment accessible to the public and therefore subject to a possible challenge by a third party (*tierce opposition*) or by appeal by the public prosecutor or the parties to the workout agreement if new money privilege is challenged.

Once approved by the court, the safeguard plan may be appealed by:

- the debtor;
- the court-appointed administrator;
- the creditors' representative;
- the works council or, in the absence of a works council, the employee delegates;
- the public prosecutor; or
- the member of the creditor classes (if any) that challenged the voting conditions.

2. POST-INSOLVENCY PROCEEDINGS

2.1 What is the objective of the proceedings?

Even though conciliation is available to solvent or insolvent companies (see section 1 above), the two main types of post-insolvency proceedings are court-monitored processes:

- rehabilitation proceedings (*redressement judiciaire*); and
- liquidation.

The objective of rehabilitation proceedings is to preserve the company's activities and prospects of recovery, to save jobs and to pay creditors. Rehabilitation proceedings are appropriate if the company is insolvent but has not ceased operating and its rescue seems possible.

Liquidation is the only possible outcome when the rescue of the insolvent company appears to be obviously impossible (either at the time of the filing or after an attempted rehabilitation). In liquidation proceedings, the objective is to sell the debtor's business, either as a whole or by line(s) of business, or to sell its assets, asset by asset, in order to satisfy creditors' claims in their order of priority.

2.2 Do all kinds of business entities qualify?

Rehabilitation and liquidation proceedings apply to all private businesses and to individuals acting as merchants, craftsmen or independent professionals such as lawyers. Those proceedings must be initiated at the request of the company (through its legal representatives) within 45 days following insolvency.

They can also be initiated if (i) the company fails to reach an agreement with its creditors during conciliation proceedings and (ii) the court agent reports that the company is insolvent.

Those insolvency proceedings can also be initiated:

- at the request of any creditor, whether secured or unsecured (regardless of the amount of its claims); or
- at the request of the public prosecutor.

2.3 What are the necessary approvals?

The board of directors does not need to approve a decision to file for insolvency unless the company's articles state otherwise. However, the company's legal representatives usually seek the board's approval as a precautionary measure. Before filing a petition, management must inform and consult with the employees' representatives. However, these representatives do not need to approve the filing.

2.4 Is it valid and binding to agree that such proceedings be a default/termination event?

The entry of a judgment opening insolvency proceedings cannot *per se* accelerate pre-filing claims that have not yet matured. As a result, any clause of a loan documentation providing that the opening of insolvency proceedings shall trigger an automatic acceleration shall be deemed null and void.

However, the question remains whether a lender could be entitled to accelerate a loan on an event of default other than the opening of safeguard proceedings.

In a court decision dated 12 June 2011, the French Supreme Court ruled that, even though the opening of insolvency could not be used as a legally acceptable cause to accelerate the loan, the lender was nevertheless entitled to accelerate it if such acceleration was based on an event of default provided for in the loan documentation other than the opening of insolvency proceedings. Assuming that this 2001 decision (even though isolated) is the present 'law' applying to this issue, one can say that any post-filing event of default (other that the opening itself), and in particular any post-filing interest payment default, should allow the lender to accelerate the loan.

2.5 What is the procedure?

In the case of a voluntary filing, the company's legal representative shall file a request with the commercial court having jurisdiction. A specific list of documents must be attached. The process is *ex parte* and creditors are not invited to participate to the hearing. The judgment opening insolvency proceedings is public and a notice is published, at the request of the clerk office of the court, in the legal gazette.

2.6 Please provide information about voluntary filings

Creditors cannot participate in the initial hearing where the court having jurisdiction will rule on the filing made by the debtor.

Creditors become aware of the existence of the opening judgment either by the notice published in the legal gazette or, as far as certain secured creditors are concerned, by a letter from the creditors' representative inviting them to file proof of claim.

The debtor does not need to have reached any sort of agreement with its creditors (term-sheet or otherwise) at the time of the filing, or to have prepared a draft restructuring plan.

2.7 How are creditors' representatives chosen?

The judgment opening rehabilitation proceedings appoints the creditors' representative from the list of sworn-in liquidators. Creditors' representatives are charged with representing the interests of creditors taken as a whole; they can be assisted by between one and five supervising creditors appointed by the court among the creditors having requested so.

Creditors have no influence of the choice of the creditors' representative.

In liquidation, the duties of the creditor's representative are entrusted with the liquidator.

2.8 Is there recourse against the opening judgment?

Rehabilitation proceedings

The opening judgment may be appealed by:

- the debtor;

- the creditor that initiated the proceedings in the case of an involuntary filing; or
- the public prosecutor.

The opening judgment is immediately enforceable and appeals lodged by the debtor or the initiating creditor (as the case may be) do not entail a stay. The debtor's protection against an unjustified opening of proceedings is a recourse to the public prosecutor, whose appeal is the only one which stays the proceedings.

As in safeguard (see section 1.5 above), a third party recourse (*tierce opposition*) can be filed against opening judgments.

Liquidation proceedings

The judgment opening liquidation may be appealed by:

- the debtor;
- the creditor that initiated the proceedings in the case of an involuntary filing;
- the works council or, in the absence of a works council, the employee delegates; or
- the public prosecutor.

Only the public prosecutor's appeal has a stay effect.

A third party recourse can also be filed against judgments opening liquidation proceedings.

2.9 What are the roles and powers of committees?

In rehabilitation (as in safeguard), classes of creditors must be set up for companies of a certain size (see section 1.10 above). The rehabilitation plan must be approved by the same majorities as those applicable to creditor classes in the framework of safeguard proceedings. In the same way as safeguard plans, in a term-out scenario, rehabilitation plans can postpone the date on which the claims of dissenting creditors (except conciliation super-senior financings) must be paid by up to 10 years (unless the initial maturity date was already in excess of 10 years). However, the court cannot impose any debt write-off to dissenting creditors. If the court considers that no restructuring plan is viable, it can approve (unlike in safeguard) a sale of all or part of the business and the creditors will be repaid with the available proceeds.

As for safeguard, any member of the class of financial institutions or of the class of major trade creditors can submit a competing alternative restructuring plan to the vote.

The above provisions are not applicable in liquidation: creditors are not invited to vote as no restructuring plan is prepared by the debtor.

2.10 What are the consequences of opening judgments for creditors?

The opening of insolvency proceedings triggers an automatic stay on enforcement actions against the company.

The same exceptions to the automatic stay as those applicable in safeguard (see section 1.8 above) apply in the framework of rehabilitation or liquidation proceedings.

In liquidation, unlike in safeguard or rehabilitation, secured creditors benefiting from a pledge can enforce their security interest through a court-monitored allocation process (*attribution judiciaire*), that is, request the court to transfer ownership of the pledged asset.

All creditors, other than employees, must file proof of claim within two months of the judgment opening insolvency proceedings being published (or four months in the case of foreign creditors).

Interest continues to accrue if it results from a loan or a contract with deferred payment having an initial term of more than one year. Interest cannot, however, be compounded.

Interest accrued during the observation period of rehabilitation proceedings is not paid in cash but added to the amount to be restructured under the plan.

2.11 What is the duration of the restructuring process?

The rules applicable to safeguard proceedings (see section 1.9 above) apply to rehabilitation proceedings.

Liquidation proceedings last until the liquidator finds that no more proceeds can be expected from the sale of the company's business or assets. After two years (computed from the judgment ordering liquidation), any creditor can request the court to order the liquidator to close the liquidation. There is a simplified form of liquidation proceedings available for small businesses that lasts for a maximum of one year.

2.12 How do creditors vote?

The rules applicable to safeguard proceedings (see section 1.10 above) apply to rehabilitation proceedings.

In liquidation, creditors are not invited to vote as no restructuring plan is prepared by the debtor.

2.13 What are the rules on clawback/voidability?

Certain transactions, payments and transfers can be challenged by the administrator, the creditors' representative (who usually becomes the liquidator if rehabilitation is ultimately converted into liquidation), the liquidator or the public prosecutor if they were entered into during the so-called hardening period (*période suspecte*).

The hardening period, if any, runs from the date on which the company is deemed to be insolvent and can be backdated by the court up to 18 months before the judgment opening the rehabilitation or liquidation. However, if the debtor and all or some of its creditors entered into a conciliation workout agreement prior to the opening of insolvency proceedings, and if the court formally approved such agreement in a judgment, the insolvency date cannot be backdated to a date prior to that of the judgment approving the workout agreement (with the limited exception of fraud).

The French Insolvency Code provides for a limitative list of transactions that are either automatically avoided by the court – assuming, of course, that the court is petitioned by the court-appointed agents (administrator or liquidator) or by the public prosecutor – or that may be avoided by the court.

Unlike for automatic clawback, the requirements for optional clawback are assessed by the court at its own discretion, according to which the court is not required to base its assessment on a damage suffered by the debtor, even if, in practice, it is always difficult to justify an avoidance action if there is no damage.

Automatic clawback

- Transactions without effective consideration for the insolvent debtor.
- Voluntary 'unusual' payments, ie:
  - any payments, in any form, made on account of debts that have not fallen due on the payment date; and
  - any payments on account of debts that have fallen due made by any means other than cash settlement, negotiable instrument, wire transfer, Dailly assignment of receivables or any other methods of payment commonly used in business transactions.
- 'Suspicious' guarantees: any mortgage or pledge (both conventional and judicial) over the company's assets on account of pre-existing debts.
- Judicial deposit and consignment-protective measures, ie:
  - any deposits or consignments of money made under Article 2350 of the French Civil Code (governing pledges over certain tangible assets) in the absence of a final judgment, it being specified that such consignment will be valid if completed in compliance with a court decision that became final before the date of insolvency; and
  - any protective measures, unless the security is registered or the attachment has occurred before the date of insolvency.
- Transactions relating to stock options: any granting, exercise or reselling of stock options made under Article L. 225-177 *et seq.* of the French Commercial Code.
- Transfers into a trust estate guaranteeing pre-existing debts.
- When the debtor is a sole proprietorship with limited liability: any allocation or change in the allocation of an asset, subject to the payment of revenues, which results in an impoverishment of the bankrupt estate to the benefit of another estate.

Optional clawback

- Any transfers of movable or immovable assets without consideration if completed within six months prior to the date of insolvency as backdated by the court (ie 18 + 6 months = 24 months in total).
- Any transactions with consideration entered into during the hardening period (18 months maximum before the insolvency judgment), but on

the condition that the other party had knowledge of such insolvency situation.
- Any payments on account of debts made during the hardening period, but on the condition that the beneficiary of the payment had knowledge of such insolvency situation.
- Any third party notification for attachment or distraint initiated by tax authorities (*avis à tiers détenteur*) and any attachment of receivables (*saisie-attribution*) may also be avoided if delivered or initiated by a creditor during the hardening period while having knowledge of the debtor's insolvency situation.

The other party's knowledge of the debtor's insolvency explains that the former will be denied specific protection and that payment of due and payable debts even made with a usual method of payment may be avoided. Proof of such knowledge may be given by any means and will be facilitated when the contracting parties or those having received payment had already entered into business relations or belong to the same group of companies.

2.14 What are the rules on set-off/netting?

Once a petition for insolvency proceedings has been filed and accepted by the court, the debtor is as a general rule prohibited from paying pre-petition claims.

Set-off

Set-off is, however, permitted and enforceable against third parties provided that claims are reciprocal and equally due and payable. Additionally, those claims must be 'connected', ie:
- they arose from one contract organising the various aspects of a business/trade relationship between the creditor, the debtor and possibly third parties; or
- they arose from separate contracts which, however, together constitute a global contractual scheme amounting to a single contract.

Close-out netting of financial obligations

Early termination and set-off provisions remain enforceable irrespective of the opening of insolvency proceedings for financial obligations resulting from:
- futures contracts, ie transactions on financial instruments when at least one of the parties to the transaction is a credit institution, an investment service provider, a public establishment, a local authority (*collectivité territoriale*), an institution, a person or an entity eligible to provide financial services (such as the French state, the *Banque de France*, insurance and reinsurance companies), a clearing house, a non-French bank with comparable status, or an international financial institution or body of which France or the European Union is a member;
- financial guarantee contracts, ie any contract giving a right to cash settlement or delivery of financial instruments when all parties belong

to certain categories of persons or entities eligible to provide financial services; or

- any contract entered into as part as an inter-bank payment systems.

Note that transactions on financial instruments include transactions on:

- shares and other securities that allow or may allow direct or indirect access to equity or voting rights;
- debt instruments other than payment instruments (*effets de commerce*) and loan notes (*bons de caisse*);
- units or shares in collective investment undertakings (*organismes de placement collectif*); and
- financial contracts, also known as forward financial instruments.

Financial obligations resulting from the above-mentioned financial instruments may be subject to early termination/acceleration provisions in the case of insolvency of the counterparty, and all debts can be set-off.

French law further provides that, as security to the above-mentioned financial obligations, the parties may provide for the transfer of title to securities, financial instruments, claims, contracts or sums of money, such transfers being binding upon third parties without any formality. Foreclosure remains possible even if one of the parties to those instruments is subject to insolvency proceedings in France or to similar judicial or amicable proceedings under foreign law.

2.15 How is exit managed?

The rehabilitation plan can combine all of the following:

- a debt restructuring;
- a recapitalisation of the company;
- a debt-for-equity swap; and
- the sale of certain assets or of portions of the business.

Rules applicable to safeguard also apply to rehabilitation proceedings.

As in safeguard, if shareholder approval is required, the court can reduce the quorum and majority rules applicable on first notice.

The court-appointed administrator can also (in rehabilitation only) vote the shares of dissenting shareholders (although only in a limited set of circumstances) to promote the conversion of debt into equity. For this purpose, shareholders must have refused to (i) restore themselves the company's net equity or (ii) vote a share capital increase to that effect. The court-appointed administrator will only have the power to vote a recapitalisation within the limit of what is the mandatory minimum under the French corporate law to restore the company's net equity (up to 50 per cent of the company's pre-existing equity and no more).

Unlike in safeguard, the administrator can make a proposal to auction the business as a whole or by line(s) if the company cannot continue to operate. In these circumstances, the sale plan is implemented within the legal framework of the rehabilitation but following the rules applicable to liquidation proceedings.

If it becomes clear that rehabilitation will not succeed, the court can order the conversion of the procedure into liquidation.

Liquidation is complete when the business (as a whole or branch by branch) and any residual assets have been sold and the proceeds distributed to the creditors by order of priority.

2.16 Are 'prepackaged' plans, arrangements or agreements permissible?

Two types of prepackaged plans are available in France to restructure a company's debt in a very short time frame:

- accelerated safeguard: a prepackaged safeguard aimed at allowing the speedy (three months maximum) reorganisation of certain eligible companies while involving both financial and trade creditors; and
- accelerated financial safeguard proceedings (SFA) involving financial creditors only.

Those two proceedings are variants of the standard safeguard, which was introduced into French law in 2005.

The purpose of those expedited safeguard processes is to restructure the company's debt within a very short time-frame, assuming that the consent of at least two-thirds of creditors voting within the creditor classes is obtained.

The major difference between accelerated safeguard and SFA is that latter has effects only *vis-à-vis* financial creditors, ie creditors gathered in the class of financial institutions and, as the case may be, bondholders. The mechanism applicable to the voting process for the adoption of the restructuring plan is the same as in safeguard, except that in SFA trade creditors are not invited to participate. It follows that other creditors, such as suppliers or tax authorities, are not affected by the opening of the SFA.

In accelerated safeguard, not only financial creditors but also trade creditors are affected and invited to vote on the restructuring plan within creditor classes.

SFA and accelerated safeguard can be opened at the debtor's request, provided that a conciliation procedure is pending (any direct access to expedited safeguard is strictly prohibited) in which at least a two-thirds majority in value of financial creditors and bondholders (as well as trade creditors for the accelerated safeguard) are likely to approve the restructuring proposals prepared by the company and the conciliateur.

Expedited safeguard processes apply to companies that are either solvent or were insolvent for less than 45 days at the time the petition for conciliation was filed provided they compile consolidated financial statements or reach one of the following thresholds:

- a minimum of 20 employees;
- a minimum annual turnover of EUR 3 million (without value added tax); or
- a minimum total balance sheet of EUR 1.5 million.

The expedited SFA must be completed within one month, renewable once for one month maximum, whereas accelerated safeguard must be completed within a maximum of three months from the date of the opening judgment.

Once approved by the creditor classes, the plan is submitted to the court for review and approval.

If any of the classes refuse to approve the plan, the court will close the proceedings. If, as a result of such closure, the company becomes insolvent, it will have no other choice than to file for rehabilitation or liquidation.

2.17 Is a public authority involved?

The public prosecutor can *inter alia*:

- petition the court to initiate rehabilitation or liquidation proceedings;
- request that the observation period in rehabilitation be exceptionally extended for an additional six months after expiry of the maximum one year period;
- request that the continuation of business operations in liquidation be extended for an additional three months;
- petition the court to order protective measures where a consolidation of estates (*confusion de patrimoines*) is set up to freeze the assets of the legal entity to which insolvency proceedings are extended, and avoid asset misappropriation;
- petition the court to rule that certain transactions be avoided pursuant to claw-down provisions; and
- initiate liable actions against directors/parent company(ies).

2.18 What is the treatment of claims arising after filing/admission?

Claims arising after the opening judgment benefit from a statutory privilege provided that they either:

- arise for the purpose of funding the observation period; or
- represent consideration due to a creditor, or to a provider of goods or services, in a business transaction directly connected to the company's activities continued during the observation period.

These post-petition claims must be paid when they fall due. If not, they rank ahead of both secured and unsecured pre-petition claims. Post-petition claims, however, always rank after arrears of wages, post-filing court costs and new money facilities extended in a court-approved conciliation workout agreement.

In liquidation, they also rank after mortgage claims.

2.19 Are there ongoing contracts?

The court-appointed administrator has the right to require the debtor's contracting party to perform ongoing contracts (such as supply agreements, leases and revolving facilities not fully drawn) in exchange of the performance of the debtor's post-petition obligations.

However, all contracts can be terminated at the option of the administrator.

The contracting party can summon the administrator to take position on the assumption of an ongoing contract which shall automatically be terminated once a formal notice has been sent to the administrator and has remained unanswered within one month (renewable once at the administrator's request), except for lease agreements.

The debtor's contracting party must perform its obligations despite the non-performance by the debtor of its own pre-petition payment obligations. The non-performance of these pre-petition payment obligations shall only give the contracting party the right to file proof of claim.

2.20 Are consolidated proceedings for members of a corporate family/group possible?

The court can order that the debts of a bankrupt company be paid from a larger consolidated pool of assets (*confusion de patrimoines*) if:

- a fictitious company (one without an independent management body) has been created in an attempt to disperse assets so that they are placed beyond the creditors' reach; or
- the estates of two or more companies are so closely connected that it is impossible to separate one company's activities from the other. This can be shown if, for example, the companies share the same management, the same assets and the same debts or bank accounts.

Since the law of 12 March 2012, it is now possible, where the consolidation of estates is ordered, to have protective measures ordered by the president of the court to freeze the assets of the legal entity to which insolvency proceedings are extended, and thereby avoid asset misappropriation.

2.21 What are the charges, fees and other costs?

In respect of court-related costs incurred within insolvency proceedings, the remuneration of the court-appointed agents represents a major part of the costs.

The fees of the administrator mainly consist of:

- a fixed amount, paid at the date of the opening judgment and determined by statutory basic rates, which vary according to the number of employees of the bankrupt company and its turnover calculated as at the date of closure of the accounting year; and
- a variable amount calculated on the basis of the pre-tax turnover generated during the observation period.

The fees of the creditors' representative usually depend on the total amount of liabilities and the number of challenges of proofs of claims.

3. LIABILITY ISSUES

3.1 What is the liability of managers/directors *vis-à-vis* creditors?

An action for mismanagement, which only applies in liquidation proceedings, can lead to an insolvent company's management being liable for all or part of its debts where, due to management errors, the company's assets are not sufficient to cover its debts. This liability can be targeted at formally appointed directors or managers with representation powers, and at any individual or entity that, though not officially a director or manager, repeatedly influenced the company's management or strategic decisions (that is, shadow (*de facto*) directors/managers).

A parent company (domestic or foreign) can also be held liable for an insolvent subsidiary's debts if it has been appointed as a director or is deemed a shadow director or manager of that subsidiary (as the case may be through an individual or individuals appointed at the shareholders' request).

More generally, any individual or entity (even if not officially a director) can be held liable for mismanagement if the individual/entity in practice repeatedly exercised an influence on management decisions.

The liquidator, the creditors' representative or the public prosecutor can initiate the action. In addition, the supervisor creditors (*contrôleurs;* appointed by the court to assist the creditors' representative/liquidator) can summon the creditors' representative/liquidator to bring an action or they can commence proceedings on their own initiative if the creditors' representative/liquidator does not do so.

Directors found liable for certain specific breaches can also (irrespective of any liability action or criminal prosecution based on the same facts) be (i) forced to assign their equity interest in the company or (ii) prohibited from managing any business for up to 15 years and from holding any public office for up to five years.

Breaches include:

- using the company's assets or credit for their own benefit, or the benefit of another corporate entity in which they have a direct or indirect interest;
- using the company to conduct and conceal business transactions for their own benefit;
- carrying out business activities at a loss to further their own interests, knowing that this would lead to the company's insolvency;
- fraudulently embezzling or concealing all or part of the company's assets; and
- fraudulently increasing the company's debts.

3.2 What is the liability of the lender?

Before the 2005 reform of French insolvency laws, there were essentially two main liability risks for the lender:

- abusive termination of ongoing credit facilities: this liability arose where a lender had abruptly stopped financing the borrower (*rupture abusive de crédit*); and
- abusive support of a bankrupt debtor: this liability arose where a lender continued financing a distressed debtor while knowing that its financial situation was obviously jeopardised, thus creating a misleading appearance of solvency in favour of a debtor which in fact was beyond any prospect of recovery, to the prejudice of other creditors (*soutien abusif*).

In 2005, the French Insolvency Code was substantially amended in relation to lender liability issues and now provides that any lender (not only financial institution) shall be exempt from liability in the framework of insolvency proceedings, except in the following circumstances:

- fraud;
- improper interference with the company's management; or
- where the lender has obtained a security interest that is disproportionate to the amount of the loan.

The Supreme Court ruled in 2012 that, in order to trigger lender liability, the following conditions should be met:

- one of the statutory triggering events occurred (ie fraud, improper interference with management or disproportionate security package); and
- the loan itself was an act of wrongdoing (see section 3.2 above regarding the pre-2005 case law on abusive support).

Germany

LADM Liesegang Aymans Decker Mittelstaedt & Partner Rechtsanwälte Wirtschaftsprüfer Steuerberater
Florian Gantenberg

1. WHAT COURT-MONITORED RESTRUCTURING PRE-INSOLVENCY PROCEEDINGS OR SCHEMES HAVE BEEN DEVISED BY THE LAW OF YOUR COUNTRY TO LIMIT VALUE DESTRUCTION FOR FAILING BUSINESS ENTITIES?

The German Insolvency Code (*Insolvenzordnung*, InsO) provides for a possibility for companies that are not yet illiquid (but imminently illiquid) to prepare an insolvency plan (*Insolvenzplan*) during the phase of preliminary insolvency proceedings and in most cases also under protection from creditors (section 270b InsO). The protective-shield proceedings, however, are available only in connection with a filing for opening of insolvency proceedings. It is administered by the insolvency court, a preliminary insolvency administrator or preliminary supervisor (*Sachwalter*) is appointed and the purpose of the proceedings is to enable the debtor to draft an insolvency plan which is to be implemented in later insolvency proceedings. The results of such protective-shield proceedings therefore take effect only within insolvency proceedings (which are described in more detail under section 2 below).

Apart from the protective-shield proceedings in preparation of insolvency proceedings, pre-insolvency restructuring in Germany is possible by mutual agreement only and German law does not provide for any specific (court-monitored) restructuring proceedings outside of (preliminary) insolvency proceedings. Discussions whether such a proceedings should be established are ongoing.

1.1 What is the objective of the proceedings?

N/A.

1.2 Do all kinds of businesses qualify?

N/A.

1.3 What are the necessary approvals?

N/A.

1.4 What is the procedure?

N/A.

1.5 Is there recourse against the opening judgment?

N/A.

1.6 What are the substantive tests/definitions?

N/A.

1.7 What is the role of a court-appointed agent?

N/A.

1.8 What protection is there from creditors?

N/A.

1.9 What is the usual duration of the restructuring process?

N/A.

1.10 Who prepares the restructuring agreement and what are the available tools?

N/A.

1.11 Are subordination agreements necessarily given full effect?

N/A.

1.12 How is exit managed?

N/A.

1.13 Who are the necessary parties?

N/A.

2. POST-INSOLVENCY PROCEEDINGS

2.1 What is the objective of the proceedings?

The objective of insolvency proceedings is, according to section 1 InsO, the collective satisfaction of the creditors' claims by liquidation of the assets and distribution of the proceeds or by reaching an insolvency plan (*Insolvenzplan*).

Thus, the insolvency plan is an alternative to liquidation proceedings within the insolvency proceedings themselves and must also aim for the (best) possible collective satisfaction of the creditors. It is important for the understanding of German insolvency plans as the 'alternative to insolvency liquidation' that an insolvency plan is only an alternative method of collectively satisfying creditors' claims but does not provide different proceedings with own provisions on filing requirements, etc. The effect of this is that the general rules of insolvency proceedings also apply in connection with an insolvency plan, eg the provisions on the filing and verifying of claims, on the fulfilment of long-term-contracts and contestation of previous actions of the debtor remain valid.

An insolvency plan may provide for deviations from the general rules of the InsO in terms of: (i) the satisfaction of the creditors entitled to separate satisfaction and of the insolvency creditors; (ii) the disposition of the insolvency estate and its distribution to the parties; and (iii) the procedural rules and debtor's liability subsequent to the termination of the insolvency proceedings. If the debtor is not a natural person, the shareholders and/or membership rights of the persons holding such rights in the debtor may be included in the plan (section 217 InsO).

It is not necessary for the insolvency plan to provide for a continuation of the business; although such a continuation is likely the most common goal, liquidation plans or plans including a (partial) asset deal transferring the business operations or parts thereof are permissible.

General remarks

Two other important principles/issues in German insolvencies shall briefly be depicted as follows:

- After the court receives an insolvency filing by a company or the sole proprietor of an enterprise, it will most often appoint an insolvency expert to review *inter alia* whether (i) the company is insolvent (ie (imminently) illiquid or overindebted) and (ii) whether the assets of the company are sufficient to cover the cost of the insolvency proceedings. The court may also take securing measures regarding the insolvency estate, such as the restriction or prohibition of any legal enforcement actions against the debtor and the appointment of a preliminary insolvency administrator. At the end of this phase the insolvency court decides on the opening of the insolvency proceedings on the basis of the expert opinion. Only if the costs of the proceedings are covered at the end of this preliminary insolvency phase will the insolvency proceedings itself be opened and its effects come into force.
- The insolvency administrator traditionally has a very strong position in Germany because he is considered a representative of the creditors. He takes most decisions in the insolvency proceedings and is the most likely party to submit an insolvency plan. German legislation has recently (in 2012) enacted new legislation intended to significantly promote the principle of a debtor-in-possession (*Eigenverwaltung*; sections 270 *et seq.* InsO). With the exceptions of claims against the individual partners or the management or contestation of transaction, the debtor (respectively its management) will remain fully entitled to act while a (preliminary) insolvency supervisor (*Sachwalter*) is appointed to merely oversee the debtor's economic situation and management and to inform the creditors' committee and the court immediately if he becomes aware of any circumstances from which a disadvantage to the creditors may be expected.

2.2 Do all kinds of business entities qualify?

Insolvency proceedings in Germany may be opened according to section 11 InsO over the assets of a natural or a legal person. An unincorporated association is deemed to be equivalent to a legal person; section 11 InsO explicitly includes companies without legal personality, eg a limited partnership (*Kommanditgesellschaft*) or a company under the Civil Code (*Bürgerliches Gesetzbuch,* BGB). Only the federation, the states (*Bundesländer*) and certain legal persons under their supervision are exempt according to section 12 InsO.

An insolvency proceedings in Germany may only be opened if there is a cause. The possible causes for the opening of insolvency proceedings are

- illiquidity (*Zahlungsunfähigkeit*): illiquidity is generally defined as the inability to pay at least 90 per cent of the debt due;
- imminent illiquidity (*drohende Zahlungsunfähigkeit*): a debtor is imminently illiquid if it will not be able to pay its expected debts when they become due; should management file for insolvency for the cause of imminent illiquidity, caution is necessary because of a much discussed final judgment by the Higher Regional Court of Munich (*Oberlandesgericht München;* judgment dated 23 March 2013, docket no. 23 U 3344/12), which held that the management of a fund in the form of a GmbH & Co. KG may be liable if filing for insolvency for imminent illiquidity without the consent of the shareholders; the complaint for non-admission of the appeal was rejected by the Federal Court of Justice (*Bundesgerichtshof* decision dated 11 February 2014, docket no. II ZR 152/13); and/or
- overindebtedness (*Überschuldung*): this is defined as the status in which the assets of the debtor no longer cover his payment obligations unless it is highly likely, considering the circumstances, that the enterprise will continue to exist.

Creditors may file for the insolvency of their debtor in cases of illiquidity and overindebtedness if they have a legal interest in insolvency proceedings and provide *prima facie* evidence for their claim and the reason why insolvency proceedings should be opened. What kind of evidence needs to be shown will depend on the individual case, but requirements are relatively high. Creditors will, however, be well prepared if they can show an executable title against the debtor and that they have already unsuccessfully attempted to execute it.

Since a recent change of law, insolvency plans may be prepared for any debtor in any insolvency proceedings – whether voluntary or involuntary. The new law explicitly permits the preparation of insolvency plans in consumer insolvency proceedings even if opened before 1 July 2014 (section 103h of the Introductory Law for the Insolvency Code, *Einführungsgesetz zur Insolvenzordnung*).

Once insolvency proceedings are opened according to the above, an insolvency plan can be submitted.

2.3 What are the necessary approvals?

Only the insolvency administrator and the debtor are entitled to submit an insolvency plan, but the creditors' assembly may request the insolvency administrator to submit an insolvency plan (section 218 InsO). The creditors' committee, the works' council, the spokesman of the executive employees (if any) and the debtor shall assist in the preparation of the insolvency plan by the insolvency administrator, but no approvals are necessary.

2.4 Is it valid and binding to agree that such proceedings be a default/termination event?

Whether an insolvency filing or (preliminary) insolvency proceedings – which is always the prerequisite of an insolvency plan – can be agreed to constitute a default/termination event is a matter of debate. The relevant provisions can be found in sections 103–19 InsO. Some of the relevant provisions stipulate an (automatic) termination upon the opening of insolvency proceedings, eg of an assignment (*Auftrag*, sections 662 *et seq.* BGB) with a relation to the estate according to section 115 InsO, of an agency agreement (*Geschäftsbesorgungsvertrag*, sections 675 *et seq.* BGB) according to section 116 InsO or of a power of representation (*Vollmacht*, sections 164 *et seq.* BGB) according to section 117 BGB. On the other hand, section 112 InsO prohibits the termination of a rent contract for nonpayment of rent for periods before the insolvency filing and/or a deterioration of the debtor's financial standing, and employment contracts continue but may be terminated – if possible under labour law rules – with a maximum termination period of three months (section 113 InsO).

The main provision regarding the termination/continuation of long-term contracts in insolvency, however, is section 103 InsO. Section 103 InsO gives the insolvency administrator a right to decide on the continuation of contracts which have not yet been fulfilled entirely by both parties. Section 119 InsO again provides that contractual deviations from sections103 *et seq.* InsO are not permissible.

Even in this context, provisions tying a termination to a delay, breach of contract or deterioration of the debtor's financial standing are generally deemed permissible (*Huber*, in *Münchener Kommentar zur Insolvenzordnung*, 3rd edn, 2013, § 119, marginal note 19). However, in 2012, the Federal Court of Justice decided that the clause providing for the automatic termination of a contract for the supply of goods or energy in the case of an insolvency filing by the client was void according to section 119 InsO (*Bundesgerichtshof* decision dated 15 November 2012, docket no. IX ZR 169/11). Prior to this decision, section 119 InsO had not been considered to be applicable before the opening of insolvency proceedings and the court argued *inter alia* that section 119 InsO would have an effect after an insolvency filing if an opening of insolvency proceedings could be seriously anticipated. Because of the reasons given by the court, the scope of the decision is widely commented on and it is currently unclear whether the decision will remain singular or will become generalised. It is also a matter of discussion whether contractual provisions not explicitly referring to an insolvency filing or the opening of (preliminary) insolvency proceedings but referring instead to, for example, a cause for the opening of insolvency proceedings or describing a state of insolvency will be upheld or considered void as being a circumvention of section 119 InsO (for more information, see eg *Huber*, in *Münchener Kommentar zur Insolvenzordnung*, 3rd edn, 2013, § 119, marginal notes 18 *et seq.*).

2.5 What is the procedure?

Insolvency plans must consist of (i) a describing part, giving all the information on the necessary measures taken in the course of the insolvency proceedings, on the basis of the insolvency plan and on the effects of the insolvency plan which are relevant to the creditors' and the court's approval; and (ii) a constructive part, describing the changes in the legal position of the parties involved.

Groups shall be formed of the different creditors who have different status. According to section 222, paragraph 1 InsO, the groups shall distinguish between:

- creditors with a right to separate satisfaction if their rights will be altered by the insolvency plan;
- the non-subordinated ('normal') insolvency creditors;
- each class of subordinated creditors, unless their claims – as in the vast majority of the cases – are deemed to be waived according to section 225 InsO; and
- the persons holding a participating interest in the debtor if their shares or membership rights are to be included in the insolvency plan.

There is no limit to the number of groups, but parties with equal rights shall be grouped in with other parties of the same economic interest and such groups shall be adequately separated from each other; the criteria for the separation into the different groups shall be illustrated in the plan. Creditors in the same group must be offered the same rights (section 226 InsO).

Once the debtor or the insolvency administrator has submitted the plan, the insolvency court shall decide within two weeks on a possible refusal of the insolvency plan *ex officio*, which is possible if

- the provisions governing the insolvency plan and its content, in particular the formation of the groups, are not complied with and the submitting party is unable to correct it or does not correct it within reasonable time;
- an insolvency plan of the debtor obviously has no chance of acceptance by the creditors or approval by the court; or
- if the claims provided for in the constructive part of the insolvency plan submitted by a debtor obviously cannot be fulfilled.

A refusal of the plan by the court may be challenged via an immediate appeal (*sofortige Beschwerde*) according to section 231, paragraph 3 InsO.

If the insolvency court does not reject the insolvency plan, it will forward it to a possible creditors' committee and the debtor for their comments if the insolvency administrator has submitted the plan, and vice versa to the insolvency administrator if the plan was submitted by the debtor. The court may also request comments from the official representative body of industry, trade, craft or agriculture competent for the debtor or other expert organisations. The deadline for comments on the insolvency plan to be set by the court shall not exceed two weeks from the request.

The insolvency plan and possible comments must be laid out for the parties' inspection in the registry of the court and the court will docket a hearing no more than one month later to discuss the insolvency plan and – if necessary – the voting rights, and to subsequently vote on the plan. The date of the hearing is to be published and the insolvency creditors who have filed claims, the creditors with a right to separate satisfaction, the insolvency administrator, the debtor, the works' council and the spokesman of the executive employees shall be summoned separately whereupon they will be informed that the insolvency plan is laid out in the registry of the court (section 235 InsO).

The party submitting the insolvency plan is entitled to modify the insolvency plan during the discussion meeting according to the results of the discussion and the vote may be taken on the modified plan at the same meeting (section 240 InsO).

If the insolvency plan is approved by the necessary majorities or the approval of disapproving groups has been inferred (see section 2.12 below), the court must also approve the insolvency plan. Before its approval, the court shall hear the insolvency administrator, the creditors' committee and the debtor (section 248, paragraph 2 InsO). Plans which are subject to specific contributions or the implementation of other measures may only be approved when these conditions have been fulfilled and shall be rejected *ex officio* if the conditions are not fulfilled after a reasonable deadline set by the court (section 249 InsO). The insolvency plan shall be refused *ex officio* if (i) the rules on the content or the procedural rules, or the acceptance by the parties and the debtor, were not complied with in an essential aspect and this cannot be corrected or (ii) the acceptance of the insolvency plan has been effected by improper means, in particular by granting an undue advantage to one party.

In order to protect minorities, the insolvency plan must also be rejected on the request of a creditor if the requesting creditor has disapproved the insolvency plan and has shown to the satisfaction of the court that he will be disadvantaged by the insolvency plan no later than in the voting meeting; the request, however, is to be rejected (ie the insolvency plan approved) if the insolvency plan provides for funds to compensate for any disadvantage of a party showing to the satisfaction of the court that it will be disadvantaged by the insolvency plan (section 251 InsO).

Once the approval of the insolvency plan has become final and unless the insolvency plan provides otherwise, the insolvency court will order the termination of the insolvency proceedings (section 258 InsO).

2.6 Please provide information about voluntary filings

No specific filing is available for a procedure regarding an insolvency plan because the insolvency plan is merely an alternative method of achieving the goal of a collective satisfaction of the creditors within insolvency proceedings.

An insolvency filing must be in written form and a filing by the debtor must include a list of the creditors. If the debtors' business operations have not yet been discontinued, the creditors' list shall include:

- the largest claims;
- the largest secured claims;
- the claims of financial authorities;
- the claims of social security agencies; and
- claims resulting from employee pension schemes.

In addition, the filing itself must include information on the balance sheet total, the turnover and the average number of employees of the previous year. The information on the creditors (largest claims, etc) is mandatory if:

(i) the debtor applies for insolvency proceedings managed by a debtor in possession (*Eigenverwaltung*– see General remarks in section 2.1 above);
(ii) the debtor fulfils at least two of the three criteria of turnover of at least EUR 4,840,000, turnover of at least EUR 9,680,000 or an annual average of 50 employees (ie corresponding to the criteria for a so-called medium-sized incorporation under section 267 of the German Commercial Code, *Handelsgesetzbuch*); or
(iii) the appointment of a preliminary creditors' committee has been requested.

The information in the filing is necessary because the court shall appoint a preliminary creditors' committee (*vorläufiger Gläubigerausschuss*) it the debtor is at least a medium-sized incorporation (see point (ii) above) or if the debtor, the preliminary insolvency administrator or a creditor applies for its appointment (section 22a, paragraphs 1 and 2 InsO).

No further information is required, but the filing must show the cause for insolvency (ie (imminent) illiquidity and/or overindebtedness) to the satisfaction of the court. A possible draft for an insolvency plan may be filed (section 218, paragraph 1 InsO), but there is no obligation.

The decisions of the insolvency courts ordering securing measures and opening insolvency proceedings are published on the website *www.insolvenzbekanntmachungen.de*. The insolvency plan is to be laid out in the registry of the court and the relevant parties are to be informed thereof (see section 2.5 above).

2.7 How are creditors' representatives chosen?

Creditors' representatives – apart from the parties to be heard by the court (see section 2.5 above) – are not an integral part of the procedure regarding an insolvency plan but are, of course, integral to the insolvency proceedings.

In insolvency proceedings, the members of the initial (preliminary) creditors' committee are often suggested by the debtor when filing for insolvency. The court may request suggestions from the debtor or a preliminary insolvency administrator. The court will often follow these suggestions, but it is not bound to do so. It may also rely on the creditors' list which is to be included in the filing materials (see section 2.6 above). Some institutional creditors have provided courts with contact persons who are able to quickly decide whether they are in a position to join a certain (preliminary) creditors' committee.

(Preliminary) creditors' committees shall comprise a representative of the creditors with a right to separate satisfaction, the insolvency creditors with the highest claims, the creditors with the smallest claims and a representative of the debtor's employees (section 67 InsO).

2.8 Is there recourse against the opening judgment?

If insolvency proceedings are opened, only the debtor may bring an immediate appeal according to section 34, paragraph 2 InsO. Creditors have no right to appeal a decision opening insolvency proceedings (see also *Kirchhof*, in *Heidelberger Kommentar zur Insolvenzordnung*, 6th edn, 2011, § 34, marginal note 8).

Because German law does not provide for separate insolvency plan proceedings, there is no separate judgment on the 'opening' of such proceedings which could be appealed separately.

2.9 What are the roles and powers of committees?

In German insolvency proceedings (including insolvency proceedings which result in the approval of an insolvency plan), the creditors' assembly is the main forum of the creditors. The first creditors' assembly normally meets six weeks to three months after the opening of the insolvency proceedings. In the first meeting, the creditors may elect a new insolvency administrator. The creditors' may also decide to elect a creditors' committee to support and supervise the insolvency administrator (section 69 InsO).

The (preliminary) creditors' committee, normally consisting of three to five representatives, must be heard on the professional and personal requirements to be met by the (preliminary) administrator before its appointment unless this would be obviously to the detriment of the debtor's assets, in which case the (preliminary) creditors' committee may unanimously elect another person in its first hearing. A unanimous vote of the (preliminary) creditors' committee on the appointment of a specific person is binding for the court unless such person is not qualified for the office. The (preliminary) creditors' committee is additionally intended to support and supervise the (preliminary) insolvency administrator (section 21, paragraph 2, no. 1a in connection with section 69 InsO) and is to be heard if an insolvency plan is submitted (see section 2.5 above).

The creditors' committee is to decide on the (dis)continuation of the debtor's business and to approve certain other 'important measures' by the insolvency administrator, including the sale of the debtor's business, a plant, the whole of its produced goods/stock or (parts of) the debtor's real estate, or the filing or joining of law suits (section 160, 161 InsO). In the absence of a creditors' committee and in special situations, the insolvency administrator will need the approval of the creditors' assembly (section 162 InsO).

The creditors pass their decisions according to section 76, paragraph 2 InsO with a majority of the voting rights of the present or presently represented creditors. A creditor has a voting right for the full amount of his claim (not subordinated according to section 39 InsO – see section 2.10 below) which has not been challenged by the insolvency administrator or another creditor. If the claim has been challenged, if the creditor has a right to separate satisfaction or if the claim is subject to a condition precedent which has not been fulfilled, this creditor, the other attending creditors with a voting right and the insolvency administrator may agree on the amount of the voting rights. If they do not reach an agreement, the court will decide on the voting right (section 77 InsO). There is no minimum number of creditors required for quorum (*Ehricke*, in: *Münchener Kommentar zur Insolvenzordnung*, 3rd edn, 2013, § 76, marginal note 15).

2.10 What are the consequences of opening judgments for creditors?

Once insolvency proceedings are opened, and independent of the question whether an insolvency plan has been or will be submitted, insolvency creditors may no longer enforce any claims on their own but may only file them with the insolvency table managed by the insolvency administrator (section 87 and sections 714 *et seq.* InsO).

The opening decision is to be served to the creditors, the third party debtors (*Drittschuldner*) and the debtor himself. In the opening decision, creditors shall be required to file their claims within a definite period of time of at least two weeks but not more than three months from the opening of the proceedings (section 28, paragraph 1 InsO). A lapse does not bar a creditor from filing his insolvency claim later, but he may have to bear the (low) cost of a separate hearing of his claim. Claims not filed before the voting meeting for an insolvency plan are time-barred no later than one year from the date on which the claim is due and the order approving the insolvency plan becomes final (section 259b InsO).

To enable the insolvency administrator to verify the claims, the filing shall include all documents evidencing the claim. Subordinated claims shall only be filed if the court requests their filing (section 174 InsO). Disputes about the validity of insolvency claims are handled in separate legal actions (sections 179 *et seq.* InsO).

Separate provisions exist for creditors having a right to separation (*Aussonderung*) or separate satisfaction (*Absonderung*) from pledges (see below). Creditors secured by such rights may claim the separation of the specific object from the estate or a separate satisfaction from the proceeds of the pledged object (sections 47–50 InsO; a claim is considered to be an object under this clause; see *Ganter*, in *Münchener Kommentar zur Insolvenzordnung*, 3rd edn, 2013, § 50, marginal note 68). In the opening decision, creditors shall be required to immediately inform the insolvency administrator of such security interests in the property or rights of the debtor; this information by the creditor can be combined with the filing of the insolvency claim.

According to section 47 InsO, creditors who are entitled to claim the separation of an object from the insolvency estate under a right *in rem* (eg ownership of an object in the possession of the estate) or a right *in personam* (eg return of an object which does not form part of the estate because it was borrowed or rented) are not considered insolvency creditors. The entitlement to separation is governed by the legal provisions outside of insolvency proceedings.

A right to separate satisfaction is granted to

- creditors holding a legal or contractual pledge or a pledge acquired by attachment (section 50 InsO);
- creditors to whom the debtor has assigned title to a movable item or a right as security; and
- other creditor groups of lesser practical importance mentioned in section 51 InsO.

According to section 166 InsO, the insolvency administrator (but not the creditor) is entitled to dispose of movable objects in his possession subject to separate satisfaction and may collect or otherwise dispose of the debtor's claims assigned as security. Before the sale of a movable object, the insolvency administrator must inform the affected creditor and permit him to prove that an alternative disposition is more beneficial to the creditors within one week (section 168 InsO). If the insolvency administrator disposes of a movable object or a claim, he may deduct the cost of identification of the object and the determination of rights to it (a flat 4 per cent of the proceeds), as well as the costs of disposition (a flat 5 per cent of the proceeds, or the actually incurred costs if these considerably exceed or fall below this amount) for the benefit of the estate (sections 170 and 171 InsO).

Creditors with a right to satisfaction from immovable objects are entitled to separate satisfaction under the rules of the Law on Forced Auction and Sequestration (*Gesetz über die Zwangsversteigerung und die Zwangsverwaltung*).

Apart from a possible separation and/or separate satisfaction, all creditors, including tax authorities, social security agencies and employees, rank equally and will receive the same quota at the end of the insolvency proceedings unless an insolvency plan provides otherwise.

Subordinated claims, ie those that are ranked below the claims of ordinary insolvency creditors (and entitled to payments only if all prior ranking claims have been fully paid) according to section 39, paragraph 1 InsO, are ranked in the following order:

(1) interest fees and late payment fines on insolvency claims accruing after the opening of the insolvency proceedings;
(2) cost of insolvency creditors for participation in the insolvency proceedings;
(3) personal monetary penalties (*Geldstrafen*), administrative fines (*Geldbußen, Ordnungsgelder*), penalty payments (*Zwangsgelder*) and other payments incidental to criminal (*Straftat*) and minor criminal (*Ordnungswidrigkeit*) offences obliging monetary payments;
(4) claims for any gratuitous performance by the debtor; and
(5) (applicable in companies where no shareholder is personally liable or such shareholder itself does not have any personally liable shareholder) claims for repayment of a shareholder loan or claims out of legal actions which economically correspond to such a shareholder loan unless

that shareholder holds less than 10 per cent of the shares and is not a member of the management body (very rigid exceptions apply for restructuring loans).

The question whether the opening of insolvency proceedings leads to a draw stop for undrawn facilities are rarely relevant in Germany because of the two-stage type of the proceedings with a prior preliminary insolvency proceedings. Most banks will make use of their extraordinary right of termination of any contractual relationship for deterioration of the debtors financial standing according to their general terms and conditions (no. 19, paragraph 3 of the General Terms and Conditions of Banks, *AGB-Banken*) during the preliminary insolvency proceedings. If they do not do so in the preliminary phase, the insolvency administrator is entitled, according to section 103 InsO, to choose the fulfilment of loan contracts (*Darlehen*) according to sections 488 *et seq.* BGB. If he does so, he will have to pay the agreed consideration out of the estate and also pay back the loan when due. Most other contracts with banks, such as keeping a negative account current (*Kontokorrentkredit*), are considered agency agreements (*Geschäftsbesorgungsvertrag*, sections 675 *et seq.* BGB), which end automatically with the opening of insolvency proceedings according to section 116 InsO (see section 2.4 above).

If the insolvency plan does not provide otherwise, the debtor is discharged of his liabilities once he has satisfied the creditors in accordance with the constructive part of the insolvency plan (section 227, paragraph 1 InsO); according to paragraph 2, this shall apply *mutatis mutandis* to the personally liable partners of a company without legal liability and a partnership limited by shares (*Kommanditgesellschaft auf Aktien*).

2.11 What is the duration of the restructuring process?

The duration of the restructuring process in insolvency or insolvency plan proceedings fully depends on the case and the provisions of the insolvency plan. There are no time limits or a statutory maximum duration, but insolvency plans submitted after the final creditors' assembly will not be considered (section 218, paragraph 1, sentence 3).

2.12 How do creditors vote?

The creditors vote on the insolvency plan in the separate groups designated by the insolvency plan (see section 2.5 above). All groups must vote in favour of the insolvency plan. A group accepts the insolvency plan if a majority of the voting creditors by number and by the sum of their claims approves it (section 244 InsO). An exception exists in the groups of subordinated creditors and shareholders where the plan is deemed to be approved if nobody votes (sections 246 and 246a InsO). If the debtor does not oppose the insolvency plan in writing no later than at the voting meeting, his consent is also implied (section 247 InsO).

If a voting group has not approved the plan with the necessary majorities, its approval is implied if:

- the insolvency plan is likely not to be disadvantageous to the members of the group in comparison to insolvency proceedings without the insolvency plan;
- the members of the group reasonably participate in the economic value available for the insolvency plan (in particular, no creditor receives economic values in excess of his claim and); and
- the majority of the groups have approved the plan with the necessary majorities.

2.13 What are the rules on clawback/voidability?

The rules on clawback/voidability (*Anfechtung*) are the same for all insolvency proceedings in Germany. According to sections 129 *et seq.* InsO, the insolvency administrator may contest transactions disadvantaging the creditors. The practically most relevant provisions are the following.

Particularly critical is the time period of three months before the insolvency filing and the time after the filing, because a contest may then be brought under sections 130 or 131 InsO. The main difference between these provisions is the question of whether the transaction to be contested was congruent or incongruent, meaning whether the other side had a right to receive the security or satisfaction in the kind and at the time that he received it (if yes, it was congruent; if not, it was incongruent). It is important to note here that under sections 130 and 131 InsO it is irrelevant if it is the debtor or a third party that has provided the security or satisfaction.

Under section 130 InsO, a transaction granting a security or satisfaction may be contested if:

- it was made in the three months before the insolvency filing, the debtor was illiquid at the time and the creditor was aware of the illiquidity; or
- it was made after the insolvency filing if the creditor was aware of the illiquidity on the date of the transaction or of the insolvency filing.

Section 131 InsO permits a contest of an incongruent transaction in particular if:

- it was made in the month prior to the insolvency filing; or
- it was made within the second or third month before the insolvency filing if the debtor was illiquid at the time.

A transaction which was made by the debtor during the last 10 years prior to the insolvency filing with the intention of disadvantaging his creditors may be contested in accordance with section 133 InsO if the other party was aware of the debtor's intention on the date of such transaction. The awareness of the other party is presumed if it knew of the debtor's imminent illiquidity and that the transaction constituted a disadvantage to the creditors.

Under section 134 InsO, a gratuitous benefit granted by the debtor may be contested if it was made during the four years prior to the insolvency filing and exceeded a usual gift of minor value. Section 135 InsO permits a contestation by the insolvency administrator if subordinated claims under section 39, paragraph 1, no. 5 InsO (claims for repayment of a shareholder loan or claims out of legal actions which economically correspond to such a shareholder loan – see section 2.10 above).

2.14 What are the rules on set-off/netting?

As a general principle, set-off (*Aufrechnung*) remains possible in German insolvency proceedings if the creditor was able to set-off his claims at the time when the insolvency proceedings were opened (section 94 InsO). If one of the claims is not yet unconditional, due or not directed at the same type of performance, the claim can only be set-off when these conditions are fulfilled but only if the creditor's claim becomes unconditional, due or directed at the same performance before the debtor's claim does (section 95 InsO). A set-off is also denied if:

- the creditor's debt originated after the opening of insolvency proceedings;
- the creditor acquired his claim from another creditor after the opening of insolvency proceedings;
- the creditor acquired his claim under circumstances which are subject to contestation (see section 2.13 above); or
- a creditor whose claim is to be fulfilled not out of the estate but out of the free assets of the debtor owes something to the estate.

2.15 How is exit managed?

Insolvency plans under German insolvency law may provide for any treatment of any creditors' claims in the groups provided for in the insolvency plan, but there must be equal treatment of the creditors within the group. If the insolvency plan is adopted, it is valid also for dissenting creditors. The approval of dissenting groups may be inferred if certain conditions are fulfilled, in particular if the creditors of such group are not disadvantaged in comparison to regular insolvency proceedings and participate reasonably in the economic values (see section 2.12 above).

Unless the insolvency plan provides otherwise, the shares and rights of shareholders/partners remain unaffected. An insolvency plan may provide for any change that would otherwise be permissible under the applicable corporate/partnership laws (section 225 InsO). In particular, the conversion of creditors' claims into shares/membership rights (but only with the consent of the respective creditor) and the decrease and/or increase of capital under exclusion of subscription rights of existing shareholders/partners and payments to excluded shareholders are permissible. If the group of shareholders does not vote on the insolvency plan, its consent is implied. If it disapproves, the consent may be implied under general rules (see section 2.12 above) whereby the group is considered to reasonably participate in the economic value if no creditor is to receive economic benefits in excess of his claim and no creditor of equal rank is to receive an advantage compared to the shareholder/partner.

Insolvency plans may also arrange for any type of asset disposal: a (partial) asset deal is possible in the same way as the continued use of all assets by the debtor. The creditors are protected by the fact that the insolvency plan must be approved by them and, if they do not approve, their approval may only be implied if their treatment under the insolvency plan is likely not to be disadvantageous in comparison to insolvency proceedings without the insolvency plan. In order to show the lack of any disadvantage, insolvency plans will always provide a comparative calculation which describes the different alternatives for the information and control of the creditors. Additionally, the creditors' committee is to assist in the preparation of the insolvency plan (section 218, paragraph 3 InsO) and will be asked for comments which will be laid out in the registry of the court for the inspection of the other creditors (sections 232 and 234 InsO). The rights of creditors entitled to separation (*Aussonderung* – see section 2.10 above) cannot be affected by insolvency plans (section 217 InsO), while the rights of creditors entitled to separate satisfaction (*Absonderung* – see section 2.10 above) remain unchanged only if the insolvency plan does not provide otherwise (section 223 InsO).

With the termination of the insolvency proceedings, the debtor is vested with the right of unhindered disposition over the insolvency estate. The constructive part of the insolvency plan may provide for the monitoring of implementation of the plan, in which case the offices of the insolvency administrator and the creditors' committee may continue until final fulfilment of all obligations under the insolvency plan (section 260 InsO).

2.16 Are 'prepackaged' plans, arrangements or agreements permissible?

So-called prepackaged insolvency plans are explicitly permitted in Germany and may be combined with the initial insolvency filing according to section 218, paragraph 3 InsO. The protective-shield proceedings according to section 270b InsO also gives an incentive to prepare an insolvency plan during the preliminary insolvency proceedings (see section 1 above).

2.17 Is a public authority involved?

Public authorities, such as tax authorities and employment agencies for insolvency payments, are regularly involved in German insolvency proceedings as creditors. Their powers are identical to those of other creditors and there are no prerogatives in favour of the public authorities (with the possible exception that taxes originating during preliminary insolvency proceedings must be paid after the opening of the proceedings under certain circumstances – section 55, paragraph 4 InsO).

2.18 What is the treatment of claims arising after filing/admission?

Claims arising after an insolvency filing but before the opening of the insolvency proceedings (ie during preliminary insolvency) are generally insolvency claims. This result is, of course, undesirable, so a number of ways have been developed in practice to effectively ensure that payment is permissible, such as payment before the opening of insolvency proceedings or a separate authorisation for certain transactions by the court (*Einzelermächtigung*), with the effect that the liabilities are considered liabilities of the estate (*Masseverbindlichkeiten*) and payment must be fully made after insolvency proceedings have been opened.

Liabilities validly entered into after the opening of insolvency proceedings are considered liabilities of the estate (*Masseverbindlichkeiten*) and must be fully paid.

The insolvency administrator must settle undisputed due claims against the estate before the termination of the insolvency proceedings (section 258, paragraph 2 InsO).

2.19 Are there ongoing contracts?

As discussed above (section 2.4), certain contracts are terminated by law with the opening of insolvency proceedings, while section 112 InsO prohibits the termination of a rent contract for nonpayment of rent for periods before the insolvency filing and/or for a deterioration of the debtor's financial standing and employment agreements are continued according to section 113 InsO. No problems exist if the insolvency administrator has chosen the fulfilment or the non-fulfilment of other long-term contracts under section 103 InsO, but it is uncertain whether the debtor can still choose the (non-)fulfilment of contracts after the termination of the insolvency plan proceedings if no declaration was made during the insolvency proceedings and the insolvency plan does not provide a solution. A clear provision for long-term contracts in the insolvency plan is therefore advisable.

2.20 Are consolidated proceedings for members of a corporate family/group possible?

German law does not (yet) provide for separate rules in insolvencies of corporate groups, but the draft for a law for the facilitation of group insolvencies is currently being discussed in Parliament (*Bundestag*). The draft provides for the jurisdiction of only one court and one judge for all group companies, as well as a coordination procedure involving a coordinator for the insolvency administrators appointed for the different companies, without questioning the separate treatment of each individual debtor and its creditors.

2.21 What are the charges, fees and other costs?

The Law on Court Fees (*Gerichtskostengesetz*) generally provides for a calculation of the court fees on the basis of the value of the estate at the time of the termination of the insolvency proceedings (section 58 *Gerichtskostengesetz*) and decreasing with the value of the estate.

The remuneration of the insolvency administrator is similarly calculated on the basis of the value of the estate, which is the subject of the final accounts of the insolvency administrator or – in proceedings with an insolvency plan – the estimated value of the estate at the end of the insolvency proceedings. The remuneration is a certain percentage of the value of the estate, and may be increased or decreased by the court if the work in the specific insolvency proceedings fell short of or exceeded the average insolvency proceedings; the submission of an insolvency plan will always justify an increase of remuneration.

3. LIABILITY ISSUES

3.1 What is the liability of managers/directors *vis-à-vis* creditors?

Where corporate/partnership laws do not provide for a personal liability of the (managing) partners, its management (including shadow management) is generally not liable for debts of the company (particularly in the common corporate forms of a GmbH, a GmbH & Co. KG or an AG) if they act with the prudence of a diligent businessman.

However, section 64 of the German Code on Limited Liability Companies (GmbHG) and sections 92 and 93 of the German Code on Stock Corporations (AktG) provide for the liability of the management for all payments made after the company has become illiquid or its overindebtedness has been determined, unless the management can prove that the respective payment was in conformity with the prudence of a diligent businessman.

The management may also be held liable, if not filing for insolvency without undue delay, for any decrease in the later quota of the creditors according to section 15a InsO in connection with section 823, paragraph 2 BGB; it may be held liable for payments out of the assets necessary to maintain the share capital (section 43 GmbHG) and payments to shareholders which necessarily led to an illiquidity (section 64 GmbHG, sections 92 and 93 AktG). In addition, the general rules of the law of torts are applicable.

The insolvency administrator is to enforce the claims of the insolvency creditors resulting from damage suffered jointly due to a reduction of the property forming part of the insolvency estate before or after the opening of the insolvency proceedings. The insolvency administrator again is liable with respect to the creditors, for any damages to the parties in case of a violation of his duties, so that it is in his best interests to pursue all existing claims of the estate.

During the course of the insolvency proceedings, creditors may therefore only bring claims for damages suffered individually (only) by the respective creditor, eg by the creditor that entered into a contract with the debtor after it became illiquid for the damage resulting from the management's failure to file for insolvency without undue delay (the damage will result from the fact that the creditor entered into the contract at all).

The management is also liable with respect to social security agencies for nonpayment of the employees' shares in the social security fees and with respect to financial authorities nonpayment of tax liabilities.

3.2 What is the liability of the lender?

The lender is generally not liable with respect to the debtor and/or the creditors unless very exceptional circumstances make him, for example, a shadow manager (*faktischer Geschäftsführer*).

Hong Kong

Deacons Philip Gilligan, Richard Hudson & Tiffany Cheung

1. WHAT COURT-MONITORED RESTRUCTURING PRE-INSOLVENCY PROCEEDINGS OR SCHEMES ARE DEVISED BY THE LAW OF YOUR COUNTRY TO LIMIT VALUE DESTRUCTION FOR FAILING BUSINESS ENTITIES?

Hong Kong does not have any specific statutory court-monitored restructuring mechanism. However, in the absence of a formal restructuring mechanism, pre-insolvency corporate rescue or restructuring may be achieved through:

- a scheme of arrangement carried out in accordance with the procedures set out under Part 13, Division 2 of the Companies Ordinance (Cap. 622) (CO); or
- provisional liquidation.

1.1 What is the objective of the proceeding?

Scheme of arrangement

A scheme of arrangement is a binding compromise or arrangement between a company and its shareholders and/or creditors (or a class of them) which, when used in an insolvency context, aims to prevent the company's liquidation. A scheme of arrangement makes it possible for there to be a compromise or arrangement which binds all of the company's shareholders and/or creditors (or a class them), even though there is a dissenting minority of such shareholders and/or creditors.

Provisional liquidation

The primary purpose of appointing a provisional liquidator is to preserve a company's assets in the interval between presentation of the petition and the making of the winding up order.

1.2 Do all kinds of businesses qualify?

Scheme of arrangement

All companies liable to be wound up under the Companies (Winding Up and Miscellaneous Provisions) Ordinance (Cap. 32) (CWUO) can enter into a scheme of arrangement. This includes companies incorporated in Hong Kong as well as foreign companies (although the courts will not exercise their jurisdiction to wind up foreign companies unless there is sufficient nexus with Hong Kong). There are no thresholds related to indebtedness, turnover or asset value that the company, its creditors or its members must meet. There is no court agent appointed to assist the company.

Provisional liquidation

The court may appoint a provisional liquidator to any company in respect of which a winding up petition has been presented. This includes companies incorporated in Hong Kong as well as foreign companies (although the courts will not exercise their jurisdiction to wind up foreign companies unless there is a sufficient nexus with Hong Kong).

The court may only appoint a provisional liquidator to a company after presentation of a winding up petition, but not if a winding up order has already been made.

There is also case law which holds that the courts will not appoint a provisional liquidator for the purposes of corporate rescue except where the assets of the company are in jeopardy.

1.3 What are the necessary approvals?

Scheme of arrangement

Once a proposal for a scheme of arrangement has been formulated by the company, the court's approval to call the relevant meetings or class meetings of the company's creditors or members is required.

The necessary approvals required at each of the relevant meetings or class meetings which are required to be held are as follows:

Privatisation or takeover schemes

For schemes of arrangement involving a general offer (ie a listed company's offer to buy back shares) or a takeover offer, approval by the members or a class of the members requires:

- approval by shareholders representing at least 75 per cent of the voting rights of the members present and voting; and
- the votes cast against the scheme at the meeting do not exceed 10 per cent of the total voting rights attached to all disinterested shares.

Other members' meetings or members' class meetings

For schemes other than privatisation or takeover schemes, approval of the members or a class of the members requires:

- approval by shareholders representing at least 75 per cent of the voting rights of the members present and voting; and
- unless the court orders otherwise, a majority in number of the members present and voting.

Creditors' meetings or creditors' class meetings

Approval of the creditors or a class of creditors requires:

- approval by creditors representing at least 75 per cent in value of the creditors present and voting; and
- a majority in number of the creditors present and voting.

Finally, the scheme of arrangement must be sanctioned by the court in order to become effective.

Provisional liquidation

The court will only exercise its discretion to appoint a provisional liquidator for corporate rescue purposes if:

- the petitioner for the winding up of the company satisfies the court that there is a good *prima facie* case for a winding up order; and
- in the circumstances, a provisional liquidator should be appointed.

The petition for the winding up of a company by the court must state at least one of six grounds, the most common of which are:

- a special resolution (ie 75 per cent of shareholders' votes cast) to wind up the company by the court is passed;
- the company is unable to pay its debts (this is presumed if it fails to satisfy a debt equal to or exceeding HK$10,000 within three weeks of service of a statutory demand, if a judgment debt is not satisfied in whole or in part, or if it is proved to the satisfaction of the court that it is unable to pay its debts taking into account contingent and prospective liabilities); and
- it is just and equitable to liquidate the company.

Whether a provisional liquidator should be appointed in the circumstances will broadly depend on the commercial realities of the case, the degree of urgency, the need for an order and the balance of convenience.

1.4 What is the procedure?

Scheme of arrangement

A company which wishes to enter into a scheme of arrangement will first formulate a proposal. Application must then be made to the court for an order authorising the convening of the relevant meetings or class meetings of the company's shareholders and/or creditors. The application is made by an originating summons, supported by an affidavit (usually by the party putting forward the proposed scheme) containing, among other things, information about the company, the proposed scheme and a draft explanatory statement (explanatory statement), and terms of the scheme. The application is made *ex parte* (although the application may be brought *inter partes* if appropriate in the circumstances), and may be made by the company, a shareholder or a creditor. However, if the company is being wound up, the application must be made by a liquidator or a provisional liquidator.

If the court orders the convening of the meetings or class meetings of the shareholders and/or creditors, the meetings are called. The court order will include directions regulating the calling of the meetings. Every notice summoning such meetings must be accompanied by an explanatory statement (or, if the notice is given by way of an advertisement, the notice must state how a creditor or member entitled to attend the meeting may obtain a copy of the explanatory statement). The scheme must be approved by the requisite majorities of creditors and/or shareholders (see section 1.3 above).

If the creditors and/or shareholders approve the scheme proposal at the meetings or class meetings, an application must then be made to the court to sanction the scheme. The application is made by petition, supported by an affidavit (which is usually made by the chairman of the creditor/shareholder meetings, who is appointed pursuant to the court order convening the meetings). The application may be made by the company, a shareholder or a creditor. However, if the company is being wound up, the application must be made by a liquidator or a provisional liquidator.

If the court sanctions the scheme of arrangement, the scheme will only take effect once an office copy of the court order has been delivered to the Registrar of Companies for registration.

Provisional liquidation

Provisional liquidation is not itself a separate procedure, but forms part of the compulsory liquidation procedure, and it has been used in Hong Kong to effect a corporate rescue or restructuring. Thus, the first step requires that a winding up petition be presented to have the company wound up compulsorily by the court.

After presentation of the winding up petition but before a winding up order has been made, any creditor or contributory, the petitioner or the company may apply to the court for the appointment of a provisional liquidator. The application is made by summons, and must be supported by an affidavit setting out sufficient grounds for the appointment of a provisional liquidator. While the court will normally take the view that applications should be heard *inter partes*, in urgent and exceptional cases, the application may be made *ex parte*.

If the court grants the application to appoint a provisional liquidator, the order appointing the provisional liquidator will bear the number of the petition, shall state the nature and a short description of the property of which the provisional liquidator is ordered to take possession, and shall set out the powers of and the duties to be performed by the provisional liquidator. The powers commonly granted by the court to provisional liquidators in the context of corporate rescue include powers to investigate misfeasance, formulate restructuring proposals and exercise rights in respect of subsidiaries.

If a winding up order is made after the appointment of a provisional liquidator, the Official Receiver or such other person appointed as provisional liquidator continues to act as the provisional liquidator until he or another person becomes the liquidator and is capable of acting as such.

If the restructuring has been successfully implemented, then, instead of proceeding with the liquidation of the company, the provisional liquidator will seek the dismissal of the winding up proceedings and his own discharge. Alternatively, a provisional liquidation also concludes at such time as the provisional liquidator or some other person is appointed as liquidator by the court (whereupon the liquidator will proceed to wind up the company).

1.5 Is there recourse against the opening judgment?

Yes, parties may lodge an appeal.

1.6 What are the substantive tests/definitions?

Scheme of arrangement

There are no substantive tests/definitions that the company, its creditors or its members must meet. It is not necessary for the company to show that it is solvent – schemes of arrangement are available to both solvent and insolvent companies.

Under the scheme of arrangement procedure, it is necessary that there is a 'compromise' or an 'arrangement'. While the term 'compromise' is not defined in the CO, it is accepted that there needs to be a pre-existing dispute whereby the creditors and/or shareholders are prepared to give up or modify some of their rights, and the term is more limited than an arrangement. An 'arrangement' is interpreted more widely to encompass any agreement modifying rights, and includes a reorganisation of the company's share capital by the consolidation of different classes of shares and/or by the division of shares into different classes.

Provisional liquidation

See section 1.3 above.

1.7 What is the role of a court-appointed agent?

N/A.

1.8 What protection is there from creditors?

Scheme of arrangement

Initiation of a scheme of arrangement does not trigger a moratorium on creditor claims. As there is no moratorium, any dissenting creditor can bring legal proceedings or present a winding up petition against the company, which could prevent a scheme from being concluded. To mitigate this, a scheme of arrangement is sometimes prepared after a provisional liquidation order has been obtained (see below).

Provisional liquidation

At any time after the presentation of a winding up petition and before a winding up order is made, the company or any creditor or contributory may apply to the court to stay or restrain proceedings against the company, and the court may stay or restrain such proceedings accordingly on such terms as it thinks fit. Further, once a provisional liquidator has been appointed, no action or proceedings may be proceeded with or commenced against the company except by leave of the court, and subject to such terms as the court may impose.

1.9 What is the usual duration of the restructuring process?

Scheme of arrangement

There is no prescribed statutory form for a scheme of arrangement (and therefore the duration of each scheme of arrangement will depend on the circumstances of each case), although, due to the court's involvement and the need to define the classes of creditors and/or members to which the scheme applies carefully, a scheme may take more than a year to conclude. Given that a scheme of arrangement is a court-monitored process, the court's timetable may also affect the duration. The scheme terms and conditions which are prepared by the company and its professional advisors will often contain provisions relating to the duration and termination of the scheme.

Provisional liquidation

As mentioned, provisional liquidation forms part of the compulsory liquidation procedure. Furthermore, the courts have taken the view that the appointment of a provisional liquidator must still always be for the purposes of the winding up of the company. Therefore, in many cases, a company in provisional liquidation will eventually be wound up. If, however, a restructuring proposal is developed within the provisional liquidation, the Hong Kong court may allow the provisional liquidator powers to continue for as long as it takes for the proposal to be implemented, with the provisional liquidator being required to return to court every few months to report on the progress of the restructuring.

1.10 Who prepares the restructuring agreement and what are the available tools?

Scheme of arrangement

The company, with the assistance of its professional advisors, will put together the explanatory statement and the terms of the scheme of arrangement.

Provisional liquidation

The company's professional advisers (who may also be appointed the provisional liquidator) will often assist the company with formulating a restructuring proposal. The provisional liquidator may also advance the proposal themselves.

1.11 Are subordination agreements necessarily given full effect?

Yes.

1.12 How is exit managed?

Scheme of arrangement

After a scheme of arrangement becomes effective (see section 1.4 above), it is binding on the company (and, if the company is being wound up, the liquidator or provisional liquidator and contributories), its creditors and/or shareholders (or a class of them) who are party to the scheme. Under the terms of the scheme, an administrator (who is usually an insolvency accountant) is appointed to implement the arrangement.

A scheme of arrangement concludes when its terms have been implemented. The terms of the scheme will usually contain provisions relating to how exit is managed, including:

- duration and termination of the scheme (eg early termination through a creditors' vote);
- payment of final dividends; and
- final arrangements on conclusion of the scheme.

On conclusion of a scheme, the scheme administrator will file a notice with the Registrar of Companies.

Provisional liquidation

If the restructuring has been successfully implemented, then instead of proceeding with the liquidation of the company, the provisional liquidator will seek the dismissal of the winding up proceedings and his own discharge. Alternatively, a provisional liquidation also concludes at such time as the provisional liquidator or some other person is appointed as liquidator by the court (whereupon the liquidator will proceed to wind up the company).

1.13 Who are the necessary parties?

Scheme of arrangement

The company and its members (generally those persons whose names are recorded in the register of members) and/or its creditors (including all creditors whose claims would be admitted to proof in the event the company is wound up).

Provisional liquidation

The company and its members (generally those persons whose names are recorded in the register of members) and/or its creditors (including all creditors whose claims would be admitted to proof in the event the company is wound up).

The Official Receiver may also be a party.

2. POST-INSOLVENCY PROCEEDINGS

In most cases, an insolvent company will be placed into liquidation. As mentioned, Hong Kong does not have any specific statutory court-monitored restructuring mechanism. However, in the absence of a formal restructuring mechanism, post-insolvency corporate rescue or restructuring of a company in liquidation may be achieved through a scheme of arrangement.

2.1 What is the objective of the proceedings?

See section 1.1 (Scheme of arrangement) above.

2.2 Do all kinds of business entities qualify?

See section 1.2 (Scheme of arrangement) above.

2.3 What are the necessary approvals?

See section 1.3 (Scheme of arrangement) above.

2.4 Is it valid and binding to agree that such proceeding be a default/termination event?

An agreement which provides that a default/termination event occurs upon (i) the entry by the company into a scheme of arrangement by the company or (ii) the presentation of a petition for the winding up of the company (and/or appointment of a liquidator) will generally be upheld by the courts to be valid and binding on the company.

2.5 What is the procedure?

See section 1.4 (Scheme of arrangement) above.

2.6 Please provide information about voluntary filings

In a scheme of arrangement, the hearing of the application to call the relevant meetings or class meetings of the company's shareholders and/or creditors is heard in chambers (ie not open to the public) and is normally heard *ex parte*.

The application must be supported by an affidavit which contains, among other things, information about the company, the proposed scheme, and a draft explanatory statement and terms of the scheme. There is no requirement for an expert opinion/report on the feasibility of the restructuring plan, but the court will not summon the relevant meetings unless it considers that the proposal is a fair one which could be supported by the relevant creditors and/or shareholders. It is common for preliminary negotiations to be held with creditors and/or shareholders prior to the actual submission of the application to ensure that the requisite majorities would be able to be obtained.

If the court orders the convening of the meetings or class meetings of the shareholders and/or creditors, the meetings are called. The court order will include directions regarding the calling of the meetings. Every notice summoning such meetings must be accompanied by an explanatory statement (or, if the notice is given by way of an advertisement, the notice must state how a creditor or member entitled to attend the meeting may obtain a copy of the explanatory statement).

2.7 How are creditors' representatives chosen?

See section 2.9 below.

2.8 Is there recourse against the opening judgment?

Yes, parties may lodge an appeal.

2.9 What are the roles and powers of committees?

The roles and powers of any committees will usually be set out in the terms of the scheme of arrangement.

2.10 What are the consequences of opening judgments for creditors?

Stay?

See section 1.8 above.

Forbidden payments?

Once a winding up order is made, any disposition of the property of the company (such as payments made to a creditor) made after commencement of the winding up is void, unless the court orders otherwise. Commencement of the winding up is deemed to be the date on which the company passes a resolution for the company to be wound up compulsorily by the court (if any) or the date of presentation of the winding up petition.

Where there is a scheme of arrangement in place, after the scheme becomes effective (see section 1.4 above), it is binding on the company (and if the company is being wound up, the liquidator or provisional liquidator and contributories), its creditors and/or shareholders (or a class of them) who are party to the scheme.

Interests accruing during the period: paid at contractual payment dates? Deferred and paid after plan is adopted? Capitalised? Is the rate necessarily the contract rate?

With respect to an insolvent company in liquidation once the winding up order is made, where the contract itself provides for payment of interest, the contractual rate of interest applies up to either (i) the date the company passes a resolution for the company to be wound up compulsorily by the court (if any) or (ii) in any other case, the date of the winding up order. There is no entitlement to interest accruing after commencement of the winding up unless the company is solvent.

Where there is a scheme of arrangement in place, the terms of the scheme will usually provide for accrual of interest on claims.

Is the opening judgment a valid draw stop for undrawn facilities?

See section 2.19 below.

Necessity to file proof of claim: are all creditors required to file proof of claim? Are secured creditors necessarily notified? Are there any time limits? Are non-resident creditors treated differently? Are there any consequences if the creditor is time-barred? Debtor discharged?

There is no requirement that creditors file a proof of claim in a scheme of arrangement. However, for a scheme to be ultimately sanctioned, it is necessary for the scheme to be properly approved by the correct classes of creditors and/or shareholders. The terms of the scheme of arrangement may provide for creditors to file proofs with the scheme administrator once the scheme is effective and binding.

Does such proceeding entail any limitation on enforcement of contractually created security?

Generally, no (except where, for example, such security is subject to a binding scheme of arrangement or a valid subordination agreement).

2.11 What is the duration of the restructuring process?

See section 1.9 (Scheme of arrangement) above.

2.12 How do creditors vote?

It is the responsibility of the applicant to determine the correct classes of creditors and/or shareholders in a scheme of arrangement. While the court may provide guidance as to the persons who should comprise a class, the constitution of classes may still be challenged at the final sanction hearing.

As to the requisite majorities required at the meetings, see section 1.3 (Scheme of arrangement) above.

2.13 What are the rules on clawback/voidability?

The following rules on clawback/voidability arise once an insolvent company is in liquidation.

Unfair preferences

An unfair preference occurs when an insolvent company does anything which puts a creditor, surety or guarantor in a better position than such person would otherwise have been in had the company gone into liquidation. A liquidator can apply to the court to set aside the unfair preference made within six months (or two years in the case where the preferred person is an associate) before the presentation of the winding up petition.

Floating charges

Floating charges created within 12 months of an insolvent company's liquidation are invalid and can be set aside by the liquidator unless money is advanced to the company at the same time as, or after, the charge is created.

Post-commencement disposals

See section 2.10 (Forbidden payments? Provisional liquidation) above.

Disclaimer of onerous property

The liquidator of a company being wound up may disclaim onerous property of the company with the leave of the court. Onerous property includes shares or stock in companies, unprofitable contracts and any other property that is unsaleable or not readily saleable by reason of its binding the company to the performance of an onerous act or payment of money. The courts are generally unwilling to sanction a disclaimer of property in cases where the rights of third parties may be adversely affected.

Fraudulent conveyance

A transaction can be set aside if a liquidator can prove to the court that it took place with the aim of defrauding creditors. The company does not need to be insolvent at the time of the transaction, or become insolvent as a result, to set aside the transaction. However, a transaction will not be avoided if the property was disposed of for valuable consideration and in good faith to a person who did not have notice of the intent to defraud the creditors.

Extortionate credit transactions

If a company is being liquidated, the court can make an order setting aside or varying the terms of an extortionate credit transaction which was entered into within three years prior to the commencement of the winding up. An extortionate credit transaction is one which involves the provision of credit to a company, the terms of which require grossly exorbitant payments to be made or otherwise grossly contravene ordinary principles of fair dealing.

Fraudulent trading

If, during liquidation, it appears that any business of the company was carried on with the intent of defrauding creditors or any other person, or for any fraudulent purpose, the court can declare that a person who was knowingly a party to that business is personally liable for the company's debts.

2.14 What are the rules on set-off/netting?

Hong Kong recognises mandatory set-off of mutual debts in the event of an insolvent company's winding up. For a set-off to apply, there must be:

- credits, debts or other dealings between the insolvent company and the creditor;
- the credits, debts or other dealings must be mutual (meaning that they must be between the same persons and in the same right); and
- the creditor's claim must be provable in the winding up.

However, a creditor shall not be entitled to insolvency set-off in any case where he had, at the time of giving credit to the insolvent company, notice that the winding up petition had been presented. The effective date at which the mutual credits, debts or other dealings must exist is at the date of the winding up order.

Neither the existence of a scheme of arrangement nor the appointment of a provisional liquidator affects the above rules on set-off.

2.15 How is exit managed?

See section 1.12 (Scheme of arrangement) above.

2.16 Are 'prepackaged' plans, arrangements or agreements permissible?

No.

2.17 Is a public authority involved?
No.

2.18 What is the treatment of claims arising after filing/ admission?
Once a liquidator has been appointed in respect of an insolvent company, no action or proceedings may be proceeded with or commenced against the company except by leave of the court, and subject to such terms as the court may impose.

2.19 Are there ongoing contracts?
By itself, the promulgation of a scheme of arrangement does not terminate the company's contracts (including any credit agreements the company may be party to). The terms of the relevant scheme of arrangement may confer power on the scheme administrator to obtain additional finance.

2.20 Are consolidated proceedings for members of a corporate family/group possible?
While there is no statutory procedure for consolidated proceedings (so that each company in a corporate group must be dealt with separately), the court is aware of the commercial and practical realities concerning group restructurings. For example, in past cases, the court has recognised that (conflicts of interest considerations aside), there are advantages of having a single liquidator in a group liquidation scenario.

2.21 What are the charges, fees and other costs?
The standard court fees will apply.

The costs of the parties of the scheme will normally be dealt with in the terms of the scheme.

3. LIABILITY ISSUES

3.1 What is the liability of managers/directors vis-à-vis creditors?

Scheme of arrangement
A responsible person of a company (which includes an officer or shadow director of a company) may be criminally liable if there is failure to comply with certain procedural requirements relating to a scheme of arrangement. For example, failure to provide the explanatory statement to the creditors and/or shareholders together with the notices summoning the relevant meetings is an offence (attracting a fine of up to HK$50,000).

Directors may also be liable for provisional liquidation, as set out below.

Provisional liquidation
Directors and officers of a company are liable to the liquidator if they commit offences such as fraud or deception. In a number of situations, a liquidator can also seek a court order requiring certain directors or officers to

either repay or restore property to the company, or provide compensation or contribute to the company's assets.

A director can be personally liable if:

- he has given a personal guarantee for company debts;
- he has breached his fiduciary duty to the creditors (which arises where the company is insolvent or near insolvency), the company and/or its shareholders;
- on the winding up of the company, it is found that the business of the company has been carried on with intent to defraud creditors (of the company or any other person) or for any fraudulent purpose, and the person is knowingly party to the carrying on of such business; or
- he has misapplied or retained the company's property for his personal benefit (misfeasance).

Directors can also be criminally liable for certain offences (such as misappropriation of property, for which they can be imprisoned). If company accounts and records are destroyed, or falsified before or after winding up begins, the party responsible (whether a past or present officer or shareholder) can be fined or imprisoned.

3.2 What is the liability of the lender?

The statutory liability of a lender where a company is in financial distress is limited (Hong Kong does not have currently any concept of 'insolvent trading' or 'wrongful trading'). Transactions entered into by lenders with the company before the commencement of its liquidation may be avoided in certain circumstances - see section 2.13 above.

More generally, liability to which lenders may be exposed may also include the following:

- breach of the loan agreement with the company may result in a claim for damages; and
- breach of its general law duties to the company (eg if the lender is a bank, breach of its fiduciary duty to the company in the provision of its services; or, if it is a secured creditor, the duties applicable to it upon enforcement of its security).

Italy

CBA Studio Legale e Tributario
Alessandro Varrenti & Daniela Sorgato

1. WHAT COURT-MONITORED RESTRUCTURING PRE-INSOLVENCY PROCEEDINGS OR SCHEMES HAVE BEEN DEVISED BY THE LAW OF YOUR COUNTRY TO LIMIT VALUE DESTRUCTION FOR FAILING BUSINESS ENTITIES?

In order to avoid bankruptcy, business enterprises which meet certain requirements, such as being in a difficult financial situation, are eligible to resort to the following pre-insolvency proceedings, regulated by Law Decree No. 267/1942 (the Bankruptcy Law) (unless otherwise indicated herein, any reference to an article of law shall be understood as a reference to the Bankruptcy Law):

- the arrangement with creditors' proceedings (*concordato preventivo*) (Articles 160–86);
- the debt restructuring agreement proceedings (*accordo di ristrutturazione dei debiti*) (Article 182 *bis*);
- the arrangement of a certified recovery plan (Article 67(3)d).

Based on Article 2221 of the Italian Civil Code and Article 1 of the Bankruptcy Law, in order to initiate one of the above-mentioned proceedings, a business entity:

- shall exercise a 'business activity' (eg production of goods and services or transportation); and
- shall not fall within the following thresholds:
  (i) total value of assets not higher than EUR 300,000.00;
  (ii) annual gross turnover not higher than EUR 200,000.00 ((i) and (ii) must be determined in relation to the last three financial years prior to the filing of the petition); and
  (iii) total indebtedness not higher than EUR 500,000.00.

In order to help enable an enterprise to solve its financial crisis by resorting to non-judicial or private solutions, the Bankruptcy Law sets up relevant advantages in case the debtor chooses one of the above-mentioned pre-insolvency proceedings.

First of all, Article 168, concerning the arrangement with creditors' proceedings, and Article 182 *bis*(3), on the debt restructuring agreement proceedings, prohibit the creditors from executing enforcement or interim measures following the publication of the petition or the agreement, respectively. The creditors are also prohibited from acquiring new privileges, unless agreed upon with the debtor.

Secondly, Article 67(3)d) and e) excludes the exercise of clawback actions in relation to deeds, payments and guarantees:

(i) executed according to a certified recovery plan;
(ii) executed according to an approved debt restructuring agreement;
(iii) executed according to an approved arrangement with creditors; or
(iv) executed following the deposit of the petition pursuant to Article 161 (see section 1.4 below).

Another important and favourable provision (Article 217 *bis*) was set out in relation to all three of the above-mentioned proceedings in order to safeguard the debtor and creditors from the risk of running into criminal liability in relation to operations executed with the objective of saving the business from bankruptcy. This provision considers Article 216 and 217, which determine the penalties in relation to the crimes connected to the bankruptcy (eg fraudulent bankruptcy), respectively, inapplicable in relation to those operations executed pursuant to an arrangement with creditors, a debt restructuring agreement or a certified recovery plan.

Arrangement with creditors

1.1 What is the objective of the proceedings?

Based on the latest amendments of the Bankruptcy Law, the arrangement with creditors' procedure (*concordato preventivo*) is intended to pursue the objective of the satisfaction of the creditors by means of a settlement measure that seeks to avoid bankruptcy. This main objective can be obtained either by (i) winding up the entire company or (ii) seeking to guarantee the recovery of the company through measures aimed at the prosecution of the business activity by the same entrepreneur or by third parties.

1.2 Do all kinds of businesses qualify?

The requirements set out by the Bankruptcy Law are those indicated in section 1 above.

By the arrangement proceedings decree, the competent court appoints an agent who, pursuant to Article 165, is considered a public official and is subject to Articles 36–39, which apply to the receiver in a bankruptcy proceedings (Article 163).

Public entities, companies exercising agricultural activities (indicated in Article 2135 of the Italian Civil Code) and artisan enterprises do not qualify in relation to this proceedings.

1.3 What are the necessary approvals?

The arrangement with creditors' procedure is initiated through the filing of a petition/proposal, which can be deposited only by the debtor and not by the creditors or any public authority.

In relation to partnerships, such petition must be approved by the partners representing more than 50 per cent of the ownership, while in the business corporations the board of directors must approve the petition.

The articles of association and the by-laws may provide otherwise.

The decision to file the petition must be adopted before a notary public and recorded in the Register of Companies.

1.4 What is the procedure?

The arrangement with creditors' procedure must be initiated through a petition, signed by the debtor and deposited at the court of the place where the filing company has its registered office (Article 161(1)).

The focal content of such petition, based on Article 161(1) and (2), is the settlement proposal and the relevant plan, including an estimate of the time and manner in which the suggested proposal will be realised.

The petition must also be accompanied by the following additional documents:

- an updated report on the financial standing of the company;
- an estimate of the assets of and a list of the creditors, the amount of their respective credits and any pre-emption rights;
- a list of holders of any land right or personal right over assets owned or possessed by the debtor; and
- the value of goods and list of the creditors of each shareholder with unlimited liability.

An advisor appointed by the debtor must verify the feasibility of the arrangement proposed in the petition and the truthfulness of the attached documents (Article 161(3)). The advisor shall meet several requirements of independence and professional qualification. The advisor bears criminal liability if the information provided is untrue or relevant information is omitted (Article 236 *bis*).

An officer of the competent court publishes the petition in the Register of Companies.

Pursuant to Article 161(6), the debtor is also granted the possibility of filing the petition, together with the balance sheets and a list of creditors and of their respective credits, within a deadline set up by the judge (between 60 and 120 days), to either:

- deposit the settlement proposal, the relevant plan and all other required documentation; or
- request the approval of a debt restructuring agreement pursuant to Article 182 *bis* (in detail below).

The court evaluates whether the requirements set out for the deposit of the petition and of the relevant documents are met and consequently issues a decree which either:

- rejects the petition (opposition to the decree is not allowed and, in the case of rejection, either a creditor or the court prosecutor can file the request for a declaration of bankruptcy of the company); or
- declares the opening of the arrangement procedure (opposition to the decree is not allowed).

In the latter case, the court appoints the judicial authorities that are competent in relation to the specific arrangement procedure (delegated judge and court-appointed agent).

The court orders the summoning of all creditors within 30 days following the issue of the decree and determines a deadline for the communication to each creditor of the same decree. The court-appointed agent must verify the correctness of the list of creditors and communicate to each of them the date on which they shall be present, the debtor's petition and the decree issued by the court by which the procedure was initiated. Such a communication can be made by registered email, registered mail or by fax.

The court also orders the deposit by the debtor of a percentage of the entire sum necessary to carry out the procedure (usually 50 per cent; not less than 20 per cent).

A specific hearing is held for the approval of the settlement proposal by the creditors. Article 177 requires that such approval must be given by the majority of all creditors (meaning more than 50 per cent) or the majority of the classes in which the creditors may be divided. The creditors may also indicate their vote by mail, telegram or email within 20 days from the closing of the voting memorandum. If no vote is expressed by a creditor, such creditor is deemed to have approved the proposal.

The proceedings ends with the approval by the court.

1.5 Is there recourse against the opening judgment?

The decree of the court determining the opening of the procedure is not subject to opposition since the existence of the requirements of the arrangement procedure is verified later at the stage of approval by the court.

At that stage, opposition can be filed by the debtor, by the court-appointed agent, by dissenting creditors or by any other interested party. The opposition may concern, for example, the feasibility of the arrangement, the requirements set out by the law, any purported fraudulent act by the debtor or the criteria based on which classes of creditors were determined.

1.6 What are the substantive tests/definitions?

The concept of insolvency is intended as an extensive notion and it mainly refers to the inability of the debtor to regularly fulfil its obligations. The notion of insolvency shall be intended not only as a patrimonial notion, but also as a financial concept.

However, the arrangement with creditors' proceedings does not apply exclusively in cases of insolvency, but also in situations of a mere financial and economic crisis of the debtor, including a temporary difficulty to pay overdue debts, insolvency risk, indebtedness or a reduction of the company's net assets to below the legal minimum.

1.7 What is the role of a court-appointed agent?

The court-appointed agent is responsible for the inventory of the debtor's assets and must carry out an evaluation of the causes of the insolvency, of the debtor's conduct, of the suggested arrangement and of guarantees offered to the creditors. The agent drafts a report on these matters and explains its conclusions during the creditors' meeting (Article 172).

The court-appointed agent has a fundamental role in relation to information to creditors and interested parties. The agent is also responsible for the supervision over the management of the debtor's assets during the procedure and over the execution of the arrangement following the court's approval (Article 167(1)).

The agent must also inform the delegated judge of any irregular transaction carried out by the debtor (eg the concealment of a part of the assets), which may cause the judge to revoke the opening decree and, if the conditions subsist, to declare the debtor bankrupt (Article 173).

1.8 What protection is there from creditors?

Further to the publication in the Register of Companies and until the approval of the decree issued by the court, the creditors are prohibited from exercising any attachment or interim measure, which would, in any case, be void, and from acquiring any pre-emption right, unless authorised by the delegated judge. Moreover, mortgages on any of the debtor's assets are ineffective towards creditors if registered within 90 days prior to the publication of the petition.

During the creditors' meeting, the creditors are authorised to object against the opening of the arrangement procedure and challenge other credits. At the same time, the debtor may reply to creditors' arguments and object to the existence or the amount of the listed credits.

Unlike in bankruptcy proceedings, any verification of the existence and amount of credits is only carried out in order to determine if the majority required for the approval of the settlement proposal is reached. Any further verification can only be requested by a creditor by filing a separate claim, which therefore gives rise to an ordinary trial.

1.9 What is the usual duration of the restructuring process?

Article 181 of the Bankruptcy Law provides a deadline of six months, starting from the deposit of the petition, for the issuance of the decree of approval. This deadline can be postponed only once, for an additional 60 days.

1.10 Who prepares the restructuring agreement and what are the available tools?

The settlement proposal and the relevant execution plan are prepared directly by the debtor (and generally by his advisors).

Article 160 of the Bankruptcy Law indicates the contents of the arrangement proposed by the debtor:

- debt restructuring and payment to the creditors, also by means of the transfer of assets, quotas, shares or other financial instruments, assumption of debt or other types of non-ordinary transactions (this last solution is not frequent);
- the assignment of the business activity to a third party (the so-called *assuntore*); and
- the determination of classes of creditors and of the possible different treatments of creditors who belong to the different classes.

The reorganisation plan submitted to the creditors must be approved by the majority of creditors who have the right to vote. All creditors without pre-emption rights have the right to vote, while privileged creditors can only vote if the plan provides only partial satisfaction of their credits and exclusively in relation to the residual unpaid amount.

If different classes of creditors are formed, the proposal must be approved by the majority of creditors within the majority of classes.

In the event that the settlement proposal requires disposal of assets, the delegated judge appoints one or more liquidators and a committee of three or five creditors, which shall assist to the relevant operations.

1.11 Are subordination agreements necessarily given full effect?

Privileged creditors must always be paid in full, but only within the limits of the value of the assets subject to the guarantee (Article 160(2)). The estimated value which must be reserved to the payment of privileged creditors shall be assessed by an expert.

The debtor can determine classes of creditors in the petition. Such determination must be verified by the court-appointed agent. The determination of classes of creditors cannot alter the preference awarded to the privileged creditors.

A different treatment is allowed by the law only among creditors that belong to different classes.

1.12 How is exit managed?

The arrangement with creditors' procedure ends with the issue of the decree of approval by the court, which must verify the compliance to any applicable law requirement and the feasibility of the plan.

In this case, an opposition (Article 180(3) and (4)) can be filed by the debtor, by the court-appointed agent, by the dissenting creditors or by any other interested party. The opposition may concern, for example, the feasibility of the arrangement, the requirements set out by the law, any purported fraudulent act by the debtor or the criteria based on which classes of creditors were formed.

1.13 Who are the necessary parties?

The only necessary party to the procedure is the debtor.

The other parties in the procedure of approval are the court-appointed agent, the dissenting creditors and any other interested party (meaning, for example and without limitation, the shareholders bearing unlimited liability, guarantors or other third parties involved in the transactions contemplated in the arrangement with creditors).

The competent judge examines all objections and either issues a decree of approval or rejects the request for approval.

Following the approval, the settlement proposal becomes binding for all creditors, both consenting and dissenting, and it must be executed under the supervision of the court-appointed agent. Article 186 of the Bankruptcy Law allows the creditors to request the termination of the arrangement procedure in case of any failure to comply with the arrangement. Such failure must be material to cause the termination.

If the delegated judge does not issue the decree of approval, bankruptcy of the debtor can be declared if the conditions subsist.

The decree of approval can be challenged before the court of appeal pursuant to Article 183.

Debt restructuring agreements

1.1 What is the objective of the proceedings?

The debt restructuring agreements, governed by Article 182 *bis*, were introduced in the Italian Bankruptcy Law as a measure to favour the non-judicial settlement of situations of insolvency and financial crisis of enterprises. The conclusion of this kind of agreement is subject to the autonomy of the parties involved (the debtor and the creditors).

1.2 Do all kinds of businesses qualify?

The same requirements as set forth in section 1 above apply to the debt restructuring agreements. However, from 2011, such agreements can also be concluded by agricultural companies.

No court-appointed agent is involved in this procedure.

1.3 What are the necessary approvals?

The debtor initiates the debt restructuring agreement proceedings by filing a petition with the competent offices of the court of the place where the filing company has its registered office, requesting the approval of the agreement entered into with the creditors representing at least 60 per cent of all the credits *vis-à-vis* the debtor. If the debtor is a company, the petition must be filed following a resolution of the board of directors.

The proceedings can be initiated only by the debtor and not by the creditors or any public authority.

1.4 What is the procedure?

The petition is accompanied by the agreement entered into with the creditors and the relevant plan, indicating the time and the manner of execution of the agreement.

Article 182 *bis* of the Bankruptcy Law also requires the debtor to file, together with the petition, the following documents:

- an updated report on the financial standing of the company;
- an estimate of the assets of and a list of the creditors, the amount of their respective credits and any pre-emption rights;
- a list of the holders of any land right or personal right over the assets owned or possessed by the debtor; and
- the value of goods and a list of creditors of each shareholder with unlimited liability.

An advisor appointed by the debtor must verify the feasibility of the arrangement provided in the petition and the truthfulness of the attached documents. The advisor must meet several requirements of independence and professionalism. As in the arrangement with creditors' proceedings,

Article 236 *bis* applies in this case, providing criminal liability of the advisor for providing false or incomplete information.

1.5 Is there recourse against the opening judgment?

Within 30 days from the publication of the agreement in the Register of Companies, the creditors and other interested parties can file an objection concerning the fulfilment of all legal requirements or the feasibility of the agreement.

1.6 What are the substantive tests/definitions?

Debt restructuring agreements are available to companies in a 'state of crisis' (Article 182 *bis*). The notion of crisis is basically financial.

1.7 What is the role of a court-appointed agent?

No court-appointed agent is involved in this procedure.

1.8 What protection is there from creditors?

For a period of 60 days following the publication of the agreement, creditors are prohibited from exercising enforcement or interim measures on the debtor's assets. They are also prohibited from acquiring new privileges in relation to their credits.

The debtor may request the court to extend such a protection also to the phase of negotiation of the agreement with creditors, which takes place prior to the signing of the agreement.

This protection aims at maintaining the stability of the value of the debtor's assets until the approval of the agreement, in order to ensure a full and successful performance of the agreement.

1.9 What is the usual duration of the restructuring process?

Within 30 days from the publication of the agreement and the execution plan in the Register of Companies, the creditors and the other parties who have a relevant interest may file an objection to the court. After examining the objections, if any, the court issues (or rejects the issuance of) a decree of approval.

1.10 Who prepares the restructuring agreement and what are the available tools?

The debt restructuring agreement has the particular nature of a private contract entered into between the debtor and its creditors, but it also has a public relevance, which justifies the control of the court by means of the procedure of approval.

The debtor and the creditors can determine freely the contents of the agreement, since no limitation whatsoever is provided for by the Bankruptcy Law.

The agreement must be entered into with creditors who represent at least 60 per cent of the credits *vis-à-vis* the debtor.

The agreement is binding only for the creditors who are a party thereto. The other creditors preserve the right to be satisfied in full.

1.11 Are subordination agreements necessarily given full effect?

As mentioned above, the agreement is binding only for the creditors who are a party thereto. The other creditors are entitled to request full payment of their credits:

- after 120 days from the issuance of the decree of approval; or
- after 120 day from the expiration of their credits, if not yet expired.

1.12 How is exit managed?

The court examines any objection filed against the debtor's petition and issues a decree, deciding on the request for approval of the debt restructuring agreement.

The competent judge must verify both the fulfilment of all requirements set out by law and the feasibility of the agreement, in particular in relation to the possibility of settlement of the credits of those creditors who did not enter into the agreement.

The proceedings of approval is governed by the provisions regarding the arrangement with creditors' procedure, if applicable.

Pursuant to Article 183 of the Bankruptcy Law, the decree which is issued by the competent court following the approval of the agreement can be challenged before the court of appeal by the debtor, by the creditors and by any other third party which participated in the proceedings, within 15 days from the publication of the decree in the Register of Companies.

Creditors who entered into the agreement may also resort to the contractual remedies provided for by the Italian Civil Code, such as, without limitation, the request for termination, annulment or declaration of nullity of the agreement.

1.13 Who are the necessary parties?

Parties are the debtor and the dissenting creditors, if any.

Certified recovery plan

Bankruptcy Law also contemplates the possibility for the debtor to issue a recovery plan, with the objective of saving the business. This measure does not entail any monitoring by the court.

Article 67(3)d) protects from the clawback action any deeds, payments or guarantees executed on the basis of a recovery plan which allows the recovery of the debtor's indebtedness and the rebalancing of its financial trend.

An independent advisor, appointed by the debtor, verifies and assesses the truthfulness of the business data and of the feasibility of the recovery plan. Also in this case Article 236 *bis*, on the criminal liability of the advisor, applies.

1.1 What is the objective of the proceedings?

The objective of the provisions on the certified recovery plan is to allow the debtor to avoid the risk of insolvency procedures. The purpose of the plan it to guarantee the continuation of the business activity, eg through new financings, the involvement in the business of strategic creditors or revision of the company's current business model. As mentioned above, the Bankruptcy Law protects the creditors from clawback actions in relation to the transactions realised on the basis of the plan.

1.2 Do all kinds of businesses qualify?

The same requirements as set forth in section 1 above apply.

No court-appointed agent is necessary, as the court is not involved in the preparation and execution of the recovery plan.

1.3 What are the necessary approvals?

The debtor prepares the recovery plan unilaterally (generally, with its financial counsel), with the approval of the board of directors.

Pursuant to Article 67(3)d) of the Bankruptcy Law, the recovery plan shall be certified and approved by an independent advisor appointed by the same debtor. In particular, the advisor must assess the truthfulness of the business data and of the feasibility of the recovery plan.

The advisor who certifies the recovery plan shall satisfy the same requirements as the receiver in a bankruptcy proceedings and as the member of a board of statutory auditors.

The law does not require the approval of the plan by the creditors, but normally the advisor assesses whether there is a sufficient consensus by the creditors in relation to the plan as a requirement for its actual feasibility.

1.4 What is the procedure?

Neither the court nor the creditors are involved in this procedure.

The law does not impose the publication of the certified recovery plan or its communication to the other parties, but, if required by the debtor, it may be recorded in the Register of Companies.

1.5 Is there recourse against the opening judgment?

In this case, the court is not involved.

1.6 What are the substantive tests/definitions?

The verification of a situation of insolvency is not required by the law. Therefore, any business entity may present a recovery plan. Clearly, as it is a precautionary measure, the debtor will resort to the certified recovery plan when he is in financial difficulty but not yet in a state of non-reversible insolvency.

1.7 What is the role of a court-appointed agent?

No court-appointed agent is involved.

1.8 What protection is there from creditors?

The creditors are not prohibited from executing enforcement or interim measures.

As mentioned above, the plan is based only on the debtor's data, the truthfulness of which is verified by the appointed advisor. In the case of disagreement about the existence and type of a specific credit, both the debtor and the creditor may start an ordinary judicial proceedings.

1.9 What is the usual duration of the restructuring process?

The recovery plan must indicate the period of time for the execution of the transactions necessary for the rebalancing of the company's financial situation. This period must be determined based on the specific situation of the business and on its indebtedness. No minimum or maximum period is set forth by the law.

1.10 Who prepares the restructuring agreement and what are the available tools?

As indicated above, the recovery plan is a non-judicial deed drafted unilaterally by the debtor, approved by its board of directors and certified by an independent advisor appointed by the debtor.

1.11 Are subordination agreements necessarily given full effect?

The contents of the recovery plan can be freely negotiated between the debtor and its creditors.

1.12 How is exit managed?

N/A.

1.13 Who are the necessary parties?

N/A.

2. POST-INSOLVENCY PROCEEDINGS

The most common post-insolvency proceedings is the bankruptcy proceedings, which is regulated by Articles 5–159 of the Bankruptcy Law.

The Bankruptcy Law also contemplates another compulsory winding up proceedings (*liquidazione coatta amministrativa,* regulated by Articles 194–215). This specific proceedings is reserved only for certain types of companies, such as banks, insurance companies and trust companies.

Furthermore, Law No. 95 of 3 April 1979 and Law No. 347 of 23 December 2003 introduced two proceedings concerning the management of large enterprises in a state of insolvency by the agents appointed by the Ministry of Economics. These proceedings apply to companies which meet certain requirements as to the dimensions and nature of their indebtedness. The main objective of these proceedings is to preserve the value of the enterprise, unlike the bankruptcy and the compulsory winding up proceedings, which aim exclusively at winding up of the insolvent company.

As the bankruptcy proceedings are by far the most common post-insolvency proceedings, and in consideration of the limited extent of this chapter, only such proceedings are described further below.

Bankruptcy proceedings

2.1 What is the objective of the proceedings?

The bankruptcy proceedings is an enforcement proceedings that is intended to safeguard the debtor's assets and to liquidate them in order to satisfy the debtor's creditors with the sales proceeds.

In this type of proceedings, saving the insolvent company and guaranteeing its continuity does not constitute a relevant objective.

A bankruptcy proceedings can also be initiated in the case of failure of one of the pre-insolvency proceedings contemplated above.

2.2 Do all kinds of business entities qualify?

The same requirements as set forth in sections 1.1 above apply to bankruptcy proceedings. However, public entities, companies exercising agricultural activities (indicated in Article 2135 of the Italian Civil Code) and artisan enterprises cannot be subject to bankruptcy.

2.3 What are the necessary approvals?

The insolvent debtor, one or more creditors and the public prosecutor are entitled to file a petition for bankruptcy of an insolvent company (Article 6). If the debtor is a company, the petition is normally filed by the board of directors, without the need for prior authorisation by the shareholders' meeting.

2.4 Is it valid and binding to agree that such proceedings be a default/termination event?

Under Article 72(6) of the Bankruptcy Law, contractual clauses providing for the termination of an agreement in the case of a declaration of bankruptcy of one of the parties are not effective.

2.5 What is the procedure?

The petition for bankruptcy shall be filed at the offices of the court where the defaulting company has its registered office (Article 9).

A judge in charge appointed by the court shall set up, by a decree, a bankruptcy hearing which shall take place no later than 45 days following the filing of the petition. The same decree must also set up a deadline of no more than seven days prior to the hearing for the parties to file their statements of defence, documents and technical reports. In particular, within the same term, the debtor shall file the balance sheets of the last three financial years and a detailed and updated documentation regarding its financial situation.

Following the process of verification of the subsistence of the requirements, the court can (i) accept or (ii) reject the claim for bankruptcy, or (iii) terminate the proceedings if the claim for bankruptcy is withdrawn by the creditor who was satisfied.

If the claim for bankruptcy is accepted, the bankruptcy proceedings starts and the court:

- appoints the judge and the receiver in charge for the prosecution of the bankruptcy procedure;
- if not yet provided, orders to the debtor to deposit the balance sheets, accounting and tax documents within three days;
- determines the date of the hearing for the assessment of the credits (*esame dello stato passivo*) within 120 days from the deposit of the decision; and
- grants a deadline of 30 days from publication of the decision, to allow the creditors and the third parties to file their claims (Article 16).

The court's decision is notified to the debtor and communicated to the receiver, the public prosecutor and the party who filed the claim for bankruptcy, then recorded in the Register of Companies.

The court may allow the temporary and monitored management of the bankrupt company and the continuation of its activity.

From the date of the declaration of bankruptcy, the debtor is no longer entitled to manage or dispose of its assets, which are managed by the receiver, under the supervision of the judge in charge and of the committee of creditors.

Once the assessment of the credits is completed, an inventory of the debtor's assets is prepared. Thereafter, the receiver drafts a plan indicating the operations and the timing for the winding up of the debtor's company (Article 140 *ter*), which shall be approved by the committee of creditors.

The receiver then carries out the sale of the assets, either as a whole (transfer of the company or of a branch) or individually.

The proceeds obtained from the sale are distributed among the creditors every four months, based on a distribution plan (Article 110) which must take into account their priority ranking.

The bankruptcy proceedings usually ends with the execution of the final distribution.

2.6 Please provide information about voluntary filings

Are creditors invited to participate in the initial hearing? If so, how are they notified?

If the petition for bankruptcy is filed by the debtor, the creditors are not invited to the first hearing. They are informed of the opening of the proceedings once the relevant decree has been issued.

Supporting documentation to be filed

The debtor must deposit the balance sheets of the last three financial years and a detailed and updated documentation regarding his financial situation.

Main restructuring principles/are proposals to be term sheeted at entry? If so, is an expert opinion or report on the feasibility of the contemplated plan needed?
No restructuring principal applies to the bankruptcy proceedings, since its only objective is the winding up of the debtor. Only a temporary management of the bankrupt company is allowed.

Publicity: how is the opening judgement rendered public? When and how are creditors deemed aware of the proceedings?
The court's declaration of bankruptcy is communicated to the creditors by the receiver and recorded in the Register of Companies.

2.7 How are creditors' representatives chosen?

Based on Article 40, a committee of creditors is appointed by the judge in charge within 30 days from the issuance of the decree of opening of the bankruptcy proceedings. The committee is composed of three or five creditors representing equally each class of credits.

The committee must monitor the activity of the receiver and in certain cases it must authorise the receiver's deeds and provide advice.

The committee also has the power to examine the accounting and other documents, and to request clarifications or information from the debtor and the receiver.

The committee's members can be replaced by the judge.

2.8 Is there recourse against the opening judgment?

The debtor and any other party who has a relevant interest can challenge the court's decision in front of the competent court of appeal within 30 days following its notification or, if no notification was executed, within six months from its publication in the Register of Companies (Article 18). Upon request by one of the parties or by the receiver, the court of appeal is entitled to suspend the liquidation of the assets of the bankrupt company (Article 19).

Within the same deadline, the filing creditor and the public prosecutor can challenge the decision of rejection of the initial claim for bankruptcy in front of the court of appeal (Article 22).

2.9 What are the roles and powers of committees?

For the compositions and the functions of the Committee of creditors, see section 2.8 above.

The Committee votes by the majority of its members.

2.10 What are the consequences of opening judgments for creditors?

Stay?
Following the issuance of the decree of opening of the bankruptcy proceedings, the creditors are not entitled to enforce their credits individually.

Forbidden payments?
Following the issuance of the decree of opening of the bankruptcy proceedings, all payments made and received by the debtor are ineffective *vis-à-vis* the debtor's creditors (Article 44).

Interests accruing during period: paid at contractual payment dates? Deferred and paid after the plan is adopted? Capitalised? Is the rate necessarily the contract rate?
Pursuant to Article 55, the accruing of interest is suspended as of the date of the decree of opening of the bankruptcy proceedings.

Privileged creditors maintain their right to the interest accrued after the opening of the proceedings, but only for a limited period of time.

Is the opening judgment a valid draw stop?
The opening judgment determines a definitive draw stop.

Necessity to file proof of claim: are all creditors required to file proof of claim? Are secured creditors necessarily notified? Are there any time limits? Are non-resident creditors treated differently? What are the consequences if a creditor time-barred? Is the debtor discharged?
All creditors must prove their individual claims and credits, by means of a specific petition.

Such petition is necessary in order to set forth a claim regarding the credit or another right *vis-à-vis* the debtor and it must describe, *inter alia*, the factual and legal arguments supporting the claim.

The petition shall be filed within 30 days prior to the hearing scheduled for the assessment of the credits.

The receiver examines all the petitions and drafts a report of verification (*progetto di stato passivo*) (Article 95), containing the list of all creditors and holders of rights over the debtor's assets. The report must be deposited at least 15 days prior to the hearing.

The creditors may file, within five days prior to the hearing, written observations and new documentation.

At the hearing, the judge in charge decides by a decree whether to accept, in whole or in part, or reject the creditors' claims.

The above-mentioned decree can be challenged by a creditor, another party claiming rights vis-à-vis the debtor or the receiver (Article 98).

The claims submitted to the court after the expiration of the deadline are admitted if set forth within one year from the issuance of the decree of the final assessment of the credits. If a claim is filed following the expiration of the one year deadline, such claim will be accepted only if the claimant proves that the delay was not due to its own fault (Article 101).

2.11 What is the duration of the restructuring process?
The duration of the entire bankruptcy proceedings is not determined by the law and it cannot be estimated in advance.

2.12 How do creditors vote?

In a bankruptcy proceedings, the approval of the creditors is not required by the law.

2.13 What are the rules on clawback/voidability?

Deeds	Relevant period of execution	Require-ments for the exercise of the claim	Type of claim	Exemptions
Deeds free of charge	2 years prior to the bankruptcy		judicial action, which can be set forth to obtain declaration of ineffective-ness (Article 64) without time limitations	
Payments of non-expired credits	2 years prior to the bankruptcy		judicial action, which can be set forth to obtain declaration of ineffective-ness (Article 65) without time limitations	
• Deeds in which the debtor's obli-gation has a total value higher by a quarter than that of the counterparty • Payment of expired credits by non-ordinary means (in particular, different from cash)	1 year prior to the bankruptcy 1 year prior to the bankruptcy	knowledge, by the counter-party, of the debtor's state of insolvency; such condition is presumed, unless contrary evidence is provided by the counterparty	clawback action pursuant to Article 67(1), to be set forth within 3 years from the opening judgment or 5 years from the execution of the deed	• usual pay-ments for the ongoing of the business; • deposits in bank accounts not consisting in a payment in favour of the bank;

• Non-judicial pledges and mortgages over existing and non-expired credits • Judicial and non-judicial pledges and mortgages over expired credits	1 year prior to the bankruptcy 6 months prior to the bankruptcy			• certain registered sales and preliminary sales contracts; • deeds, payments and guarantees executed based on a certified recovery plan;
• Payment of expired credits • Deeds executed against a performance or a service by the counterparty • Establishment of a guarantee in relation to a contextual assumption of a debt	6 months prior to the bankruptcy	the receiver must prove that the counterparty had knowledge of the debtor's state of insolvency	clawback action pursuant to Article 67(2), to be set forth within 3 years from the opening judgment or 5 years from the execution of the deed	• deeds, payments and guarantees executed pursuant to Article 182 *bis* (debt restructuring agreements) or in relation to an arrangement with creditors' proceedings; • payments of worker's or collaborator's salaries; • payments of expired debts, when necessary to enter into an arrangement with creditors' proceedings
Deeds, which cause damages to creditors		the receiver must prove that the deed damages the creditors and that the counterparty had knowledge of the debtor's insolvency	ordinary clawback action pursuant to Article 2901 of the Italian Civil Code, to be set forth within 5 years from execution of the deed	

The creditors who, as a consequence of the clawback actions, had to return the amount obtained, can set forth a claim against the bankruptcy to compete with the other creditors in obtaining satisfaction over the debtor's assets.

2.14 What are the rules on set-off/netting?

Article 56 allows the creditors to set off their debts towards the bankruptcy with their respective credits, even if the latter have not yet expired prior to the opening judgment.

However, in relation to non-expired credits, no set-off shall operate in the event that the credit was assigned to the creditor following the declaration of bankruptcy or within one year prior to such a declaration.

2.15 How is exit managed?

As indicated above, the bankruptcy proceedings normally ends with the execution of the final distribution. It can also finish before, if all the creditors have been paid in full or if the proceedings does not allow the creditors to be satisfied even in part.

The bankruptcy proceedings may also end as a consequence of the initiation of an arrangement with creditors within the bankruptcy proceedings under Articles 124–54.

2.16 Are 'prepackaged' plans, arrangements or agreements permissible?

Prepackaged plans or agreements are not allowed.

2.17 Is a public authority involved?

The public authorities involved are the public prosecutor, the court and the judge in charge.

Powers?

Article 7 allows the public prosecutor to file a petition requesting the opening of a bankruptcy proceedings if he has become aware of the insolvency during a criminal trial or due to the information provided by a civil court during a civil trial.

Section 2.5 above presents details in relation to the role of the court and of the judge in charge.

Does it have to rule on the debtor's eligibility to the court protection?

As indicated in section 2.5 above, the court examines all evidence, directly requests whatever further evidence or information is required and verifies the requirements for the opening of a bankruptcy proceedings.

The judge in charge monitors the activity of the receiver and authorises his actions.

2.18 What is the treatment of claims arising after filing/admission?

These claims are paid with priority.

2.19 Are there ongoing contracts?

The execution of ongoing contracts is suspended in the event of bankruptcy of one of the contractual parties. The receiver, upon authorisation of the committee of creditors, can decide to replace the debtor in the contractual relationship (Article 72(1)).

Upon the request of the counterparty, a contract is automatically terminated if the receiver does not enter into it within the deadline assigned by the judge in charge (no longer than 60 days).

In case of termination of a contract, the contractual party can set forth a claim against the bankruptcy, requesting the payment of its credits arising from the contract.

2.20 Are consolidated proceedings for members of a corporate family/group possible?

Bankruptcy of a group of companies is not contemplated by the Italian law. Therefore, in a bankruptcy proceedings, each company must be considered as autonomous.

If there are shareholders with unlimited liability, the declaration of bankruptcy of the company also determines the bankruptcy of such shareholders.

2.21 What are the charges, fees and other costs?

The receiver's fees, determined by the judge in charge, and the costs of the proceedings are deducted from the proceeds of the sale of the debtor's assets (Article 109).

3. LIABILITY ISSUES

3.1 What is the liability of managers/directors *vis-à-vis* creditors?

The directors of a company are jointly liable towards the company for damages caused by breaching their duties. Pursuant to Article 2392 of the Italian Civil Code, the liability is excluded only for those directors who did not act negligently and communicated their dissent in a timely manner.
A liability action against the directors can also be initiated by a relevant minority of shareholders or by the company's creditors.

In the case of insolvency proceedings, the liability action can be exercised by the receiver, the liquidator or the agent, as the case may be, which represents the insolvent company, its shareholders and the creditors (Article 2394 *bis* of the Italian Civil Code).

The Bankruptcy Law contains a number of specific provisions governing the criminal liability of the directors (Articles 216–37).

3.2 Lender's liability

A qualified lender may incur liabilities by maintaining a credit line in favour of an enterprise in financial difficulty and, in particular, in the case of a risk of bankruptcy.

The appearance of solvency deriving from an unjustified maintenance of the credit line by a qualified lender may give rise to a request for damages by other creditors. In Italy, case law has confirmed that a bank can be deemed liable *vis-à-vis* the other creditors of the same debtor for maintaining an unjustified appearance of solvency of the latter.

When filing such a claim against the lender, the plaintiff must prove:

- the actual fault and negligence of the lender in creating the situation of appearance;
- the damage suffered by the plaintiff; and
- the fact that the damage was directly caused by the appearance of solvency.

The lender may also incur criminal liability, eg in the following cases:

- when, by maintaining a credit line, the lender allows the debtor to delay the opening of a bankruptcy proceedings (ordinary bankruptcy); or
- when the lender simulates the existence of privileges, pledges, mortgages or other priority rights (eg a repurchase option) over certain credits (preferential bankruptcy).

Malta

Fenech & Fenech Advocates Nicolai Vella Falzon

1. WHAT COURT-MONITORED RESTRUCTURING PRE-INSOLVENCY PROCEEDINGS OR SCHEMES HAVE BEEN DEVISED BY THE LAW OF YOUR COUNTRY TO LIMIT VALUE DESTRUCTION FOR FAILING BUSINESS ENTITIES?

While Maltese law distinguishes between different types of 'business entities', the rules relating to restructuring pre-insolvency proceedings apply only to limited liability companies regulated by the Companies Act. Sole traders are regulated by the Commercial Code and are subject to bankruptcy rules, which are different in scope and extent to rules of insolvency. Businesses set up as commercial partnerships (*en nom collectif* or *en commandite*) are also regulated by the Companies Act but are not subject to the rules relating to restructuring and insolvency that apply to limited liability companies. Company reconstruction procedures are dealt with in Title VI of the Companies Act and comprise:

- the power of a company to enter into a compromise or arrangement with creditors;
- provisions for facilitating company reconstructions or amalgamations; and
- the right to apply for the protections afforded by a court-monitored company recovery procedure.

1.1 What is the objective of the proceedings?

Compromise or arrangement

The objective of this procedure is to obtain the sanction of the court to a scheme of arrangement or compromise between a company and its creditors or between a company and its members where the requisite majority of creditors or members has agreed to implement such scheme, thereby making it binding on all creditors or members of the company and on the company itself (or, in the case of a company in dissolution, on the liquidator). While this procedure can be availed of when a company is already in dissolution in order to facilitate the liquidation process, it is a useful tool with which to facilitate the recovery of a company in distress.

Reconstruction or amalgamation

This procedure is intended to complement the compromise or arrangement procedure where a restructuring or amalgamation of the company is being proposed in order to address the company's distressed situation. Accordingly, where the compromise or arrangement has been proposed for the purposes of or in connection with a scheme for the restructuring of the company or for its amalgamation with one or more other companies and the scheme proposes to transfer all or some of the company's business or property to another company, the court may be requested to make provision for a number of matters, all of which are intended to facilitate the restructuring or amalgamation process by minimising the formality, expense and time required for the implementation of the scheme. In particular, it enables the company to implement its restructuring or amalgamation with the support of the majority of its creditors and with the sanction of the court.

Company recovery procedure

The objective of this procedure is to apply for a court-sanctioned moratorium in favour of a company with a view to protecting it from its creditors for a period of time (usually one year) sufficient to enable it to recover from a period of financial distress. Amongst other things, during the period in which the company recovery procedure is in force, monetary claims against the company and interest accruing thereon are stayed, the company is protected from the enforcement of security over its assets and judicial proceedings cannot be instituted against the company, in each case without leave of court.

1.2 Do all kinds of businesses qualify?

Is there a threshold related to indebtedness, turnover or asset value?

All limited liability companies qualify for the compromise or arrangement procedure and for the company reconstruction procedure without any limitations or thresholds relating to indebtedness, turnover or asset value. As far as the company recovery procedure is concerned, 'small companies' do not qualify for this procedure unless they have more than EUR 465,874 owing to creditors. A 'small company' is one which, at its balance sheet date, does not exceed the limits of two of the three following criteria:

- balance sheet total: EUR 2,562,310.74;
- turnover: EUR 5,124,621.48; or
- average number of employees during the accounting period: 50.

Is a court agent necessarily appointed to assist the company? If so, how is it chosen?

In the event of a company recovery procedure, the court will nominate and appoint a special controller, who will effectively take charge of the management of the company for the duration of the period of the company recovery order.

1.3 What are the necessary approvals?

Compromise or arrangement/reconstruction or amalgamation

A compromise or arrangement (whether or not in the context of a proposed reconstruction or amalgamation of the company) may be proposed by a company, by its members or by its creditors. The company, members or creditors may file an application in court requesting that a meeting of the creditors be summoned. Where a company is already in liquidation, a scheme of arrangement or compromise can also be proposed by the liquidator, who is entitled to apply to the court for its sanction. The court will only sanction a proposed scheme (thus making it binding on all creditors or members, as the case may be) if it has been approved by a majority of creditors or members representing three-quarters in value of the creditors or members (as the case may be) present and voting at the meeting so summoned.

Company recovery procedure

A company recovery application can be made by:

- the company, following an extraordinary resolution of the shareholders;
- a resolution of the board of directors; or
- creditors of the company representing more than half in value of the company's creditors.

This procedure may not be availed of if the company is already in liquidation and therefore, unlike an application for the sanction of a compromise or arrangement, it may not be made by a liquidator.

1.4 What is the procedure?

Compromise or arrangement/reconstruction or amalgamation

The procedure for obtaining the sanction of the court for a compromise or arrangement is commenced by virtue of an application filed in the registry of the First Hall of the Civil Court. The application may be filed by the company itself or, if it is already in liquidation, by the liquidator on behalf of the company. It may also be filed by a creditor in the case of a proposed compromise or arrangement between the company and its creditors, or by a member in the case of a proposed compromise or arrangement between the company and its members. The application will request the court to summon a meeting of the creditors or members of the company, as the case may be. The manner in which the meeting is summoned is left to the discretion of the court.

The court can only proceed to sanction the proposed compromise or arrangement if approved by the majority in number representing at least three-quarters in value of the creditors or members (as the case may be) that are present and voting at the meeting summoned by the court. The court has the discretion to approve or reject the proposed compromise or arrangement. If sanctioned, the proposed compromise or arrangement will be binding on all creditors or members, as the case may be, and on the company. A copy of the court's decision must be filed with the registrar of companies in order to take effect.

There is no specific requirement for the filing of any documents with the court application, but it is implied that a statement explaining the effect of the proposed compromise or arrangement must be prepared and, if possible, filed with the application. In particular, the statement must refer to any material interests of the directors of the company (whether as directors, members or creditors of the company, or otherwise), and the effect on those interests of the compromise or arrangement.

Where the proposed compromise or arrangement affects the rights of debenture holders of the company, the statement shall give the same explanation as regards the holders of any security for the issue of the debentures as it is required to give as regards the company's directors.

If the statement is not filed with the application, it must be made available to the creditors or members of the company, who must be informed where they can obtain the statement when given notice of the meeting.

Company recovery procedure

An application requesting the court to place a company under the company recovery procedure may be filed by:

- the company following an extraordinary resolution of the shareholders;
- the directors following a decision of the board of directors; or
- creditors of the company representing more than half in value of the company's creditors.

The application must give the full facts, circumstances and reasons which led to the company's inability or likely imminent inability to pay its debts. It must also state how the financial and economic situation of the company can be improved in the interests of its creditors, employees and the company itself as a viable going concern.

If the person applying to be put under the company recovery procedure is the company itself, then, together with the application, it must submit:

- a statement of the company's assets and liabilities made up to a date not earlier than the date of the application by more than two months;
- a list containing the names and addresses of the creditors, together with an indication of the amount due to each such creditor; and
- the security, if any, of the respective creditors.

If filed by creditors, the application must be accompanied by appropriate supporting documentation and statements supporting the creditors' claims.

There is no requirement for any third parties to be served with the acts of the proceedings. The court must hear the application with urgency and a decision must be taken within 20 working days from the date that the application is filed. Accordingly, while the court may, using its discretion, request creditors or other persons to attend to give evidence, there is no requirement for them to be served with the acts, or for them to object or make representations in the course of the proceedings.

Proceedings are held in open court and the acts of the proceedings are available to the public through the registry of courts.

1.5 Is there recourse against the opening judgment?

There is no provision for a right of appeal from a decision with regard to any of the procedures mentioned above. While we are not aware of any judgments relating to the right of appeal, our view is that the right to request a review of a decision of the court with regard to a request for the implementation of any one of the procedures mentioned above can only be made by the filing of a new action (by virtue of a sworn application filed in the same court) requesting the revocation of the previous decision of the court.

1.6 What are the substantive tests/definitions?

The substantive test is that the company is 'unable to pay its debts'. This is the test of solvency applied by Maltese law. The term 'unable to pay its debts' is defined in the Companies Act, which states that a company shall be deemed to be unable to pay its debts if:

- a debt due by the company has remained unsatisfied in whole or in part after 24 weeks from the enforcement of an executive title against the company by any of the executive acts specified in the Code of Organization and Civil Procedure; or
- it is proved to the satisfaction of the court that the company is unable to pay its debts, account being taken also of contingent and prospective liabilities of the company.

1.7 What is the role of a court-appointed agent?

Where the court has admitted a company recovery procedure, it will appoint a special controller, whose principal function is to take over, manage and administer the business and property of the company for the period (up to 12 months) specified by the court. The special controller must be an individual who the court has ascertained to be of proven competence and experience in the management of businesses, who has the requisite experience and who is not conflicted. His functions and powers will be determined by the court.

During the company recovery period, the company will continue to carry on its normal activities under the management of the special controller. Accordingly, the special controller takes into his custody or under his control all the property of the company and is thenceforth responsible for the management and supervision of its activities, business and property. He has a duty to examine the assets, affairs and business performance of the company, and to ascertain and verify whether there is a reasonable expectation of the company's recovery and continuation as a viable going concern. Indeed, he must submit an initial report about the company's viability to the court not later than two months from the date of his appointment.

On the appointment of the special controller, all powers conferred by law or the memorandum and articles of association (M&As) on the company, its directors or its officers are suspended, although the special controller may give permissions to exercise such powers either generally or in relation to a particular case or cases. Duties conferred on the company, its directors or its officers, whether by the Companies Act or the M&As, are assumed and exercised by the special controller. The special controller is obliged to perform his functions fairly and equitably, taking into account the best interests of the company, its shareholders and creditors, together with the interests of any other interested party.

Other particular powers of the special controller are:

- to remove any director of the company and to appoint any individual to serve as a manager (after informing the court);
- to engage persons for the provision of professional or administrative services, and to commit the company to the payment of their respective fees or charges; and
- to call any meeting of the members or creditors.

Insofar as limitations of authority are concerned, the special controller cannot, without the prior authorisation of the court:

- engage the company in any commitment of more than six months' duration;
- terminate the employment of company employees if he considers it necessary for ensuring the continuation of the company as a viable going concern in whole or in part; or
- sell or otherwise dispose of property of the company to himself, his spouse or other relatives.

Within one month from his appointment, the special controller must convene a meeting or meetings of creditors and members, whether separately or jointly, for the purposes of:

- laying before them for their information and review a comprehensive statement of the company's affairs, together with preliminary proposals on the future prospects and management of the company; and
- appointing a joint creditors and members committee, consisting of not more than three creditors and not more than three members, to render such advice and assistance as the special controller may require in the management of the affairs, business and property of the company and its recovery as a viable going concern.

1.8 What protection is there from creditors?

The provisions regulating the company recovery procedure provide for certain protective measures for the company during the period when the company recovery procedure is in force. Accordingly, during the relevant time:

- any pending or new application for the winding up of the company will be stayed and no resolution for the dissolution and consequential winding up of the company may be passed or given effect to;
- the execution of claims of a monetary nature against the company and any interest that may otherwise accrue thereon will be stayed;
- during the tenure of a lease, no landlord or other person to whom rent is payable may exercise any right of termination of lease in relation to premises leased to the company in respect of a failure by the company to comply with any term or condition of its tenancy of such premises, except with leave of the court;
- no other steps may be taken to enforce any security over the property of the company, or to repossess goods in the possession of the company

under any hire-purchase agreement, except with the leave of the court; and

- no precautionary or executive act or warrant mentioned in the Code of Organization and Civil Procedure may be made against the company or any property of the company except with leave of the court and no judicial proceedings may be commenced or continued against the company or its property except with leave of the court.

1.9 What is the usual duration of the restructuring process?

The company recovery period is established by the court but cannot exceed 12 months. However, the court may, upon good cause being shown, extend the period up to a maximum of a further 12 months.

1.10 Who prepares the restructuring agreement and what are the available tools?

Compromise or arrangement/reconstruction or amalgamation

A compromise or arrangement can be proposed either by the company itself or by any creditor or shareholder of the company. If a company is being wound up, the compromise or arrangement can also be proposed by the liquidator. The proposal must be submitted to the court by virtue of an application and thereafter the court will order a meeting of the creditors (or of the shareholders, as the case may be) to be summoned. Typically, the compromise or arrangement will be proposed between the company and its creditors, and therefore a meeting of the creditors will need to be summoned. In order for the proposed compromise or arrangement to become binding, it must be approved by at least three-quarters of the creditors present and voting at the meeting (duly summoned) and must also be sanctioned by the court.

There is nothing to limit the creditors from proposing the appointment of brokers or banks where the proposed scheme provides for the transfer of assets of the company. The court will then have the discretion to accept or reject such proposals. In general, the court has very wide powers in connection with such matters, and is in fact empowered to make provision for such incidental, consequential and supplemental matters as are necessary to secure that the reconstruction or amalgamation is fully and effectively carried out.

Company recovery procedure

The person(s) applying for the company recovery procedure will generally propose the terms thereof. It is required that the application give the full facts, circumstances and reasons which led to the company's inability or likely imminent inability to pay its debts, together with a statement as to how the financial and economic situation of the company can be improved in the interests of its creditors, employees and the company itself as a viable going concern.

In deciding whether to accept or reject an application for the procedure, the court is bound to confirm that the company is or is imminently likely to become unable to pay its debts (as defined above) and that the making of the order would be likely to achieve the survival of the company as a viable going concern in part or in whole; or to sanction a compromise or arrangement between the company and any of its creditors or members.

1.11 Are subordination agreements necessarily given full effect?

Subordination agreements are specifically recognised and permitted in terms of Article 1996A of the Civil Code of Malta, and will generally be given full force and effect. Indeed, such agreements are not affected by the insolvency of any person bound by or entitled under such agreement and will not be affected by the insolvency of the company (as debtor).

1.12 How is exit managed?

Any compromise or arrangement, company reconstruction or amalgamation, or company recovery procedure must be sanctioned by the court. Except in relation to a scheme of compromise or arrangement proposed in the course of a winding up, the scope of the court's review will generally be to verify that the proposed process is likely to achieve the survival of the company.

1.13 Who are the necessary parties?

The necessary parties are usually the company and its creditors. However, where a compromise is proposed between a company and its shareholders, then the shareholders are also necessary parties, and in the case of a proposed scheme of arrangement or compromise in the course of the winding up of a company, the liquidator becomes a necessary party too. See section 1.5 above regarding appeal.

2. POST-INSOLVENCY PROCEEDINGS

2.1 What is the objective of the proceedings?

A compromise or arrangement process, reconstruction or amalgamation, or company recovery procedure can be availed of before a company is technically insolvent and after its insolvency. However, the company recovery procedure cannot be availed of if the company has been put into voluntary dissolution or if a winding up order has been issued by the court.

For the objective of the proceedings, see section 1.1 above.

2.2 Do all kinds of business entities qualify?

Yes. All business entities qualify subject to what is stated in section 2.1 above. See also section 1.2 above.

2.3 What are the necessary approvals?

See section 1.3 above.

2.4 Is it valid and binding to agree that such proceedings be a default/termination event?

Yes.

2.5 What is the procedure?

See section 1.4 above.

2.6 Please provide information about voluntary filings

Compromise or arrangement/reconstruction or amalgamation

Where an application to sanction a scheme of arrangement or compromise with creditors has been filed by a company, there is no particular requirement for the creditors to be served with the acts of the proceedings or to participate in the initial hearing. However, the objective of the proceedings, in the first instance, is to request the court to summon a meeting of the creditors with a view to obtaining the consent of the creditors to the proposed scheme.

The law does not specifically request the filing of any supporting documentation, term sheet or expert opinion when applying to sanction a scheme of arrangement or compromise, whether in the context of a reconstruction or amalgamation of the company or otherwise, although it is good practice to file documentation relevant to and supporting the declarations made in the application. In the event that the court orders and summons a meeting of the creditors or shareholders, as the case may be, then there is an obligation to send with the notice of the meeting a statement explaining the effect of the compromise or arrangement. This must include a declaration with regard to any material interests of the directors of the company and the effect of those interests on the proposed compromise or arrangement. The court has the discretion to appoint experts if it deems fit.

In terms of publicity, where a court accepts to convene and summon a meeting of creditors or members, as the case may be, for the purposes of approving a scheme of arrangement or compromise (whether in the context of a reconstruction or amalgamation of the company), a copy of the court order must be sent to the registry of companies within seven days for publication on the company's register, which must be publicly accessible. There are no other particular rules relating to publicity. However, all known creditors must be served with the notice of the meeting, and the law allows the publication of notices through advertisements in daily newspapers.

Company recovery procedure

Where an application to place a company into recovery has been filed by the company following an extraordinary resolution of its shareholders or by its board of directors, there is no particular requirement for the creditors to be served with the application; nor does the law impose on the court an obligation to invite the creditors to participate in the proceedings. The court is, however, specifically obliged to take the best interests of the creditors into account when considering the application.

The application must, as far as possible, give the full facts, circumstances and reasons which led to the financial situation of the company, together with a statement by the applicants as to how the financial and economic situation of the company can be improved in the interests of its creditors, employees and the company itself as a viable going concern.

Where an application is made by the company itself, the application must include:

- a statement of the company's assets and liabilities made up to a date not earlier than the date of the application by more than two months;
- a list containing the names and addresses of the creditors, together with an indication of the amount due to each such creditor; and
- the security, if any, of the respective creditors.

Where the application is made by the creditors, the law merely states that it must be accompanied by 'appropriate supporting documentation and statements', without specifying what those documents are.

The court has the discretion to appoint experts if it deems fit, but there is no mandatory requirement to do so.

The decision of the court to place a company into recovery does not need to be publicised, though it must be publicly available. The creditors of the company do not need to be notified of the decision, but the special controller must convene, within one month from his appointment, a meeting of the creditors for the purpose of laying before them a comprehensive statement of the company's affairs, together with preliminary proposals on the future prospects and management of the company, and appoint a joint creditors and members committee. Notice of the meeting must be given at least 14 days in advance to all the known creditors of the company and a notice of the meeting must also be published in a daily newspaper circulating wholly or mainly in Malta.

2.7 How are creditors' representatives chosen?

Creditors' representatives may be appointed in the course of the company recovery procedure. At the meeting referred to in section 2.6 above, the creditors will be invited to appoint up to three representatives to sit on the joint creditors and members committee, along with up to three representatives of the shareholders. These appointments will be made on a majority vote and if, for any reason, they do not appoint their representatives, the special controller has the right to proceed without them. The powers of the representatives are not specifically defined in the law, but their role is to render such advice and assistance as the special controller may require in the management of the affairs, business and property of the company and its recovery as a viable going concern.

2.8 Is there recourse against the opening judgment?

See section 1.5 above.

2.9 What are the roles and powers of committees?

Committees are contemplated only in the context of the company recovery procedure. With regard to their roles and powers, see section 2.7 above. The law does not stipulate how creditor majorities are computed but by analogy to other provisions of the law, majorities should be computed by reference to the value of the debts. In fact, Article 323 of the Companies Act, which applies in relation to winding up procedures, states that where the court requires a meeting to be held in order to ascertain the wishes of creditors or members of a company in the course of its winding up, at such meetings, in the case of creditors, regard will be had to the value of each creditor's debt; and in the case of contributories, regard will be had to the number of votes conferred on each member by the memorandum or articles of the company.

2.10 What are the consequences of opening judgments for creditors?

Compromise or arrangement/reconstruction or amalgamation

The purpose of the opening judgment following an application for the sanctioning of a scheme of compromise or arrangement is merely to decide whether or not to order that a meeting of the creditors or the shareholders (as the case may be) be convened. Unlike in the case of the company recovery procedure, there is no stay or freeze affecting creditors or liabilities of the company. It will be up to the creditors to agree, subject to a three-quarters majority, to implement the proposed terms and conditions of the proposed scheme of arrangement or compromise (whether or not including terms for the restructuring or amalgamation of the company,) and any stay or freeze or other conditions that may be proposed will only become binding once approved by the creditors as aforesaid and (subsequently) sanctioned by the court.

Company recovery procedure

See section 1.8 above.

2.11 What is the duration of the restructuring process?

The company recovery period is established by the court but cannot exceed 12 months. However, the court may, upon good cause being shown, extend the period up to a maximum of a further 12 months.

2.12 How do creditors vote?

The provisions of the law regulating the company recovery procedure refer to creditors of the company generally and, while the law does not stipulate how creditor majorities are computed, by analogy to other provisions of the law, majorities should be computed by reference to the value of the debts.

The provisions dealing with compromise or arrangement, however, do refer to classes of creditors and classes of shareholders, so that a compromise or arrangement can also be proposed between a company and any class of its creditors or even between a company or any class of its shareholders. The law does not define the term 'class', nor does it establish what constitutes a class of creditors/shareholders. Accordingly, it is left to the discretion of the court on a case-by-case basis to determine whether a group of creditors or shareholders constitutes a class for the purposes of the relevant provisions of law.

2.13 What are the rules on clawback/voidability?

There is a legal presumption that every privilege, hypothec or other charge, or transfer or other disposal of property or rights, any payment, execution or other act relating to property or rights made or done by or against a company and any obligation incurred by the company within six months before the dissolution of the company is a fraudulent preference against its creditors (whether it is of a gratuitous nature or an onerous nature) if it constitutes a transaction at an undervalue or if a preference is given, unless the person in whose favour it is made, done or incurred proves that he did not know and did not have reason to believe that the company was likely to be dissolved by reason of insolvency. Accordingly, when a company is being dissolved, every such transaction is deemed to be void and subject to clawback.

In terms of general principles of civil law, any transaction made by a debtor in fraud of his creditors claims is subject to clawback by virtue of the so-called *actio pauliana*. In such cases where the transaction was performed under an onerous title (ie for consideration), it will be up to the creditor to prove that there was fraud on the part of both contracting parties to the transaction, but where the transaction was gratuitous it will be sufficient to prove fraud only on the part of the debtor. The relevant action for the clawback of fraudulent transactions is barred by the lapse of 30 years.

2.14 What are the rules on set-off/netting?

As a general rule, set-off operates *ipso iure* (by operation of law) where two persons are mutual debtors, even without the knowledge of the debtors, and the moment two debts exist simultaneously they are mutually extinguished to the extent of their corresponding amounts (provided their subject matter is a sum of money which is certain and due). However, set-off will not take place where it causes prejudice to the rights of a third party. Accordingly, the general rule is that it would cease to operate in the context of an insolvent company.

In terms of the Set Off and Netting on Insolvency Act, notwithstanding the general civil law rules, any close-out netting provision or any other provision in any contract providing for or relating to the set-off or netting of sums due from one party to another in respect of mutual credits, mutual debts or other mutual dealings is rendered enforceable in accordance with its terms, whether before or after bankruptcy or insolvency, in respect of mutual debts, mutual credits or mutual dealings which have arisen or occurred before the bankruptcy or insolvency. Of course, this exception to the general rule does not apply in respect of any close-out netting agreement entered into at a time at which the other party knew or ought to have known that an application for the dissolution and winding up of the company by reason of insolvency was pending, or that the company has taken formal steps to bring about its dissolution and winding up by reason of insolvency.

2.15 How is exit managed?

See sections 1.9 and 1.10 above.

In addition, with reference to schemes of compromise or arrangement, which include proposals for the restructuring or amalgamation of the company, including term-out and asset disposal programmes, the court will review, sanction and direct the relevant processes. The court is given very wide powers in this respect and may, either by the order sanctioning the compromise or arrangement requested or by any subsequent order, make provision for a number of matters, namely:

- the transfer to another company of the whole or any part of the undertaking and of the property or liabilities of the company;
- the allotment or appropriation by another company of any shares, debentures, securities or other like interests in that company which under the compromise or arrangement are to be allotted or appropriated by that company to or for any person;
- the continuation by or against another company of any legal proceedings pending by or against the company;
- the dissolution of the company and the striking off of its name, without its having to be wound up;
- the provision to be made for any persons who, within such time and in such manner as the court directs, dissent from the compromise or arrangement; and
- all such incidental, consequential and supplemental matters as are necessary to secure that the reconstruction or amalgamation is fully and effectively carried out.

Where the court order provides for the transfer of property or liabilities, then that property or liability will be transferred by virtue of the order itself and will vest in the transferee company. The court order may direct that the property will be transferred and will vest in the transferee company free from any charge or other burden which will, by virtue of the compromise or arrangement, cease to have effect.

Once a scheme of compromise or arrangement is approved by a three-quarters majority of the creditors and is sanctioned by the court, it becomes binding on all creditors of the company and accordingly will be enforceable against them. Any person having a juridical interest in the proper implementation of the scheme will have a right to request that it be enforced according to its terms and according to the relevant court orders, and to seek judicial intervention for this purpose.

In all cases it is possible for the creditors of the company to initiate the relevant restructuring process and, once sanctioned by the court, it will become binding on all other creditors, on the shareholders and on the company itself. Note that, in the case of an application for a company recovery procedure, this can be filed only if the application has been filed by or on behalf of at least half in value of the company's creditors.

2.16 Are 'prepackaged' plans, arrangements or agreements permissible?

N/A.

2.17 Is a public authority involved?

No. The only public authority 'involvement' relates to the registrar of companies, who must be given notice of an order of the court calling for a meeting of the creditors or shareholders of the company for the purposes of a compromise or arrangement (whether or not including a proposed restructuring or amalgamation).

Similarly, on the submission of a company recovery application, the issue of a company recovery order, the appointment and termination of the appointment of a special controller and the appointment of a replacement thereof, the submission of an application for the termination of a company recovery order and the order of the court terminating the company recovery procedure for any reason, a copy of the relevant application, of the relevant court order or of any other relevant document must be submitted to the registrar of companies for registration.

2.18 What is the treatment of claims arising after filing/admission?

The relevant provisions of law dealing with company reconstructions do not specifically contemplate or address this situation. In the context of a scheme of compromise or arrangement that has already been sanctioned by the court, a claim arising subsequently ought not to affect the scheme unless the creditor concerned seeks judicial intervention to prevent the scheme from being implemented. Similarly, the claim itself ought not to be affected by the scheme in the sense that, provided that the claim arose subsequently to the approval of the scheme, the creditor concerned will have a right to prosecute his claim against the company.

Similarly, in the context of a company recovery order, a claim arising subsequently will not affect or be affected by the procedure except that, for as long as the company recovery procedure is in effect, the rights of the creditor concerned to enforce its claim against the company will be stayed.

2.19 Are there ongoing contracts?

In the context of a scheme of distribution or arrangement, these matters will typically be provided for in the proposed scheme. In the context of a company recovery procedure, once an application requesting to put a company into recovery has been filed and for as long as the company recovery procedure is in force, the execution of claims of a monetary nature against the company and any interest that may otherwise accrue thereon will be stayed.

2.20 Are consolidated proceedings for members of a corporate family/group possible?

The law does not contemplate such proceedings. Accordingly, each member of the corporate group wishing to avail itself of the relevant procedures will need to file a separate application for the required purpose.

2.21 What are the charges, fees and other costs?

Judicial fees and costs associated with the relevant applications are established with reference to tariffs set out in the schedules to the Code of Organisation and Civil Procedure. Additional, minor expenses may be incurred in connection with any advertisements required to be made in terms of law. There are no other mandatory charges or fees in connection with the various restructuring procedures referred to herein except the fees payable to the special controller appointed when a company recovery order is made. The fees of the special controller will be established by the court depending on circumstances.

3. LIABILITY ISSUES

3.1 What is the liability of managers/directors *vis-à-vis* creditors?

As a general rule, directors act as agents of the company and therefore their acts are binding on the company, and it will be the company, as the principal, that will be responsible for such acts. A director cannot be held personally liable for acts performed on behalf of the company except in those special circumstances stipulated by law.

The Companies Act provides for a number of instances in which the directors of a company may render themselves personally liable towards creditors of the company. Of relevance in the context of companies which are insolvent or imminently so are the provisions dealing with fraudulent trading, which provide that a director of a company which is being wound up may be held personally liable for all or any of the debts of a company if it appears to the court that any of the company's business was carried out with intent to defraud creditors or for any fraudulent purpose. Moreover, in such a case, the director will be guilty of an offence and liable to a fine and imprisonment. Similarly, the provisions relating to wrongful trading provide that, where a company has been dissolved and is insolvent and it appears that a person who was a director of the company knew, or ought to have known, prior to the dissolution of the company that there was no reasonable prospect that the company would avoid being dissolved due to its insolvency, the court may declare that director liable to make a payment towards the company's assets as the court thinks fit. Other, instances of personal responsibility exist in more specific legislation, such as the Investment Services Act 1994, the Insider Dealing Act of 1994 and the bye laws issued by the Malta Stock Exchange for application to listed companies.

In addition to this, general principles of law can also apply to impose personal liability on directors, in particular, where a director has acted in a fraudulent manner to the determinant of a third party or creditor of the company he represents.

Where such personal liability exists, any person affected (typically creditors) by the relevant act will have standing to sue the director(s). Similarly, the liquidator of a company in dissolution will also have the right and duty to take recourse against the directors in terms of the relevant provisions of the law where in the course of the liquidation it becomes apparent to the liquidator that fraudulent or wrongful trading has been committed by the director(s).

Similarly, if, during such time as the company recovery procedure is in force, it appears that any business of the company has been carried on with intent to defraud creditors or for any fraudulent purpose, the special controller may apply to the court requesting that it declare that any persons who were knowingly parties to the carrying on of the business in such manner be personally responsible, without any limitation of liability for all or any of the debts or other liabilities of the company as the court may direct.

Furthermore, the special controller may also request the court to order that a director or directors of the company who continued to trade when they knew, or ought to have known, that the company was unable to pay its debts or was imminently likely to become unable to pay its debts be directed to make a payment towards the company's assets as the court thinks fit.

The relevant action is competent to the special controller and not the creditors in these cases, and the law does not contemplate a right competent to creditors to join in the action filed by the special controller if he chooses to do so. Nevertheless, in practice it is likely that the creditors will have considerable influence over the discretion of the special controller to take such action where circumstances permit and the special controller will be mindful of his legal obligations to perform his functions fairly and equitably, taking into account the best interests of the company, its shareholders and creditors, together with the interests of any other interested party.

3.2 What is the liability of the lender?

Lenders are unlikely to assume any liability towards other creditors of the company unless, for instance, the loan/credit was set up at a time when the lender knew that the company was insolvent or if it was set up in fraud of other creditors' claims. In such cases the transaction will be subject to impeachment (at the instance of any creditor affected thereby), but a lender would also be exposed to liability for any damages caused in terms of general principles of law (tort law). Similarly, loans/credits set up within the six month period preceding the insolvent dissolution of a company will be deemed to be a fraudulent preference and may be subject to impeachment, although the law does not contemplate any additional liability on the part of the lender in such a case. Other than this, lenders are not generally exposed to liability – unless, of course, they act in breach of the contractual provisions underlying the relevant loan/credit.

The Netherlands

RESOR N.V. Lucas Kortmann & Niels Pannevis

1. WHAT COURT-MONITORED RESTRUCTURING PRE-INSOLVENCY PROCEEDINGS OR SCHEMES HAVE BEEN DEVISED BY THE LAW OF YOUR COUNTRY TO LIMIT VALUE DESTRUCTION FOR FAILING BUSINESS ENTITIES?

At the time of writing, one restructuring procedure is codified under Dutch law. This is the suspension of payments (*surséance van betaling*) procedure. Although this procedure is included in Annex A of the Insolvency Regulation (Regulation 1346/2000) and as such could be considered formal insolvency proceedings, it is aimed at reorganisation rather than liquidation.

Draft legislation has been proposed to introduce two proper pre-insolvency restructuring procedures:

- the procedure of silent administration (*stille bewindvoering*), possibly including the preparation before bankruptcy of an asset sale in bankruptcy; and
- the pre-insolvency scheme (*gerechtelijk dwangakkoord buiten insolventie*).

This draft legislation is expected to come into force in 2015. Meanwhile, there is an established practice of silent administration, albeit without statutory basis. The text below on these pre-insolvency proceedings is based on the most current legislative drafts as of September 2014.

Special proceedings exist for banks and insurance companies. These are not addressed in this contribution.

1.1 What is the objective of the proceedings?

A debtor who expects not to be able to continue to discharge his liabilities as and when they fall due may apply for suspension of payments. The goal of suspension of payments is twofold. First, it instantly provides the debtor with a suspension (moratorium) of unsecured, non-preferential payment obligations. Secondly, it provides the opportunity to restructure unsecured, non-preferential debts by implementing a restructuring plan (*akkoord*) through a mechanism in which a majority of the creditors can bind a dissenting minority (cram down).

Silent administration serves to prepare the insolvency proceedings by appointing a silent trustee (*stille bewindvoerder*). The silent trustee is the anticipated (to be appointed) insolvency trustee in case the debtor subsequently files for the opening of formal insolvency proceedings. This allows the silent trustee to be informed of the situation the debtor is in prior to the opening of (formal and thus public) insolvency proceedings. As such, the silent trustee can be informed of anticipated restructuring plans and can assist in the preparation of the insolvency, which can include the preparation of a prepackaged asset sale, ie a transaction in which relevant assets of the company are transferred to a different company and which transaction is to be executed directly after the opening of the insolvency proceedings. In principal, the debts remain with the insolvent debtor.

The pre-insolvency scheme is aimed at (financial) restructuring outside of insolvency proceedings through a restructuring of the debt of the company. The procedure includes voting in classes, cram down possibilities and confirmation by the court.

1.2 Do all kinds of businesses qualify?

All businesses except for banks and insurance companies qualify for all three types of proceedings. There are no limitations as to the size or asset value of the business. Natural persons, who do not conduct an independent profession or business, cannot apply for any of these proceedings.

1.3 What are the necessary approvals?

The suspension of payments procedure can only be requested by the debtor. The management board does not need shareholder permission to file such a request unless the articles of association of the company contain a provision to the contrary.

The opening of silent administration can also only be requested by the debtor. In principle, no shareholder permission is needed.

A pre-insolvency scheme can be offered by the debtor. Any statutory or contractual obligation for the board of the debtor company to obtain the approval of shareholders before entering in such proceedings is void. Creditors can propose a pre-insolvency scheme only after the debtor has refused to do so.

1.4 What is the procedure?

The suspension of payments can only be requested by the debtor. The request to the court has to be supported by a cash-flow forecast and an up-to-date balance sheet. The procedure is initially *ex parte* (ie no creditors will be heard by the court). After the request, the suspension of payments is immediately granted provisionally. This decision is made public. In practice, the court-appointed administrator informs the major creditors after opening of the procedure. After two to four months, the ordinary creditors vote on whether the suspension of payment proceedings should be granted definitively. The court then decides whether the suspension of payments is granted. It must refuse further suspension of payments if:

- more than one-third of the creditors, or creditors holding more than 25 per cent of the claims, oppose the continuation of the suspension of payments;
- there is just reason to believe the debtor will prejudice the creditors during such proceedings; or
- there is no prospect that the debtor will be able to satisfy his creditors. This satisfaction does not necessarily include full payment.

Silent administration can only be requested by the debtor. The request to the court has to be accompanied by a cash-flow forecast and a balance sheet. The procedure is *ex parte*. Formally, creditors are not informed, and cannot influence the opening of silent administration in any way. The decision to appoint a silent trustee is not made public. In practice, creditors who may be essential for a restructuring (such as secured lenders) will often be involved in the request for silent administration, though they do not play a formal role in the decision to grant silent administration and appointment of the silent trustee.

The pre-insolvency scheme can be filed for by the debtor, or by a creditor if the debtor has refused to do so upon the creditor's request. Any petition to open insolvency proceedings is suspended during the pre-insolvency scheme. The draft of the pre-insolvency scheme must be filed with the court. It is voted upon no sooner than eight days after the filing. The debtor, creditors and/or shareholders can request the supervisory judge for a preliminary ruling on the division into classes, the valuation of claims and/or the voting procedure.

1.5 Is there recourse against the opening judgment?

Suspension of payments is immediately and automatically granted upon request, albeit provisionally. There is no recourse against this provisional suspension of payments. However, creditors can appeal the later decision by the court to definitively grant suspension of payments. If the suspension of payments is not granted, the debtor can appeal this decision. In the case of silent administration, the creditors are not aware of the opening of such proceedings and have no option to appeal such a decision.

The process of a pre-insolvency scheme starts with the debtor filing a petition to execute the scheme. At this point, no judgments by the court are required. The court's interference is only warranted if, after the voting procedure, the court is asked to confirm the scheme. On the appeal against such a judgment, see section 1.13 below.

1.6 What are the substantive tests/definitions?

Suspension of payments can be granted if the debtor foresees that he will not continue to be able to pay his debts as they fall due. This is a future cash-flow test.

The procedure of silent administration can be opened if the debtor demonstrates that this is in the best interests of the creditors (ie the silent administration will benefit the recovery rate for creditors in the subsequent insolvency proceedings) or in the public interest (eg good for employment).

In the current draft legislation, there is no substantive test that has to be met before the debtor can offer a pre-insolvency scheme to its creditors. However, a creditor can request the debtor to offer a pre-insolvency scheme if the creditor foresees that the debtor will not be able to continue to pay his debts as they fall due.

1.7 What is the role of a court-appointed agent?

In suspension of payments proceedings, the court appoints one or more administrators (*bewindvoerder*), usually a lawyer specialised in insolvency. The administrator manages the estate together with (the managing directors of) the debtor, their mutual cooperation being required to perform any legal acts concerning the estate of the debtor. Although the debtor can (informally) suggest candidates, the court ultimately decides who is appointed.

In silent administration, the court appoints one or more silent trustees (*stille bewindvoerder*, or *beoogd curator*), usually a specialised insolvency lawyer. When requesting the opening of silent administration, the debtor can suggest candidates to be appointed as silent trustee. Usually the court willingly considers such suggestions. The silent trustee has very few statutory powers, yet significant influence. He does not have any formal control within the company, but he will resign from his position if he cannot come to an agreement with the debtor/management on the best course of action. Such disagreement will severely reduce the opportunity of reaching a successful restructuring. It is instrumental to involve the silent trustee in the preparation of the transaction that is to be executed after the opening of formal insolvency proceedings. Furthermore, the silent trustee can indicate whether, should he be appointed as trustee, he will challenge certain actions as voidable based on fraudulent preference. This is an important indication that certain transactions will or will not be challenged in a potential insolvency procedure.

The process of a pre-insolvency scheme does not include a court-appointed agent, but, upon request, the court can appoint a supervisory judge. This supervisory judge can be requested by the debtor, creditors and/or shareholders to render a view on the division into creditor voting classes, the valuation of claims and/or the voting procedure. Furthermore, he can be requested to rule on whether the scheme must reasonably be amended in order for creditors/shareholders to form a proper judgment as to the proposed amendment of their rights.

1.8 What protection is there from creditors?

During a suspension of payments procedure, the ordinary creditors cannot enforce their claims. Preferential creditors, including the tax collector and the employees, are not bound by this moratorium. Suspension of payments proceedings are aimed at providing the debtor with relief through a moratorium, and the possibility of restructuring its debts through an agreement or plan. During these proceedings, the appointed administrator has no special avoidance powers. Also, the creditors are only requested to substantiate their claims once the debtor proposes a plan to restructure its debts. In that case, the supervisory judge rules on the admittance of claims.

The procedure of silent administration offers no protection or moratorium against creditors exercising their rights (since the procedure is silent and not to be made public). The debtor may be forced to continue to pay his debts as they fall due. The silent trustee has no special avoidance powers and, since there is no scheme or plan to be presented to creditors in these proceedings, no proof of claims takes place at this stage.

If a pre-insolvency scheme is pending, the court may suspend the hearing of any bankruptcy petition against the debtor. There is no other protection from the creditors taking recourse. However, due to the swiftness of the process and the impossibility of filing for insolvency, disgruntled creditors may in practice be stalled during the pre-insolvency scheme. The court can also take whatever measures it deems necessary to protect the interests of the debtor or its creditors. However, the suspension of a bankruptcy petition will be lifted if the court has reason to believe that the scheme will not be accepted by the required majority of creditors, or if a creditor whose claim has become due and payable after the proposal of the scheme explicitly requests that the suspension be lifted.

1.9 What is the usual duration of the restructuring process?

The suspension of payments is immediately granted provisionally by the court. The creditors vote two to four months later, and the court decides on the definitive approval of the suspension of payments for a fixed term of at most 18 months. This term can be extended one or more times, to a maximum of another 18 months. A restructuring through an agreement in suspension of payments proceedings will in practice take anywhere between four weeks and six months.

The procedure of silent administration can last between two weeks and three months, though it usually it takes no longer than three weeks. The court can set a term for the silent administration, which is usually no longer than two months.

As there is currently no established practice for pre-insolvency schemes, it is difficult to estimate how long it will take. However, the process was specifically designed to be swift and efficient. After proper preparations, it should be possible to complete the process within weeks.

1.10 Who prepares the restructuring agreement and what are the available tools?

In the suspension of payments procedure, the debtor is entitled to file a restructuring plan together with the application for suspension of payments proceedings or thereafter. Only the debtor can offer a plan. A restructuring plan can be characterised as an agreement concluded between the debtor and its ordinary creditors. Hence, the content of the plan is governed by the principle of freedom of contract. This provides the parties with a high degree of flexibility to negotiate the terms of a possible restructuring plan. Such plans regularly include deferral of payment maturities, partial payment of debts against a waiver of remaining liabilities and debt for equity swaps. In determining the content of the restructuring plan, debtors must also consider the mandatory reasons for a court to deny confirmation (as discussed below). The plan is accepted if a majority of the ordinary creditors that hold a majority of the claims vote in favour of the plan. If at least 75 per cent of the creditors vote in favour of the plan but the necessary majority in amount of claims is not met, the court can decide to deem the plan accepted if the opposing creditors have acted unreasonably. This is decided by means of a 'best interest of creditors' test.

The process of silent administration is essentially the preparation of a transaction that is to be executed directly after the opening of an insolvency procedure. The creditors do not get to vote on the transaction. However, the transaction must be approved by the supervisory judge. This usually takes no longer than a day or two.

The pre-insolvency scheme can also be characterised as an agreement between the debtor, his creditors and/or shareholders. Similar to the plan during suspension of payments, the parties are largely free to determine the contents of the plan, within the limits set by the confirmation procedure. The voting on the pre-insolvency scheme takes place in classes of creditors or shareholders, where the division into classes is based upon the reasonably similar positions that the parties hold. The scheme is accepted if, in every class that is affected by the scheme, a simple majority of creditors holding two-thirds of the claims votes in favour, cramming down dissenting creditors. If this is not the case, the plan can still be accepted through the intervention of the court. This is possible if the opposing class(es) could not have reasonably voted against the plan, which is decided by the court on the basis of a best interest of creditors test.

1.11 Are subordination agreements necessarily given full effect?

The plan during a suspension of payments procedure is an agreement between the debtor and his ordinary creditors. It does not involve classes within the ordinary creditors, nor does it bind secured or preferential creditors. Preferential creditors need to be paid in full or otherwise agree to a settlement on the basis of unanimity. We deem it possible to give effect to subordination agreements in such a plan, although no legislation exists and case law is scarce. It is not formally allowed to give preferential treatment to specific ordinary creditors, but plans providing for a better treatment of smaller creditors have been accepted in the past.

There is no specific statutory law or case law on early bird fees. An agreement offering early bird fees would not, in our opinion, be approved by the court in case the early bird fees are paid from the insolvent estate, though we deem early bird fees possible when paid by a third party (eg a purchaser).

Since the execution of a restructuring through silent administration eventually takes place through an insolvency proceedings, the distribution of proceeds is done accordingly. Subordination agreements are given full effect in this distribution process.

The pre-insolvency scheme provides for voting in classes. The subordinated creditors will usually form a separate class. The voting rights of relatively subordinated creditors can be exercised by the economic beneficiary of the subordination. With regard to the possibility of early bird fees, the same applies as to the agreement in a suspension of payments procedure.

1.12 How is exit managed?

In suspension of payment proceedings, the court has to confirm (*homologeren*) the restructuring plan, for which purpose a hearing is held. The hearing usually takes place about two weeks after the creditors' meeting. The court is obliged to deny confirmation under certain circumstances, including where:

- the liquidation value of the assets of the estate is greater than the amount offered to the creditors;
- the performance of the plan is not sufficiently guaranteed;
- the plan came into place through fraud or unfair preference of certain creditors; or
- the administrator has not been paid.

Furthermore, the court can deny confirmation based on other grounds (at its discretion). The confirmation is in principle a marginal test regarding the 'fairness' of the composition, not a test of whether the plan is the best deal achievable for the creditors. The court will in principle respect the majority vote. If the court sanctions the plan and the decision becomes final, the plan becomes binding on all ordinary unsecured creditors, including those that have voted against, and the suspension of payment proceedings comes to an end. The company continues to exist in its restructured form. Appeal can take place in two instances (appellate court and Supreme Court), and can take two to twelve months, depending on the courts' agendas. Should the required majority of creditors' votes not be obtained or should the court deny confirmation of the plan, the court is authorised to declare the company bankrupt. It should be noted that a restructuring plan can be offered only once.

A procedure of silent administration is aimed at restructuring that is to be executed directly after the opening of bankruptcy proceedings. Hence, silent administration usually results in bankruptcy proceedings. The restructuring is often achieved through an asset sale directly after the opening of the bankruptcy.

A pre-insolvency scheme has to be confirmed by the court, much like the restructuring plan in suspension of payments proceedings. The test is essentially the same. However, since a pre-insolvency scheme is voted on in classes, the court can be called on to cram down one or more classes. In this assessment, the court considers whether the crammed down creditors could reasonably oppose the plan, taking into account the value they could expect to receive in case of a liquidation of the debtor's estate.

1.13 Who are the necessary parties?

Since the suspension of payment proceedings only concern ordinary creditors, the cooperation of secured creditors or preferential creditors is not strictly necessary. However, in practice, a successful restructuring through suspension of payment proceedings usually only takes place if preferential creditors (mainly the tax authorities) also accept a certain haircut and if secured creditors cooperate.

If the court refuses confirmation of a restructuring plan in suspension of payments proceedings, both the debtor and the creditors that voted in favour of the plan can appeal within eight days. If the court approves the plan, the creditors that voted against it and those that were not present at the vote can appeal within eight days. This procedure is usually concluded within two months. After that, it is possible to appeal such a decision at the Supreme Court. This will take roughly as long as the original appeal.

The process of silent administration followed by an asset transaction directly after the opening of the bankruptcy leaves no room for the creditors to appeal. Creditors can try to claim damages if they believe their rights were not duly observed in the process. Such claims could (in theory) be brought against the parties involved in the transaction, such as directors of the company, the (silent) trustee and potentially any creditors involved in the transaction.

The pre-insolvency scheme can be limited to certain classes of creditors only, and can also include secured creditors and even shareholders of the debtor. Thus, which parties are involved depends greatly on the contents of the scheme. The possibilities for appeal during a pre-insolvency scheme are similar to those regarding the restructuring plan in suspension of payments, albeit that these apply to the parties that are involved in the scheme only. Depending on the decision, the outvoted creditors and/or the debtor can appeal against the decision to grant or deny approval of the pre-insolvency scheme. The decisions made by the supervisory judge on valuation, the formation of the classes and the voting procedure are not open to appeal, but they will be taken into account by the court in the confirmation procedure.

2. POST-INSOLVENCY PROCEEDINGS

2.1 What is the objective of the proceedings?

Dutch law contains one type of post-insolvency proceedings (formally) for liquidation purposes: bankruptcy. Special procedures exist for over-indebted natural persons, and banks and insurance companies. These will not be considered here.

Bankruptcy proceedings are aimed at liquidation, but are also used for restructuring and reorganisation, mostly through an asset sale. Bankruptcy proceedings also provide for a plan procedure, which is comparable with the restructuring plan during the suspension of payments described above.

2.2 Do all kinds of business entities qualify?

All businesses except banks and insurance companies qualify for bankruptcy proceedings. Both the debtor and creditors can file for insolvency. Bankruptcy proceedings can be opened if the debtor has ceased to pay its debts as they fall due. This entails a cash-flow test, rather than a balance-sheet test. To prove that a company has ceased to pay its debts, it is necessary that there are at least two creditors, of which at least one has a claim that is due and payable. Further circumstances can be taken into account. The claims only need to be proven *prima facie*, although courts generally deny the opening of bankruptcy proceedings if the claim is hard to verify or very uncertain (eg when the claim is subject of pending legal proceedings).

2.3 What are the necessary approvals?

The debtor (usually represented by its director(s)) can file for voluntary opening of bankruptcy proceedings. Limited liability companies (*Besloten Vennootschap*, or B.V.) and public limited companies (*Naamloze Vennootschap*, or N.V.) cannot file for insolvency without approval of the general meeting of shareholders.

Creditors can also file for (involuntary) bankruptcy as well as the public prosecutor, who can request bankruptcy proceedings being opened in the public interest.

2.4 Is it valid and binding to agree that such proceedings be a default/termination event?

In principle, a contract may (and often will) provide for opening of bankruptcy proceedings being an event of default or ground for termination. However, certain limitations exist regarding provisions that would unilaterally burden the debtor with significant debts or extinguish his entitlements or rights (to assets) on the sole basis of his insolvency.

2.5 What is the procedure?

Once the court has declared the debtor bankrupt, a bankruptcy trustee is appointed who is charged with the administration of the bankrupt estate. Furthermore, a supervisory judge is appointed to supervise the trustee and whose consent is required for certain actions by the trustee.

Formally, the bankruptcy trustee must liquidate the assets of the debtor and divide the proceeds amongst the creditors in accordance with their ranking.

Consequently, restructuring through bankruptcy is mostly achieved using an asset sale transaction. The bankruptcy trustee sells all, or part of, the assets to a new company, which usually also hires (a portion of) the employees of the debtor. Rules of transfer of undertaking do not apply in bankruptcy proceedings. Thus, the healthy part of the business continues in the new company, and the trustee distributes the purchase price among the creditors of the debtor. The asset sale can be prepared using the process of silent administration (see above). The prospective bankruptcy trustee is thus involved before the opening of the bankruptcy procedure so that he can be informed of and involved in the preparation of the asset sale, which can then take place directly after the opening of the bankruptcy (thus safeguarding the value of the business).

Alternatively, it is possible to restructure through a restructuring plan in bankruptcy which, *mutatis mutandis*, is very similar to the restructuring plan described above, albeit that a plan and subsequent revival of the legal entity is rare in bankruptcy.

If restructuring through either of these procedures is not a viable option, the assets of the company will be liquidated. The trustee then distributes the proceeds between the creditors (in accordance with their ranking).

2.6 Please provide information about voluntary filings

The debtor can voluntarily file for insolvency proceedings. The filing is treated behind closed doors. Creditors are not informed or invited. The opening judgment is made public by publication in an online register and the Official Gazette (*Nederlandse Staatscourant*). Furthermore, the bankruptcy trustee will inform the known creditors of the bankruptcy.

If the debtor is declared bankrupt, this takes effect as of 00.00h on the day the court opens the proceedings. This means that any legal acts performed by the debtor on the day of the opening of the bankruptcy are not binding upon the bankrupt estate.

The debtor can offer a composition plan to the creditors prior to the first meeting of creditors. It is not necessary for the plan to already be presented with the filing for bankruptcy.

2.7 How are creditors' representatives chosen?

The bankruptcy trustee must take the interests of the joint creditors into account and, as such, he can be considered as a representative of the joint creditors. The court appoints the trustee from a list of selected attorneys specialised in insolvency law. Creditors can request certain trustees, but the court ultimately decides. Creditors can also apply to the court to replace a trustee, although this does not often happen in practice.

If the nature or complexity of the estate requires a creditors' committee, such a committee may be formed by the court on its own initiative or upon request by a creditor. Such committee consists of one to three creditors. The court decides which creditors can take a place on the committee. The creditors' committee must be granted full access to all information regarding the bankruptcy. Essentially, it is an advisory body to the trustee, who must obtain the advice of the committee to decide on certain actions, such as the initiation of legal proceedings, the continuation of the business or the cancellation of employment contracts. In practice, a creditors' committee is rarely formed. Reasons for the court not to form a creditors' committee could be that the bankruptcy is not complex and thus the trustee does not require such assistance, or that it is not expected that ordinary creditors will receive a distribution from the bankruptcy (in which case there is no justification for having a committee to represent their interests).

2.8 Is there recourse against the opening judgment?

The debtor and each creditor can appeal against the opening of the bankruptcy within eight days. After that, the decision of the appellate court can be challenged before the Supreme Court. Both instances usually take no longer than two months.

The appellate court will again consider whether the debtor has 'ceased to pay its debts'. This is judged according to the situation at the time of the decision in the appellate proceedings. A successful defence for the debtor may be to pay the claim of the creditor requesting bankruptcy. After this, the creditor will no longer have standing to request the bankruptcy.

2.9 What are the roles and powers of committees?

Since creditors' committees are hardly ever installed, they do not play an important role in Dutch insolvency proceedings. If such a committee is formed, its job is to advise the trustee on important decisions (see also section 2.7 above).

2.10 What are the consequences of opening judgments for creditors?

Unsecured (ordinary and preferential) creditors cannot enforce their rights during a bankruptcy. They have to file their claims with the trustee for verification. Pending legal proceedings against the debtor are suspended and only continued if, after the claim to which such proceedings relate is filed for verification, such claim is contested. Attachments or garnishments cease to have effect. Creditors holding a claim against the estate (estate creditors) and secured creditors are exempt from this rule. Estate creditors include creditors with claims incurred by the trustee (see section 2.18 below). Secured creditors do not need to file their claim, but can take recourse as if there were no insolvency. However, if a temporary stay is ordered (with a maximum period of two months, which can be extended for a maximum of another two months), the secured creditors cannot (yet) foreclose on their collateral without permission of the supervisory judge. Furthermore, the trustee can set a (reasonable) deadline for secured creditors to take foreclosure on collateral. After the lapse of that period, the trustee can liquidate the asset, in which case the secured creditor only receives the proceeds thereof, after the deduction of a share in the bankruptcy costs.

Interest accrued during bankruptcy cannot be claimed in the bankruptcy, but secured creditors can also apply proceeds of foreclosed collateral to pay post-bankruptcy interest.

The trustee will notify all (known) creditors of the opening of the bankruptcy proceedings. If and when it is conceivable that a distribution to ordinary creditors can take place, ordinary creditors are then invited to submit their claims for verification, jointly with substantial evidence of that claim. Such verification process does not apply to secured creditors and the tax authorities/social services (in relation to their preferential claim), but the trustee will also require such creditors to provide proof of their claims, to establish that their exceptional position is justified.

In Dutch bankruptcy proceedings, there is no differential treatment for local and foreign creditors.

2.11 What is the duration of the restructuring process?

There is no fixed time-frame for a restructuring through bankruptcy proceedings. The time-frame for a successful restructuring will largely depend on the question whether the bankruptcy trustee has sufficient liquidity available in the bankrupt estate (or can obtain financing for the estate) to effectuate such restructuring.

If an asset sale is prepared before the opening of the bankruptcy, ie through silent administration beforehand, the transaction can take place hours or days after the opening of the bankruptcy. The business can then continue as a going concern without much interruption. An unprepared restructuring through bankruptcy usually takes several weeks or months, depending on the type of company (certain companies cannot survive operationally if the restructuring takes too long).

2.12 How do creditors vote?

If the restructuring takes place through an asset sale transaction, the creditors do not get to vote on the transaction.

If the restructuring takes place through a plan within bankruptcy, the voting procedure is similar to that of the above described plan within suspension of payments. The plan is accepted if a majority of the ordinary creditors that hold a majority of the claims vote in favour of the plan. If at least 75 per cent of the creditors vote in favour of the plan but the necessary majority in amount of claims is not met, the court can decide to deem the plan accepted if the opposing creditors have acted unreasonably. This is decided by means of a 'best interest of creditors' test.

The plan within bankruptcy is an agreement between the debtor and its creditors. Since preferential creditors rank higher in priority to ordinary creditors, a plan offering partial payment to ordinary creditors would imply full payment of preferential creditors. In practice, the most important preferential creditor, the Dutch Tax Administration, usually cooperates with any plan in which it receive a payment on its claim which amounts to double the percentage that ordinary creditors receive. Secured creditors are not involved in the plan, but they may be allowed to vote on the plan for the part of their claim for which they cannot take recourse on their security.

Dutch bankruptcy law does not distinguish different classes within the ordinary creditors.

Shareholders are not allowed to vote. However, it is not possible to create new shares in Dutch companies without the consent of the existing shareholders, meaning that a plan that would involve a debt for equity swap would also require the cooperation of shareholders.

2.13 What are the rules on clawback/voidability?

The bankruptcy trustee can declare void any (i) voluntary legal act (ii) performed by the debtor before opening of the insolvency proceedings which (iii) prejudiced the possibilities of the joint creditors to take recourse, and of which both (iv) the debtor and (v) the counterparty knew that the act would result in such prejudice.

A voluntary legal act includes entering into an agreement and payment of outstanding debt that was not due.

In most avoidance actions, the crucial point is whether the trustee can prove that both the debtor and the counterparty knew that the transaction would prejudice the (other) creditors. Such prejudice exists if the overall estate has been diminished by the transaction, but can also exist if the estate was not diminished as such but certain creditors were put in a better position (eg through set-off possibilities) at the expense of other creditors. For a successful avoidance action, the bankruptcy trustee will have to prove the knowledge of such prejudice by demonstrating that both the bankruptcy and the fact that not all creditors would be paid in full were foreseeable with a reasonable degree of certainty.

Furthermore, knowledge that the act would prejudice the creditors is deemed to exist in transactions that the debtor entered into within a year prior to the bankruptcy (i) with a related party, (ii) not at arms' length or (iii) which include the debtor providing payment or security for a debt that is not due.

If the legal act considered was performed at no cost to the counterparty (ie gifts), it is not necessary for the trustee to show that the counterparty was aware that this act would prejudice the creditors.

Much stricter norms apply when there was a legal obligation to perform the contested act, eg the payment of debts that are due and payable. Such acts can only be challenged if the counterparty was aware that the bankruptcy petition was already pending or the payment was the result of an agreement between the debtor and creditor aimed at favouring the creditor at the expense of other creditors. This is a heavy burden of proof, which is applied strictly by the courts.

Other than certain other jurisdictions, Dutch law does not provide for a certain period of time prior to the bankruptcy, during which acts are automatically subjected to clawback or are suspect. The one year mentioned above merely relates to a shift in the burden of proof. In theory, clawback can apply to acts that took place several years prior to the bankruptcy (be it that the trustee will have difficulty proving the knowledge of prejudice).

2.14 What are the rules on set-off/netting?

The possibilities for setting off claims are expanded by the opening of bankruptcy proceedings. In bankruptcy, set-off is allowed if both claims originate before the bankruptcy proceedings or are the direct result of acts performed by the debtor before insolvency. However, claims cannot be set off if the creditor has obtained the claim in bad faith, ie with the sole purpose of setting off the claims during the insolvency. The possibility of set-off can be excluded by contract.

2.15 How is exit managed?

The bankruptcy can end through the acceptance of a restructuring plan, or by liquidation of the assets (possibly through an all encompassing asset sale) followed by distribution of the proceeds.

The rules on voting on the plan are discussed in section 2.12 above. The composition plan essentially is an agreement between the debtor and the creditors, meaning that the principle of freedom of contract applies and parties are free to shape the plan according to their wishes, albeit that the dissenting minority is also bound (crammed down) by the majority voting in favour. Most plans are so-called percentage plans, in which the debtor offers payment of a certain percentage of each claim in exchange for full discharge of any remaining claims.

If the plan is confirmed by the court, the bankruptcy ends and the plan is subsequently executed by the debtor. However, if the debtor fails to execute the plan, the composition plan can be dissolved and the bankruptcy will be reopened.

It is not possible to execute a plan including a debt-for-equity swap without the consent of the shareholders. However, this is possible in the pre-insolvency scheme.

2.16 Are 'prepackaged' plans, arrangements or agreements permissible?

Restructuring through a prepackaged insolvency usually involves a prepackaged asset sale, which was prepared during a period of silent administration (see section 1 above).

2.17 Is a public authority involved?

Other than the supervisory judge who oversees the bankruptcy trustee, no public authority is involved. Major decisions, such as an asset sale, have to be approved by the supervisory judge. This is usually done within one or two days.

2.18 What is the treatment of claims arising after filing/ admission?

Claims against the debtor originating after the opening of the bankruptcy cannot be admitted in the bankruptcy. However, there are two exceptions to this rule.

First, Dutch law applies the concept of estate claims, which are claims against the estate that arise after the opening of bankruptcy. These claims are paid with preference over pre-bankruptcy creditors. A claim can be classified as an estate claim when:

- it was incurred by the bankruptcy trustee in his capacity as trustee;
- it is prescribed by law (eg rent and wages after opening of the proceedings); or
- it is a claim for damages due to the bankruptcy trustee breaking a rule that applies to him in his capacity as a trustee.

Secondly, claims originating after the opening of the bankruptcy but arising directly out of a contract that was entered into before the bankruptcy can be admitted in the insolvency as ordinary pre-bankruptcy claims.

2.19 Are there ongoing contracts?

As a matter of principle, the opening of bankruptcy proceedings does not affect existing contracts of the debtor. However, if the contract has not been fully performed by both parties, the counterparty of the debtor can request the trustee to declare whether he intends to uphold the contract. If the trustee decides to do so, he must provide security for the execution of the contract. If the trustee decides not to uphold the contract, he can no longer demand the execution thereof from his counterparty. On the other hand, the trustee is not obliged to honour contracts, meaning he cannot be forced to perform contractual obligations.

Special rules apply to labour contracts and rental agreements. If the debtor is an employer, all labour contracts can be terminated on six weeks' notice. If the debtor is a tenant, any rental agreement can be terminated with three months' notice.

If the debtor is a borrower under a finance agreement, the trustee cannot draw under the finance agreement unless he can provide security for his obligations thereunder (ie security to repay). Therefore, in practice, new financing agreements must be entered into by the trustee if he requires liquidity.

2.20 Are consolidated proceedings for members of a corporate family/group possible?

Dutch bankruptcy law does not contain rules for substantive consolidation of insolvency proceedings. In practice, the concept of substantive consolidation is therefore only recognised in a situation where it is (virtually) impossible to separate the estates of different legal entities.

2.21 What are the charges, fees and other costs?

The bankruptcy trustee is paid an hourly rate, which is determined by the court. For an experienced trustee, this is around EUR 300 per hour. The costs of the bankruptcy must be paid from the estate. Thus, if the estate holds insufficient funds, the trustee may be forced to terminate the bankruptcy due to lack of funds.

3. LIABILITY ISSUES

3.1 What is the liability of managers/directors *vis-à-vis* creditors?

There is no concept of disqualification in Dutch law (although there are qualification tests for certain financial institutions such as banks). A legislative proposal regarding a civil law-based director disqualification (*civielrechtelijk bestuursverbod*) is currently pending.

Under Dutch law, a company's managing board is collectively charged with the management of the company. As a general rule, directors are not personally liable for obligations incurred by, on behalf of or for damage inflicted upon the company. Under certain circumstances, however, they may become personally liable – individually or jointly – towards the company, its shareholders, the bankrupt estate or third parties (eg creditors). Each managing director has a statutory duty towards the company to properly perform the duties assigned to him. There is only a failure under that duty if it is established that the director has failed in the performance which could be reasonably expected under the specific circumstances. Failure does not automatically lead to liability, but will do so if it is severely reproachable (*ernstig verwijtbaar*). Whether a failure was severely reproachable is determined on a case-by-case basis, taking into account all the relevant circumstances. All managing directors of a company are, in principle, jointly and severally liable. An individual director may be discharged if he can prove that:

- he cannot be held responsible for the failure; and
- he has not been negligent in – actively – preventing the consequences thereof.

A director may be held liable in tort (*onrechtmatige daad*) by a creditor on the grounds that he entered into a transaction on behalf of the legal entity while at the time he knew or should reasonably have known that the company would not be able to meet its obligations arising from that transaction, and would not offer sufficient recourse either. It is not sufficient that there was a more than negligible risk that the legal entity would not be able to meet its obligations. Liability arises only if the director should have anticipated that the risk would actually materialise. A managing director can also be held liable in tort if he allowed or effectuated that the legal entity did not meet its obligations under an earlier commitment and consequently caused damage to its counterparty.

A claim in tort as described above can also be brought by the receiver in bankruptcy on behalf of the joint creditors of the company. If a legal entity does not provide sufficient recourse to pay all creditors on its bankruptcy, the directors shall be jointly and severally liable for the entire deficit in the bankruptcy if:

- it is apparent that the management has not discharged its duties properly; and
- it is likely that the bankruptcy was caused by mismanagement by the board of directors.

This is referred to as manifestly improper performance of duties (*kennelijk onbehoorlijke taakvervulling*). Only manifestly improper performance of duties during the three years preceding the bankruptcy is taken into account. Manifestly improper performance of duties means that no reasonably acting entrepreneur would have acted similarly in equivalent circumstances and with the same knowledge as the director had (or should have had) at the time.

If the management has failed to keep its books properly or has failed to publish the annual accounts with the Chamber of Commerce in a timely manner, improper performance of duties is (irrefutably) deemed to have occurred and such improper performance is (refutably) presumed to have been an important cause of the bankruptcy. If manifestly improper performance of duties by the board is established, all managing directors are, in principle, jointly and severally liable for the entire deficit of the bankrupt estate (although the court can mitigate damages).

Lastly, managing directors can become liable to the tax collector or, if applicable, the branch pension fund for tax, social security and pension debts of the company. In particular, the managing directors have a duty to immediately (within two weeks) inform the tax authorities that the company is unable to meet its payment obligations. If the company breaches its obligation to notify the tax collector, the director is liable for manifestly improper management and it is assumed that he is to be blamed for such management.

If both an individual creditor and the trustee bring separate claims against a director for tort liability, the court may suspend the legal proceedings initiated by the individual creditor until after the court has ruled on the claim brought by the trustee.

Similar grounds for liability apply for supervising directors and *de facto* directors.

3.2 What is the liability of the lender?

Lenders are in principle free to terminate a credit agreement according to the provisions of the agreement. Such a termination can be challenged on the grounds that such termination would be unreasonably and unfair in the specific circumstances. Under certain circumstances, a termination (in particular, on short notice) can be considered invalid. A court may then annul the termination of the credit agreement or decide that the contract will end only after a specific time period, usually no more than a few months. The court will consider all relevant factors, such as the length and nature of the relation between the lender and the borrower, the conduct of the borrower, whether or not the borrower is or has been at default, the associated credit risk, the odds of survival of the borrower, the decision-making process and communication by the lender.

Lenders are only held liable for early termination of credit agreements in exceptional cases (where such termination was unreasonable and unfair). There is no specific statutory framework for such liability, but case law has developed on the basis of general tort provisions. Moreover, the borrower/debtor must prove that it suffered damage because of this termination, rather than due to other circumstances that may have led to the financial distress.

Norway

Advokatfirmaet Selmer DA Jon Skjørshammer

1. WHAT COURT-MONITORED RESTRUCTURING PRE-INSOLVENCY PROCEEDINGS OR SCHEMES HAVE BEEN DEVISED BY THE LAW OF YOUR COUNTRY TO LIMIT VALUE DESTRUCTION FOR FAILING BUSINESS ENTITIES?

Norwegian law has adopted a pre-insolvency proceedings called 'debt settlement proceedings'. This procedure consists of either a voluntary or a compulsory debt settlement.

The advantage of initiating a court-monitored debt settlement proceedings is that, contrary to a voluntary arrangement made with the creditors, a proceedings under the Bankruptcy Act involves mechanisms that more easily render the debt settlement plan binding on all creditors. A voluntary arrangement with the creditors will, in most cases, only be feasible in cases with few creditors, and where the creditors have a clear, common interest in seeing the debtor survive the short (or long)-term financial distress.

Debt settlement and bankruptcy proceedings are regulated by the Bankruptcy Act (BA; *Konkursloven*) and the Creditors Security Act (CSA; *Dekningsloven*). The BA contains the procedural rules and the CSA contains the substantial rules, including rules regarding clawback, priority and debtor's agreements.

1.1 What is the objective of the proceedings?

The objective of the proceedings is to provide the debtor with an ability to negotiate with creditors for a solution consisting of either a voluntary or a compulsory settlement. The proceedings allow the debtor to avoid bankruptcy proceedings.

1.2 Do all kinds of businesses qualify?

All business entities and private individuals may qualify.

Is there a threshold related to indebtedness, turnover or asset value?

To be eligible for debt settlement proceedings, the debtor must be illiquid. This means that the debtor is unable to satisfy its financial obligations as they come due (BA, § 1). There is no requirement concerning turnover or asset value. In contrast to a bankruptcy petition, it is not necessary for the debtor's liabilities to exceed the value of the debtor's assets.

Is a court agent necessarily appointed to assist the company?
Once the ruling on debt settlement proceedings is announced, the court will appoint a debt settlement committee (the Committee) (BA, § 7).

1.3 What are the necessary approvals?

Only the debtor can petition for debt settlement proceedings pursuant to BA, § 1. If the debtor is a corporation or other legal entity, the petition must be filed by the competent authority. For limited liability companies and public limited liability companies, the competent authority is the board.

The court makes the decision regarding whether or not debt settlement proceedings shall be commenced (BA, § 4).

1.4 What is the procedure?

The petition for debt settlement proceedings must be submitted in writing to the district court (BA, § 2). The petition must state whether the debtor submits a voluntary or a compulsory settlement. The debtor must submit the following information:

- a brief statement of the reasons for the payment problems and a plan for the debt settlement;
- a list of the debtor's assets and liabilities, and information about the creditors and any security interests; and
- a brief overview of booking and accounting information.

The court decides whether debt settlement proceedings shall be opened (BA, § 4). In principle, the creditors have no decisive influence on the decision; however, the court may discuss the debtor's petition with the creditors (BA, § 4(2)).

The court's decision is public (BA, § 6), but in certain circumstances the court may choose not to publicly announce the debt settlement proceedings.

1.5 Is there recourse against the opening judgment?

A ruling that grants the petition cannot be appealed. A ruling that dismisses the petition can, on the other hand, be appealed (BA, § 4(3)).

1.6 What are the substantive tests/definitions?

The main condition is that the debtor is illiquid, meaning that it is unable to pay its obligations when they are due (BA, § 1). To assess whether a debtor is illiquid, the court applies a pure cash-flow test.

1.7 What is the role of a court-appointed agent?

The Committee is led by a chairman, typically an attorney, and consists of one to three additional members, usually selected from the body of creditors and their representatives. At least one of the members of the Committee should have knowledge about the nature of the debtor's business.

The role and the structure of the Committee is outlined in BA, § 7. The role of the Committee is to assist the debtor during the debt restructuring proceedings and ensure that the creditors' common interests are taken care of. The Committee should also, to the extent possible, make sure that the interests of employees and the public at large are protected.

The debtor retains possession and control over the assets and its business during the proceedings (BA, § 14). The debtor's business activities are subject to the Committee's supervision, and the debtor is obligated to comply with the Committee's instructions.

1.8 What protection is there from creditors?

Protection from creditors

The two primary advantages of the debt settlement proceedings are protection from creditors through the automatic stay and avoidance (clawback) powers.

The debtor is protected against creditors that petition for bankruptcy or seek to initiate other debt enforcement proceedings. As a general rule, bankruptcy proceedings cannot be opened against the debtor as long as the debt settlement proceedings are in progress (BA, § 16). However, a bankruptcy petition filed by at least three creditors with claims amounting to at least two-fifths of the total amount of known claims is not subject to the stay (BA, § 16).

A creditor is also prohibited from filing for attachment of the debtor's assets or initiating other debt enforcement proceedings (BA, § 17). If the debtor's petition is legally disapproved, then any petition for attachment will be expedited by the court. If debt settlement proceedings are opened, the petition for attachment will be rejected.

The Committee has the same clawback powers as a trustee in bankruptcy (BA, § 38; CSA, chapter 5); cf. section 2.13 below.

Creditors' claims

The Committee must promptly notify all known creditors and request that they submit information about any claims, security interests, or jointly and severally liable persons or entities, with supporting proof (BA, § 19). A creditor's failure to respond or provide sufficient proof will not by itself lead to the inadmissibility of the claim, but it could result in a challenge to the claim.

The court shall terminate the debt settlement proceedings and open bankruptcy proceedings when certain conditions are present. If a settlement is not reached within six months, the court will terminate the settlement proceedings and open bankruptcy proceedings. The court may extend the deadline upon request from the Committee, but only as long as the negotiations are making progress (BA, § 57(1), (4)).

1.9 What is the usual duration of the restructuring process?

The duration of the debt settlement proceedings is six months (BA, § 57(4)). However, the court may choose to grant the Committee's request for extension of the proceedings. There is no maximum statutory time frame.

1.10 Who prepares the restructuring agreement and what are the available tools?

The debtor is responsible for preparing and presenting the debt settlement plan, but in practice the plan will be prepared in conjunction with the Committee (BA, § 22). The Committee shall conduct an interim assessment of the likelihood that the debtor will be able to achieve a voluntary or compulsory debt settlement (BA, § 21). The Committee has the authority to accept, reject or set conditions for the approval of the agreement.

The available tools for debt settlement proceedings depend on whether the procedure is voluntary or compulsory. The tools in a compulsory debt settlement are limited to those enumerated by BA, § 30:

- a payment extension (moratorium);
- a percentage reduction of the debt;
- a liquidation of the debtor's assets (wholly or partly) with a release of the creditor for the uncovered part of the debt, as long as the creditors receive a minimum 25 per cent recovery; or
- a combination of these options.

A voluntary debt settlement proceedings provides the debtor with the same alternatives as for a compulsory proceedings, but also includes other options that may be used alone or in combination (BA, § 23). For instance:

- a term-out/conversion of short- to long-term debt;
- replacing old debt with new debt (refinancing);
- cancellation of debt in exchange for equity in the company;
- payment by instalments; or
- asset disposal, investment in bonds, etc.

The debtor is free to suggest any of these options in addition to those listed in § 23.

1.11 Are subordination agreements necessarily given full effect?

Norwegian bankruptcy law presumes an equal distribution of the debtor's assets, but this is subject to several exceptions (BA, § 23). Creditors are given different priorities, which dictate their order in the distribution:

1. priority: claims for unpaid salary;
2. priority: tax and duties;
3. priority: general creditors;
4. priority: interest on claims accruing after commencement of the proceedings, gifts, etc.

Secured claims will be treated outside the chain of priority to the extent that the security covers the outstanding debt.

In a voluntary debt settlement, the creditors may agree to receive a smaller dividend than they would be entitled to under a statutory distribution (BA, § 23). It is assumed that the same also applies under a compulsory debt settlement.

The size of the proposed dividend to the creditors determines the number of creditors that must support the proposition for it to be legally binding on all creditors.

1.12 How is exit managed?

Voluntary debt settlement proceedings

The debt settlement proposition is adopted when all the covered creditors have accepted the proposition (BA, § 25). The Committee shall notify all creditors who will not receive full recovery under the proposed plan, and should also send the approved proposal to the court (BA, § 27).

Upon the debtor's request, after the expiration of the time limit in BA, § 19, the court may suspend the debt settlement proceedings by ruling, subject to the written consent of all creditors except creditors with fully secured claims (BA, § 56).

The court may also suspend the debt settlement negotiations and open bankruptcy proceedings in the debtor's estate pursuant to BA, § 57 if the debt settlement proves to be unsuccessful; cf. section 1.8 above.

Compulsory debt settlement proceedings

The size of the proposed dividend determines the number of creditors that must vote in favour of the proposition for it to be legally binding on all creditors. Within a week of the creditors' vote, the Committee must submit the proposal to the court together with a statement regarding the outcome of the vote (BA, § 45). The court will set a date to confirm or reject the proposal (BA, § 52). The court will summon the debtor, the Committee and, usually, the creditors (BA, § 46).

If the court dismisses the proposal, the court shall suspend the debt settlement negotiations and open bankruptcy proceedings in the debtor's estate (BA, §§ 52 and 57). However, upon the debtor's request, after the expiration of the time limit in § 19, the court may suspend the debt settlement proceedings by ruling, subject to the written consent of all creditors except creditors with fully secured claims (BA, § 56).

1.13 Who are the necessary parties?

Once a voluntary debt settlement is accepted by the creditors included in the debtor's proposition, it will be considered a legally binding agreement between the debtor and the creditors included in the proposition. If the court approves the voluntary debt settlement plan, both the debtor and the creditors have a right to appeal the ruling (BA, § 52).

In a compulsory debt settlement proceedings, the approved settlement will be binding on all creditors except those with claims that are secured, prioritised or subject to set-off (BA, § 55). The court's decision to suspend the debt settlement negotiations and to open bankruptcy proceedings in the debtor's estate may also be subject to an appeal (BA, § 57).

2. POST-INSOLVENCY PROCEEDINGS

2.1 What is the objective of the proceedings?

The objective of the bankruptcy proceedings is to convert the debtor's assets into cash and ensure a fair distribution between the debtor's creditors. An important reason for bankruptcy proceedings is to counteract incidental and unreasonable differences between the creditors.

2.2 Do all kinds of business entities qualify?

All business entities and private individuals may qualify for post-insolvency proceedings, as long as their centre of main interest (COMI) is in Norway. Venue determination is based on international COMI rules.

To open bankruptcy, the debtor must be insolvent (BA, § 60). Insolvency consists of two requirements: illiquidity and insufficiency (BA, § 61). Illiquidity exists when the debtor is unable to meet its obligations as they come due, unless the payment problems can reasonably be assumed to be temporary. Insufficiency exists when the debtor's debt exceeds the debtor's assets (balance deficit). If both these conditions are met, the debtor will be presumed insolvent unless the debtor's combined assets and income provides sufficient coverage for the debt.

A petition for bankruptcy may be filed by the debtor or its creditors (BA, § 60). A creditor is prohibited from petitioning for bankruptcy if:

- the creditor has a receivable secured by a satisfactory pledge over the debtor's assets;
- the creditor has a receivable secured by a satisfactory pledge over a third party's assets and a bankruptcy petition is inconsistent with the terms of the security guarantee; or
- the creditor's receivable is not yet due and is secured or will be secured by a satisfactory pledge in a third party's assets (BA, § 64).

2.3 What are the necessary approvals?

If the debtor is a corporation or other legal entity, the petition must be filed by the competent authority, ie the board. The debtor's creditors may initiate bankruptcy proceedings, but subject to the limitations in BA, § 64. Public authorities, in the capacity of being a creditor, can also petition for bankruptcy.

When the court receives a petition for bankruptcy proceedings by party other than the debtor, notice of hearing shall be served, with a two-day notice to the debtor and the petitioning creditor (BA, § 70).

The court shall, as soon as possible, announce a ruling on whether to commence bankruptcy proceedings (BA, § 72).

2.4 Is it valid and binding to agree that such proceedings be a default/termination event?

The parties may agree that the opening of bankruptcy is a trigger for default. An agreement that only gives one contracting party a right to terminate due to insolvency is not generally binding on the estate (CSA, § 7-3).

2.5 What is the procedure?

The procedure depends on whether the petition is filed voluntarily by the debtor or by a creditor. When the petition is filed voluntarily by the debtor, a court will usually handle the petition within one day. A petition filed by a creditor will be subject to a more comprehensive review, and the treatment will depend on the complexity of the petitioning creditor's claim and the level of default by the debtor. Straightforward claims are usually handled by the court in six weeks, while more complex and disputed claims may last for several months.

When bankruptcy proceedings are opened, the court immediately appoints a trustee (usually a lawyer), who will be in charge of the bankruptcy administration (BA, § 77). The court may also appoint one or several creditor representatives to form a creditors' committee. The trustee and the creditors' committee will together form the board of trustees. The court may also appoint an estate auditor.

2.6 Please provide information about voluntary filings

The petition must be submitted in writing to the district court and must give the reasons on which it is based (BA, § 66). The petition must also include:

- a list of the debtor's assets and liabilities, and information about the creditors and any security interests; and
- a brief overview of booking and accounting information.

Creditors are not invited to the initial hearing. The court must promptly issue a public notice and notify all known creditors (BA, § 78).

2.7 How are creditors' representatives chosen?

The court may appoint one or several creditor representatives to form a creditors' committee. The committee members are usually appointed upon a request from the trustee after having considered the complexity and the means of the estate.

2.8 Is there recourse against the opening judgment?

If the court dismisses the petition, the petitioning creditor may appeal the court's ruling with the debtor as the opposing party. If the court grants the petition, the debtor may appeal the ruling. Both the petitioner and the estate will be opposing parties (BA, § 72).

The appeal will not suspend the bankruptcy proceedings (BA, § 72). The deadline for filing an appeal is one month (BA, § 153).

2.9 What are the roles and powers of committees?

The trustee and the creditors' committee together form the board of trustees that administers the estate. The board of trustees ensures the creditors' common interests (BA, § 88). The committee shall supervise the activities of the executive trustee.

2.10 What are the consequences of opening judgments for creditors?

The two primary consequences of bankruptcy are the automatic stay and avoidance (clawback) powers.

Stay?

The opening of a bankruptcy proceedings prohibits creditors from initiating debt enforcement actions. The stay covers both the creditor's access to file for attachment and to carry out a forced sale or other kind of enforcement proceedings on the debtor's assets. Attachments made within three months of the filing have no legal effect against the estate (CSA, § 5-8; BA, §§ 17 and 117).

Forbidden payments?
Bankruptcy deprives the debtor of the authority to act on its own behalf, including control over assets (BA, § 100). This includes payments to creditors.

Certain payments made prior to the opening of the bankruptcy can be subject to clawback by the estate (CSA, chapter 5); cf. section 2.13 below.

Interests accruing during period: paid at contractual payment dates? Deferred and paid after the plan is adopted? Capitalised? Is the rate necessarily the contract rate?
Only claims that arose before the opening of the bankruptcy are admissible (CSA, § 6-1). Interest on admissible claims that has accrued during the proceedings is admissible, but ranks last in priority (CSA, § 9-7). The interest rate is set at the same level as the standard interest on late payments (CSA, § 9-7; Act Relating to Interest on Overdue Payments, § 3).

Is the opening judgment a valid draw stop (for undrawn facilities)?
The opening judgment prevents the debtor from acting on behalf of the company in all matters, including making use of undrawn facilities. The bankruptcy estate is also prohibited from making use of any undrawn facilities.

Necessity to file proof of claim: are all creditors required to file proof of claim? Are secured creditors necessarily notified? Are there any time limits? Are non-resident creditors treated differently? Are there consequences if a creditor is time-barred? Is the debtor discharged?
After opening bankruptcy, the court shall request all creditors to file claims with the trustee by a specific deadline. Claims filed after the deadline are still admissible, but the court can demand that the late-filing creditor reimburses the estate for any extra costs incurred as a result of the late filing (BA, § 115).

In cases where creditors do not file a claim, the debtor (both individuals and legal entities) is not discharged, but remains responsible for the debt even after the end of the bankruptcy. However, in practice, limited liability entities will in most cases be dissolved as a result of the bankruptcy, and therefore the creditors will not have any debtor to pursue. On the other hand, individual debtors will naturally continue to exist, and will still be subject to the creditor's debt enforcement.

The claims shall be accompanied by sufficient documentation (BA, § 109). The trustee will keep a list of all filed claims (BA, § 110). Creditors can file a claim with sparse or no documentation, but the trustee may refuse to admit claims that are not sufficiently documented. The trustee will give the creditor a deadline for filing the necessary proof of claim and, if the creditor fails to supply further information, the trustee will report the lack of proof to the court with the trustee's decision. The court will then give the creditor three weeks' notice to dispute the trustee's decision before the trustee's decision to dismiss the claim will be made effective (BA, § 114).

Non-resident creditors are treated equally as resident creditors.

Does such proceedings entail any limitation on enforcement of contractually created security?

The opening of bankruptcy proceedings limits the enforcement of security interests. The Mortgages and Pledges Act will control the validity of the security interests. The security interest may be subject to avoidance rules; cf. section 2.13 below.

2.11 What is the duration of the restructuring process?

There is no statutory maximum for the duration of the insolvency proceedings. The duration depends on the size and complexity of the estate. The duration of the process can range from around three months in smaller estates to several years in larger estates.

2.12 How do creditors vote?

Once proceedings are opened, the rest of the proceedings follow a specific procedure outlined in the BA. There is no room for the debtor to present a 'restructuring plan' in the insolvency proceedings, unlike the Chapter 11 process in the United States.

The BA distinguishes between different priority claims (CSA, chapter 9); see section 1.11 above. This distinction is only given effect if the estate has sufficient funds for a distribution to the creditors.

The creditors are represented by the creditors' committee. The creditors' committee is entitled to vote on matters in the board of trustees (BA, § 89). The creditors' committee can demand that specific matters concerning the bankruptcy proceedings are submitted to the board of trustees for a vote (BA, § 88).

The creditors generally have the right to vote at creditors' meetings, subject to certain exceptions related to matters regarding the creditor itself, as well as secured and prioritised claims (BA, §§ 94–95).

2.13 What are the rules on clawback/voidability?

The CSA distinguishes between 'objective' and 'subjective' clawback rules.

The purpose of the objective clawback rules is to ensure a simple and straightforward application of the rules that can be applied to many dispositions that are presumptively disadvantageous to the body of creditors. Objective clawback does not require a detailed assessment of the debtor's financial situation at the time of the disposal or payment, or an evaluation of the other party's good faith. Attachments and liens established for securing old debt, gifts and, in certain cases, set-off are voidable when the disposition is made less than three months before the bankruptcy petition. The estate's claim is limited to the other party's enrichment (CSA, § 5-11).

The subjective clawback provisions apply to a wider range of dispositions, and contains both objective and qualified subjective assessments (CSA, § 5-9). The time limit is extended to 10 years and the estate's claim is not limited to the other party's enrichment, but to the loss to the estate (CSA, § 5-12).

2.14 What are the rules on set-off/netting?

A creditor can use a claim against the debtor to set off any claim the debtor has against the creditor during the bankruptcy proceedings, when certain conditions are present. First, the creditor's counterclaim must have arisen prior to the opening of the bankruptcy. Secondly, the creditor cannot use the counterclaim for set-off when the debtor's (principal) claim was due before the opening of the bankruptcy and the counterclaim is due after the opening (CSA, § 8-1).

To ensure consistency in the regulations, the creditor cannot use a (counter)claim for set-off prior to the opening of the bankruptcy if this would be prohibited during the bankruptcy proceedings (CSA, § 5-6).

2.15 How is exit managed?

Before terminating the bankruptcy, the estate should convert the debtor's assets into cash. This includes assessing the possibility of selling the business as a going concern, selling the debtor's hard assets and recovery of outstanding claims against third parties.

The creditors may submit their own proposal on how to dispose of the debtor's assets, but ultimately the decision remains with the trustee. The trustee is obligated to dispose of the debtor's assets in the most profitable way to protect the common interest of the creditors (BA, §§ 85 and 117). Existing pledges and charges will continue to exist over the debtor's assets, but subject to the clawback rules; cf. section 2.13 above.

Credit-bidding is possible, but it is in the trustee's discretion to set the conditions of a sale. The estate will usually demand cash payment to ensure a quick and safe settlement.

When the estate has made its best efforts to dispose of the debtor's assets, the trustee will initiate the exit of the bankruptcy. The BA outlines three types of exits, depending on the financial status of the estate.

In most cases, the estate only has sufficient funds to cover the estate's own administrative costs. In such cases, the bankruptcy proceedings will be terminated without any further action by the estate (BA, § 135).

If the estate has sufficient funds to cover the administrative costs and full or partial coverage of the claims, the estate should carry out an examination of the submitted claims. The estate should submit the proposed distribution to the court, and distribute the funds to the creditors with the court's approval if no creditors have objected within the deadline (one month from the trustee's announcement of the allotment) (BA, §§ 128 and 130).

The debtor may request to regain control of the estate ('handed back'). The debtor must cover the estate's administrative costs and:

- Obtain written consent from all unsecured creditors; or

- Prove that all such claims are covered in full (BA, § 136).

As an alternative to the three options outlined above, the bankruptcy estate may also be converted to a compulsory debt settlement upon court approval. This gives the debtor the possibility to 'cram down' dissenters if the plan is approved by a sufficient majority (see BA, §§ 123–24, 130 and 140–44). The compulsory debt settlement plan is not binding on some preferential and secured creditors (BA, § 55). The available tools in a compulsory debt settlement are described in section 1.10 above.

There is no room for combining the exit of a bankruptcy proceedings with arrangements other than those prescribed above, such as a term-out or an asset disposal programme.

2.16 Are 'prepackaged' plans, arrangements or agreements permissible?

Prepackaged plans, arrangements and agreements are normally not binding on the estate. Arrangements that seek to distribute the debtor's assets in a way other than prescribed by law will not have any effect on the estate. The procedure for the distribution of assets is mandatory (CSA, chapter 9). The debtor may force a proposition in accordance with the rules on compulsory debt settlement; cf. section 1.10 above.

2.17 Is a public authority involved?

The public authority involved is the county court in the district where the debtor is registered with its main address (BA, § 146). The court will make an assessment of whether or not the conditions for the opening of bankruptcy are met (BA, § 60 et seq.).

The court's powers also include the treatment of any disputes concerning the existence, size or priority of submitted claims, as well determining issues of voidability (BA, § 145).

2.18 What is the treatment of claims arising after filing/admission?

Claims arising before the bankruptcy are entitled to dividend payment if the estate has sufficient funds (CSA, chapters 6 and 9). Claims arising after the opening of bankruptcy proceedings are generally treated as preferential claims and will take precedence over all other claims (CSA, § 9-2).

2.19 Are there ongoing contracts?

The bankruptcy estate can choose to assume any executory contracts of the estate (CSA, § 7-3). The choice of acceding to the agreement is in the trustee's discretion. If the estate chooses to assume a contract, it will have the same rights and obligations under the contract as the debtor (CSA, § 7-4).

The estate is not entitled to accede to certain types of contracts due to the nature of the contract, eg contracts that are highly dependent on the debtor's person or the debtor's continued (solvent) operations. Accordingly, credit agreements are not subject to the estate's accession.

2.20 Are consolidated proceedings for members of a corporate family/group possible?

There are no formal provisions that make it possible to consolidate bankruptcy proceedings. The group companies will be treated as separate estates with separate assets and administration. In practice, the same trustee will usually be appointed if several companies in a corporation are taken under bankruptcy, due to the practical benefits of jointly administrating the estates.

2.21 What are the charges, fees and other costs?

The petitioner must guarantee the estate's costs (BA, §§ 67 and 73). However, the liability is limited to a maximum of approximately NOK 43,000.

Certain costs must be covered upon exiting a bankruptcy. For estates without funds that only cover the estate's own administrative costs, the estate must pay NOK 10,750 in court fees. This is one of the administrative costs, along with the necessary insurance and various other costs. Additionally, the trustee's fee must be paid. In estates with insufficient funds to cover all these costs, the fee must be drawn from the petitioner's guarantee.

In estates with sufficient funds to cover the administrative costs and full or partial coverage of the claims, the estate must pay NOK 21,500 in court fees.

In both cases, the estate's administrative costs, including the trustee's salary, will be preferential claims (CSA, § 9-1).

3. LIABILITY ISSUES

3.1 What is the liability of managers/directors *vis-à-vis* creditors?

Can management/directors (de jure or shadow) be held personally liable? What are the prerequisites?

Norwegian law imposes both civil and criminal liability on directors for breach of fiduciary duties. The legal basis for holding directors personally liable is found in the Limited Liability Companies Act and the Public Limited Liability Companies Act, in addition to general tort rules. General tort rules are wider and allow all parties that have suffered a loss from the directors' or management's actions to commence suit.

For instance, criminal liability for failure to petition for bankruptcy when the company is insolvent is imposed under the Criminal Code, § 284. This rule usually only extends to directors of the company, not management.

Who has standing to sue? Can creditors force the court agent to introduce an action? How? Can creditors join in the court agent's action? Under what conditions? Is there a need to prove specific loss (different from the one suffered by the creditors collectively)?

The trustee of the estate has the primary authority to sue on the estate's behalf. The creditors may not directly force the trustee to pursue any particular cause of action. Safeguards exist, as the trustee may be held personally liable for failure to pursue clearly beneficial claims without any justifiable excuse. However, a high bar is set for imposing liability on the trustee.

It is the responsibility of each individual creditor to pursue a cause of action personally held by the creditor.

3.2 What is the liability of the lender?

The concept of lender liability is not prevalent in Norwegian law. Lender liability may be imposed indirectly, through the clawback provisions, or directly, through the tort rules. Although not well tested in Norwegian law, the lender could, in theory, be held liable where acts of the lender amount to an exercise of control over the company. For example, if the creditor influences the company through its board or management so that the bankruptcy petition is postponed until after the expiration of the limitation period for fraudulent preferences, the bankruptcy court may hold the debtor liable to other creditors for the loss suffered from the delay in filing.

Poland

Sołtysiński Kawecki & Szlęzak
Marcin Olechowski & Borys D Sawicki

1. WHAT COURT-MONITORED RESTRUCTURING PRE-INSOLVENCY PROCEEDINGS OR SCHEMES HAVE BEEN DEVISED BY THE LAW OF YOUR COUNTRY TO LIMIT VALUE DESTRUCTION FOR FAILING BUSINESS ENTITIES?

The only pre-insolvency proceedings is the restructuring proceedings regulated by the Act of 28 February 2003 on the Law of Bankruptcy and Restructuring (LBR).

1.1 What is the objective of the proceedings?

The aim of the restructuring proceedings is to recover the debtor's ability to compete on the market. The aim is reached through the conclusion of a restructuring arrangement agreed during a creditors' meeting.

1.2 Do all kinds of businesses qualify?

In general, the restructuring proceedings is available for all types of entrepreneurs (including, among others, individual entrepreneurs, partnerships and commercial companies), regardless of their turnover or the value of their assets.

The restructuring proceedings may be started only if the entrepreneur is facing a risk of insolvency, ie if, despite not being insolvent yet, it is obvious, based on a reasonable assessment of its financial standing, that the entrepreneur will be insolvent shortly. This prerequisite is not, however, connected to any fixed threshold. Needless to say, the restructuring proceedings is not admissible if the entrepreneur is already insolvent.

The restructuring proceedings cannot be conducted with respect to the entrepreneur who:

- had previously conducted restructuring proceedings, if less than two years has passed since their discontinuation;
- had been subject to an arrangement concluded within restructuring proceedings or bankruptcy proceedings, if less than five years has passed since the performance of the arrangement;
- had been subject to a liquidation bankruptcy or a liquidation arrangement, if less than five years has passed since the final and non-appealable conclusion of such proceedings; or
- had an application for the declaration of his bankruptcy dismissed or had his bankruptcy proceedings discontinued due to insufficient assets to cover the costs of proceedings, if less than five years has passed since the proceedings have become final and non-appealable.

1.3 What are the necessary approvals?

There is no statutory requirement for the approval of any corporate bodies and the request for commencement of the restructuring proceedings may be submitted by any duly authorised representative of the entrepreneur (usually, a member of the management board or a commercial proxy). While the articles of association may stipulate the requirement of the approval of another governing body, such a requirement does not affect the validity of the request itself and failure to obtain it may only constitute grounds for civil/corporate liability towards the company of the person(s) acting contrary to the articles of association.

1.4 What is the procedure?

The only way to start the restructuring proceedings is to submit a statement of the commencement of restructuring proceedings to the court.

Along with the statement, the entrepreneur shall submit:

- a statement on the non-existence of negative prerequisites of the restructuring proceedings;
- a restructuring plan;
- a list of assets with their valuation;
- the balance sheet as of a day within 30 days preceding the submission of the statement;
- a list of creditors and their receivables;
- a list of security interests;
- a statement on the repayment of obligations within six months preceding the submission;
- a list of the entrepreneur's debtors and their debts;
- a list of enforcement titles against the entrepreneur; and
- information regarding the proceedings related to encumbrances over the entrepreneur's assets.

The entrepreneur shall also submit a signed statement confirming the accuracy of the data provided in the above-listed documents, witnessed by a notary public.

Within 14 days from the submission of the statement, the court may forbid the start of the restructuring proceedings. Following the lapse of the deadline for the court decision (if the court does not forbid the start of the proceedings), the entrepreneur shall publish the statement of the commencement of the proceedings in *Monitor S dowy i Gospodarczy* (MSiG; a Polish official journal dedicated to entrepreneurs' announcements) and in at least two other (one local, one countrywide) daily newspapers. The day of publication of the statement in the MSiG is deemed to be the day of commencement of the restructuring proceedings.

The restructuring of an entrepreneur's debts requires the creditors' meeting to adopt the arrangement. The entrepreneur shall notify its creditors on the date and place of the creditors' meeting at least two weeks prior to the meeting. The notification shall be sent by registered mail or delivered in any other way with confirmation of receipt of delivery.

The entrepreneur shall also deliver the restructuring plan along with the notification.

1.5 Is there recourse against the opening judgment?

Since there is no opening judgment, no recourse is available. If the court issues a decision forbidding the start of the restructuring proceedings, the entrepreneur may appeal against it. The second-instance decision is usually issued within a few months (there is no statutory deadline for the court's decisions and time frames vary between different courts).

1.6 What are the substantive tests/definitions?

As mentioned above, the restructuring proceedings is available for entrepreneurs facing the risk of insolvency, which means that they are still solvent; however, based on the reasonable assessment of their financial standing, it is obvious that they will shortly become insolvent.

An entrepreneur is deemed to be insolvent if:

- it fails to perform its due financial obligations; or
- the sum of its liabilities exceeds the value of its assets (the entrepreneur has negative own capital).

The second prerequisite applies only to a debtor who is a legal person (eg a commercial company) or an organisational unit with legal capacity (eg a partnership).

1.7 What is the role of a court-appointed agent?

Restructuring proceedings involve a 'court supervisor'. The court supervisor has the authority to supervise the entrepreneur's activities and his enterprise at any time during the restructuring proceedings, and, if the court so determines, during the performance of the arrangement. The supervisor may also verify whether an entrepreneur's assets that do not constitute part of an enterprise are sufficiently protected against deterioration. The court supervisor also acts as the chairman of the creditors' meeting, and determines with the debtor the date and venue of the creditors' meeting.

1.8 What protection is there from creditors?

As of the day when the restructuring proceedings starts:

- performance of the entrepreneur's obligations and accrual of interest are suspended;
- deduction (set-off) of reciprocal claims of the entrepreneur and creditors is limited (generally, to the claims which arose prior to the commencement of the restructuring proceedings);
- execution (debt enforcement) proceedings, as well as proceedings to secure claims, cannot be brought against the entrepreneur; and
- pending proceedings are suspended (except proceedings pertaining to claims which are not included in the arrangement).

If, during the restructuring proceedings, a creditor files an application to declare an entrepreneur bankrupt, such application may be considered once the restructuring proceedings has been completed or jointly with the court's approval of an arrangement with creditors in the restructuring proceedings.

1.9 What is the usual duration of the restructuring process?

The arrangement with creditors shall be concluded within four months (three months in the case of small or medium entrepreneurs) from the start of the restructuring proceedings, otherwise the proceedings is discontinued.

The conclusion of an arrangement is not, however, the end of the restructuring proceedings as it is subject to the court's approval. There is no statutory deadline for the court's decision, and the time in which the decision is adopted depends on a given court's practice. Usually it takes approximately 1–2 months.

The duration of restructuring process is set out in the restructuring arrangement. The LBR does not indicate the maximum time of the restructuring process.

1.10 Who prepares the restructuring agreement and what are the available tools?

The proposal of the restructuring arrangement is prepared by the entrepreneur. Neither the creditors nor any other participant to the restructuring proceedings (eg the court supervisor) has the right to present a competing proposal.

The restructuring arrangement is adopted by the creditors' meeting. Adoption of the restructuring arrangement requires a majority vote of the creditors entitled to participate in the creditors' meeting holding jointly at least two-thirds of the total amount of receivables, which give voting rights. If the creditors are divided into separate classes of interest (see section 1.11 below), the consent of each group is required. However, the arrangement will also be adopted despite not being accepted by a part of the groups if the majority of creditors voting in other groups holding at least two-thirds of the total value of claims voted for the arrangement and if creditors in groups against the arrangement will be satisfied with the arrangement to a degree at least equal when compared to bankruptcy involving liquidation.

Each creditor entitled to participate in the creditors' meeting may object against the adopted restructuring arrangement. Objections may also be raised by a creditor not entitled to participate in the creditors' meeting provided such creditor proves that the arrangement may impede the pursuit of its claims.

If the proposal regarding the restructuring arrangement has been rejected, the creditors' meeting may be convened again and new/amended restructuring arrangements may be presented.

The restructuring arrangement shall determine the restructuring of debts, assets and employment in the enterprise. The proposal of debt restructuring may include in particular:

- the deferment of payments,
- the payment of debts in instalments;
- the reduction of debts;

- the conversion of claims into shares; and
- the modification, exchange or cancellation of security interests.

1.11 Are subordination agreements necessarily given full effect?

The LBR does not stipulate specific provisions regulating subordination agreements. A subordination agreement has only contractual effect and is not binding *vis-à-vis* third parties in either restructuring or bankruptcy proceedings.

All creditors shall be treated equally; however, the LBR provides for some exemptions, the most important being that the creditors may be divided into separate classes of interest (one of the classes may include shareholders). In such case, there is a possibility that different categories of creditors will be treated unequally. Also, certain groups of creditors are excluded from voting on the arrangement (see section 2.9 below).

1.12 How is exit managed?

Following the adoption by the creditors' meeting, the restructuring agreement is subject to the court's approval. The court issues a decision after a hearing. The date of the hearing is announced in the MSiG, a local daily newspaper and the court building, and both the entrepreneur and creditors who raised objections are notified.

The court examines the admissibility of the restructuring proceedings and will refuse to approve the arrangement if there are no grounds for the proceedings. The court shall also refuse approval if the entrepreneur has failed to submit the required documents (or if the information provided was untrue) or to notify all known creditors of the date of the creditors' meeting. Moreover, the following circumstances constitute grounds for refusal:

- the court supervisor had no possibility of exercising supervision;
- provisions of law have been violated in a manner which might affect the way in which creditors vote;
- the entrepreneur has disposed of or encumbered his assets contrary to the provisions of the LBR;
- the circumstances of the case imply that the arrangement will not be performed;
- the arrangement is detrimental to the creditors, who have raised objections; or
- the restructuring plan does not ensure the recovery of the entrepreneur's ability to compete on the market.

The arrangement is binding for all creditors notified of the creditors' meetings as well as those who reported their participation in the creditors' meeting, unless the entrepreneur denied the existence of their claims.

The court may appoint a court supervisor for the time of the performance of the arrangements.

If the entrepreneur does not perform the restructuring arrangement or if the grounds for refusal of the arrangement become known after the court's positive decision, the arrangement may be revoked by the court.

1.13 Who are the necessary parties?

The conduct of the restructuring proceedings requires the participation of (i) the entrepreneur and (ii) his/her/its creditors, both included in the list of creditors and receivables attached to the statement of the commencement of restructuring proceedings and those who later reported their participation in the creditors' meeting. The creditors act through the creditors' meeting.

The appointment of a court supervisor is mandatory (see section 1.7 above for more details).

The new Restructuring Law

At the beginning of October 2014, the Polish government submitted to the Parliament a draft of the new Restructuring Law.

According to the proposal, the restructuring regulations would be extracted from the LBR into a separate act, while the LBR itself would be significantly revised. The key goals of the proposed amendment are to improve the efficiency and pace of the restructuring proceedings and to deliver effective means of conducting a restructurisation process to entrepreneurs and their contractors, while at the same time increasing the protection of creditors and, finally, remodelling of the bankruptcy proceedings (under the amended LBR) into a last resort procedure to be employed in case of failure of the (new) restructurisation process, with the latter obtaining priority as means of assistance to businesses in distress. The latter goal is of particular practical importance because currently the provisions on restructuring included in the LBR are virtually dead, with only a few successfully completed restructurisations over the 10 years of the act being in force.

2. POST-INSOLVENCY PROCEEDINGS

2.1 What is the objective of the proceedings?

The objective of the bankruptcy proceedings is to satisfy creditors' claims at the highest possible level and to save the enterprise of the debtor if reasonably possible. Bankruptcy proceedings may involve either the liquidation of the debtor's enterprise or the conclusion of an arrangement. The decision on the type of bankruptcy proceedings to be conducted in a given case is made by the court.

Bankruptcy proceedings with the possibility of an arrangement are conducted if it becomes apparent that a debtor will be able to satisfy creditors to a higher degree when compared to a bankruptcy involving the liquidation of the debtors' assets. The type of bankruptcy proceedings may be changed by the court in the course of the proceedings. In this brief summary we focus on the regulations pertaining to the bankruptcy with the possibility of an arrangement; however, some of the LBR's provisions are common to both types of proceedings.

2.2 Do all kinds of business entities qualify?

In general, bankruptcy proceedings are available for all types of entrepreneurs (including, among others, individual entrepreneurs, partnerships and commercial companies), regardless of their turnover or the value of their assets. Bankruptcy proceedings start upon an application pertaining to the insolvent debtor.

As an exemption, bankruptcy may not be declared with respect to:

- the State Treasury;
- local government units;
- independent public health care institutions;
- institutions created by statutory law or in fulfilment of an obligation imposed by statutory law (*inter alia* the Warsaw Stock Exchange, the National Securities Depository, the National Bank of Poland – Poland's central bank, and the Polish Enterprise Development Agency);
- an individual person operating an agricultural farm; or
- higher education institutions (eg universities).

Bankruptcy proceedings are involuntary, which means that the debtor is required by law to file an application for the declaration of bankruptcy if it is deemed to be insolvent under the LBR. By operation of law, it will also be a party to the bankruptcy proceedings if the application is filed by other entitled parties (eg creditors).

The debtor (the entrepreneur) is deemed to be insolvent if it fails to perform its due and payable financial obligations. If a debtor is a legal person or an organisational unit with legal capacity, it is also deemed to be insolvent when the total amount of liabilities exceeds the value of its assets (the debtor has negative own capital). The LBR does not indicate the method of assessment of the value of liabilities or assets; however, in practice, the balance sheet value is primarily taken into consideration. If the balance sheet value of the debtor's own capital is negative, the debtor may try to avoid bankruptcy by proving that the actual market value of its liabilities and assets differ to the balance sheet value and therefore there are no grounds to deem it insolvent and declare bankruptcy.

The court may dismiss the application to declare bankruptcy if the delay in the fulfilment of the entrepreneur's due and payable obligations does not exceed three months and the value of the non-performed obligations does not exceed 10 per cent of the balance sheet value of the enterprise, unless the non-performance of the due and payable obligations is constant or the dismissal of the application could place the creditors in a less favourable position.

The court will, as a matter of course, dismiss an application for bankruptcy if the debtor's assets are not sufficient to cover the costs of proceedings. The same applies if the debtor's assets are encumbered with a mortgage, a pledge or other preferred security interest to such a degree that the remaining assets are not sufficient to satisfy the costs of the proceedings.

2.3 What are the necessary approvals?

The application to declare bankruptcy may be filed by the debtor or by any of its creditors. With respect to the following entities, the LBR also entitles other persons to submit an application:

- in the case of partnerships – by partners who are personally responsible for the partnership's liabilities;
- in the case of legal entities and organisational units with legal capacity – by their duly authorised representatives;
- in the case of a state enterprise – by the founding body;
- in the case of a sole shareholder company of the State Treasury – by the Minister of State Treasury;
- in the case of legal entities and partnerships in liquidation – by any of the liquidators;
- in the case of legal entities entered into the National Court Register (eg commercial companies and partnerships) – by a curator, if appointed by the register court; or
- in the case of a debtor who has received public aid (state aid) exceeding EUR 100,000 – by the entity granting the aid.

2.4 Is it valid and binding to agree that such proceedings be a default/termination event?

Contractual provisions according to which, in the event of bankruptcy, a legal relationship with a debtor is subject to change or termination are null and void under the LBR.

There is a possibility of structuring a contract in a manner that enables the other party to amend or terminate the legal relationship with a debtor in the case of the debtor's insolvency or bankruptcy. However, those solutions may be challenged as a circumvention of the law. Despite this risk, such contractual clauses are fairly common in practice in Poland.

2.5 What is the procedure?

Bankruptcy proceedings begin upon an application for the declaration of bankruptcy.

Together with the application, the applicant shall submit a statement on the entrance of the debtor into the relevant register. If the application is filed by the debtor, it should indicate whether it is applying for the declaration of bankruptcy involving liquidation or with the possibility of concluding an arrangement. If the latter is the case, the debtor should attach the following documents:

- a list of assets with their valuation;
- the balance sheet prepared as of a day within 30 days preceding the submission of the application;
- a list of creditors and their receivables and security interests;
- a statement on the repayment of obligations within six months preceding the submission of an application;
- a list of his debtors and their debts;
- a list of enforcement titles against the debtor;
- information regarding proceedings related to encumbrances upon the entrepreneur's assets;
- information on the place of residence of the debtor's representatives and liquidators;

- an arrangement proposal together with a proposal of how to finance it;
- a cash-flow statement for the last 12 months (if the debtor was obliged to keep the necessary documentation); and
- a statement confirming the accuracy of the data provided in the application.

If the debtor is not able to provide any of the above-mentioned documents, it should present and substantiate an explanation.

If the application for bankruptcy with the possibility of concluding the arrangement is submitted by the creditor, the creditor should substantiate its claim and present a preliminary arrangement proposal.

Participants to the proceedings regarding the declaration of bankruptcy are the debtor and each entity who has filed the application. The statutory deadline for the court's decision is two months from the day of submission of the application. The court hearing is optional and conduct of the hearing is subject to the court's discretional decision. The court may appoint an expert to examine the current status of the enterprise and the fulfilment of the debtor's and its representatives' obligation of filing the application within the statutory deadline.

The court may convene a preliminary creditors' meeting. The preliminary creditors' meeting may adopt a resolution on the type of bankruptcy proceedings (with the possibility of concluding an arrangement or involving liquidation) and on the appointment of the creditors' council. The initial creditors' meeting may conclude an arrangement if at least half of the creditors jointly holding three-quarters of the total sum of claims, confirmed by enforcement titles, made probable or unquestionable participate in the meeting. Only creditors whose claims are confirmed by an enforcement title may participate in the preliminary creditors' meeting; creditors whose claims are unquestionable or made probable may participate upon the court's consent. The initial creditors' meeting may render an opinion concerning the appointment of a court supervisor or administrator. The court is bound by the resolutions regarding the type of the proceedings and the appointment of the creditors' committee unless they are contrary to the provisions of law.

Upon an examination of the application to declare bankruptcy, the court may issue a decision on the declaration of bankruptcy. The decision indicates the type of bankruptcy proceedings.

In the case of a bankruptcy proceedings with a possibility of concluding an arrangement, the court decides if, and to what extent, the debtor will remain in management of its assets. If allowed to do so, the bankrupt is obliged to provide the judge-commissioner and appointed court supervisor with any required explanations concerning assets which are subject to the proceedings and to enable the court supervisor to examine its enterprise, in particular its accounting books. If the bankrupt is prohibited from the management of his assets, the court appoints an administrator instead of a court supervisor. In that case, the bankrupt is obliged to reveal and release all his assets and documents related to his business to the administrator. He/

she is also obliged to provide required explanations. The court also appoints the judge-commissioner.

The court summons creditors to file claims within a time limit not shorter than one month and not longer than three months.

The date on which the decision is issued is the date of the bankruptcy. The decision shall be immediately published in MSiG and in local daily newspapers and delivered to the bankrupt, court supervisor or administrator and the creditor(s) who filed an application to declare the bankruptcy.

2.6 Please provide information about voluntary filings

There are no material differences between bankruptcy proceedings initiated by the debtor and those initiated by the creditor. Because of the debtor's obligation to file for the declaration of bankruptcy in case of its insolvency, even the bankruptcy proceedings initiated by the debtor may not be deemed voluntary.

Once the debtor has been declared bankrupt, bankruptcy proceedings are focused on the protection of creditors rather than of the debtor. Slight differences between proceedings commenced upon an application of the debtor and those commenced following the creditor's filing are indicated *inter alia* in sections 2.5 above and 2.15 below.

2.7 How are creditors' representatives chosen?

The only body which may be referred to as the creditors' representatives is the creditors' council. The creditors' council may be appointed either at the preliminary creditors' meeting or, after the declaration of bankruptcy, by the judge-commissioner if the judge considers such appointment necessary. The judge-commissioner is also obliged to appoint the creditors' council upon the request of creditors representing one-fifth of the total value of claims acknowledged or made probable. Only creditors may be appointed as members and deputies of the creditors' council. The judge-commissioner may replace the members of the creditor's council and their deputies if they neglect their duties. Creditors representing one-fifth of the total value of the above-mentioned claims may request a change of the council's composition. If the judge-commissioner does not accept the request, the request is considered by the creditors' meeting. If the creditors representing the majority of the total value of claims support the request, the judge-commissioner is obliged to change the composition of the council in accordance with the request.

Creditors do not have any influence on the appointment of court supervisors and administrators, but the creditors' meeting and creditors' council may apply for their removal and appeal against a refusal by the court to do so.

The creditors' council provides assistance to the court supervisor or administrator, supervises their activities, monitors the bankruptcy estate's funds and expresses opinions in other matters if so requested by the judge-commissioner, court supervisor or administrator. The creditors' council grants permission to:

- encumber the bankruptcy estate with a mortgage, maritime mortgage, pledge, registered pledge or treasury pledge in order to secure the claims not included in the arrangement;
- encumber the bankruptcy estate with other rights;
- incur a credit facility or loan by an administrator; and
- allow an administrator or court supervisor to perform other actions which require the creditors' council's consent due to the decision of the judge-commissioner.

The creditors' council (and each member of the council) may submit remarks on the activities of a court supervisor or administrator to the judge-commissioner, and request the judge-commissioner to remove them. The creditors' council may also demand explanations from a court supervisor or administrator, and review the ledgers and files concerning the bankruptcy.

2.8 Is there recourse against the opening judgment?

The decision declaring bankruptcy may only be appealed by the bankrupt, whereas the decision dismissing the application to declare bankruptcy may be appealed only by the applicant. The appeal should be examined within one month from the delivery of the case file to the second-instance court. The second-instance court cannot declare bankruptcy; thus, if the appeal is granted to the applicant, the case is reconsidered by the first-instance court.

2.9 What are the roles and powers of committees?

Informal creditors' committees have no legal standing. Instead, creditors vote at the creditors' meeting. The most important role of the creditors' meeting is the acceptance or refusal of the arrangement.

According to the general rule, only creditors whose claims have been acknowledged may participate in the creditors' meeting. They vote with the value of claims recorded in the list of claims. A claim is acknowledged if a court supervisor or an administrator has entered it into the list of claims, which is then approved by the decision of the judge-commissioner (the list of claims may be changed or supplemented by the judge-commissioner). Upon a creditor's request and after hearing the debtor, the judge-commissioner may admit the creditor whose claims are probable or are subject to conditions precedent to participate in the creditors' meeting. In that case, the judge-commissioner indicates the value according to which the creditors' vote is counted.

Each creditor has one vote which represents the value of its claims. The required majority is counted in accordance with the number of votes and the value of the claims which they represent. Claims which arose after the declaration of bankruptcy (including accrued interest) are not taken into consideration.

The following creditors cannot vote on the arrangement:

- the bankrupt's spouse;
- certain relatives of the bankrupt;
- if the bankrupt is a partnership – a partner who is personally liable for the bankrupt's debts;

- if the bankrupt is a partnership or a commercial company – persons authorised to represent it;
- creditors who have acquired the claims after the declaration of bankruptcy;
- if the bankrupt is a partnership or a commercial company – affiliated, subsidiary and dominant companies and their representatives; or
- if the bankrupt is a commercial company – individual shareholders holding at least 25 per cent of shares in the share capital.

2.10 What are the consequences of opening judgments for creditors?

As of the day of declaration of bankruptcy, the bankrupt's assets become bankruptcy estate, which serves to satisfy creditors.

During the period between the declaration of bankruptcy and the court's approval of the arrangement (or discontinuation of the proceedings), neither the bankrupt nor the administrator (if appointed) can satisfy claims included in the arrangement.

2.11 What is the duration of the restructuring process?

The duration of the restructuring process is subject to the restructuring arrangement. The LBR does not indicate a maximum duration for the restructuring process.

2.12 How do creditors vote?

After the approval of the list of claims, the judge-commissioner may decide that the creditors will vote on the arrangement in groups. Otherwise, all creditors vote jointly at the creditors' meeting.

If the first option is chosen, the judge-commissioner divides creditors into groups and prepares separate lists of claims for each group. The groups may constitute, in particular:

- employees who accepted the inclusion of their claims in the arrangement;
- farmers whose claims are connected with the delivery of agricultural products from their farms;
- secured creditors who accepted the inclusion of their claims in the arrangement;
- shareholders holding at least 5 per cent of voting rights at the shareholders' meeting of the bankrupt; or
- other creditors.

The above example of a list of groups is not binding and the judge-commissioner may divide the creditors in other ways, taking into account other differences between their interests.

If creditors vote in groups, the required majority has to be reached in each group.

If the LBR does not state otherwise, a resolution of the creditor's meeting is adopted with the majority of votes representing at least one-fifth of the total value of the claims of the creditors entitled to participate in the meeting.

2.13 What are the rules on clawback/voidability?

The LBR provides for various clawback rules which differ as to time frames and prerequisites.

The basic rule is that all legal actions (including court settlements, acknowledgement of lawsuits and waiver of claims) performed by the bankrupt within a year prior to the filing of the application to declare bankruptcy, on the basis of which the bankrupt has disposed of his assets, are ineffective towards the bankruptcy estate if such actions were performed gratuitously or if the value of the bankrupt's performance significantly exceeds the value of the reciprocal consideration.

Also, any security established to secure, or payment made on account of, an undue debt by the bankrupt within two months prior to the filing of the application to declare bankruptcy are considered ineffective. However, the other party may pursue recognition of the above-mentioned actions as effective if it is able to prove its lack of awareness of the existence of grounds for declaring bankruptcy at the moment at which the actions took place.

Moreover, legal actions for consideration are ineffective if performed by the bankrupt within six months prior to the filing of the application to declare bankruptcy with, *inter alia,* their spouse or certain relatives, partners and shareholders, affiliated companies and their shareholders, as well as the company's dominant companies.

Also, if the remuneration for the work of the bankrupt's representative is significantly higher than the average remuneration for this type of service and the same is not justified by the workload, the remuneration – in part for up to six months before the submission of the application to declare bankruptcy – shall be declared ineffective by the judge-commissioner. The judge-commissioner may also declare ineffective part or all of the remuneration for a representative's work and services due after the declaration of bankruptcy if it is no longer justified by the work input because of the introduction of the administrator's management. The judge-commissioner acts *ex officio* or upon the court supervisor's or administrator's motion.

The court supervisor or administrator may file a motion with the judge-commissioner to declare ineffective, mortgages, maritime mortgages, pledges or registered pledges that were established within a year prior to the submission of an application to declare bankruptcy and if the bankrupt was not personally liable towards the secured creditor and did not receive appropriate consideration for the establishment of the above-mentioned encumbrances.

Lastly, under the general rules of civil law, the court supervisor or the administrator may challenge the bankrupt's legal actions performed to the detriment of creditors (so-called *actio pauliana,* which corresponds to the concept of fraudulent conveyance).

2.14 What are the rules on set-off/netting?

During the course of bankruptcy proceedings, until their discontinuation or conclusion in any other way, deduction (set-off) of reciprocal claims of the debtor and creditor is limited.

Set-off is inadmissible if the creditor has become a debtor of the bankrupt after the declaration of bankruptcy. It is also inadmissible if the creditor, being the bankrupt's debtor, has become his creditor upon the acquisition (through assignment or endorsement) of claims which arose prior to the declaration of bankruptcy.

However, the set-off of reciprocal claims is admissible if the acquisition of the claim has been effected as a result of paying off the debt for which the acquirer was liable and if the acquirer's liability for the debt had arisen before the day the application to declare bankruptcy was filed.

The creditor who intends to exercise the right to set-off shall make a relevant declaration at the time of notifying his claim at the latest.

In the case of the declaration of bankruptcy of a participant of a payment system or a securities settlement system, legal effects of a settlement order and netting are legally binding for a third party only if the order was entered into the system prior to the declaration. If, however, the settlement order has been entered into the system after the declaration of bankruptcy, legal effects of the settlement order and netting are legally binding for third parties provided that an operator of the system proves that, at the time when the order became irrevocable (in accordance with the rules of a given system), it was not, nor could not be, aware of the declaration of bankruptcy.

2.15 How is exit managed?

After the declaration of bankruptcy with the possibility of an arrangement, if an arrangement proposal has not been submitted, the bankrupt is obliged to present it within one month (the judge-commissioner may extend the deadline up to three months). Within the same time frame, the court supervisor or administrator may also file arrangement proposals. An arrangement proposal may be presented by the creditor who was an applicant and who filed the initial arrangement proposal.

If the court-declared bankruptcy involves liquidation, the bankrupt, a trustee or the creditors' council may present an arrangement proposal. In such case, the court changes the type of bankruptcy proceedings if there are grounds for such change.

The bankrupt has the right to propose amendments or supplements to the arrangement during the creditors' meeting.

The creditors' meeting shall take place within one month from the approval of the list of claims. The proposal of the arrangement and information regarding the creditors' division into groups of different interest is delivered to the creditors along with notification of the creditors' meeting. Creditors whose claims are disputable cannot participate in the meeting. On the other hand, creditors who present to the judge-commissioner a non-appealable court or administrative ruling confirming their claims may participate despite not being recorded in the list of claims.

The proposal of the restructuring arrangement describes the manner of the debt restructuring and contains a justification. The proposal of debt restructuring may include, in particular:

- the deferment of payments;
- the payment of debts in instalments;
- the reduction of debts;
- the conversion of claims into shares; or
- the modification, exchange or cancellation of security interests.

The arrangement may include satisfaction of creditors' claims through the liquidation of the bankrupt's assets (liquidation arrangement).

The conditions regarding restructuring should be equal for all creditors or, if they are divided into groups, for creditors in the same group, unless a given creditor accepts less favourable treatment. More favourable restructuring terms may be granted to creditors with small claims and those who granted or agreed to grant a facility required to perform the arrangement.

The adoption of a restructuring arrangement requires the majority vote of the creditors entitled to participate in the creditors' meeting holding jointly at least two-thirds of the total amount of receivables, which give voting rights. If the creditors are divided into separate classes of interest (see section 1.11 above), the consent of each group is required. However, the arrangement will also be adopted despite not being accepted by a part of the groups if the majority of creditors voting in other groups holding at least two-thirds of the total value of claims voted for the arrangement and if creditors in groups against the arrangement will be satisfied with the arrangement to at least an equal degree when compared to bankruptcy involving liquidation.

Participants in the bankruptcy proceedings may raise objections against the arrangement (one week after the creditors' meeting at the latest).

If the arrangement has been refused, the court will immediately change the proceedings into a bankruptcy proceedings involving liquidation. In such case, a return to the bankruptcy proceedings with the possibility of an arrangement is impossible.

Following the adoption of the creditors' meeting, the arrangement is subject to the court's approval. The court issues a decision after the court hearing. The court will refuse to accept the arrangement if it is contrary to law or it is obvious that the arrangement will not be performed. The court may also issue a negative decision if the terms of the arrangement are grossly harmful to the creditors who voted against the arrangement and raised an objection. The court's decision may be appealed.

Only claims which arose before the declaration of bankruptcy are included in the arrangement. Claims subject to a condition which has been fulfilled during the performance of the arrangement will be included in the arrangement. The LBR lists specific types of claims which are excluded from the arrangement (eg claims secured with a mortgage and certain other security interests, social insurance premiums, alimonies). The arrangement is binding for all creditors whose claims are included within the arrangement pursuant to the LBR, even if their claims were not recorded in the list of claims (unless the bankrupt deliberately did not reveal their claims and they did not participate in the creditors' meeting). As of the day the arrangement becomes non-appealable, all injunction and enforcement proceedings against the bankrupt and concerning claims included in the arrangement are discontinued.

The arrangement does not infringe any mortgages, maritime mortgages, pledges, registered pledges or treasury pledges which encumber the bankrupt's assets (unless the secured creditor agreed to include his claims in the arrangement).

If the arrangement includes the conversion of debts into shares, the approved arrangement replaces the actions required by commercial companies law for the increase of share capital and constitutes a sole ground for the registration of the increase of share capital in the commercial register.

The arrangement may establish a supervision over the bankrupt and compulsory management of the bankrupt's assets.

When the court's decision approving the arrangement becomes non-appealable, the court issues a decision on conclusion of the bankruptcy proceedings. Upon conclusion of the proceedings, the bankrupt recovers the management of his assets within the scope described in the arrangement.

The arrangement may be amended only if an extraordinary change in economic relationships has occurred. If the entrepreneur does not perform the arrangement or it is obvious that the arrangement will not be performed, the court may revoke the arrangement upon the request of the bankrupt, creditor or supervisor indicated in the arrangement.

2.16 Are 'prepackaged' plans, arrangements or agreements permissible?

Prepackaged plans, arrangements or agreements are not regulated by the LBR. If any such agreement were concluded between the debtor and creditors, it would have only a contractual *inter partes* effect and would not have a binding effect on the bankruptcy proceedings (in particular, if a debtor is insolvent within the meaning of the LBR, then any creditor or officer of the debtor can validly file for declaration of bankruptcy even if he/she was part to a 'prepackaged' arrangement).

2.17 Is a public authority involved?

No public authorities are involved in standard bankruptcy proceedings (subject to some exceptions of minor relevance).

However, the LBR provides specific regulations regarding the bankruptcy of banks, cooperative savings and credit funds (entities similar to banks), insurance and reinsurance companies which involve participation of the Polish financial markets regulator or, in some cases, the representative of the Ministry of the State Treasury.

In addition, public authorities are obliged to assist the judge-commissioner in the performance of his duties.

2.18 What is the treatment of claims arising after filing/ admission?

Only claims which have arisen prior to the day of declaration of bankruptcy are included in the arrangement. Other claims, especially those which arose after declaration, are not included. In effect, the latter claims are not subject to the prohibition of performance by the bankrupt/administrator, and therefore shall be satisfied on a current basis. The creditor may also pursue the performance of those claims through court litigation, which is not subject to suspension.

2.19 Are there ongoing contracts?

A landlord, until the discontinuance of bankruptcy proceedings, the conclusion of the arrangement or a change in the type of bankruptcy proceedings from arrangement proceedings into liquidation proceedings, may not, without the consent of the creditors' council (or the judge-commissioner if the council has not been appointed), terminate lease and commercial lease agreements regarding properties in which the bankrupt conducts business. Moreover, the arrangement may envisage that this prohibition is binding until the arrangement has been fully performed. The same applies to leasing, property insurance, bank accounts and licence agreements, as well as to sureties, guarantees and letters of credit.

Claims which arose under ongoing contracts after the declaration of bankruptcy are not included in the arrangement and shall be fulfilled on a current basis.

2.20 Are consolidated proceedings for members of a corporate family/group possible?

There are no consolidated proceedings for members of a group under the LBR.

2.21 What are the charges, fees and other costs?

The costs of bankruptcy proceedings consist of court fees and expenses necessary to conclude the proceedings. The costs are paid out from the bankruptcy estate. After the conclusion of the bankruptcy proceedings, the bankrupt pays the costs not paid out from the bankruptcy estate.

Fixed court fees apply to:

- the application to declare bankruptcy (PLN 1,000);
- the application to declare bankruptcy of an individual person (PLN 200);
- an appeal against the court's decision (PLN 200);
- an objection to the acceptance or refusal of acceptance of notified claims (PLN 200);
- an objection to the arrangement (PLN 100); and
- the application to revoke or amend the arrangement (PLN 100).

The typical expenses of the proceedings include:

- remuneration and expenses of court supervisor or administrator and their deputies;
- remuneration and expenses of members of the creditors' council;

- expenses related to the creditors' meetings;
- costs of delivery of notifications;
- costs of announcements;
- taxes and other public levies due for the period following the declaration of bankruptcy; and
- expenses related to the management of the bankruptcy estate.

The above list does not indicate all the expenses that may emerge during the proceedings and even a general estimation of the cost of a typical bankruptcy proceedings is very difficult, if not impossible.

3. LIABILITY ISSUES

3.1 What is the liability of managers/directors *vis-à-vis* creditors?

Persons authorised to represent the debtor are obliged to submit an application for the declaration of bankruptcy to the court within two weeks from the date on which the grounds for the declaration have arisen (ie the debtor has become insolvent within the meaning of the LBR). If they fail to comply with this obligation within a statutory time frame, they are liable for the damages caused as a result.

To pursue the liability of persons authorised to represent the debtor, one who has suffered damages has to prove specific loss (the negative difference between one's current financial standing and the financial standing which one would have if the application for the announcement of bankruptcy had been submitted within the statutory deadline) and the causal relationship between the representatives' infringement and the loss.

Usually the loss is suffered by creditors through the deterioration of the debtor's financial standing and the subsequent lower degree of satisfaction of their claims during bankruptcy proceedings when compared to bankruptcy proceedings which started without delay.

Creditors may pursue compensation only in a separate litigation.

Specific rules of liability apply to members of management boards of limited liability companies (*spółka z ograniczoną odpowiedzialnością*). If enforcement against a limited liability company proves ineffective, members of the company's management board are jointly and severely liable for its obligations. A member of the management board may avoid liability only if he/she proves that:

- the application for the declaration of bankruptcy was filed, or the restructuring proceedings were commenced, in due time;
- the failure to comply with the obligation was not his/her fault; or
- despite the infringement, no damage was done.

This severe regime changes the burden of proof in litigation against a member of the management board.

3.2 What is the liability of the lender?

N/A.

Portugal

Gómez-Acebo & Pombo (Portugal)
Mafalda Barreto & Carlos Soares

1. WHAT COURT MONITORED RESTRUCTURING PRE-INSOLVENCY PROCEEDINGS OR SCHEMES HAVE BEEN DEVISED BY THE LAW OF YOUR COUNTRY TO LIMIT VALUE DESTRUCTION FOR FAILING BUSINESS ENTITIES?

The Portuguese Insolvency Act provides court-monitored restructuring pre-insolvency proceedings, named Special Revitalisation Process (*Processo Especial de Revitalização*, PER), which was introduced by Act No. 16/2012, dated 20 April.

Failing business entities may also engage in an out-of-court pre-insolvency procedure, called SIREVE (*Sistema de Recuperação de Empresas por Via Extrajudicial*).

1.1 What is the objective of the proceedings?

The PER is a pre-insolvency in-court procedure whereby a financially distressed (or imminently insolvent) debtor (that is not in an actual state of insolvency and that has not yet been held insolvent) with realistic prospects for revitalisation may, under the supervision of a court-appointed administrator (the Provisional Judicial Administrator), establish negotiations intended to devise a restructuring plan for a maximum period of three months to avoid the opening of insolvency proceedings and its effects.

1.2 Do all kinds of businesses entities qualify?

The PER can be applied to all kind of business entities, with the exception of:

- public entities;
- insurance companies;
- credit institutions;
- financial companies;
- investment firms; and
- collective investment undertakings.

Is there a threshold related to indebtedness, turnover or asset value?

No threshold is defined by law or applied by the courts.

Is a court agent necessarily appointed to assist the company? If so, how is it chosen?

During the PER, the debtor is assisted by the Provisional Judicial Administrator appointed by the judge. The debtor is entitled to suggest to the judge one name among the public list of judicial administrators.

1.3 What are the necessary approvals?

Only the board of directors' approval is required to initiate the process.

The power to initiate the process lies exclusively with the debtor together with at least one of its creditors.

1.4 What is the procedure?

Must a petition be filed? Must it be *ex parte*?

The PER begins with a petition filed by the debtor together with at least one of its creditors before the commercial court with jurisdiction over the location of the company's registered office.

Are there any other procedural documents? Must supporting documentation be filed with the application?

The debtor shall attach to its petition the following documents:

- a list of its creditors and the amount of each claim;
- annual accounts for the prior three financial years;
- a brief summary of the current status of the company and of its chances of recovery;
- a list of its assets;
- a list of its employees; and
- a written and signed statement in which the debtor declares that it complies with all the conditions required for its recovery.

Are creditors invited to participate? If so, how are they notified? What influence do they have, if any?

All the creditors are invited to file their claims and take part in the negotiations of the restructuring agreement. Creditors are notified both directly by the debtor, by means of a registered letter, and through a publication on the official website (*www.portalcitius.pt*).

Creditors who filed their claims and those who were listed by the debtor will be allowed to vote on the restructuring agreement.

Publicity/confidentiality? Access to petition + documents? How? When?

The restructuring process is entirely public.

Any lawyer may have access to the proceedings' file, which includes the petition and all supporting documents. Lawyers may consult the proceedings' file before the court at any time after the announcement of the appointment of the Provisional Judicial Administrator by the court.

The main events of the PER are published on the official website, which is publicly accessible online.

1.5 Is there recourse against the opening judgment?

In the event that the judge rejects the opening of the proceedings, the debtor is entitled to appeal against that decision to the second instance (appellate) court (*Tribunal da Relação*). The grounds of the appeal shall be compliance with the legal requirements to apply for the PER.

The decision of the appeal would take approximately one to three months.

Conversely, the decision to open the PER is not appealable.

1.6 What are the substantive tests/definitions?

If being still solvent is the test, what constitutes insolvency? Is there a pure cash-flow test? Is there a mix?

Under Portuguese law, restructuring may only be filed if the company is in a difficult economical situation or imminent distress but not yet insolvent. Under the Portuguese Insolvency Act, a company is in distress/state of insolvency whenever it is unable to meet its obligations (cash-flow criteria) or whenever its assets are insufficient to satisfy its liabilities (balance sheet or assets criteria).

1.7 What is the role of a court-appointed agent?

According to the law, the Provisional Judicial Administrator has the following main role and powers:

- receiving the claims and preparing a provisional list of all the creditors and the amount of their claims;
- supervising the negotiations of the restructuring agreement between the debtor and the creditors;
- authorising the debtor to perform acts of a certain relevance or with impact on the management of the company;
- presenting to the creditors the restructuring plan prepared by the debtor;
- receiving and counting the creditors' votes on the restructuring plan; and
- submitting the restructuring plan to the court's approval (homologation).

1.8 What protection is there from creditors?

What protection is there from creditors? Stay?

After the judge has accepted the opening of the PER, all legal actions aimed at collecting debts filed against the debtor are suspended, as well as any pending insolvency proceedings. Moreover, throughout the duration of the PER for insolvency, no applications or new collecting debts actions can be filed against the debtor.

In order to ensure the restructuring of the companies, the restructuring agreement approved by the court binds all creditors, notably those creditors that did not make claims in the proceedings, those who did not take part in the negotiations and those who voted against the plan.

Furthermore, submission to PER proceedings will avoid management liability for failing to file for insolvency (as described in more detail in sections 2.2 and 3.1 below).

Are there avoidance or other powers?

Contrary to what the law provides for insolvency proceedings (as will be better described below), the Provisional Judicial Administrator does not have any avoidance powers within the PER.

Is proof of claims necessary? If the proof is challenged, who rules on the challenge? Timing?

Any document that proves the existence of the claim, such as agreements, invoices or credit notes, shall be attached by the creditors to the claims.

The creditors have a 20-day period after the announcement of the appointment of the Provisional Judicial Administrator to file their claims.

After receiving and analysing the claims and the respective proof, the Provisional Judicial Administrator prepares and files with the court, within a five-day period, a list of the creditors recognised and the amount of their respective claims. Such list can be challenged before the court by any creditor and by the debtor within a five-business-day period after its publication on the official website.

The law sets forth a five-business-day period for the judge to decide on challenges submitted. However, considering that courts are currently flooded with judicial claims, one should not expect this deadline to be observed by the judge. In any event, the negotiations of the agreement are not suspended by the challenging of the list of claims.

1.9 What is the usual duration of the restructuring process?

The PER takes approximately four to six months. The negotiations of the restructuring plan between the debtor and the creditors shall have a maximum duration of two months, starting from the publication of the list of claims, which is extendable by prior written agreement between the Provisional Judicial Administrator and the debtor for an additional month.

Even though the time periods of the proceedings are established by law, the statutory time limits are frequently not met by the judge.

1.10 Who prepares the restructuring agreement and what are the available tools?

The debtor is the party responsible for preparing the restructuring agreement. The Portuguese Insolvency Act does not limit the contents of such agreement; however, restructuring agreements usually incorporate the following measures:

- waiver of interest and/or of part of the principal;
- extension of the maturity of the claims (no statutory limit for the extension);
- liquidation of some of the debtor's assets;
- conversion of the claims into equity; and
- share capital increase by the shareholders and/or the creditors.

The agreement may also contain alternative solutions for creditors to opt for; for example, creditors may choose between a haircut and a debt-equity swap.

If term-out?

If at the end of the statutory time limit for the negotiations an agreement is not reached, the PER is extinguished and, in case the debtor is insolvent, the provisional judicial administrator shall request the court to open insolvency proceedings.

Is a majority needed? That provided in the finance documents? What if unanimity is the rule?

For the restructuring agreement to be approved, a quorum of at least one-third of all claims (with voting rights) and a twofold majority of the votes is required, comprising:

- more than two-thirds of the total votes cast; and
- more than half of the votes cast by unsubordinated creditors.

The criteria for approval are established by law.

In the case of assets disposal, can the creditors choose the broker/ investment bank?

Yes. If the restructuring plan provides for the disposal of assets, the terms and conditions of such disposal may be set out in the plan.

1.11 Are subordination agreements necessarily given full effect?

The subordination agreements do not necessarily take full effect, considering that the restructuring agreement may affect agreements entered into prior to the PER (ie determining their amendment).

Is it possible to discriminate between categories of creditors? Is an early bird fee/preferential treatment possible?

The different categories of creditors are set out in the law (see section below) and apply both to PER and to general insolvency proceedings. However, Portuguese law allows discrimination within the same category of creditors, provided that such discrimination has objective grounds.

Those creditors that, during the PER, have financed the debtor's activity by providing fresh money for its revitalisation shall be granted a general privilege over the movable assets of the insolvent's asset pool, ranking senior to the general privilege over the movable assets granted to employees.

Contrary to the insolvency proceedings, the PER does not recognise early bird fees.

1.12 How is exit managed?

The restructuring agreement is approved by the creditors, but a subsequent court sanction is mandatory.

The court shall not sanction the restructuring agreement if any procedural provision has been breached or the agreement contains unlawful provisions. Moreover, any creditor may ask the court to refuse to sanction the restructuring agreement based on the following grounds:

- if the creditor's position would be better ensured if no restructuring agreement had been approved; or

- if, under the terms of the agreement, any creditor is granted a more favourable position than the nominal value of its claim.

Nevertheless, there are few cases of non-approval by the court.

1.13 Who are the necessary parties?

The parties in these proceedings are the debtor, its creditors and the Judicial Provisional Administrator that will assist the debtor throughout the proceedings.

Is recourses possible? If so, who has standing?

In general, the judicial decisions may be appealed to the second instance court (*Tribunal da Relação*) and, in limited cases, to the Supreme Court of Justice (*Supremo Tribunal*).

The appeal of the court decision on the restructuring agreement is possible in the following cases:

- if the court sanctions the restructuring agreement, the creditors that voted against such agreement are entitled to lodge an appeal; and
- if the court has refused to sanction the restructuring agreement, both the debtor and the creditors that voted in favour of the agreement are entitled to lodge an appeal.

In any of the above described scenarios, the appeal should be lodged within 15 days from the court's decision.

2. POST-INSOLVENCY PROCEEDINGS

2.1 What is the objective of the proceedings?

A company is in a state of insolvency whenever it is unable to meet its obligations (cash-flow criteria) or whenever its assets are insufficient to satisfy its liabilities (balance sheet or assets criteria).

The objective of the insolvency proceedings is to ensure that the debtor's creditors are satisfied either (i) through the sharing of the proceeds resulting from the liquidation of the debtor's assets or (ii) through an insolvency plan to be approved by the creditors and that may include the debtor's restructuring. The debtor's restructuring is therefore seen as merely instrumental to the satisfaction of the creditors' interests.

2.2 Do all kinds of business entities qualify?

Any company in a state of insolvency is under the obligation to file for insolvency proceedings before the court within a 30-day period following the date it becomes aware (or should be aware) of its insolvency status. The director's lack of compliance with such provision significantly increases the possibility of being held personally liable.

The insolvency proceedings apply to all kinds of business entities and to individuals, with the exception of:

- public entities;
- insurance companies;
- credit institutions;
- financial companies;

- investment firms; and
- collective investment undertakings;

Is there a threshold related to indebtedness, turnover or asset value?
No threshold is defined by law or applied by courts.

Are involuntary proceedings a possibility? Is action available to all creditors? Under what conditions?
Third parties may also file for the debtor's insolvency. In this case, the debtor is granted a 10-day period to object to such insolvency petition.

Any creditor holding an overdue claim is able to instigate insolvency proceedings, irrespective of the amount of the claim or the percentage such amount represents in the overall amount of assets/liabilities of the debtor. However, the court shall only open insolvency proceedings if the debtor is in a state of insolvency (see section 2.1 above). The only exception to this rule is the claim resulting from shareholders' loans (*suprimentos*), which do not entitle the respective creditor (shareholder) to instigate insolvency proceedings.

2.3 What are the necessary approvals?

Only the board of directors' approval is required.

Apart from the debtor, acting through its directors, only the creditors and the entities which are liable under the law for the debtor's liabilities (and, in certain cases, the Public Prosecutor's Office – *Ministério Público*) are entitled to instigate insolvency proceedings.

2.4 Is it valid and binding to agree that such proceedings be a default/termination event?

The Portuguese Insolvency Act prevents the parties from setting forth the termination of a contract based on an event of insolvency of either party. Provisions of this nature will, as a general rule, be considered null and void.

2.5 What is the procedure?

The filing for insolvency shall be presented to the commercial court with jurisdiction over the location of the debtor's registered office or its centre of main interests through a petition in which the debtor or the creditor, depending on the party that has filed the same, describes the relevant facts (notably the debtor's state of insolvency and the creditor's claim) for the opening of insolvency proceedings.

Such request shall contain the identification of the debtor's directors and its five major creditors (other than the creditor that has filed the petition for insolvency proceedings, if applicable), and shall have attached a copy of the debtor's commercial certificate. If the petition is filed by the debtor, it may also include an insolvency plan. Regarding the remaining supporting documentation, see the next section.

If the court deems the petition for insolvency proceedings complete, it will decide on its admissibility. If, on the contrary, the court considers that the application is in any way incomplete, it will grant the applicant a period no longer than five days to cure the same.

If the insolvency proceedings have been instigated by the debtor and the court considers that there is clear evidence of a state of insolvency situation, the judge will issue a court order opening insolvency proceedings.

On the other hand, if the proceedings are filed by a creditor, the court will admit the petition provided it meets all the procedural requirements. The debtor will then be notified to accept the opening of insolvency proceedings or to file its objection within a 10-day period. Nevertheless, the court shall dismiss the petition if the debtor is subject to a PER.

If the debtor files its objection to the opening of insolvency proceedings, the judge shall schedule a court hearing to be held within the five following days. At the hearing, the judge will hear witnesses and review any other evidence admitted in order to rule on the insolvency. Burden of proof of solvency lies with the debtor.

The state of insolvency is effective from the date on which the court order opening insolvency proceedings is made. From such moment on, the proceedings, as well as notice and formalities of the same, will be made public by different means.

In addition, once the insolvency proceedings have been opened, the court will have to appoint an insolvency administrator (the Insolvency Administrator), who will manage the insolvent's asset pool and liquidate it in the event that the creditors do not decide against the liquidation.

The Insolvency Administrator shall be selected by the court from amongst those individuals publicly listed to perform such duties. The party that filed for the insolvency proceedings (either the debtor or a creditor) may suggest to the judge the name of an Insolvency Administrator.

2.6 Please provide information about voluntary filings

Are creditors invited to participate to the initial hearing? If so, how are they notified?

Creditors are not invited to participate in the initial hearing, irrespective of who had the procedural initiative.

Supporting documentation to be filed

The debtor shall attach to its request for insolvency filed before the court the following documents:

- a list of its creditors and the amount of their claims;
- a list of all pending judicial proceedings filed against it;
- a brief summary of its business activity for the prior three years, containing a reference to its establishments, offices or other business premises, if any;
- a brief summary of the current status of the company;
- a list of the company's directors, shareholders and anyone that can be held liable for the insolvency;
- a list of its assets;
- annual accounts for the prior three financial years;

- management reports and audit reports; and
- a list of its employees.

Main restructuring principles/are proposals to be term sheeted at entry?

In practice, the majority of insolvency proceedings result in a liquidation of the debtor's assets. In particular, after the entering into force of the law which has introduced the PER, few of the insolvencies end up in restructuring.

In the context of insolvency proceedings, the debtor's restructuring is achieved through an insolvency plan, which the creditors (see below for required majority) are called to vote on and approve.

The debtor may attach an insolvency plan to its petition for insolvency proceedings filed before the court. In any case, such plan can be filed at a later stage.

Apart from the debtor, the insolvency plan may also be submitted by:

- the insolvency administrator;
- anyone that can be held liable for the insolvency; or
- a creditor (or a group thereof) representing at least one-fifth of the unsubordinated claims.

The Portuguese Insolvency Act does not limit the contents of an insolvency plan. As a result, such plan may include a variety of measures, such as:

- write-offs;
- maturity extensions;
- payment deferrals; and
- debt-for-equity swaps.

Even though the contents of the insolvency plan are not specifically regulated, it must abide by the principle of equality of creditors without prejudice to different treatments based on objective criteria.

Unless the insolvency plan expressly states otherwise, the following shall mandatorily apply:

- the rights arising out of security *in rem* and privileges are not affected by the insolvency plan;
- the subordinated claims are fully written off; and
- the debtor's compliance with the insolvency plan shall release the debtor and its legal representatives from all of the debtor's remaining debt.

For the insolvency plan to be approved, a quorum of at least one-third of all claims with voting rights and a twofold majority of the votes is required, comprising:

- more than two-thirds of the total votes cast; and
- more than half of the votes cast by unsubordinated creditors.

The following shall not have voting rights:

- creditors whose claims are not modified by the insolvency plan; and
- subordinated creditors of a certain ranking if the insolvency plan provides for full waiver of the claims of the subordinated creditors

ranked below and does not attribute any economic value to the debtor and its shareholders (eg if the company does not continue as a going concern and the insolvency plan includes a reduction of the shareholders' shares to zero).

If yes, is an expert opinion or report on the feasibility of the contemplated plan needed?

In either of the cases referred to above, an expert opinion or report on the feasibility of the envisaged plan is not required.

How is the opening judgment rendered public?

The insolvency proceedings are made public by different means from the date on which the court order opening the insolvency is made. In fact, the order can be consulted on the official website (*www.portalcitius.pt*), before the court where the proceedings are pending and also in the Register of Companies (available online at *www.portaldaempresa.pt*).

When and how are creditors deemed aware of the proceedings?

The creditors are deemed aware of the proceedings through the publication of the court order opening the insolvency proceedings on the official website (*www.portalcitius.pt*). Additionally, the court shall send a notification letter to the debtor's five major creditors.

2.7 How are creditors' representatives chosen?

As referred to above, once the insolvency proceedings are held opened, the court will appoint an Insolvency Administrator, who will manage the insolvency pool under the supervision of the creditors' committee.

After being appointed, the Insolvency Administrator shall perform his duties using reasonable care, skill and diligence, and is under the obligation to act as a loyal representative of the insolvent in the best interests of its creditors.

In any case, the Insolvency Administrator can be replaced by the creditors' decision. The court can only refuse such replacement on the following grounds:

- the Insolvency Administrator appointed by the creditors has no ability or experience to perform his duties;
- the remuneration awarded by the creditors to the appointed Insolvency Administrator is clearly excessive; or
- if the creditors appoint an Insolvency Administrator whose name is not part of the public list of individuals available to perform such duties and such choice is not justified considering the size of the company, its area of activity or the complexity of the proceedings.

Under the terms of the Portuguese Insolvency Act, the Insolvency Administrator has the following role and powers:

- management of the insolvent's asset pool, including the decision to maintain or terminate ongoing contracts;
- to prepare a report to be presented to the creditors regarding:

  - the company's activity during the prior three years and its current situation;
  - the company's accounts and financial information; and
  - the viability of the company and the convenience and consequences of approving an insolvency plan;
- to represent the debtor in all judicial claims where the debtor is a party;
- to prepare a list of the creditors' claims;
- clawback powers – the Insolvency Administrator is entitled to, at its own initiative, unwind certain agreements (either those entered into within the hardening periods or those that are detrimental to the debtor – see section 2.13 below);
- to liquidate the insolvent's asset pool; and
- to prepare an insolvency plan.

Once the insolvency proceedings are held open, the court shall appoint the members of a creditors' committee, comprising between three and five creditors representing different ranking claims, presided over by the debtor's major creditor. This committee shall cooperate with the insolvency administrator and is responsible for supervising the performance of the duties of the latter.

2.8 Is there recourse against the opening judgment?

The decision of the judge to allow or refuse the opening of insolvency proceedings is subject to appeal to the second instance (appellate) court and, in very limited cases, to the Supreme Court of Justice.

The creditor that has filed the petition for insolvency proceedings is entitled to appeal against the order deciding not to open the debtor's insolvency proceedings. The debtor, the entities which are liable under law for the debtor's liabilities, any creditor and any shareholder of the debtor may appeal against the decision opening insolvency proceedings. If the debtor itself has requested its own insolvency proceedings, it may appeal against the decision that rejects the petition.

In the appeal against the court order, the creditor or the debtor, as appropriate, shall attempt to prove the existence or not of a certain claim or that the debtor is or is not in a state of insolvency.

The appeal must be filed within a 15-day period after the court order has been notified to the parties. The decision on the appeal will take approximately one to three months.

2.9 What are the roles and powers of committees?

Apart from the creditors' committee referred to above, the Portuguese Insolvency Act also provides for the existence of a creditors' general meeting, with the following roles and powers:

- to ask the insolvency administrator for all information deemed relevant;
- to revoke the decisions of the creditors' committee;
- to replace the creditors' committee;
- to request the replacement of the Insolvency Administrator;
- to analyse the report prepared by the Insolvency Administrator;

- to approve and amend the insolvency plan;
- to decide on the maintenance or closing-down of the establishments, offices and other debtor's business premises;
- to authorise the execution of the most relevant decisions regarding the company's activity during the course of the insolvency proceedings in those cases where a creditors' committee has not been appointed; and
- to decide on the management of the asset pool by the debtor itself.

As a general rule, the majority required in the creditors' general meeting is a simple majority of the votes of the unsubordinated creditors present or represented (irrespective of the ranking of the claims).

However, for the insolvency plan to be approved, a group of creditors representing one-third of all claims with voting rights must vote and a twofold majority of the votes is required, comprising:

- more than two-thirds of the total votes cast; and
- more than half of the votes cast by unsubordinated creditors.

Each creditor holds a number of votes in proportion to the amount of its claim.

Interest accruing on claims after the opening of the insolvency will be subordinated. The exception to this rule is interest on secured claims up to the amount of the proceeds resulting from the sale of the encumbered asset – such interest is also secured. Although there is no specific provision, interest accruing after the opening of insolvency proceedings are not usually taken into account in determining the number of votes.

Shareholders' loans (*suprimentos*) are deemed subordinated claims. Subordinated creditors are not allowed to vote at the creditors' general meeting except in respect of the approval of an insolvency plan (with the limitations referred to above).

2.10 What are the consequences of opening judgments for creditors?

Stay?

The opening of insolvency proceedings has several effects on pending and future proceedings, as follows:

- all pending enforcement proceedings filed against the debtor are stayed;
- any new enforcement proceedings filed against the debtor will be rejected by the court; and
- several pending judicial proceedings can be attached to the insolvency proceedings, namely:
  - judicial proceedings filed against the debtor or against a third party that may have a direct impact on the value of the insolvent's asset pool;
  - judicial proceedings of a financial nature filed by the debtor; and
  - insolvency proceedings of any of the debtor's subsidiaries or affiliates.

See also section 2.19 below.

Forbidden payments?

In general, creditors shall only be paid with the liquidation of the insolvent's asset pool, with the following exceptions:

- payments to counterparties in ongoing agreements which the Insolvency Administrator decided to continue performing; and
- debts resulting from the management of the insolvent's asset pool.

Creditors benefiting from security *in rem* are paid with the proceeds of the sale of the encumbered assets as they are sold.

Interests accruing during the period: paid at contractual payment dates? Deferred and paid after the plan is adopted? Capitalised? Is the rate necessarily the contract rate?

According to the law, interest accruing after the opening of insolvency proceedings is deemed a subordinated claim (except for those claims with security *in rem*, up to the amount of the proceeds resulting from the sale of the encumbered asset). The payment of such interest will only take place after the liquidation of the debtor's assets provided that there are still any funds available or, instead, as set out in the insolvency plan.

Interest shall not be capitalised.

The rate is necessarily the contractual rate, unless the insolvency plan sets forth otherwise.

Is the opening judgment a valid draw stop?

The general rule under the Portuguese Insolvency Act is that agreements with reciprocal obligations pending on both parties on the date of the opening of insolvency proceedings (such as credit facilities with undrawn commitments) shall be suspended until the Insolvency Administrator decides to terminate or maintain them (see section 2.19 below).

Nevertheless, a decision of the Insolvency Administrator deciding to continue to perform a credit facility with undrawn commitments and requesting further drawdowns would be considered clearly abusive as the insolvent's asset pool could not, in principle, meet the obligations deriving therefrom – such a decision by the Insolvency Administrator would be challengeable.

Necessity to file a proof of claim: are all creditors required to file a proof of claim?

All creditors shall attach to their claims sufficient proof of the existence of the same, such as invoices, credit notes or any document in which the debtor recognises the amount in debt.

Are secured creditors necessarily notified? Are there any time limits? Are non-resident creditors treated differently?

The five major creditors, the tax authorities and the social security are notified of the opening of insolvency proceedings, generally by means of registered letter sent by the court. In case one of the major five creditors is a non-resident entity, it shall be notified by way of registered letter. The remaining creditors are notified through a publication on the official website (*www.portalcitius.pt*) and through a public announcement posted in the debtor's registered office, establishments, offices or business premises, if any, as well as in the court.

The known creditors residing in another member state of the European Union shall be notified as set out in EC Regulation No. 1346/2000.

The judge establishes a period of up to 30 days for the creditors to file their claims.

What are the consequences if a creditor is time-barred? Is the debtor discharged?

After the time limit granted for submitting the claims has elapsed, the creditors are granted a last opportunity to make their claims, within a specific procedure named 'subsequent claim'. Claims shall be filed within the six months after the *res judicata* of the court's decision opening the insolvency proceedings.

The debtor is not automatically discharged if the creditors do not meet the time limits set forth by law to make their claims. However, these creditors cannot be paid within the insolvency proceedings.

Does such proceedings entail any limitation on the enforcement of contractually created security?

After the opening judgment, no judicial or out-of-court civil enforcement against the debtor may be initiated and any action in course shall be stayed as of the date of the opening judgment. Therefore, the enforcement of security and payment to the secured creditors will be made within the insolvency proceedings.

There are no stays on enforcement during insolvency proceedings (eg prohibition to sell the assets required for the maintenance of the debtor's operation for a certain time frame).

However, it must be noted that, at the first creditors' general meeting, the creditors may either decide to liquidate the debtor's assets (and consequently sell the secured assets) or decide on the preparation of an insolvency plan to be approved on a subsequent creditors' general meeting. Such insolvency plan may include limits on the enforcement and sale of any secured assets.

2.11 What is the duration of the restructuring process?

There is no statutory deadline for the restructuring process.

As mentioned above, the creditors can approve an insolvency plan which may (i) contain the measures to be carried out for the restructuring of the debtor and/or (ii) lay down specific rules for the payment of creditors' claims through the liquidation of the insolvent's asset pool.

2.12 How do creditors vote?

The insolvency plan can be submitted to the creditors, *inter alia*, by the debtor, by the Insolvency Administrator or by any creditor (by itself or as a group) representing at least one-fifth of the unsubordinated claims. The insolvency plan shall be approved at the creditors' meeting or, instead, through a written vote within a period not exceeding 10 days from the date of submission.

The court cannot determine the number of classes of claims based on case by case criteria. All claims are classified according to specific criteria set out by law, as follows:

- Secured and preferential claims (*créditos garantidos e privilegiados*): those that benefit from a security *in rem* arrangement on specific assets of the debtor (these have preference over specific assets of the debtor) and those which hold a general legal preference in respect of the assets of the debtor (eg social security contributions or employment-related claims).
- Subordinated claims:
  - claims where subordination has been agreed;
  - interest of any kind to the extent that it is unsecured;
  - claims held by related parties (ie directors or shareholders holding, directly or indirectly, a share interest in the debtor in excess of certain thresholds, companies of the same group as the debtor or having dominant influence, etc)
  - claims resulting from a clawback by the Insolvency Administrator against bad faith counterparties; and
  - shareholders' loans (*suprimentos*).
- Ordinary claims: all claims that are neither secured/preferential nor subordinated.

The shareholders are not a specific class of creditors.

2.13 What are the rules on clawback/voidability?

In general terms, all prejudicial actions of the debtor carried out within two years preceding the opening of insolvency proceedings may be subject to clawback.

As an exception to the rule of evidence, transactions with related parties within the two-year period preceding the opening of insolvency proceedings only require evidence of prejudice. In this case, bad faith is presumed (rebuttable presumption).

However, the following transactions from companies are subject to clawback regardless of any other circumstances:

Specific transaction	Hardening period – ie prior to the date of the beginning of the insolvency proceedings (PBIP)	Bad faith	Prejudice
Acts of the debtor without consideration, with the exception of donations in accordance with social practice	Within 2 years PBIP	Regardless	Regardless
(i) New securities in respect of pre-existing obligations or of others in lieu of pre-existing obligations (ii) Personal guarantees with no actual interest for the debtor (iii) Prepayment of liabilities in unusual terms of legal transactions and which the creditor could not claim (iv) Prepayment of liabilities falling otherwise due after the opening of insolvency proceedings	Within 6 months PBIP	Regardless	Regardless
	From 6 months to 2 years PBIP	Required	Presumed (NRB)
New security *in rem*	Within 60 days PBIP	Regardless	Regardless
	From 60 days to 2 years PBIP	Required	Presumed (NRB)
Acts of the debtor for consideration where its obligations significantly exceed those of the counterparty	Within 1 year PBIP	Regardless	Regardless
	From 1 to 2 years PBIP	Required	Presumed (NRB)
Repayment of shareholders loans	Within 1 year PBIP	Regardless	Regardless
	From 1 to 2 years PBIP	Required	Presumed (NRB)

2.14 What are the rules on set-off/netting?

The set-off/netting of claims by the creditors is only admissible in limited situations expressly provided for by law. In general terms, for a creditor to be entitled to set off its credit over the insolvent's asset pool, one of the requirements below must be met:

- legal set-off requirements must have been fulfilled prior to the declaration of the insolvency; or
- the creditor's claim shall be the first to have met the general set-off requirements, ie before the debtor's claim has fulfilled those legal requirements.

In any case, subordinated creditors and those which have acquired the claim after the opening of the insolvency proceedings cannot be set off.

2.15 How is exit managed?

Simple term-out; is a majority needed?

There is no specific deadline for the termination of insolvency proceedings. Insolvency proceedings may normally end with the liquidation of the insolvent's asset pool or, if applicable, the judicial sanction of the insolvency plan.

Is it possible to cram down dissenters?

The insolvency plan approved by the referred twofold majority of the creditors and sanctioned by the court crams down dissenters.

The court shall not approve the restructuring agreement if any procedural provision has been breached or the agreement contains unlawful provisions. Moreover, any creditor may ask the court to refuse approval of a restructuring agreement based on the following grounds:

- if the creditor's position would be better ensured if no insolvency plan had been approved; or
- if, under the terms of the insolvency plan, any creditor is granted a more favourable position than the nominal value of its claim.

Term out + asset disposal programme: should the programme be completed before the adoption of the plan? Can it be postponed and be part of the plan? Will sanctions be imposed if not completed? Is it possible for creditors to monitor the process?

The insolvency plan may also aim at the ordered liquidation of the insolvent's asset pool. As a result, if agreed by the required majority of creditors, it is possible to include an asset disposal programme and all its relevant features, including the conducting of the disposal programme, within an insolvency plan.

The insolvency plan may allow the insolvency administrator to monitor the compliance thereof. In such case, creditors are entitled to be updated annually by the insolvency administrator on the compliance of the insolvency plan and to ask the insolvency administrator for further information on the compliance.

In the case of debt conversion(s), what approvals are necessary? Is it possible to force shareholders' consent?

As a general rule, the approval of the affected creditor is required by law for debt conversions. However, the approval shall not be required if some prerequisites set forth in the law are met that ensure the marketability of the shares.

The share capital increase of the debtor may be part of the insolvency plan and may waive existing shareholders' pre-emption rights provided that:

- the share capital is previously reduced to zero; or
- this share capital increase does not entail the devaluation of the shareholdings held by the existing shareholders.

Sale of the business as a going concern to an entrepreneur

The Portuguese Insolvency Act provides for the possibility of selling the business as a going concern to an entrepreneur. The business as a going concern will be sold as a whole, unless no satisfactory proposal of purchase is presented or the liquidation or sale of separated parts of the business is more satisfactory.

Do creditors have the right to make their own proposal? Is credit-bidding possible?

Any person, including any creditor, is entitled to present an offer. Credit-bidding is possible if the creditor holds a security *in rem* over the asset being sold. The creditor can credit-bid up to the amount of its claim provided that there are no higher ranked secured creditors.

Automatic release/survival of existing pledges and charges

There is an automatic release of all existing pledges and charges over the assets sold within the proceedings. The secured creditors shall be paid by the proceeds of the sale.

2.16 Are 'prepackaged' plans, arrangements or agreements permissible?

According to the Portuguese Insolvency Act, prepackaged plans, arrangements or agreements are not permissible (contrary to what is provided for in restructuring proceedings). The debtor may nonetheless file an insolvency plan proposal together with its filing for insolvency.

2.17 Is a public authority involved?

The Public Prosecutor's Office (*Ministério Público*) is the only public authority that can be involved in insolvency proceedings. The Public Prosecutor's Office, within its general powers of representation of the state, may represent Portuguese public entities, notably public creditors, in such proceedings.

The Public Prosecutor's Office may also be involved in the classification (characterisation) of the insolvency as at-fault and the assessment of the Insolvency Administrator accounts, and can take part in creditors' general meetings.

The Public Prosecution Service plays mainly a supervisory role and is therefore not entitled to rule on the debtor's eligibility to the court protection, nor must it approve/opine upon the feasibility/sustainability of the plan.

2.18 What is the treatment of claims arising after filing/admission?

Such claims, namely those resulting from the management of the insolvent's asset pool, are pre-deductible.

2.19 Are there ongoing contracts?

The Portuguese Insolvency Act sets out a general principle according to which the performance of any ongoing contract (that has not yet been fulfilled by either of the parties) is suspended until the Insolvency Administrator decides that it will be performed or, instead, chooses to refuse its performance. The Insolvency Administrator is prevented from choosing the performance of an agreement whenever it is highly unlikely that the insolvent's asset pool will be able to fully comply with the obligations under the agreement.

The counterparty is entitled to grant the Insolvency Administrator a reasonable deadline to announce its option. If the Insolvency Administrator does not meet such deadline, refusal is assumed.

A decision of the Insolvency Administrator deciding to continue to perform a credit facility with undrawn commitments and requesting further draw downs would be considered clearly abusive as the insolvent's asset pool could not, in principle, comply with the obligations deriving therefrom – such a decision by the Insolvency Administrator would be challengeable.

2.20 Are consolidated proceedings for members of a corporate family/group possible?

According to the law, the Insolvency Administrator may request that the judicial proceedings regarding the insolvency of members of a corporate family/group be ruled together.

What are the consequences with regard to pooling of assets and liabilities? Do creditors have a right to challenge such pooling?

The pooling of assets and liabilities of two or more related debtors into a single big pool to pay creditors is not allowed.

2.21 What are the charges, fees and other costs?

The insolvency proceedings are subject to the payment of court fees, namely an initial court fee, which shall be paid when the petition for insolvency proceedings is filed, and a subsequent fee due at the end of the proceedings.

The court fees regulation determines the obligation of the payment of the court fees due if the request for insolvency is withdrawn or if such request is rejected by the court, such payment to be made by the applicant.

In all other cases, it is the insolvent's asset pool that is held liable for the payment of the court fees. Furthermore, the insolvent's asset pool is also responsible for the payment of the Insolvency Administrator's fees.

3. LIABILITY ISSUES

3.1 What is the liability of managers/directors *vis-à-vis* creditors?

Can management/directors (*de jure* or shadow) be held personally liable? Are there any prerequisites?

In general terms, the debtor's managers/directors (*de jure* or shadow) are liable before the creditors for damages caused by its acts or omissions that caused or aggravated the insolvency situation and/or that reduced the value of the debtor's assets, frustrating payment to the creditors.

The duties on which managers/directors' liability is grounded are deemed to have been breached in the following circumstances:

- destruction, damage, concealment of all or of a considerable part of the debtor's assets;
- disposal of the debtor's assets for the managers/directors own benefit or for the benefit of third parties;
- reduction of the debtor's profits, or cause or increase its losses, leading to detrimental agreements entered into by the debtor for the managers/ directors' own benefit or for the benefit of people specially related to them;
- using the debtor's credit or its assets for purposes contrary to its interests, for the managers/directors' own benefit or for the benefit of third parties, namely in order to favour another company in which the managers/directors have an direct or indirect interest;
- mismanagement, being aware that it would lead to the debtor's insolvency;
- breach of the obligation to keep the debtor's accounts organised; or
- breach of the obligation to file the petition for insolvency proceedings within 30 days from the date it becomes aware of the debtor's state of insolvency.

Who has standing to sue? Can creditors force the court agent to introduce an action? How?

Both the Insolvency Administrator and creditors are entitled to bring an action against the managers/directors.

The creditors may request the Insolvency Administrator to bring an action against the debtor's managers/directors.

In particular, the debtor's managers/directors can be held responsible through three different routes.

*Specific proceedings aimed at classifying the insolvency as at-fault (*qualificação da insolvência*)*

These specific proceedings takes place within the insolvency proceedings, and are intended to determine if the insolvency is no-fault or, instead, at-fault.

The insolvency situation shall be deemed as at-fault if the debtor's managers/directors committed any act with malicious intent or wilful misconduct that caused or aggravated the debtor's insolvency situation.

According the Portuguese Insolvency Act, managers/directors have acted with wilful misconduct in the following situations:

- when they have destroyed, damaged, rendered useless, hidden or got rid of the debtor's patrimony, either in its entirety or in a considerable part;
- when they have created or artificially aggravated liabilities or losses, or reduced profits, leading the debtor to enter into loss-making

transactions, to its own benefit or to the benefit of those with whom it has a special relationship with;
- when they have purchased goods on credit, in order to sell them or use them as payment at a price considerably lower than current prices, before the obligation is satisfied;
- when they have used the debtor's assets for their personal benefit or for the benefit of third parties;
- when they have exercised, under the corporate veil, an activity for personal gain or for third parties gain, damaging the company;
- when they used the debtor's credit or assets in a way contrary to its interests, to their own benefit or to the benefit of third parties, namely in order to favour another company in which they have a direct or indirect interest;
- when they have pursued, in their own interest or in the interest of third parties, a loss-making operation while being aware or with the obligation to be aware that such operation would most likely lead to an insolvency situation;
- when they have failed to substantially comply with the obligation to keep the company's accounts, kept altered books or a dual accounting system, or committed any irregularity in respect of the assessment of the debtor's assets and liabilities and financial position; or
- when they have repeatedly failed to comply with their duties to report and to collaborate until the date of the report drawn up by the Insolvency Administrator.

In addition, the existence of malicious intent will be presumed, in the absence of evidence to the contrary, when the managers/directors:
- have breached the duty to request the debtor's insolvency; or
- have breached the duty to prepare annual accounts, within the legal time limit, and to submit them to audit or deposit them with the Register of Companies.

Pursuant to the Portuguese Insolvency Act, the court's decision to classify the insolvency as tortious shall order the debtor's managers/directors (*de jure* or shadow), during the three years prior to the date of the opening of insolvency proceedings, to pay to the debtor's creditors the amount of its claims that they have not received within the liquidation of the debtor's assets (ie the total amount or only a part of such claims). All the managers/directors have joint and several liability.

'Collective' civil action

In case of breach of the duties above referred, during the insolvency proceedings the Insolvency Administrator is entitled to bring an action against the debtor's managers/directors on behalf of the creditors, asking for a compensation for the damages caused by the decrease of the insolvent's asset pool (either before or after the opening of insolvency proceedings). This action can be filed by the Insolvency Administrator at its own initiative or by creditors' request, being attached to the insolvency proceedings.

Criminal judicial procedure

If there is any evidence of a crime committed by the debtor's managers/ directs, the court shall inform the Public Prosecutor's Office, so that an investigation is opened.

The criminal offences that may arise from the debtor's managers/directors are:

- fraudulent insolvency;
- concealment of assets;
- negligent insolvency; or
- granting advantages to certain creditors.

These criminal offences are punishable with imprisonment or a fine, under the terms of the Portuguese Criminal Code.

Can creditors join in the court agent's action? Under what conditions?

In general terms, the creditors cannot join in the action filed by the Insolvency Administrator. However, any creditor having specific losses may be entitled to file a separate claim. In this case, the creditor needs to claim and provide evidence of its specific loss.

3.2 What is the liability of the lender?

The Portuguese Insolvency Act has no specific provision regarding the liability of a lender or akin, nor are we aware of any case law decision where such matter is discussed.

Romania

Kinstellar Bogdan Bibicu

1. WHAT COURT-MONITORED RESTRUCTURING PRE-INSOLVENCY PROCEEDINGS OR SCHEMES HAVE BEEN DEVISED BY THE LAW OF YOUR COUNTRY TO LIMIT VALUE DESTRUCTION FOR FAILING BUSINESS ENTITIES?

Both pre-insolvency and insolvency proceedings are currently regulated by Law No. 85 from 25 June 2014 regarding proceedings for the prevention of insolvency and insolvency (the Insolvency Code).

The Insolvency Code recognises the procedure of moratorium (*concordat preventiv*), which basically represents a restructuring agreement concluded as part of a pre-insolvency proceedings. However, it cannot be deemed court-monitored to a full extent, as court intervention is limited to certain circumstances or scenarios.

The Insolvency Code also regulates the *ad hoc* mandate (*mandatul ad-hoc*), which consists in the appointment of an *ad hoc* proxy having the objective to reach within 90 days, on behalf of the debtor, an agreement between the latter and one or more of its creditors with a view to safeguarding the debtor, overcoming its financial difficulties, preserving its employees and satisfying the receivables against it. So far the *ad hoc* mandate has had very little (if any) applicability in practice (we are not aware of any case law related to the implementation of the *ad hoc* mandate regarding a debtor in financial difficulties). In addition, it does not represent court-monitored restructuring proceedings *per se* (since it strictly involves a specific representation, the *ad hoc* proxy being empowered only to negotiate, on behalf of the debtor, with its creditors, just as the debtor would do absent the *ad hoc* proxy). Therefore, the focus of this chapter is only on the moratorium procedure.

1.1 What is the objective of the proceedings?

The objective of moratorium proceedings is to readjust and satisfy a debtor's receivables as an expression of its and its creditors' joint efforts to overcome the financial difficulties the debtor experiences.

1.2 Do all kinds of businesses entities qualify?

All kinds of businesses qualify for the moratorium proceedings regulated by the Insolvency Code. Thus, most debtors in financial difficulty may use the moratorium procedure, the exceptions being:

- debtors who have benefited from a moratorium that failed during the last three years;

- if the respective debtors or their shareholders or directors were sentenced for the perpetration of certain criminal offences within the last five years; and
- if the directors or members of the supervising/managing bodies of the debtor were personally held liable on the account of the debtor's liabilities).

A 'debtor in financial difficulty' is considered a debtor which, although it performs or is capable of performing its outstanding obligations, has a low liquidity ratio on a short-term basis and/or a high indebtedness level on a long-term basis that may impact the performance of its contractual duties by reference to either the resources generated from the operational activity or the resources raised through its financial activity.

There is no threshold related to indebtedness, turnover or asset value.

When submitting a request for opening of the moratorium procedure, a receiver (*administrator concordatar*) must be proposed by the debtor from amongst the insolvency practitioners authorised according to the law. The receiver is appointed by the bankruptcy–global change judge and is responsible, together with the debtor, for drafting the creditors' list and the moratorium offer.

1.3 What are the necessary approvals?

No special approval is required by the Insolvency Code before the initiation of the moratorium procedure. However, given that the moratorium is an agreement concluded between the debtor and its creditors, the latter usually require in practice that the debtor pass a resolution approving the terms of the moratorium (such as rescheduling payments).

No parties other than the debtors themselves (acting through their legal or conventional representatives) are allowed to initiate the moratorium procedure.

1.4 What is the procedure?

Must a petition be filed? Must it be *ex parte*? Are there any other procedural documents? Must supporting documentation be filed with the application?

The debtor must file a request for opening the moratorium procedure with the competent court. The parties are subpoenaed within 48 hours thereafter.

There are no specific documents required by the Insolvency Code to accompany the request for opening the moratorium procedure.

Are creditors invited to participate? If so, how are they notified? What influence do they have, if any?

The receiver is obliged to notify creditors via registered post or other means of fast communication which ensure confirmation of receipt. The above notification will include the moratorium offer.

Publicity/confidentiality? Access to petition + documents? How? When?

For opposability purposes, the moratorium offer will be filed with the competent court, where it will be registered in a special register held by that court. The fact that it has been registered in the respective register is also mentioned in the register where the debtor is registered (such as the Commercial Register).

In order for creditors to vote on the moratorium, the debtor may organise one or more meetings to negotiate with its creditors, in the presence of the receiver. Such meetings may also be initiated by creditors or the shareholders of the debtor who have control over the latter.

In extraordinary circumstances, the receiver is entitled to summon a general assembly of all creditors of the debtor.

As a rule, creditors vote by correspondence with respect to the moratorium and their vote must be communicated to the debtor within a maximum of 60 days from the date they received the moratorium offer.

1.5 Is there recourse against the opening judgment?

All rulings pronounced by the competent courts in relation to moratorium proceedings (including opening judgments) are executory and may be appealed within seven days from the moment they are pronounced or communicated (as the case may be).

Any interested person has legal standing to appeal the opening judgment.

As, in practice, there have not been many cases in which the moratorium procedure has been used, it is very hard to assess a timeline for the issuing of judgments.

1.6 What are the substantive tests/definitions?

The 'debtor in financial difficulty' is defined in section 1.2 above, according to which a mixed test (ie an indebtedness test as well as a liquidity test) should be borne in mind when assessing whether a debtor may be considered in financial difficulty.

1.7 What is the role of a court-appointed agent?

The role and powers of receivers are as follows:

- drafting of the creditors' list;
- preparing, together with the debtor, the moratorium offer (including the recovery plan);
- acting in order to amicably solve any dispute between the debtor and its creditors or among creditors;
- requesting the bankruptcy judge to sanction the moratorium;
- supervising the fulfilment by the debtor of its obligations assumed in the moratorium and informing the creditors of the improper fulfilment or non-fulfilment of such obligations;
- drafting and sending to the assembly of creditors which are parties to the moratorium monthly or quarterly reports regarding the activity of the debtor;

- summoning the assembly of the creditors which are parties to the moratorium;
- requesting the court the closing of the moratorium proceedings; and
- any other powers established by the law or conferred by the bankruptcy judge.

1.8 What protection is there from creditors?

Generally, there are two phases provided by the Insolvency Code with respect to the implementation of the moratorium.

A. Approval of the moratorium (*aprobarea concordatului*)

The moratorium is deemed approved following a vote by creditors representing at least 75 per cent of the aggregate value of the accepted and undisputed receivables.

B. Sanction of the moratorium (*omologarea concordatului*)

The moratorium is sanctioned by the bankruptcy judge if:

- the moratorium may be deemed approved by creditors (as detailed under section 1.8(A) above); and
- the value of the disputed and/or challenged receivables does not exceed 25 per cent of the aggregate value of the receivables against the debtor.

From the date the sanctioned moratorium is communicated to creditors, all enforcement proceedings against the debtor initiated by the creditors who have signed the moratorium are suspended. Also, the lapse of the limitation period related to creditors' right to start enforcement against the debtor is suspended as well.

The accruing of interest, penalties or other expenses related to receivables is not suspended with respect to the creditors signing the moratorium unless the latter express in the moratorium their written consent for the suspension.

In addition, upon request from the receiver, the bankruptcy judge may decide on the postponement, for a maximum 18 month period, of the maturity of the receivables held by the creditors who did not sign the moratorium, subject to the debtor granting guarantees in this regard. During such period, no interest, penalties or expenses will accrue with respect to such receivables.

Throughout the period of the sanctioned moratorium, no insolvency procedure may be initiated against the debtor.

1.9 What is the usual duration of the restructuring process?

According to the Insolvency Code, the period during which negotiations may take place with respect to the moratorium proposed by the debtor cannot exceed 60 calendar days.

The maximum restructuring term established for the satisfaction of the receivables included in the moratorium is 24 months from the date the moratorium was sanctioned, with the possibility of prolongation for a maximum of 12 months. During the first year, a minimum 20 per cent of the value of the receivables set forth in the moratorium must be repaid by the debtor.

1.10 Who prepares the restructuring agreement and what are the available tools?

The moratorium is prepared by the receiver and the debtor and communicated to creditors as detailed above.

As mentioned above, the moratorium is deemed approved following a vote by creditors representing at least 75 per cent of the aggregate value of the accepted and undisputed receivables (irrespective of the majority provided in the finance documents).

There is no limitation in the Insolvency Code as to the means by which asset disposal should be achieved as part of the moratorium proceedings. It all depends on the result of the negotiations between the debtor and its creditors.

1.11 Are subordination agreements necessarily given full effect?

Romanian law does not recognise the concept of subordination agreements as these are typically regulated in other jurisdictions. Therefore, such type of contractual arrangements is unlikely to be given full effects by Romanian court if they were to assess them on merits/substance.

1.12 How is exit managed?

As mentioned above, the moratorium is sanctioned by the bankruptcy judge if (i) the moratorium is approved by creditors and (ii) the value of the disputed and/or challenged receivables does not exceed 25 per cent of the aggregate value of the receivables against the debtor.

The request for sanctioning the moratorium may be rejected by the bankruptcy judge only for legality grounds.

1.13 Who are the necessary parties?

The parties to the moratorium proceedings are the competent courts, the receiver, the debtor and the creditors approving the moratorium.

In addition to our answer to section 1.5 above, creditors that voted against the approval of the moratorium may file a request for invalidation within 15 days from the date the moratorium was sanctioned by the bankruptcy judge. If the grounds for invalidation trigger the absolute nullity of the moratorium, the request for invalidation is time-barred to within six months from the date the moratorium is sanctioned. The bankruptcy judge may suspend the moratorium if the aforementioned creditors so request.

If a material breach by the debtor of its obligations assumed in the moratorium is ascertained, the assembly of the creditors who signed the moratorium or, separately, the creditor holding more than 50 per cent of the accepted and undisputed receivables may decide to file a claim for the termination of the moratorium. Should such claim for termination be decided to be filed, the moratorium proceedings are automatically suspended.

With respect to delays to appeal, please see our answer under section 1.5 above.

2. POST-INSOLVENCY PROCEEDINGS

2.1 What is the objective of the proceedings?

The purpose of insolvency proceedings is to implement a collective procedure (ie a procedure in which creditors participate together in the pursuit and recovery of their receivables) ensuring, if and when possible, the debtor's chance for recover.

2.2 Do all kinds of business entities qualify?

All kinds of businesses qualify for the insolvency proceedings regulated by the Insolvency Code.

A minimum threshold related to indebtedness must be observed when filing for insolvency. Thus, any request for opening the insolvency proceedings must refer to a receivable having a minimum value of RON 40,000 (approx. EUR 9,000).

Creditors are allowed to file for insolvency with respect to receivables they hold against their debtors, subject to the following conditions:

- the minimum threshold referred to above is observed;
- the creditors' receivables are certain and determined, and have been due for more than 60 days; and
- the debtor's insolvency is presumed, ie the debtor has not paid its debts to the creditors for more than 60 days from the due date.

Creditors' request for opening the insolvency proceedings must contain the following:

- the amount and source of its receivable;
- (if relevant) any lien or other preferential rights the creditor enjoys, either based on the law or created by the debtor in its favour;
- any interim measures regarding the debtor's assets; and
- a statement by which the creditor manifests its intention to participate in the reorganisation of the debtor and the means contemplated in this regard.

The creditor must attach supporting documents regarding its receivable and the documents creating the privileges, liens and preferential rights it enjoys with respect to the debtor' assets.

All requests for opening insolvency proceedings filed by creditors with respect to the same debtor are joined in the same file.

2.3 What are the necessary approvals?

As a rule, there is no need for shareholder or board approval before the debtor files for insolvency. However, if the debtor requests the application for the simplified insolvency procedure (ie to enter directly into bankruptcy, with no prior reorganisation phase), the resolution of the general meeting of shareholders approving the simplified procedure must be attached to the insolvency proceedings opening request.

The Insolvency Code sets forth that debtors in a state of insolvency are obliged to file for opening the insolvency proceedings within 30 days from the date when the insolvency state occurred. If, at the expiry of the above 30 day term, the debtor is engaged in good faith in non-judicial negotiations for the restructuring of its debts, it is obliged to file for the opening of insolvency proceedings within five days from the moment the respective negotiations failed.

The Insolvency Code also states that even debtors in an imminent state of insolvency are allowed to file for the opening of insolvency proceedings. The insolvency is deemed imminent when it is proved that the debtor will not be able to pay its due debts at maturity with the funds available at that time.

The debtor's request must be signed by the persons having representation powers according to its constitutive act or statute.

As mentioned under section 2.2 above, creditors are also entitled to file for insolvency. Further, the Financial Supervisory Authority and the National Bank of Romania are entitled to file requests for the opening of insolvency proceedings with respect to entities regulated and supervised by them, subject to the conditions set forth in the special regulations regarding the insolvency of such entities.

2.4 Is it valid and binding to agree that such proceedings be a default/termination event?

The underlying principle governing the insolvency procedure is that ongoing agreements are deemed to be maintained, unless the judicial receiver cancels them for not being fully or at least substantially performed by its parties, with a view to maximising the value of the debtor's patrimony. The judicial receiver's right of cancellation may be exercised within three months from the date the insolvency proceedings are opened.

Thus, the Insolvency Codes stipulates that any contractual clauses allowing or imposing the termination of ongoing agreements, disenfranchisements from the benefit of term or the acceleration/early repayment of outstanding obligations as an effect of the opening of insolvency proceedings are void.

Qualified financial agreements (such as agreements regarding operations with derivative instruments, repo and reverse repo agreements) and bilateral set-off operations based on bilateral netting agreements (such as ISDA master agreement) are exempted from the above principle.

2.5 What is the procedure?

Given that the formalism-related queries concerning pre-insolvency proceedings under section 1.4 above are practically identical to the ones listed under sections 2.6 and 2.7 below, I will address the most important aspects related to the formalism of insolvency proceedings by answering to the respective questions.

2.6 Please provide information about voluntary filings

Are creditors invited to participate to the initial hearing? If so, how are they notified?

If the request for opening the insolvency proceedings is filed by the debtor, the bankruptcy judge rules on such request urgently, within 10 days from filing, with no parties (eg creditors) being subpoenaed.

If the debtor's request observes the requirements established by the law, the bankruptcy judge decides to open the insolvency proceedings and rules that the judicial receiver must serve notices to creditors no later than 10 days before the deadline for filing the requests for admission of receivables. In the event that, within 10 days from receipt of notification, certain creditors oppose the opening of the insolvency proceedings, the bankruptcy judge will summon a meeting within five days thereafter to which the judicial receiver, the debtor and the creditors opposing the opening of the insolvency procedure are subpoenaed. The creditors' opposition may be either sustained (in which case the decision opening the insolvency proceedings is revoked) or overruled (in which case the insolvency proceedings resume).

Supporting documentation to be filed

The debtor's request for opening the insolvency proceedings must be accompanied by the following documents:

- the latest annual financial statements, certified by a director and auditor and the balance sheet for the previous month;
- a complete list of all its assets (including bank accounts);
- a list and details of all its creditors, the amounts owed to them and any liens or preferential rights;
- a list of all payments and transfers made by the debtor within the last six months;
- a profit and loss account related to the preceding year;
- if relevant, a list of the members of the economic interest group (*grup de interes economic*), or the associates with unlimited liability for partnerships (*societate in nume colectiv*) or limited partnerships (*societate in comandita*);
- a declaration whereby the debtor expresses its intention to apply for the simplified insolvency procedure of reorganisation based on a plan, by other restructuring its activity of winding-up its assets;
- a brief description of the means considered for reorganising its activity;
- an affidavit (notarised or certified by a lawyer) or a certificate issued by the relevant registry (such as the Commercial Registry) stating whether, within the last five years prior to the opening of the insolvency proceedings, the debtor was subject to reorganisation procedure provided by the Insolvency Code;
- an affidavit (notarised or certified by a lawyer) evidencing that the debtor or its directors, managers and/or associates/shareholders have not been sentenced for the perpetration of certain criminal offences (such

as patrimonial offences, corruption or forgery) within the last five years prior to the opening of the insolvency proceedings;
- if relevant, a certificate of admission to trading on a regulated market;
- if relevant, a declaration evidencing that the debtor is a member of a group of companies;
- proof of the debtor's sole registration code; and
- proof that the competent fiscal authorities have been notified with respect to the insolvency proceedings.

Main restructuring principles/are proposals to be term sheeted at entry? If so, is an expert opinion or report on the feasibility of the contemplated plan needed?

As mentioned above, one of the documents that the debtor must attach to its request for opening the insolvency proceedings is a brief description of the means considered for reorganising its activity. The Insolvency Code does not require an extended plan/term sheet or an expert opinion/report to be submitted at this stage.

A detailed reorganisation plan may be submitted at a later stage (ie after the publication of the final receivables table) by the debtor, the judicial receiver or one or more creditors together holding at least 20 per cent of the aggregate value of receivables evidenced in the final receivables table.

How is the opening judgment rendered public?

The judicial receiver serves notice of the opening of insolvency proceedings to all creditors mentioned in the list filed by the debtor, as well as the relevant registry where the debtor is registered (eg the Commercial Registry). The above notification is published in a widely distributed newspaper and in the Insolvency Proceedings Bulletin (IPB).

All acts and correspondence issued by the debtor and/or the judicial receiver must mandatorily comprise, with visible characters, the wording *'in insolventa'*, *'in insolvency'* or *'en procedure collective'*.

Also, if the debtor holds or manages one or more internet web pages, its management must publish on such pages, within 24 hours from the date the decision regarding the opening of insolvency proceedings is communicated to the debtor, all information related to the new status of the debtor, as well as the number and date of the insolvency ruling and the court having issued it.

2.7 How are creditors' representatives chosen?

During insolvency proceedings, creditors are represented by two organisational structures: the creditors' meeting and the creditors' committee, each holding a distinct set of prerogatives when appointed, in accordance with provisions of the Insolvency Code.

The creditors' meeting will include all known creditors which have filed a documented request for registration of their receivables against the debtor with the judicial receiver and were approved registration of their receivables by the judicial receiver, either in full or in part, in the preliminary table of receivables, based on the justifying documentation submitted to this effect and the verification process carried out by the judicial receiver.

The designation and structure of the creditors' committee is optional, depending on the decision of the bankruptcy judge and the total number of creditors. The bankruptcy judge may appoint three or five creditors from creditors with voting rights which hold either secured receivables or budgetary and unsecured receivables of the highest value. If the number of creditors is low, the judge may consider it unnecessary to appoint a creditors' committee. In this particular case, the attributions of the creditors' committee will be exercised by the creditors' meeting. Based on the proposal of the creditors, the bankruptcy judge also appoints the president of the creditors' committee.

The creditors, rather than the judicial receiver, can directly influence the choice of creditors' representatives. During the first meeting, the creditors' meeting has the right to designate a new committee of creditors, which will replace the previous one appointed by the bankruptcy judge. The newly approved committee will be formed by three or five creditors, selected from the first 20 creditors with voting rights, based on the highest voting percentage corresponding to the present debts. If the majority is not secured, the previous committee designated by the bankruptcy judge will be maintained.

For further details on the role and powers of the creditors' committee, see section 2.9 below.

2.8 Is there recourse against the opening judgment?

An opening judgment of insolvency proceedings against the debtor is subject to appeal upon different grounds and under different conditions, depending on the person that requested the opening of insolvency proceedings.

If such request was made by the debtor, the creditor(s) will have standing to file an opposition, within a period of 10 days from the date when the creditor(s) received the notification from the judicial receiver regarding the opening of insolvency proceedings.

If a creditor has filed such request, the debtor has standing to challenge the request of the creditor within 10 days from the date of receipt of the creditor's request for the opening of insolvency proceedings.

In addition, any person holding a legitimate interest (eg shareholders who opposed the decision of the debtor to open insolvency proceedings) may appeal the opening judgment or can submit intervention requests in their own interest within the case already pending.

As a general rule, the grounds for challenge relate to the legal requirements to be observed for the filing of insolvency (threshold of indebtedness, conditions attached to creditors' receivables). For further details on the relevant legal requirements see section 2.2 above.

Although the Insolvency Code may provide recommended legal terms within which appeals against opening judgements may be brought (eg creditors' oppositions must be solved within a maximum term of 10 days from the expiry of the opposition submission term), in practice, delays may occur depending on procedural incidents, such as intervention requests submitted by other interested parties and oppositions filed by a large number of creditors.

2.9 What are the roles and powers of committees?

The creditors' meeting represents all the rightful creditors which take part in the procedure, collectively managing creditors' rights throughout insolvency proceedings and deciding by majority. Meetings legally take place in the presence of creditors holding receivables which amount to a minimum aggregate value of 30 per cent of the value of receivables with voting rights and decisions are adopted by express vote of the creditors holding the majority of the present receivables with voting rights. The judicial receiver may be elected by qualified majority exceeding 50 per cent of the total value of receivables with voting rights within the first creditors' meeting.

The creditors' committee comprises three or five creditors with voting rights which hold secured receivables or the highest value budgetary and unsecured debts. The committee decides by a simple majority of members.

The main powers of the creditors' committee (which will be performed by the creditors' meeting if a creditors' committee has not been appointed, as explained above) are as follows:

- to analyse the debtor's financial status and to make recommendations to the creditors' meeting in respect of the debtor's activity;
- to analyse the reports drafted by the judicial receiver or judicial liquidator and, as the case may be, to challenge such reports;
- to draft reports on the measures taken by the judicial receiver or by the judicial liquidator, to present said reports to the creditors' meeting and make new recommendations if the case;
- to request the withdrawal of the debtor's right to manage its business; and
- to file court actions for cancellation of fraudulent acts and operations made by the debtor to the prejudice of the creditors pursuant to provisions of the Insolvency Code when such actions have not been filed by the judicial receiver or judicial liquidator.

2.10 What are the consequences of opening judgments for creditors?

Stay?

Once the insolvency proceedings are opened, with the exception of some specific situations, both judicial and extrajudicial actions and enforcement procedures are automatically suspended.

Agreements concluded with service providers for supply of electricity, natural gas, water and other types of facilities will not be changed or suspended during the period of observation or reorganisation, provided the debtor is a captive consumer pursuant to the law (ie a consumer which benefits by a regulated agreement with its supplier).

Forbidden payments?
Except for payments related to the regular conditions for carrying out current activity, those authorised by the bankruptcy judge and those endorsed by the judicial receiver, any other act, operation or payment made by the debtor after the opening of the insolvency proceedings is null by effect of the law.

Interests accruing during the period: paid at contractual payment dates? Deferred and paid after the plan is adopted? Capitalised? Is the rate necessarily the contract rate?
After the insolvency proceedings are opened, no accessory (interest, penalty or any other expense) can be added to the previous debts.

After the reorganisation plan is confirmed, the interests, penalties or incidental expenses relating to obligations arising after the opening of the general procedure are paid in accordance with the provisions set forth by the documents which generated them and in accordance with the payments programme.

Is the opening judgment a valid draw stop?
Under Romanian law, there is no express legal provision that undrawn facilities can no longer be drawn once the insolvency proceedings are opened, and contractual provisions have to be observed in this respect as well. Nevertheless, note should be taken that the activities that the debtor can undertake within the insolvency period are subject to the 'business as usual' rule, any other activities being conditioned by the prior approval of the judicial receiver and the favourable vote of the creditors' committee, and any financing activity undertaken for performance of activities within normal course of business will be always subject to the prior approval of the creditors' meeting.

Since the judicial receiver or the judicial liquidator has to ensure that the value of the debtor's assets is maximised, they are vested with powers to decide whether a particular ongoing agreement is to be terminated or renegotiated (possibly also including credit facilities considered to have onerous terms for the debtor).

Necessity to file a proof of claim: are all creditors required to file a proof of claim? Are secured creditors necessarily notified? Are there any time limits? Are non-resident creditors treated differently? What are the consequences if a creditor is time-barred? Is the debtor discharged?
All creditors holding receivables prior to the initiation of the insolvency procedure must submit a debt admission claim, within the term provided in the opening judgment, with the exception of employees, whose rights are registered based on internal accounting records. However, creditors holding receivables which have arisen after the opening of insolvency or bankruptcy procedure are not required to file a debt admission claim.

The term for submission of debit admission claims will not exceed 45 days from the opening of insolvency proceedings and known creditors (including secured creditors) must be notified to this effect with a minimum of 10 days before the submission deadline.

Non-resident creditors are bound by the same obligations as resident creditors within an insolvency procedure. The writs, convenings and notifications will be communicated to the parties having their headquarters, domicile or residence abroad, in accordance with the provisions of the Civil Procedure Code, corroborated with the provisions of the Council Regulation (EC) No. 1346/2000 on insolvency proceedings and of Regulation (EC) No. 1393/2007 of the European Parliament and of the Council on the service in the member states of judicial and extrajudicial documents in civil or commercial matters. However, if such creditors have local representatives, the notification will be sent to them.

If a creditor is time-barred, it will lose the right to participate in the insolvency procedure. Pursuant to the recent amendments introduced by the Insolvency Code, the debtor appears to be automatically discharged from its debts towards these creditors, as the law clarifies that the respective creditor(s) will no longer have the right to recover the debts following the termination of the insolvency proceedings. These creditors will nevertheless be entitled to challenge rejection of their claim and request the reinstatement in their right to submit a debt admission claim, provided that they can prove the justified reasons set forth by the Insolvency Code.

Does such proceedings entail any limitation on the enforcement of contractually created security?

The creditors having secured receivables benefit from priority during the insolvency period. However, according to the law in force, enforcement is possible only in case of the receivables arising after the initiation of the procedure.

2.11 What is the duration of the restructuring process?

The duration of the restructuring process depends on the duration of the reorganisation plan, which will be initially proposed by the person proposing the reorganisation measures (the debtor, one or more creditors or the judicial receiver). The reorganisation plan will be subject to the prior approval of the creditors' meeting and decision by the bankruptcy judge.

Pursuant to explicit provisions of the Insolvency Code, when the restructuring process of the insolvent company is made according to a reorganisation plan, the implementation of the measures proposed within the reorganisation plan must be completed within a maximum statutory period of three years. The implementation period is not renewable, but it may be extended to a maximum of four years from the date of initial confirmation.

The restructuring process will also include an additional period of a maximum 12 months, known as the observation period, set between the opening of the insolvency proceedings and the confirmation of the reorganisation plan.

Consequently, the maximum duration of the restructuring process will not exceed a period of five years from the date of the opening judgment.

2.12 How do creditors vote?

Each creditor has a voting right, which may be used within the class of receivables corresponding to its debt.

The Insolvency Code provides that the following types of receivables will be grouped in five different classes:

- receivables having preference rights;
- salary receivables;
- budgetary receivables;
- receivables of the indispensable creditors; and
- unsecured receivables.

The plan will be considered accepted by a class, if it will be voted by the absolute majority of the creditors within that class.

There are specific rules regarding the approval of the plan when several categories of creditors are involved. In cases where five classes are involved, the plan will be considered accepted if:

- it is voted for by at least three categories
- at least one of the three categories is considered disadvantaged; and
- at least 30 per cent of the total amount of the receivables accept the plan.

In cases where there are three categories, the plan will be accepted if:

- it is voted for by at least two categories;
- at least one of the two categories is considered disadvantaged; and
- at least 30 per cent of the total amount of the receivables accept the plan.

When two or four categories of receivables are involved, the plan will be considered accepted if:

- it is voted for by at least half of the categories;
- at least one of the categories is considered disadvantaged; and
- at least 30 per cent of the total amount of the receivables accept the plan.

2.13 What are the rules on clawback/voidability?

The judicial receiver/liquidator can request the annulment of the fraudulent acts or operations concluded by the debtor over a period of two years prior to the opening of the insolvency proceedings, such as:

- gratuitous agreements (except for humanitarian sponsorships);
- operations where the debtor's performance obviously exceeds the other party's performance, concluded within the last six months;
- acts which reflect the intention of all contracting parties to endanger the creditors' rights;
- the setting of a preference right for an unsecured debt; and

- anticipated payment of the debts, if its due date was subsequent to the opening of the insolvency proceedings.

2.14 What are the rules on set-off/netting?

The opening of the insolvency proceedings does not affect the right of any creditor to invoke the netting of its receivable against the debtor if the conditions provided by the law concerning the legal netting are fulfilled when the proceedings are opened. This provision may also be applied to mutual debts that have arisen after the initiation of the proceedings.

2.15 How is exit managed?

Simple term-out; is a majority needed? Is it possible to cram down dissenters?

If the creditors receive the owed receivables or if they withdraw their requests, the bankruptcy judge will render the completion of the procedure.

Term out + asset disposal programme: should the programme be completed before the adoption of the plan? Can it be postponed and be part of the plan? Will sanctions be imposed if not completed? Is it possible for creditors to monitor the process?

The judicial receiver is entitled, at any time during insolvency, to sell those unsecured assets of the debtor that are not significant for the reorganisation in order to sustain the costs related to the procedure.

Until the creditors' committee meets, the decision regarding such sale may be taken by the judicial receiver. However, any interested party may challenge the recovery proposal within three days from when such decision was published in the IPB.

In the case of debt conversion(s), what approvals are necessary? Is it possible to force shareholders' consent?

The conversion is only possible with the approval of the general meeting of the shareholders. However, during the insolvency procedure, the activity of the debtor is conducted by the judicial receiver. Although conversions are not expressly indicated by law, in practice, such procedure is performed.

Sale of the business as a going concern to an entrepreneur: do creditors have the right to make their own proposal? Is credit-bidding possible? Automatic release/survival of existing pledges and charges

It is not common in practice for the business of the debtor to be sold and the law does not expressly specify such option. However, if such action were to be taken, according to general legal provisions, the mortgages related to the assets of the debtor should survive regardless of the buyer.

2.16 Are 'prepackaged' plans, arrangements or agreements permissible?

The only forms regulated under the Insolvency Code which may amount to 'prepackaged arrangements' are the *ad hoc* proxy and the moratorium procedure. For an overview of the conditions applicable to this procedure, see section 1 above.

Following the commencement of insolvency proceedings, the activity of the debtor may be organised pursuant to a reorganisation plan, which may be proposed by the debtor, the judicial receiver and/or one or more creditors. Once the reorganisation plan has achieved a favourable vote in the creditors' meeting and has been accepted by the bankruptcy judge, the plan will be implemented.

2.17 Is a public authority involved?

As a general rule, public authorities are not involved in the general insolvency procedure, other than in their capacity as creditors holding receivables against the debtor.

Particular provisions of the Insolvency Code regulate the insolvency of, for example, credit institutions and companies traded on regulated markets, where the National Bank of Romania and the Financial Supervisory Authority are also involved in the procedure.

2.18 What is the treatment of claims arising after filing/admission?

Receivables arising after the opening of the insolvency proceedings/bankruptcy proceedings, during either the observation period or the reorganisation period, will be paid in accordance with the documents which generated them, without it being necessary for creditors to file an admission claim to this purpose.

If the bankruptcy proceedings are opened after the observation period or after the reorganisation period, the creditors will request the registration of the due receivables that have arisen after the opening of the insolvency proceedings in a supplementary table.

2.19 Are there ongoing contracts?

The ongoing agreements are maintained after the date of the opening of the insolvency proceedings. Any clauses which stipulate the termination of such agreements, the loss of a grace period or the anticipation of the payment date upon the opening the insolvency proceedings are null and void. In the event that an agreement is unilaterally terminated, the other contracting party can file a claim for damages against the debtor, except for specific exemptions provided by law (eg qualified financial agreements).

In brief, the following matters are of interest with respect to ongoing agreements.

In order to maximise the value of the debtor's assets, the judicial receiver/liquidator is able to unilaterally terminate, within three months from the opening of the insolvency proceedings, any agreement, whether an unexpired lease or any other long-term agreement, as long as these agreements have not been fully or substantially executed.

Further, the judicial receiver/liquidator must respond, within 30 days from receipt, to any request from a co-contractor of the debtor regarding the unilateral termination of such agreement filed within the first three months from the opening of the insolvency procedure. The lack of such response from the judicial receiver/liquidator renders the agreement terminated.

In respect of the credit agreements concluded by the debtor, the judicial receiver can modify the clauses thereof with the consent of the co-contracting party in order for such clauses to ensure the equivalence of future performances.

The judicial receiver/liquidator can immediately terminate the individual labour agreements of the debtor's employees or lease agreements concluded by the debtor as leasee, complying with the legal notice term and with the relevant employment legislation.

The judicial receiver may also assign ongoing agreements (except for *intuitu personae* agreements, as provided under the Civil Code) for the maximising of the debtor's wealth or when such agreements can no longer be performed.

2.20 Are consolidated proceedings for members of a corporate family/group possible?

Under Romanian law, the general insolvency legislation is applicable for groups of companies, except for certain provisions expressly provided under national law.

For instance, if a common request for opening of insolvency proceedings with respect to several members of the same group of companies has been filed, the competent court of law is the tribunal situated in the administrative district of the headquarters of either the parent company or the member of the group having the largest turnover. A separate file, separate lists of creditors and separate reorganisation plans will be created for each member of the group, but will be analysed by the same judge.

Under Romanian law, a group of companies contains two or more companies interconnected through control and/or holding of qualified participation.

A common request for opening insolvency proceedings against a group of companies may be filed:

(a) by two or more debtors which are members of the same group of companies;
(b) one or more members of a group of companies which, in order to avoid a future request for opening insolvency proceedings, even if not insolvent and not imminently insolvent, may decide to subscribe to a request filed as per (a) above; or
(c) a creditor having receivables against two or more members of the same group of companies under the legal provisions.

The committees of creditors of each member of the group under insolvency proceedings will meet at least four times a year in order to establish recommendations with respect to the respective members and their reorganisation plans.

Throughout the insolvency proceedings, the judicial receivers of each member of the group under insolvency proceedings have an obligation to cooperate with each other.

Certain matters that may be discussed between the respective judicial receivers include clawback and voidability requests and, with a view to approving compatible and coordinated reorganisation plans, the drafting of the reorganisation plans with respect to each member of the group.

2.21 What are the charges, fees and other costs?

All charges related to the insolvency proceedings – including, but not limited to, the costs generated by the convening of the creditors' meeting, the notification and the communication of the procedural acts – are to be paid by the debtor.

The summoning of the parties and the communication of any procedural acts are performed through the IPB. In order to cover the publishing expenses, a tax of 10 per cent of the taxes paid for the constitution, authorisation or registering in the Trade Registry is required from the debtor.

The notification of the creditors regarding the opening of the insolvency proceedings is also covered by the debtor.

3. LIABILITY ISSUES

3.1 What is the liability of managers/directors *vis-à-vis* creditors?

Can management/directors (*de jure* or shadow) be held personally liable? Are there any prerequisites?

The managers/directors of the company can be held personally liable if they had an inappropriate attitude which led to the company's insolvency, such as:

- using the assets of the company for their own benefits;
- carrying out production or commercial activities for their own profit, benefiting from the fact that such activities are considered performed by the company;
- deciding to continue activities which obviously led to the impossibility to pay the debts;
- keeping false records;
- disposing of part of the company's assets or fraudulently extending the company's liabilities;
- using ruining methods to obtain funds for the company;
- deciding to pay a creditor preferentially, in prejudice of the other creditors, during the month prior to the interruption of payments; or
- any other intended action which contributed to the debtor's insolvency.

A manager/director will not be held personally liable if he voted against the decision which caused the insolvency of the company.

Are there any prerequisites?

Personal liability of the managers/directors will be incurred if it can be proved that these persons performed an action which determined the insolvency of the company.

If the insolvency is contemporary with or set before the period when these persons exercised their mandate, they may be held jointly liable.

Who has standing to sue? Can creditors force the court agent to introduce an action? How?

In order for managers/directors to be personally liable, certain conditions need to be fulfilled.

Such persons should have performed actions which determined the insolvency of the company. If the insolvency is contemporary with or prior to the period when they exercised their mandate, all of them will be held jointly liable.

If the judicial receiver/liquidator does not indicate the liable persons, the president of the creditors' committee, a creditor designated by the creditors' meeting or a creditor holding over 50 per cent of the debt's value has the right to submit the case to the court.

A manager/director will not be held personally liable if he voted against the decision which caused the insolvency of the company.

Can creditors join in the court agent's action? Under what conditions?

The insolvency law does not expressly provide such procedure as regards the collaboration between creditors and a court agent. According to the general procedure, in order for a claim of the creditor to be admitted by the court, it is necessary for the due receivables to be proven.

3.2 What is the liability of the lender?

The law specifically provides for the liability of the director and of any other person responsible for the insolvency of the debtor. As any person may be held liable, the lender may in theory incur liability under similar conditions. From preliminary searches carried out, there is little public information available on similar claims brought against a lender.

Singapore

Rajah & Tann Singapore LLP Sim Kwan Kiat

1. WHAT COURT-MONITORED RESTRUCTURING PRE-INSOLVENCY PROCEEDINGS OR SCHEMES HAVE BEEN DEVISED BY THE LAW OF YOUR COUNTRY TO LIMIT VALUE DESTRUCTION FOR FAILING BUSINESS ENTITIES?

The two key court-monitored restructuring regimes in Singapore are:

- judicial management; and
- scheme of arrangement.

1.1 What is the objective of the proceedings?

Schemes of arrangement and judicial management are aimed at providing a company in financial difficulty with the opportunity to recover its financial footing and carry on its business. Schemes of arrangement allow the management of the company to retain control over the debt restructuring process, whilst judicial management involves the appointment of a third party judicial manager by the court who will replace the directors and take possession and control of the company's assets and business.

1.2 Do all kinds of businesses qualify?

Generally all types of businesses may apply to be placed in judicial management or schemes of arrangement. However, special considerations may apply in specific industries, such as insurance and banking. There is no special requirement on the level of indebtedness, turnover or asset value.

For judicial management, a court-appointed judicial manager takes charge of the restructuring process. With respect to schemes of arrangement, the management of the company retains management control. However, once a scheme is approved, a scheme manager is appointed to implement the scheme.

1.3 What are the necessary approvals?

A creditor of the company, or the company itself, may apply to court to place the company under judicial management. For schemes of arrangement, it is typically the company that applies to court for the necessary orders.

1.4 What is the procedure?

Judicial management

The company itself or its creditors may file an application to put the company into judicial management. The application is by way of an originating summons, which is supported by an affidavit setting out the grounds for the application.

The applicant will nominate a judicial manager, who has to be a public accountant but not the auditor of the company, though the creditors may oppose the nomination by a majority in number and value.

However, the court will dismiss a judicial management application if a receiver and manager have been appointed or will be appointed by a secured creditor under a debenture, creating a floating charge over the whole or substantially the whole of the company's assets.

Thereafter, in a case where the applicant is a creditor, notice of the application must be given to the company, and to the holders of debentures where there is a power to appoint a receiver and manager under the debentures.

A moratorium comes into effect once an application for judicial management is filed. The company may not resolve to wind itself up, nor may a winding up order be made. No creditor can enforce any security over the company's property and no execution or other legal process may be commenced against the company without the leave of court.

At the hearing of the application, the court must be satisfied that the judicial management order is likely to achieve:

- the survival of the company or the whole or part of its undertaking as a going concern;
- the approval under section 210 of the Companies Act of a compromise or scheme of arrangement; or
- a more advantageous realisation of the company's assets than would be effected on a winding up.

Schemes of arrangement

An application to court for an order permitting the convening of a scheme meeting (or meetings) of the creditors or classes of creditors will need to be filed. In practice, this application is made by way of an *ex parte* originating summons accompanied by a supporting affidavit.

A scheme meeting is then held to secure the required majority, which is a majority in number representing three-quarters in value of each class of creditors who are present and voting at the meeting.

Once the scheme is approved by the requisite majority of creditors, an order of the court sanctioning the scheme has to be obtained. In deciding whether to sanction the scheme, the court will have to be satisfied that the statutory procedures and requirements have been complied with, that there is no coercion of the minority creditors by the majority creditors, and that the scheme is a fair and reasonable one. Once the court has sanctioned the scheme, it becomes binding on all the creditors whether they voted in favour of it or not.

Once the court has sanctioned the scheme, the Order of Court is extracted and lodged with the Registrar of Companies. The order only takes effect and is binding on all parties from the date of lodgment or such earlier date as the court may provide.

Before the necessary resolutions are passed or before the court approves the scheme, it is possible to apply to court for an order for proceedings against the company to be stayed (section 210(10) of the Companies Act).

1.5 Is there recourse against the opening judgment?

Subject to the directions of the court, a party with an interest in the outcome of the judicial management or scheme of arrangement generally has recourse to a right of audience before the court. Such parties include creditors of the company. In addition, the court retains a supervisory role over the judicial management or scheme of arrangement process. In practice, this means that it is generally possible for the judicial manager, the scheme manager, the company or its creditors to seek further directions from the court on matters relating to the judicial management or scheme of arrangement.

1.6 What are the substantive tests/definitions?

An insolvent company may be placed in judicial management by the court for one or more of the following purposes:

- to rehabilitate the company's business;
- to effect a scheme of arrangement between the company and its creditors; or
- to carry out a more advantageous realisation of the company's assets than from a winding up.

There is no single appropriate test for insolvency. Regard is given to all evidence relevant to the question of solvency, and it is a question of fact. However, the two key tests are the balance-sheet test and the cash-flow test.

The balance-sheet test deems a company insolvent when its current liabilities exceed its assets, where the company's liabilities include its contingent and prospective liabilities. Contingent liability refers to liability/loss arising out of an existing legal obligation or state of affairs, but which is dependent on the happening of an event which may or may not occur. Prospective liability refers to a debt which will certainly become due in the future, either on some date which has already been determined or on some date determinable by reference to future events. It embraces liquidated and non-liquidated claims.

The cash-flow test deems a company insolvent when it cannot meet its obligations as and when they fall due. Relevant factors are:

- what all of the company's debts are at the time in question, in order to determine when those debts were due and payable;
- all the assets at the time, to determine which assets are liquid or realisable within a time-frame which will allow debts to be paid as and when they are payable;
- what the company's expected net cash flow is at the time (by deducting cash expenses from projected future sales); and
- whether any shortfall in liquid/realisable assets can be made up from borrowings repayable at a later time.

In determining whether a company is insolvent, the court does not rely solely on any single test, but looks at all of the circumstances of the case.

For a scheme of arrangement, there is no strict requirement for a company to be insolvent. However, in many cases where a company seeks to restructure its debts by way of a scheme of arrangement, the company would have been insolvent.

1.7 What is the role of a court-appointed agent?

A judicial manager takes over the management and control of the company's affairs and business. The officers of the company must cooperate with the judicial manager so that he can carry out his proposals. The directors and secretary of the company must submit a statement of affairs to the judicial manager. Generally all officers and employees of the company must also give the judicial manager all information which he reasonably requires.

In addition, the judicial manager has the power of investigation, and may look into the past transactions of the company and the past conduct of the company's officers. Where necessary, the judicial manager may try to recover any of the company's assets that were improperly disposed of prior to the judicial management. The judicial manager has the power to unravel such wrongful transactions as unfair preference and transactions at an undervalue.

The powers of a scheme manager are generally set out in the terms of the scheme. The powers typically involve the implementation of the scheme rather than any investigative powers.

1.8 What protection is there from creditors?

For judicial management, the statutory moratorium is wide and is effective at protecting the company from most types of creditor action. However, the exercise of contractual rights is not caught by the moratorium. Thus, when a company enters into judicial management, contracts which the company is a party to are not automatically terminated by virtue of the order of judicial management *per se*. As such, contractual rights such as a right of set-off or a right to terminate the contract which can properly be invoked in the circumstances can still be exercised and would probably not be prohibited by the statutory moratorium. For instance, banks' self-help right of set-off against the company's funds in account is not subject to the statutory moratorium (*Electro Magnetic (S) Ltd (under judicial management) v Development Bank of Singapore Ltd* [1994] 1 SLR(R) 574).

For the avoidance powers of a judicial manager, see section 1.7 above.

With respect to a scheme of arrangement, before the necessary resolutions are passed or before the court approves the scheme, it is possible to apply to the court for an interim order for proceedings against the company to be stayed.

Both judicial management and schemes of arrangement involve the filing of proofs of debt with the judicial manager or scheme manager. A challenge against the adjudication of the proof of debt may be made in the court.

1.9 What is the usual duration of the restructuring process?

The judicial management order will be in force for a period of 180 days from the date the order is made, but this time period may be extended by the court on application by the judicial manager.

When a judicial manager is appointed, he has 60 days to send a statement of his proposals to the members and creditors of the company. Within this period, a meeting of creditors must be called for the approval of the proposals, giving at least 14 days' notice to the creditors. At this meeting, the proposals must be approved by the majority of the creditors in number and in value. If this requisite majority is not achieved, the court may discharge the judicial management order. However, if the proposals are approved, the judicial manager must then manage the company according to his proposals.

A scheme of arrangement is subject to a more flexible timeline. The court may grant a few months for the company to convene the creditors' meeting to vote on the scheme. Usually, however, the court takes into account, and monitors the status and progress of, the restructuring in determining the timeline.

1.10 Who prepares the restructuring agreement and what are the available tools?

Generally, the judicial manager prepares the restructuring agreement. As for a scheme of arrangement, the proposed scheme manager typically works together with the management of the company in preparing the restructuring agreement.

The levels of approval required for a proposal under a judicial management and for a scheme of arrangement are set out in section 1.4 above.

1.11 Are subordination agreements necessarily given full effect?

Subordination agreements validly entered into before the commencement of judicial management are generally given effect. It is up to the judicial management, however, to consider proposals to the creditors which may impact on the rights and obligations under subordination agreements.

Where a company with existing subordination agreements enters into a scheme of arrangement process, whether a subordination agreement will be given full effect will depend on the terms of the scheme.

1.12 How is exit managed?

Once the scheme is approved by the requisite majority of creditors, an order of the court sanctioning the scheme has to be obtained. In deciding whether to sanction the scheme, the court will have to be satisfied that the statutory procedures and requirements have been complied with, that there is no coercion of the minority creditors by the majority creditors, and that the scheme is a fair and reasonable one. Once the court has sanctioned the scheme, it becomes binding on all the creditors, whether they voted in favour of it or not. The exit mechanism under a scheme depends on the terms of that scheme. The scheme usually comes to an end once it has been fully implemented, or if the scheme is breached or terminated.

A judicial management order may be discharged once the purposes of the judicial management have been fulfilled or, alternatively, if the court is satisfied that such purposes are no longer achievable.

1.13 Who are the necessary parties?

See section 1.5 above.

2. POST-INSOLVENCY PROCEEDINGS

2.1 What is the objective of the proceedings?

If the restructuring attempted by way of judicial management or a scheme of arrangement fails, the company is typically placed in liquidation (ie wound up).

2.2 Do all kinds of business entities qualify?

To commence a winding up application against the company, it must be proved that the company is insolvent. For the test of insolvency, see section 3.3 above.

To invoke the presumption of insolvency by serving a statutory demand on the company, the amount demanded must be more than S$10,000.

2.3 What are the necessary approvals?

N/A.

2.4 Is it valid and binding to agree that such proceedings be a default/termination event?

Yes. It is fairly common to see clauses in, for instance, facility agreements which state that the commencement of such proceedings will be regarded as a default or termination event.

2.5 What is the procedure?

The steps for a creditor to commence a compulsory liquidation (pursuant to the issuance of a statutory demand) are as follows:

(a) Upon the expiry of the 21 day statutory period under the statutory demand, the creditor may file an application to court to wind up the company. In practice, this application is made by way of a companies' winding up originating summons accompanied by a supporting affidavit. A date for the hearing of the winding up application is usually fixed within three to four weeks from the date of filing of the application.

Under the winding up application, a creditor may nominate the Official Receiver or a private liquidator to be the liquidator of the company. If a private liquidator is nominated, a consent to act as liquidator will need to be signed and filed on behalf of the nominee.

(b) At any time after the making of a winding up application, the court may, upon the application of any creditor or contributory of the company and upon proof by affidavit of sufficient ground for the appointment of a provisional liquidator, appoint a provisional liquidator (who shall have and may exercise all the functions and powers of a liquidator) upon such terms as the court shall think just of necessary: section 267 of the CA and Rule 35(1) of the Companies (Winding-Up Rules) (Cap. 50, 1990 Rev Ed, R 1) (the CWR).

(c) The winding up application and supporting affidavit shall be served upon the company at the registered office of the company and the Official Receiver in accordance with the requirements of Rule 26(1) of the CWR. A copy of the winding up application and supporting affidavit is usually also served on ACRA as well.

(d) The winding up application shall be advertised in the prescribed form, seven clear days (or such longer time as the court may direct) before the hearing, once in the gazette and once at least in one English and one Chinese local daily newspaper or in such other newspapers as the court may direct: Rule 24 of the Companies (Winding-Up Rules) (Cap. 50, 1990 Rev Ed, R 1).

(e) After the winding up application has been filed and prior to the hearing of the application, the applicant or his solicitor must appear before a court registrar to satisfy him that the statutory requirements under the Companies Act have been complied with and to extract a memorandum signed by the registrar confirming the same. If a memorandum is not extracted, no order, except an order for the dismissal or adjournment of the winding up application, shall be made on the application of any person making the winding up application who has not, prior to the hearing of the winding up application, appeared before the registrar to extract the memorandum: Rule 32(2) of the Companies (Winding-Up Rules) (Cap. 50, 1990 Rev Ed, R 1).

On the date set for the hearing of the application, the court will decide whether to grant the application or dismiss it (section 257(1) of the Companies Act). The court also has a wide discretion to adjourn the proceedings and to make interim orders. If the court grants the application, an order for the winding up of the company will be made.

2.6 Please provide information about voluntary filings

Interested parties (eg other creditors of the company) may appear at the hearing of a winding up application by serving on the applicant or his solicitor a notice of such intention. The notice shall be served not later than 12 noon of the day prior to the day appointed for the hearing of the winding up application.

Generally, the liquidation process does not contemplate a restructuring proposal for the company. The objective of the liquidation is to wind down the affairs of the company and realise the assets of the company for the benefit of the creditors.

As a general rule, a winding up application is heard in open court. The notice of the hearing date is usually available on the website of the Singapore Supreme Court.

2.7 How are creditors' representatives chosen?

There is no strictly prescribed manner of choosing creditors' representatives. The creditors may on their volition constitute a committee of inspection (COI). A COI consists of no more than five persons, whether creditors or not, with the function of authorising the liquidator to make certain major decisions in the liquidation process.

2.8 Is there recourse against the opening judgment?

Any party whose interest may be affected by the winding up may appear and be heard in court upon filing the necessary notification of their intention to appear.

2.9 What are the roles and powers of committees?

See section 2.7 above.

2.10 What are the consequences of opening judgments for creditors?

Upon the making of the winding up order, there is a stay of all legal action and enforcement against the company.

The liquidator has to exercise his best endeavours to convert all the assets of the company into money.

The liquidator has a duty to determine the debts and liabilities of the company and the identities of its creditors by examining its books and records. The liquidator also has to advertise to invite persons who wish to assert a claim against the company to lodge a proof of debt within 14 days and to adjudicate on any such proof of debt which is duly lodged. The liquidator shall cause all ascertained debts and liabilities to be discharged (including obtaining tax clearance if necessary).

The distribution of dividends is prescribed under Section 328 of the Companies Act. After secured creditors, preferential creditors (such as the Central Provident Fund, to which employees contribute), workmen's compensation and tax have priority in distribution. Thereafter, all unsecured creditors rank on a *pari passu* basis, ie all unsecured creditors share in the company's assets in proportion to the size of their claims.

Secured creditors are not subject to the *pari passu* principle but are entitled to priority over the unsecured creditors.

There are also certain preferential debts which are given priority over unsecured creditors and debts secured by floating charges, namely:

- costs and expenses of the winding up;
- wages and salaries of employees, up to S$7,500 per employee;
- retrenchment benefits and *ex gratia* payments of employees, up to S$7,500 per employee;
- amounts due in respect of workmen's compensation;
- amounts due in respect of contributions payable in a stipulated period to employees' superannuation or provident funds;
- remuneration payable in respect of vacation leave for employees; and
- tax assessed, including goods and services tax.

Distribution to shareholders

After the discharge of the debts and liabilities of the company, the liquidator will distribute the surplus assets of the company to its shareholders.

Final meeting and dissolution

As soon as the affairs of the company are fully wound up, the liquidator has to prepare final accounts and convene a final meeting of shareholders to present the final accounts. The relevant form has to be filed with the Registrar of Companies and the Official Receiver within seven days of the final meeting. Upon the expiry of three months from the final meeting (unless an extension of time is granted by the court), the company will be dissolved and the winding up will be completed.

2.11 What is the duration of the restructuring process?

There is no fixed timeline for a liquidation process.

2.12 How do creditors vote?

The creditors generally vote by reference to the amount of debt owed to them. There is no provision for classification of creditors in a liquidation.

2.13 What are the rules on clawback/voidability?

The two main modes of clawback or avoiding antecedent transactions are:

- unfair preference transactions under section 329 of the Companies Act read with sections 99 and 100 of the Bankruptcy Act – this refers to transactions which put the transferee in a better position than he would otherwise have been had the company been wound up – that occurred within two years (if the transferee is an associate of the company) or six months prior to the commencement of the winding up of the company. The company must be insolvent when these transactions occurred and be influenced by a desire to put the transferee in a better position than the latter would be if the company was wound up. Such transactions are voidable by the liquidator; and
- undervalue transactions under section 329 of the Companies Act read with sections 98 and 100 of the Bankruptcy Act – this refers to transactions which are at an undervalue – that occurred within five years prior to the commencement of the winding up and the company was insolvent at the time or became insolvent as a consequence of the transaction. Such transactions are voidable by the liquidator.

2.14 What are the rules on set-off/netting?

Once a company is wound up, the mandatory insolvency set-off rules automatically apply (section 88 of the Bankruptcy Act read with section 329 of the Companies Act). Only mutual debts and credits between the company and its creditor in the same capacity may be set off.

The mandatory insolvency set-off rules cannot be contracted out.

2.15 How is exit managed?
Exit is managed by the liquidator of the company. The liquidator decides on whether the affairs of the company have been fully addressed, after which he will make application. The company will then be dissolved and the liquidators discharged.

2.16 Are 'prepackaged' plans, arrangements or agreements permissible?
Generally, no.

2.17 Is a public authority involved?
N/A.

2.18 What is the treatment of claims arising after filing/ admission?
This depends on the nature of the claim. As a general rule, post-liquidation claims are not provable in the liquidation.

2.19 Are there ongoing contracts?
N/A.

2.20 Are consolidated proceedings for members of a corporate family/group possible?
There is no strict rule that automatically consolidates proceedings for members of a corporate group, but they are possible. The general rule is that each member is a separate legal entity. A separate application for judicial management or a scheme of arrangement should be made for each member of the corporate group.

2.21 What are the charges, fees and other costs?
There are certain mandatory charges, such as a deposit with the Official Receiver (S$5,300) and advertising fees (around S$2,800). The exact amount of charges, fees and costs would depend on the nature of the matter.

3. LIABILITY ISSUES
3.1 What is the liability of managers/directors *vis-à-vis* creditors?
A director has, *inter alia*, a statutory duty, under section 157(1) of the Companies Act, to act honestly and use reasonable diligence in the discharge of his duties at all times and a general common law duty to act in good faith in the best interests of the company as a whole. The statutory obligation to 'act honestly' encompasses the following duties:

- a duty to act in the company's interests;
- a duty not to place himself in a position where his duty to the company and his personal interests may conflict; and
- a duty not to place himself in a position where his duty to the company conflicts with his duty to another principal.

If a company's directors are found to have breached the fiduciary duties owed to the company, they would be liable to the company for any profit made by them or for any damage suffered by the company as a result of the breach of fiduciary duty.

In the case of an insolvent company, apart from a director's usual common law and statutory duties to the company, a director would have to act in the interest of the creditors of the company as well, and not take any action that could adversely affect the interests of the creditors: *Chip Thye Enterprises Pte Ltd (in liquidation) v Phay Gi Mo and others* [2004] 1 SLR 434, citing *West Mercia Safetywear Ltd v Dodd* [1988] BCLC 250. In this regard, it may be argued that, in undertaking a transaction for an insolvent company, the directors of the company are required to try and maximise value for the benefit of the creditors through the medium of the company. Where a transaction is not in the interest of an insolvent company's creditors, it may also be argued that the directors had acted in breach of their duty as directors to keep the property of the company inviolate in order to pay its creditors.

A director of an insolvent company also faces potential liability for the following:

- transactions between a company and its directors: where the company purchased any property, business or undertaking from a director for a cash consideration within a period of two years before the commencement of the winding up of the company, the liquidator may recover any amount by which the cash consideration for acquisition exceeded the value of the property, business or undertaking: see section 331(1) of the Companies Act. Similarly, where the company sold any property, business or undertaking to a director for cash consideration within a period of two years before the commencement of the winding up of the company, the liquidator may recover the amount by which the value of the property, business or undertaking exceeded the cash consideration: see section 331(2) of the Companies Act;
- Fraudulent trading under sections 340(1) and 340(5) of the Companies Act: the directors may face a criminal offence and, contingent upon the finding of an offence having been committed, personal liability for all or any of the liabilities of the company if directors were aware that the business of the company had been carried on with the intent to defraud creditors or for any other fraudulent purpose. To succeed in a claim against the company's directors for personal liability for fraudulent trading, the liquidator (or any creditor or contributory of the company) would have to show dishonest intention on the part of the company's directors: see generally *Tang Yoke Kheng (trading as Niklex Supply Co) v Lek Benedict* [2005] 3 SLR 263. This is not a burden of proof that is easily discharged, as the court would not be inclined to accept a serious allegation of fraud in the absence of compelling evidence; or
- insolvent trading under sections 339(3) and 340(2) of the Companies Act: the directors may face a criminal offence and, contingent upon the finding of an offence having been committed, personal liability for

the whole or any part of the debt incurred by the company if directors caused the debt to be incurred at a time when there was no reasonable or probable ground of expecting the company to repay the debt.

3.2 What is the liability of the lender?

N/A.

Spain

Gómez-Acebo & Pombo Abogados
Fermín Garbayo & Julio Pernas Ramírez

1. WHAT COURT-MONITORED RESTRUCTURING PRE-INSOLVENCY PROCEEDINGS OR SCHEMES HAVE BEEN DEVISED BY THE LAW OF YOUR COUNTRY TO LIMIT VALUE DESTRUCTION FOR FAILING BUSINESS ENTITIES?

The pre-insolvency court-monitored procedure existing in Spain is the court approval (sanctioning) of refinancing or restructuring agreements (RAs) envisaged in additional provision 4 (AP 4) of the Spanish Insolvency Act 22/2003 of 9 July (IA).

Non-sanctioned RAs (out-of-court restructuring) may still obtain protection against clawbacks (avoidance) if the requirements set out in Article 71 bis IA are met but no extension on dissenters is achieved. Also, Article 231 IA contains a regime for out-of-court restructuring for individuals and small companies. These processes bear no court monitoring and therefore are excluded from our analysis.

Both the eligibility requirements of an RA to deserve the above said court approval and the content of the RA itself that could – as a consequence of such approval – be imposed on dissenters have been subjects of a number of legal reforms since 2009. Judges have also played a significant role in defining the features, limits and reach of court approvals. To illustrate the volatility of our insolvency regime, a new reform of the IA is currently been enacted and published (RDA 11/2014), this time mostly in connection with the voting regime and the effects of the composition of creditors in insolvency. Reference to this new regime shall be made in section 2 below.

What is described below is a summary of the court approval (CA) as it stands pursuant to the law and case law at the time of writing. Some of the issues remain subject to legal debate and discrepancies between the different commercial courts, especially those new provisions established by RDA 11/2014 in connection with which no court pronouncements yet exist.

Some of the matters discussed below have been simplified for easier reading.

1.1 What is the objective of the proceedings?

A CA aims at overcoming the rigidity of Spanish law to reach a consensual RA. Until 2009, the principle of *'pacta sunt servanda'* could only be overturned in Spain in the context of actual insolvency proceedings by a composition of creditors, and even in this case, until the reform carried out by RDA 11/2014, only in connection with unsecured lenders. Before the onset of insolvency proceedings, any RA could only bind the parties consenting to become so bound. Dissenters could just stick to their claims and jeopardise the attempts of the majority to rescue viable distressed debtors.

The changes made to the IA by means of Royal Decree Act 3/2009 and Act 38/2011 introduced for the first time in Spain the possibility of imposing on dissenters – creditors that either did not vote for or that voted against – the terms of an RA agreed by the majority outside of an insolvency scenario. The way the terms of the RA would be imposed on such minority dissenters would be the approval of the RA by the Spanish commercial court that would otherwise be in charge of the insolvency of the company.

1.2 Do all kinds of businesses qualify?

Is there a threshold related to indebtedness, turnover or asset value?

All businesses qualify and, as a general rule, there is no threshold.

Credit institutions have a specific regime contemplated in Act 9/2012.

Is a court agent necessarily appointed to assist the company? If so, how is it chosen?

Regarding the general regime of pre-insolvency refinancing, no court agent (ie receiver) is appointed to assist the company in the process. Only the court agent (procurador) mentioned in section 1.4 below is required.

1.3 What are the necessary approvals?

The debtor has the legal standing to request the CA. Pursuant to general company law principles, it is the management body of the company (the board of directors/sole director) that has the capacity to resolve to apply for a CA.

The creditors that had signed the RA may also request the CA.

1.4 What is the procedure?

Must a petition be filed? Must it be *ex parte*? Are there any other procedural documents?

The RA has to be filed through a court agent and a qualified Spanish lawyer. The jurisdiction to approve the RA, as well as to conduct insolvency proceedings lies with the commercial courts located in the territory where the debtor has its centre of main interests (Article 10 and AP 4 IA).

The court agent must provide evidence of capacity to represent the debtor, or the creditor by means of a power of attorney. This request may also contain a request for an injunction to stay any enforcement proceedings (unless the stay has been requested as part of the Article 5 bis filing described in section 1.8 below).

In order to be eligible for the CA and henceforth be imposed on dissenters, RAs submitted to the judge need to abide by the following requirements under Article 71 bis IA, namely:

- the RA should (i) significantly increase the funds available to the debtor and/or (ii) extend the tenor of such loans or reorganise the terms of the indebtedness in accordance with a viability plan of the debtor that allows the company to continue as a going concern in the short and mid-term;

- the RA must be executed before a Spanish Notary Public and recorded in a deed containing a copy of all documents proving compliance with the requirements for CA; and
- the auditor of the company or, if the company does not have such an auditor, an ad hoc auditor appointed by the companies house with which the debtor is registered, certifies the achievement of the majorities mentioned in section 1.10 below.

The extension of the effects of RA may only be imposed on dissenters holding financial indebtedness regardless of whether or not such creditor is an entity subject to financial supervision (eg a bank).

Holders of claims arising out of commercial transactions and creditors regulated by public law shall not be affected by the RA.

Should supporting documentation be filed with the application? Are creditors invited to participate?

In the request for approval filed with the court, the debtor shall include the following documents:

- a copy of the RA;
- the certificate issued by the auditor in connection with the majorities required by the relevant features of the RA as described in section 1.10 below;
- any reports drawn by the independent experts pursuant to Article 71 bis IA;
- certificates issued by the company in connection with any share capital increase required in the context of the restructuring; and
- certificates or appraisals issued in the context of the appraisal of assets required for the calculation of the value of the assets as described in Section 1.10 below.

The debtor freely decides the creditors that will take part in the negotiations of the RA, bearing in mind the percentage of the debt held by each of them.

1.5 Is there recourse against the opening judgment?

The commercial court, after a preliminary examination of the debtor's request for approval, shall issue an order allowing the petition. This preliminary decision gives rise to a publication in the Spanish Official Gazette (BOE) and the Public Registry of Insolvencies. The IA does not envisage any appeal against the opening court order; however, creditors may submit allegations against the approval (eg majorities not being reached).

1.6 What are the substantive tests/definitions?

There is no formal test to be made for the CA.

1.7 What is the role of a court-appointed agent?

N/A.

1.8 What protection is there from creditors?

The IA protects the negotiation process against a number of risks the crystallisation of which could potentially jeopardise the objectives pursued with a CA, namely:

- The liability of directors for breach of the duty to file a petition for insolvency proceedings in the two -month period following the date in which they became aware or should have become aware of an insolvency trigger event.

  Pursuant to Article 5 IA, a company is bound to file for insolvency within the 2 months following the date on which it became aware or should have become aware of the grounds for effective insolvency. The Insolvency Act presumes that the debtor knew of the insolvency event in any of the following circumstances:

  (i) generalised inability to pay debts;
  (ii) executions against property affecting the debtor's assets and liabilities as a whole;
  (iii) undervalued transactions and preferences; or
  (iv) generalised breach of certain tax, social security or employment obligations/

  Failure to make this filing within this two-month period could potentially trigger the liability of directors and other debtor representatives (see section 3.1 below). This threat of liability generates a race against the clock that plays against the likelihood of success of the whole negotiation process.

  Article 5 bis of the Insolvency Act provides for a notice that – if made by the debtor before the lapse of the aforementioned two-month period – gives the company a further three-month window (that will start to count on the date of the notice served under Article 5 bis) to conclude the refinancing or restructuring negotiations. Within the month following the lapse of this three-month period, the company should file for insolvency if the grounds for such filing persist.

  This filing is generally known as the 5 bis notice, and has to be served on the commercial court that would otherwise be competent for the insolvency of the debtor.

- Insolvency filings by third parties.

  Any petition for insolvency proceedings filed by third parties will be frozen by the court as long as the debtor is under the protection of the above-mentioned Article 5 bis IA, as set out in Article 22 IA.

- Debt recovery actions and security enforcement by third party creditors.

  Pursuant to Article 5 bis (4) IA, , other than in respect of public law claims, no individual enforcement proceedings on assets that are necessary for the continuation of the activity of the debtor shall commence – and those already commenced shall be stayed – from the date of submission of the 5 bis filing, until there is a court decision on the approval of the refinancing or restructuring agreement but, in connection with financial indebtedness, subject to providing evidence that at least 51 per cent of the providers of such financial indebtedness have expressly accepted the commencement of the restructuring negotiations and have agreed not to initiate or continue enforcement proceedings during the negotiation process.

- Protection against clawbacks.

  Regardless of the majorities required for the extension of the terms of the RA on dissenters as described in section 1.10, if the RA obtains the support of at least 51 per cent of the financial indebtedness, it shall be shielded against clawback actions to be brought by other creditors (note that the receiver in insolvency may still bring this action once insolvency proceedings have begun) provided that, at the time of entering into the RA, the three conditions listed in section 1.4 above are met.

1.9 What is the usual duration of the restructuring process?

The IA does not establish a specific duration of the process. In this regard, the duration of the restructuring process varies substantially from case to case as it depends on elements such as the complexity of the indebtedness, the nature of the creditors and their willingness to engage into restructuring negotiations. Some restructuring processes extend over a long period of time as shareholders or other stakeholders support the debtor with the necessary cash to avoid a payment default or the occurrence of any of the circumstances defined in section 1.8 above that would trigger the duty of directors to effectively file for insolvency.

What is relevant in this case, however, is that, once the company hits an insolvency event of the kind described in section 1.8 above, the clock starts ticking for directors to take action. So, in terms of timing, the debtor would need to serve a notice under section 5 bis IA within the two-month period referred to above. Once this is done the debtor will have the 3+1 month window described in section 1.8 to conclude negotiations.

1.10 Who prepares the restructuring agreement and what are the available tools?

The restructuring agreement is normally prepared by an ad-hoc steering committee created by a group of creditors frequently holding the majority of the financial indebtedness to assure the success of the RA or by the debtor itself.

In order to be eligible for CA, the RA needs the support of a majority, which varies depending on two elements, namely:

- the nature of the measures to be imposed on dissenters; and
- the features of the claims held by such dissenters.

In respect of (i) unsecured dissenters and (ii) secured dissenters with regard to their claim exceeding the value of the security (as defined below), the RA has to be approved by:

(i) 60 per cent of the financial indebtedness for 'mere payment deferrals' or extensions not exceeding five years, or the conversion of that claim into a profit sharing loan for the same maximum period; or

(ii) 75 per cent of the financial indebtedness for:

- extensions in excess of five years (with a limit of 10 years);
- debt write-off;
- debt for equity swaps, in which case dissenters may opt for a write-off equivalent to the nominal value of the shares to be given in exchange of the loans, plus any premiums;
- conversion of the claims into profit-sharing loans for more than five years (with the same 10-year limitation), convertible bonds and other similar instruments, including subordinated debt instruments and other debt instruments with features different than the original debt; or
- payments in kind.

In connection with the aforementioned 'mere payment deferrals', the judgments of the Barcelona Commercial Courts No. 6 and 3, of 5 June 2012 and 29 July 2014, respectively, have interpreted the meaning of the term 'deferral' to be not restricted to the mere postponement of the maturity date under a debt instrument but, rather, to involve the amendment of the specific financing agreement to reflect the new maturity date, hence curing the effects of any event of default that could stand in the way of further drawdowns on unused credit facilities at the time of the restructuring.

In respect of the part of claims of secured creditors covered by the value of the security (as defined below), the refinancing or restructuring agreement has to be approved by:

- 65 per cent for the features described in (i) above; or
- 80 per cent for the measures described in (ii) above.

In this case, the majority to be achieved is calculated on the basis of the proportion that the value of the security voting for the restructuring represents of the global value of the security (all the security interest created by the debtor).

The value of the security is calculated as 90 per cent of FV – PC, where FV is the fair value of the asset and PC is the claims holding a security or right over the asset preferential on the security being appraised.

The fair value of an asset shall be calculated as follows:

- the fair value of securities listed in an official or regulated market or money market instruments shall be calculated as the weighted average price during the three-month period preceding the onset of negotiations with creditors;
- real estate shall be valued by an official appraiser registered with the central bank of Spain (*Banco de España*);
- other assets shall be valued by an independent appraiser pursuant to the rules applicable in each case;
- in the case of security arrangements created indistinctly over a number of assets, the fair value of the overall package shall be calculated as the sum of the fair value of each asset but always bearing in mind that the global value of the security shall not exceed that of the claim held by the creditor; and
- for security arrangements indistinctly created for the benefit of a number of creditors, the value of the security allocated to each creditor

shall be determined by the percentage of the claim held by each of them but always bearing in mind the rules relating to syndicated claims described below.

Where syndicated facilities are involved, all lenders under the facility shall be deemed to have voted for the restructuring if (i) 75 per cent or (ii) the lower threshold established in the syndicated loan/intercreditor agreement for the approval of the particular features of the RA vote for it. So any majority rule in excess of 75 per cent shall be disregarded for the purposes of this approval.

For the purposes of the calculation of the majorities described above, the claims held by related parties as defined in Article 93(2) IA shall be disregarded. Despite this, the effects of the RA could still be imposed on them, provided that their claim qualifies under the definition of financial indebtedness mentioned below.

Regardless of the CA, dissenters will retain their rights against third party guarantors of the debtor.

1.11 Are subordination agreements necessarily given full effect?

Preferences are specifically regulated in the IA and therefore creditors do not have the capacity to alter the order of payments established by operation of said preferences (Article 100.3 and 154 *et seq* of the IA). So both the composition of creditors and the liquidation of the assets of the company in case of insolvency must abide by the said rules.

In connection with subordination agreements, Article 92 contains a list of seven types of claim the subordination of which will be recognised in insolvency. Payment of those claims shall be made in the order they are respectively listed in Article 92, beginning in 92.1 and ending with those in 92.7.

92.2 specifically refers to *'claims that have been* conventionally subordinated to all other claims *against the debtor'.*

On the basis of the above, subordination agreements shall be respected by the insolvency tribunal provided that they relate to all other creditors of the company (general subordination).

Nevertheless, the issue arises in connection with subordination arrangements with a less broad reach (ie subordination agreements of some creditors (the B claims) in respect of one or various specific groups of other creditors (the A claims)). In connection with these, it is commonly accepted that these provisions are valid and should be respected by the receivers/ tribunal, but:

- the B claims shall not be deprived of their initial ranking (secured, ordinary or otherwise);
- the receiver in insolvency and the judge shall respect the subordination arrangements and only pay the B claims once the A claims have been paid; and
- the conclusion above would lead to another effect, which is that other creditors of the same class as the A creditors shall benefit from the subordination arrangement despite it not being initially addressed to

them. So, in practice, if the A claims and the B claims are all ordinary claims, the B claims shall only be paid once all the ordinary creditors have been paid. But (see the first bullet above) B claims shall remain ordinary claims and therefore be paid before any subordinated creditor under Article 92 is satisfied.

1.12 How is exit managed?

Which court must approve the restructuring agreement?

The same commercial court that preliminarily examined the debtor's request for approval (see section 1.4 above) has to finally rule on the substance of the petition within 15 days from the opening order (see section 1.5 above).

What is the scope of the court's review?

The commercial court will approve the RA provided that the formal requirements described in section 1.4 above are met. Further, the court shall extend the effects of the RA to the dissenters subject to receiving a certificate drawn by the auditor confirming that the majorities described in section 1.10 have also been achieved.

1.13 Who are the necessary parties?

The decision to approve the RA will be published both in the Spanish Official Gazette and in the special public registry of insolvencies.

Within 15 days of the publication, dissenters affected by such decision may challenge the court approval through the filing of an insolvency procedural plea. Dissenting creditors may challenge the CA on very limited grounds, namely:

- the breach of the majorities required for the court approval as described in section 1.10 above; and
- the burden (sacrifices) imposed on them being disproportionate.

No further appeal shall be accepted by the court.

The judgment of Commercial Court No. 6 of Barcelona of 5 June 2012 determined that, in order to evaluate the burdens imposed on dissenters, special attention should be paid to the financial situation of each creditor, the amount of its claim, the existence of encumbrances on the debtor's sizeable assets and the security package agreed in the refinancing agreement. Further, the judge ruled that a refinancing agreement could legitimately maintain the right of the debtor to carry out additional drawdowns on credit facilities made available by dissenters (preservation of existing disbursement rights), but could not impose on such credit providers the increase in the amounts available under those facility arrangements.

The judgment of Commercial Court No. 3 of Barcelona of 29 July 2014 established further that it should be relevant to compare the outcome of the CA not only with what dissenters would otherwise achieve in the winding up of the debtor, but also other elements, such as discrimination in respect of the creditors accepting the RA (including situations of unequal treatment of the same kind of creditors or more onerous conditions imposed on creditors with better ranking). The court also seems to conclude that: (i) a proportionally small group of dissenting creditors (in this case less than 5 per cent of the financial indebtedness) helps in the analysis of the fairness of the terms of the RA; and (ii) the fact of dissenters not sharing the guarantees and security given to creditors accepting the RA does not in itself qualify as a disproportionate burden for unequal treatment, despite the fact that those security arrangements cover pre-existing claims as well as new loans under the RA.

2. POST-INSOLVENCY PROCEEDINGS

For ease of reference in the following sections, I include below the general structure of insolvency proceedings under the IA. Reference is made to the specific section of this paper that provides further detail of each of the milestones of the overall process.

An insolvency filing may be made by the debtor (voluntary insolvency) or by any of its creditors (compulsory insolvency) (see sections 2.2 and 2.3 below).

The insolvency is effective as from the date of the court order declaring the institution of insolvency proceedings. The onset of insolvency proceedings is publicised as described in section 2.10 below and determines the consequences described in the same section.

The insolvency court shall appoint receivers (see section 2.7 below) and will publicise the insolvency so that all creditors may file their claims.

Common phase

The so-called common phase commences with the rendering of a Court Order declaring the institution of insolvency proceedings, an excerpt of which is published both in the Spanish Official Gazette and the Public Registry of Insolvencies. This excerpt shall summon all creditors to lodge their claims before the appointed receivers.

The main purpose of this phase is to determine the amount and ranking of all claims against the debtor (the liabilities of the estate) and the assets that belong to the estate (the assets of the estate – see section 2.10 below). The process to determine the estate can be summarised as follows:

- with the information received from creditors and that arising from the petition filed by the debtor, as well as from the debtor's own books, receivers shall produce an interim report within the two-month period following their appointment (the Interim Report). This Interim Report is made available to all creditors appearing before the court;
- creditors will have a 10-working-day period to challenge the content of the Interim Report; and
- after all challenges have been heard and resolved, receivers shall produce a final report of assets and liabilities (the Final Report), closing the common phase and leading to the solution of the insolvency either through the opening of the composition of creditors phase or through the opening of the winding-up phase.

Exit of the insolvency

Insolvency proceedings may normally end in two different ways:

- the fulfilment of a composition agreed with the creditors and approved by the commercial court (see sections 2.11 *et seq*); or
- failing the approval of a composition or, if the composition approved is breached or the debtor so requests, insolvency proceedings shall end by winding-up.

Exceptionally, insolvency proceedings may also come to an end in cases of (i) insufficient assets to pay claims against the asset pool and (ii) full satisfaction of all claims.

2.1 What is the objective of the proceedings?

The objective of insolvency proceedings is to maximise the recovery of creditors of distressed debtors either by means of a composition that creditors shall vote and agree upon or by the winding up of the company and sale of all assets for the satisfaction of the said claims. The preservation of the business of the company to the extent that it is viable also plays a critical role in the decisions of the receiver and the judge dealing with the insolvency. The rules regarding the content of a composition, the enforcement of claims and the transfer of business units discussed below are inspired by this principle of preservation.

In achieving the objective of maximisation of recovery, the principle of *par condition creditorum* plays a critical role. Once insolvency proceedings have begun, all creditors deserve in principle the same treatment (ie same payment deferrals, write-offs, etc). Only the specific exceptions contemplated in the IA allow for a different treatment (see section 2.10 in this respect).

Also as a consequence of this principle of maximisation of recovery and preservation of the equal treatment of all creditors, the law sets forth some specific rules to set aside transactions carried out during the two-year hardening period, as described in section 2.12 below.

2.2 Do all kinds of business entities qualify?

Is there a threshold related to indebtedness, turnover or asset value?

All kinds of debtors, both legal persons and individuals, and some foundations may seek the protection of insolvency proceedings. However, the state (and its departments), public bodies and other public administration entities may not, as provided in Article 1.3 IA. In the case of financial institutions and financial services providers, the public supervisors (ie European Central Bank, Bank of Spain, FROB) may initiate resolution proceedings, with strong public intervention, in lieu of the general insolvency proceedings set forth in the IA. Those alternative proceedings are regulated under the provisions of the Royal Decree Act 24/2012 of 31 August on the restructuring and resolution of credit institutions and Regulation (EU) No. 806/2014 of the European Parliament and of the Council of 15 July 2014. This is similar to the insurance regime which has an alternative to the insolvency proceedings regulated by the Royal Legislative Decree 6/2004 of 29 December, approving the consolidated text of the Private Insurance Supervisory Act.

Notwithstanding the foregoing, there are also specific characteristics, both inside and outside the IA, for the insolvency proceedings of the following entities:

- sport clubs;
- financial institutions and financial services providers when they file for an insolvency proceedings; and
- concessionaires of public works and services and public procurement contractors.

Are involuntary proceedings a possibility?

Insolvency proceedings can be initiated both by the debtor and by any of its creditors.

A creditor may file an insolvency petition against a debtor based on current grounds of insolvency only. The circumstances that allow a creditor to make this insolvency filing are defined in Article 2(4) IA, ie if after enforcement of a particular claim the creditor cannot seize assets sufficient for a full recovery or based on any of the circumstances listed in section 1.8 above (necessary filing).

The debtor itself may seek the protection of the insolvency regime not only in cases of current insolvency as defined above but also based on potential insolvency grounds (in the event of anticipating that it shall not be able to meet its obligations as they fall due in the ordinary course of business; voluntary filing).

The claim of the creditor making the necessary filing referred to above shall be enhanced with a general preference amounting to 50 per cent of the claim (see section 2.10 below).

Is action available to all creditors? Under what conditions?

Article 3.2 IA withholds the right of filing a debtor into insolvency from those creditors that, within the six-month period prior to the said filing, acquired by contract an individual claim already fallen due and payable from its holder.

2.3 What are the necessary approvals?

Board, shareholders, others

The voluntary filing has to be approved by the management body of the debtor. There is no need to provide evidence of a shareholders' agreement to file for insolvency.

According to Article 2(3) IA, shareholders, members and parties who are legally liable for the debts of a debtor shall also be entitled to file a voluntary filing.

Parties other than the management/board entitled to initiate the process (secured/senior creditors)

Regarding the creditors' standing, see section 2.2 above. Neither auditors nor public authorities may force a legal person to file for insolvency. They cannot make the filing by themselves either. Only the public prosecutor may inform the creditors about their right to do so, when instituting criminal actions grounded on certain felonies against the property and against the social-economic order, such as at-fault insolvency.

2.4 Is it valid and binding to agree that such proceedings be a default/termination event?

Article 61(3) IA contains a general rule setting forth that termination events consisting exclusively of the onset of insolvency proceedings shall be ineffective.

Nevertheless, Articles 11(1), 15(4) and 16(1) of Royal Decree Act 5/2005 provide for an exceptional regime applicable to closing out netting and financial collateral arrangements the provisions of which shall not be affected by the onset of insolvency proceedings. In respect of these, the initiation of insolvency proceedings shall be valid grounds for termination, provided that the arrangements and the parties thereto comply with the eligibility requirements established in RDL 5/2005.

2.5 What is the procedure?

Voluntary filings are analysed below; here, I make brief reference to the procedure of necessary filing.

A necessary filing should be addressed by any of the creditors to the court of the place in which the debtor has its centre of main interests.

The petition shall contain a description (and documentary evidence) of the origin, nature, amount, dates of acquisition and maturity and present status of the claim that supports the petition. Witness evidence of an insolvency event alone shall not suffice.

Other parties with standing to make the filing must state in their petition the capacity in which they are acting, and produce documentary evidence thereof.

If the debtor has made a 5 bis filing as examined in section 1.8 above, all insolvency petitions submitted during the negotiation period with creditors shall only be decided upon once the period of one month provided in that section has elapsed. If, during such one-month period, the debtor files for insolvency, such a petition shall prevail; that is to say, the insolvency will qualify as a voluntary filing.

Similarly, no insolvency proceedings shall be onset on credit institutions affected by a recovery or resolution process contemplated in Act 9/2012.

Once an insolvency petition has been admitted, the commercial court shall serve a notice on the debtor. The debtor shall bring any challenges against such petition within the five-working-day period following the notice. The court sometimes calls the parties to a hearing prior to taking a decision on the petition.

A necessary filing shall be admitted and the court shall issue an order opening the insolvency proceedings in the following cases:

- acceptance by the debtor (either expressly or by making a subsequent voluntary filing);
- failure of the debtor to object to the filing in the five-working-day period mentioned above; or
- if the court rejects any challenges filed by the debtor after holding the hearing mentioned above.

2.6 Please provide information about voluntary filings

Voluntary filings are those initiated by the debtor itself. However, when the public supervisors opt for different proceedings, financial institutions, financial services providers and insurance companies may not be authorised to file for insolvency, as examined in section 2.2 above.

The court shall decide on the opening of insolvency proceedings in light of the documentation produced by the debtor (ie evidence is provided on any of the indicators described in section 2.3 above to justify a necessary filling).

If the court understands that the documentation produced is insufficient, it shall grant the debtor a term not exceeding five days to provide complementary documentation. Otherwise, it will directly issue the opening judgment declaring the insolvency with the effects depicted in section 2.10 below.

Are creditors invited to participate in the initial hearing? If so, how are they notified?

In the case of a voluntary filing, it is not necessary for the court to hear the creditors in order to open the insolvency proceedings.

What supporting documentation should be filed?

The petition shall be accompanied by the following documents:

- special power of attorney of the individual or entity appearing on behalf of the debtor executed before a Spanish Notary Public. This power of attorney may also be replaced by one executed *apud acta*, that is to say, in the presence of the court clerk;
- a memorandum describing: (i) the historical and legal background of the debtor; (ii) activities during the preceding three-year period; (iii) establishments, offices or operating facilities; (iv) grounds of insolvency; and (v) the assessment made by the debtor regarding its viability and the potential solutions to the insolvency. If the debtor is a legal person, the report shall identify all registered shareholders or members, directors or liquidators and, when appropriate, the accounts' auditor, as well as whether it is part of a group of companies, listing the companies that belong to such group of companies, and whether it has issued securities listed on an official secondary market;
- an inventory of property and rights, stating nature, location, particulars of registration if any, acquisition value, valuation corrections and

estimation of the current real value. An indication shall also be given of the encumbrances, liens and charges;
- a list of creditors, by alphabetical order, stating the identity of each one of them, as well as the amount and maturity of the respective claims and the security *in personam* or *in rem* they may hold. If any creditor has claimed payment judicially, the relevant proceedings shall be identified and described; and
- a list of employees and, if any, any employee representative body.

If the debtor is legally bound to keep accounts, the following documents shall also be attached:
- annual accounts and, where appropriate, management reports or audit reports for the last three business years;
- information on any significant changes that occurred in its assets following the closing of the last deposited annual accounts and any transactions outside the debtor's ordinary course of business;
- in the case of debtors subject to a duty to deposit interim financial statements with any regulatory or supervisory body, the interim financial statements produced after the annual accounts referred to above; and
- in the event of the debtor being part of a group of companies, as the parent company or as a controlled company, the consolidated annual accounts and management report of the last three business years and the audit report issued with regard to those accounts, as well as a report stating the transactions performed with other companies of the group during that same period.

Are the main restructuring principles/proposals to be term sheeted at entry? If so, is an expert opinion or report on the feasibility of the contemplated plan needed?

As a general rule, no term sheet of a restructuring or composition is filed alongside the petition of insolvency. Article 104 IA, however, allows the debtor to file an advanced composition proposal (*propuesta de convenio anticipado*, or ACP) at any point in time between the request for voluntary insolvency or the declaration of necessary insolvency and the deadline for notification of claims referred to in the preamble to section 2 above.

For the ACP to be admitted, section 106.1 of the IA establishes that it must count with the support of creditors of any kind holding claims in excess of one-fifth of the liabilities of the debtor. Alternatively, if the ACP is submitted together with the request for voluntary insolvency, the support of the creditors holding one-tenth of the liabilities of the debtor shall suffice.

Pursuant to Article 100.5 IA, a feasibility report issued by the debtor shall have to be filed alongside the petition if compliance with the terms of the composition requires the use of the proceeds generated by the activity of the debtor.

Pursuant to Article 105 IA, the debtor is barred from filing an ACP in the following cases:

- if the debtor (or, in the preceding three year period, its directors or liquidators) has been condemned for forgery or offences against property, the social-economic order, the tax agency, the social security or the rights of workers; or
- if the debtor has breached its obligation of depositing annual accounts in any of the preceding three years.

Note that there are special rules regarding insolvency proceedings of concessionaires of public works and services and public procurement contractors, in general, according to which the public administration shall also be entitled to make proposals for compositions.

How is the opening judgment rendered public? When and how are creditors deemed aware of the proceedings?

The opening of insolvency proceedings shall be made public through the State Official Gazette (see the preamble to section 2 above) and through the Public Registry of Insolvencies.

Despite this general publication, the receiver shall serve individual notices on creditors that are identified in the list attached to a voluntary filing (see section 2.6 above) and on those the identity of which can be obtained from the books of the debtor.

The judgment declaring the insolvency is public and all creditors appearing before the court shall be entitled to obtain a copy of it.

2.7 How are creditors' representatives chosen?

The insolvency administration shall, as a rule, be a single-person body (the receiver). The receiver shall be appointed by the commercial court from individuals or legal entities duly registered in the special public registry of insolvencies.

However, in insolvencies with a duly justified public interest and at the request of a public law creditor, an additional receiver shall be appointed amongst public law creditors.

In the case of insolvency of financial institutions, there are particular rules on the appointment of receivers and the intervention of the relevant supervisory and regulatory bodies.

Can creditors (or administrators/trustees) influence the choice?

No, but they have several grounds for recusal and may bring actions for liability.

What is their role and powers?

In the case of a voluntary filling (see section 2.6 above), the debtor shall retain, as a general rule, the ability to manage the business and, therefore, will also maintain the powers of management and disposal over assets, the exercise of which will only be subject to intervention/approval by the insolvency receivers.

In the case of a necessary filing, however, as a general rule, the capacity of the debtor to manage the business and/or dispose of assets will be suspended and substituted by the receiver/s mentioned above.

In any event:

- In general terms, the powers of the receiver will be tailored and supervised by the court.
- Particularly, the receivers have limited powers to sell assets during the insolvency proceedings.
- During the common phase, only certain urgent sales may be entered into by the receiver and only after court authorisation, as provided for in Article 43 IA with two basic exceptions:
  - the sale of assets to obtain the cashflow strictly required for the continuation of the activities of the debtor or to ensure the continuation of the insolvency proceedings, provided that notice is promptly given to the judge together with justification of the need thereof; and
  - the sale of assets not required for the continuation of the activity of the debtor at a price not substantially different to that allocated to the asset in the inventory contained in the Interim Report referred to in section 2 above.
- Relevant management and disposal actions therefore shall require court consent and will be subject to challenges by any creditors and other interested parties in case the requirements set forth under the IA are not met.

Receivers also draft the three reports mentioned in the preamble to section 2 above.

2.8 Is there recourse against the opening judgment?

In case of rejection of a voluntary filing, the debtor may challenge this decision only before the same court.

By contrast, in case of rejection of a necessary filing, the petitioner may file an appeal before the provincial commercial court in the 20-day period following the date of the resolution rejecting the opening of insolvency proceedings.

In case of an opening judgment declaring the onset of insolvency proceedings, either the debtor or any interested party may file an appeal against the declaration of insolvency before the provincial commercial court in the twenty day period following the date of the resolution at stake.

Finally, a particular decision contained within the opening judgment declaring insolvency, distinct from the declaration of insolvency itself, may be challenged before the same court but not appealed.

As a rule, the recourses discussed above shall not stay the judgment (eg avoiding the effects of insolvency declaration as examined in section 2.10 below) unless, exceptionally, the court, either by motion or on its own, decides a partial or complete stay of said effects.

2.9 What are the roles and powers of committees?

Pursuant to Article 116 IA, creditors shall meet at the creditors' meeting that shall be chaired by the insolvency judge. The creditors' meeting is subject to a quorum of at least 50 per cent of the ordinary claims against the debtor.

The insolvency receivers and the debtor must be present at the creditors' meeting.

To determine compliance with the quorum requirement, the list of creditors contained in the final report by the receiver (see the preamble to section 2 above), once approved by the court, shall be used.

Creditors shall vote their claims on the basis of the amount of each of them. The first proposal of composition to be voted on is that of the debtor (if any). After that, other proposals, beginning with those signed by the holders of the larger claim amounts, shall be voted on.

RDA 11/2014 has removed the voting right restrictions previously applicable to non-subordinated post-insolvency purchasers of debt. These shall now vote as any other unsubordinated creditor.

Interest accrual is suspended upon the opening of insolvency proceedings unless there is, and to the extent covered by, a security arrangement and therefore these shall be disregarded in the calculations to be made in the creditors' meeting (Article 56 of the IA).

In terms of majorities for the approval of a composition of creditors, the following rules apply:

- Ordinary creditors (those holding a claim that is neither subordinated nor preferential over the assets of the debtor by operation of a security arrangement or a preference as established in Article 91 IA) shall be bound by the terms of a composition provided that at least the holders of 50 per cent of all the ordinary claims vote for it.

  The content of the composition is limited to write-offs not exceeding 50 per cent of the claims, mere payment deferrals or maturity extensions not exceeding five years or, in respect of creditors other than those holding employment or public administration claims, the conversion of the claim into a profit sharing loan (for the same maximum period) with the following exceptions:

  (i) where the composition consists of the full satisfaction of ordinary claims in a period not exceeding three years or the immediate payment of all due and payable ordinary claims with a haircut not exceeding 20 per cent, the voting threshold is reduced to a simple majority approval (more valid votes for than against the composition); and

  (ii) the aforementioned 50 per cent rule is increased to 65 per cent where the content of the composition includes measures such as write-offs exceeding 50 per cent of the claims, payment deferrals or maturity extensions exceeding five years but always subject to a maximum limit of 10 years or, in respect of creditors other than those with employment or public administration claims and in the context of an alternative proposal of composition only, the conversion of the claim into a profit sharing loan subject to the same limit, subordinated loans and debt for equity swaps. Although not entirely clear yet, this majority rule also applies in case of transfer of assets and/or business units.

The alternative proposals of composition need to be put forward alongside another that merely contains a payment deferral and/or a write-off within the limits and subject to the majorities described above.

As a general rule, the effects of the composition of creditors are restricted to ordinary creditors. Nevertheless, subordinated creditors shall also be subject to the same write-offs and payment deferrals. Payment deferrals applicable to subordinated creditors shall only count from the date the composition of creditors is fully complied with in respect of ordinary creditors.

Pursuant to the reform of the IA carried out by means of RDA 11/2014, preferential creditors may also be bound by the composition subject to a regime that very much resembles that applicable in respect of secured creditors in the context of the CA (see section 1 above).

For the purposes of the extension of the effects of the composition of creditors, the RDA 11/2014 has defined four classes of preferential creditors, namely:

- employment creditors: those creditors that hold a preferred employment claim other than a claim under an employment contract of senior management for amounts exceeding the limit set out in Article 91(1) IA;
- public administration creditors: those creditors holding a claim governed by public law;
- financial creditors: those creditors of financial indebtedness, regardless of whether or not they are subject to financial supervision; and
- remaining creditors: including creditors under commercial indebtedness and any other creditors not included in any of the classes mentioned above.

Based on the above, preferential creditors shall also be bound by the terms of the composition if they so accept, or provided that the following majorities calculated in respect of each of the said classes is reached:

- 60 per cent if the measures to be extended are any of those referred to in the paragraph immediately preceding (i) above; and
- 75 per cent if the measures to be extended are any of those referred to in (ii) above.

In the case of secured preferential creditors, the majority to be achieved is calculated within each of the aforementioned classes on the basis of the proportion that the value of the security voting for the composition represents on the aggregate value of the security for each class.

The value of the security is calculated as 90 per cent of FV – PC, as defined in section 1.10 above.

No appraisal shall be required for real estate assets that had been so appraised within the six-month period prior to the onset of insolvency proceedings or in respect of cash, claims for the balance of current accounts, term deposits or electronic money.

Subordinated creditors (including all related parties) shall not have voting rights. Loans by and between group companies shall qualify as subordinated as well as loans made by shareholders that at the time of making the loan hold, directly or indirectly, a share interest in excess of 10 per cent of the debtor (5 per cent if the debtor has issued listed shares or debt instruments).

2.10 What are the consequences of opening judgments for creditors?

- All creditors shall be pooled together as liabilities of the estate of insolvency (*masa pasiva*).

  Some payments due by the insolvent debtor are, however, specially protected in insolvency, being paid at their maturity as if the debtor had not entered insolvency proceedings (eg wages for the last 30 days prior to insolvency, court fees, and charges and costs generated by the exercise of the debtor's professional or business activity after the onset of proceedings). Those listed cases are essentially claims arising as a result of the insolvency proceedings or for the sake of the continuity of the debtor´s activity (claims against the asset pool).

  By contrast, all other payments shall be stayed and only made pursuant to the terms agreed in the composition or in the winding up of the company (insolvency claims). Insolvency claims are classified as follows:
  - secured claims (*créditos con privilegio especial*): those that benefit from any security arrangement on specific assets of the debtor (mortgages, pledges or otherwise), claims under financial lease contracts and under sale and purchase agreements subject to retention of title provisions, or explicit termination clauses to the extent covered by the value of the security. These hold a preference on specific assets of the debtor, but only to the extent of the value of the security;
  - preferred claims (*créditos con privilegio general*): some claims for unsecured salaries, 50 per cent of all tax and social security claims, extracontractual civil liability claims, fresh money to the extent that it does not qualify as a claim against the asset pool, and 50 per cent of the claim of the creditor that instigated the insolvency proceedings. These hold a general preference on all assets of the debtor not affected by any security arrangement;
  - subordinated claims: claims notified out of time; interest of any kind to the extent unsecured; claims held by related parties (ie directors or shareholders holding, directly or indirectly, a share interest in the debtor in excess of certain thresholds, companies of the same group as the debtor, etc); and
  - ordinary claims: all claims that are neither secured/preferred nor subordinated.
- Stay on legal actions and enforcement proceedings, namely:
  - judges before whom any civil or labour law actions may be brought after the opening judgment shall instruct the parties to

bring the proceedings before the insolvency judge. Actions brought with this purpose before the opening judgment may be joined to the insolvency proceedings or carried out before the same courts;
- commercial courts shall reject any claims filed after the opening judgment against the directors of the debtor which should have not fulfilled their obligations in case of concurrence of a ground for termination. Actions brought with this purpose before the opening judgment shall be stayed;
- first instance courts shall reject any claims filed after the opening judgment in connection with the provisions contained under Article 1,507 of the Spanish Civil Code. Actions brought with this purpose before the opening judgment shall be stayed;
- contentious administrative, labour and criminal courts before which any action affecting the estate of the debtor may be brought after the opening judgment shall summon the receivers, accepting them as party to the proceedings if they decide to be so (Article 50 IA);
- stay on any individual enforcement actions and administrative or tax seizures on the assets of the debtor (Article 55 IA); and
- stay of any enforcement proceedings of security arrangements entered into by the debtor on assets that are necessary for the continuation of its activity (Article 56 IA). Actions aimed at the recovery of assets sold subject to retention of title provisions, availed to the debtor under financial lease contracts or aimed at the termination of sale and purchase agreements of real estate for breach of payment obligations shall also be stayed.

- Prohibition of offsetting (Article 58 IA). See section 2.14 in this respect.
- Suspension of interest bearing (Article 59 IA), other than (i) to the extent secured under a security arrangement and (ii) interest for unpaid salaries, within the limits established by the law and the annual state budget. However, if a composition is agreed with no writing off of claims, the total or partial payment of (until then) suspended interest may be agreed. In the event of a winding-up, if a remainder is left after payment of all the insolvency claims, interest shall be paid too.
- Suspension of any retention rights on assets integrated in the asset side of the insolvency estate (Article 59 bis IA).
- Interruption of time-barring of claims against the debtor.

Is the opening judgment a valid draw stop (for undrawn facilities)?

The general rule, as described in section 2.19 below, is that contracts with reciprocal obligations pending on both parties (such as credit facilities with undrawn commitments) shall remain in full force and effect after the declaration of insolvency (Article 61.2IA).

Accordingly, undrawn commitments shall be preserved even upon declaration of insolvency of the debtor. Attention should also be paid by creditors with pending drawdowns to Article 92.7IA, which subordinates the claim of a creditor under this type of contract (contracts with pending reciprocal obligations on both parties thereto) if such creditor is found to be repeatedly obstructing the fulfilment of the contract against the interest of the insolvency estate.

In connection with this, see section 1.10 above and the court definition of 'payment deferral'.

Article 68 IA allows the insolvency receiver to rehabilitate facility agreements terminated during the three-month period preceding the onset of insolvency proceedings for breach of payment obligations provided that (i) notice of such rehabilitation is served on the lender prior to the lapse of the period for presenting claims in the insolvency, as described in section 2.6 above, and (ii) amounts due and payable are immediately paid and subsequent payments secured as a claim against the asset pool.

Necessity to file a proof of claim: are all creditors required to file a proof of claim? Are secured creditors necessarily notified? Are there any time limits? Are non-resident creditors treated differently? What are the consequences if a creditor is time-barred? Is the debtor discharged?

All creditors shall file a proof of claim before the receivers, including documentary evidence of the claim (see section 2.5 above). Notwithstanding the above, there are several rules to ensure that the most significant claims are taken into consideration despite their actual lodging. This is the case for, among others, secured claims and those arising from arbitral awards or judicial rulings, regardless of being final, as well as those that have been recorded in a public deed or official documents of acknowledgement of public works.

However, and in parallel to the lodging of the claims before the receivers, creditors have the option of appearing directly before the court, which gives them the advantage of getting access to the whole dossier of the proceedings.

Not only secured creditors but all creditors with claims that are reflected within the books of the debtor shall be notified by the receivers, generally by e-mail. Pursuant to Article 214 IA, notifications to be made to non-resident creditors shall have to contain certain additional information regarding the insolvency proceedings.

Creditors are given, as a rule, a one-month period from the publication of the opening judgment to lodge their respective claims (see section 2.6 above) directly. Note that this term shall also apply to non-resident creditors pursuant to Article 217 IA.

Extemporary lodging determines the subordination of the claim, as a rule.

Does such proceedings entail any limitation on the enforcement of contractually created security?

After the opening judgment, no judicial or out-of-court civil enforcement against the debtor may be initiated and any action in process shall be stayed from the date of the opening judgment. Public administration creditors (ie the state, inland revenue, etc) are treated more favourably.

Particularly, pursuant to Article 55 IA, attachments levied over the debtor's assets as a consequence of enforcement proceedings carried out by such public administrations shall not be released until the winding up is opened, provided that the attached assets are not necessary for the continuance of the activity of the debtor. In contrast, in respect of any other attachments, the receiver may request the commercial courts to lift any attachment levied over the debtor's assets as a consequence of pending enforcement proceedings, in the interest of the insolvency proceedings. The court will also hear the counterparty to such proceedings.

As to security arrangements (mortgages or pledges over goods, rights or receivables), once proceedings have commenced, secured creditors shall be subject to the stay on enforcement referred to above. This stay shall last until the earlier of (i) the agreement on a composition the content of which does not affect the exercise of the enforcement and (ii) the lapsing of one year from the date of commencement of proceedings without the winding up of the company being ordered

Once the winding-up phase is started, ongoing foreclosures and other enforcements over pledges can continue but cannot be commenced. Otherwise the assets affected by the security arrangement will be liquidated pursuant to the normal regulations of the winding-up phase and the proceeds used for the payment of the secured claim.

2.11 What is the duration of the restructuring process?

The duration of the insolvency proceedings is neither fixed by the law nor set forth by the court. It depends mostly on how long it takes for the commercial court to close the so-called 'common phase' (see section 2 above).

Two special rules should be mentioned:

- Article 96 IA sets out a mechanism by means of which the court may accelerate the proceedings and finish the common phase pending challenges affecting less than 20 per cent of the inventory and the list of creditors; and
- in the case of the abbreviated proceedings, all time limits set out in the IA are significantly reduced, as provided in Article 191 IA. The court may apply this especially simplified procedure when, in the light of available information, it understands that the insolvency proceedings are not particularly complex, based on the following circumstances:
  - the list submitted by the debtor includes fewer than 50 creditors;
  - the initial estimate of liabilities does not exceed five million euros; and
  - the valuation of the aggregated assets does not reach five million euros.

The judge may also use the abbreviated proceedings where the debtor presents, together with the voluntary filing, an advanced composition proposal (see section 2.6 above) that includes either a structural modification with disposal of all its assets and liabilities or a winding-up plan that contains a binding written offer to buy the single production unit in operation or where the debtor has ceased business and has no contracts in force.

2.12 How do creditors vote?

See section 2.10 above regarding the classes of creditors under the IA and section 2.9 above on how majorities work.

2.13 What are the rules on clawback/voidability?

Article 71 IA sets forth the general principle that all actions of the debtor carried out within the two-year period preceding the onset of insolvency proceedings may be set aside if evidence is provided that they were prejudicial to the asset pool.

This clawback rule is based solely on prejudice and disregards the intention of the parties to the particular transaction. Aside from this clawback rule, the general principles of voidability of fraudulent dealing remain applicable. these not being subject to the two-year hardening period mentioned above and requiring evidence of fraudulent intent.

As a general rule, the alleged prejudice has to be evidenced by the party bringing the claim. Only two exceptions to this general rule exist:

- *iuris tantum* presumption of prejudice (the burden of proof is shifted to the parties to the transaction whom will have to provide evidence that there was no prejudice to the insolvent's estate). This is applied *inter alia* to:
  - the prepayment of secured loans the maturity of which would otherwise fall after the opening of insolvency proceedings;
  - the transfer of assets for consideration for the benefit of related parties; and
  - the creation of security for pre-existing liabilities or for new liabilities assumed in substitution of any pre-existing liabilities; and
- *iuris et de iure* presumption of prejudice (these shall be automatically set aside), which is applicable to disposals of assets without consideration and prepayments of unsecured loans the maturity of which would otherwise fall due after the opening of insolvency proceedings.

The definition of 'prejudice' has been the subject of a number of interpretations, some more restrictive than others. The prevailing interpretation currently among Spanish insolvency courts is that not only should a reduction in the insolvent's assets be analysed against the rules of prejudice (restrictive interpretation), but so should any unjustified action for the benefit of one creditor that diminishes the likelihood of satisfaction of the claims of the others (broad interpretation). This broad interpretation seeks to ensure that all creditors are treated equally in the case of insolvency (*par conditio creditorum*) (see section 2.1 above). It also implies that contracts that determine a reduction in liabilities of the debtor associated with a parallel reduction in the assets may be set aside on the basis of prejudice if, as a consequence of such transaction, there is a diminution of the chances of recovery of other creditors (see, among others, the judgments of the

Provincial Insolvency Court of Madrid dated 19 December 2008 and of the Insolvency Court of Murcia No. 1 dated 18 April 2013).

The resolution of the Insolvency Court of Murcia No. 1 dated 18 April 2013 further states that, in the assessment of the existence of justification for a particular transaction, the proximity of the action to the date of the insolvency filing and the circumstances of the debtor at the time of entering into the contract at stake need to be considered. In this particular case, the insolvent debtor (EYMO, S.L.) transferred to one of its creditors a receivable against a third party for the satisfaction of the claim of the said creditor. This transfer was made on a date (August 2010) not specially close to the opening of insolvency proceedings (July 2011) but close enough to the filing under Article 5 bis (December 2010) (see section 1.8 above) to understand that on the date of the transfer the company was already 'in a situation of severe disruption in the satisfaction of the amounts due to the other creditors'.

The Provincial Insolvency Court of Vizcaya No. 4, in a judgment dated 30 July 2010, understood that there was no prejudice implied (in other words, the sacrifice imposed on other creditors was justified) in the EUR 625,000 mortgage loan made by Banco Vasconia to Umaran Sociedad Cooperativa regardless of the fact that part (approximately 40 per cent) of the loan was to be used for the repayment of a pre-existing claim of the same creditor while the rest was to be used for the payment of other amounts due from the debtor to third parties. The court understood that the new loan provided the debtor with a lower interest rate and extended the maturity of the indebtedness by one year, thereby allowing the company to survive for a longer time. A similar reasoning is followed by the Provincial Insolvency Court of Barcelona No. 15 in a judgment dated 6 February 2009.

In connection with secured loans, Spanish courts seem to have accepted the possibility of setting aside the security arrangement only.

In respect of security arrangements entered into as security of indebtedness of other companies belonging to the same group of companies, it is normally accepted that there is some implicit consideration received by the parent while securing or guaranteeing the debts of the subsidiary. Thus, such guarantee or security does not amount *per se* to a 'disposal of assets without consideration' (see the *iuris et de iure* presumption of prejudice above). In contrast with this, upstream security (ie the subsidiary guaranteeing the liabilities of the parent) requires a specific consideration beyond that 'group interest' to avoid the clawback described above (judgment of the Commercial Court of Alicante dated 7 May 2010).

Article 71 IA also provides for a safe harbour against clawback for, *inter alia*:

- contracts and arrangements in the ordinary course of business of the debtor carried out under normal circumstances; and
- out-of-court RAs compliant with some requirements set forth in Article 71 bis IA.

The ordinary course of business of the debtor should be understood not as what the company does on a regular basis but rather as the activity of the company in the context of the business in which the company operates. It should not be confused with acts carried out on a regular basis with no necessary connection with the preservation of the business. The Commercial Court No. 9 of Madrid, in a judgment dated 18 November 2010, clarified that an intragroup offsetting of claims may have been a general and regular policy of the group of companies to which the debtor belonged, but it certainly did not qualify for the purposes of the safe harbour against clawbacks as it did not have a connection with the business of the company.

Further to that, the safe harbour requires that the particular transaction be carried out under 'normal conditions'. Normal conditions should not be interpreted only as arm's length conditions, but should be assessed by contrast with:

- what the insolvent debtor had done previously or subsequently to the transaction at stake;
- discriminatory treatment awarded to other creditors in similar circumstances;
- the form of the transaction to abide with the company's customary practice; and
- the proximity of the insolvency filing and awareness of the debtor of the grounds of insolvency.

See the judgment of the Provincial Commercial Court of Murcia dated 23 March 2009, endorsed by the judgment of the Commercial Court of Alicante No. 1 dated 16 July 2010.

Finally, some protection is also awarded against clawback to the mortgages created under Article 10 of the Mortgage Market Act (*Ley 2/1091 del Mercado Hipotecario*, dated 25 March), which may only be set aside in the case of fraud. Despite the loose language used in this act, it seems to be generally accepted that only mortgages used as collateral in the context of issuances of mortgage-secured instruments qualify for this protection.

Voidance of a contract under Article 71 IA determines the recovery of the consideration given and received by both parties to the transaction. As a general rule, the claim of the counterparty to the transaction so set aside would be a claim against the asset pool (Articles 73(3) and 84(8) IA) and satisfaction of this claim shall take place simultaneously to the recovery of the consideration received by such counterparty (Article 73(3)). Only one exception to this rule is contemplated in the IA, namely, the subordination of the counterparty that the insolvency court found had acted in bad faith.

In connection with the definition of bad faith that would automatically trigger the subordination mentioned above, the Spanish Supreme Court in, among others, judgments dated 16 September 2010, 27 October 2010 and 26 October 2012 has clarified that no fraudulent intent is required, only (i) the awareness of the financial distress of the debtor and of the fact that by entering into said transaction the interests of the remaining creditors would be jeopardised together with (ii) a conduct of the affected creditor susceptible to ethical reproach.

Judgments such as that of the Commercial Court of Valencia dated 14 July 2014 have introduced some disturbing elements for financial entities in the context of the assessment of the bad faith that may trigger the subordination described above, holding that *'it cannot be denied that it is precisely the banker lender who is better informed of the financial and asset situation of its clients'.*

2.14 What are the rules on set-off/netting?

Set-off shall not operate once insolvency proceedings have begun, unless the conditions for such compensation had been met before the opening of insolvency proceedings (Article 58 IA).

The fact that Article 58 IA allows the offsetting of reciprocal claims provided that the conditions for such offsetting have been met before the opening of insolvency proceedings does not isolate said compensation from scrutiny under Article 71 IA (see section 2.13 above on clawbacks). The Commercial Court No. 9 of Madrid, in a judgment dated 18 November 2010, set aside the compensation of reciprocal claims carried out by and between group companies on the grounds that it was indeed prejudicial to the interest of the insolvent's assets as it cancelled by compensation a claim of a group company that would have otherwise been ranked as subordinated under Article 93 IA (subordination of claims of related parties such as group companies).

Also, as described in section 2.4 above in respect of valid termination grounds and in section 2.10 above in respect of stays on enforcement, the closing out of netting arrangements made under Spanish Royal Decree 5/2005, dated 11 March, shall not be affected by the aforementioned restrictions.

2.15 How is exit managed?

Simple term-out

There is no specific deadline for the termination of insolvency proceedings. Insolvency proceedings may normally end with the fulfilment of a composition agreed with the creditors or by winding up (see the preamble to section 2 above). Although some effects of the insolvency declaration disappear after the judicial approval of the composition of creditors, the court will supervise the compliance of such composition.

In case (i) a composition of creditors is not reached, (ii) it is breached by the debtor or (iii) the debtor, instead of proposing a composition, requests the opening of the winding-up phase, the insolvency will transform into a winding-up process that will only end with the complete liquidation of the debtor's assets (see section 2 above). IA provides a number of guidelines to the winding up. Besides such guidelines, the framework of the winding up is a liquidation plan filed by the receiver, when approved by the court, which is not subject to special rules regulating the sale of the assets. with some exceptions that we shall briefly describe below.

Term out + asset disposal programme: should the programme be completed before the adoption of the plan?

See section 2.9 above for the different contents of the composition of creditors. Disposals of assets in the context of a composition are only acceptable after the reform of the IA carried out through the recent RDL 11/2014.

In a nutshell, the most noteworthy of the last legal developments on the content of the composition proposal are the following:

- the disposal of assets and rights attached to the debtor's business or professional activity, or of certain productive units, is expressly allowed; and
- the transfer of assets or rights to the creditors in payment of their claims is also allowed, provided that the assets or rights assigned are not necessary for the continuity of the debtor's business or professional activity.

Despite this, the general rule is that no composition of creditors may imply the *de facto* liquidation of the debtor. Thus, an asset disposal programme as content for a composition of creditors is something exceptional that may happen only in the following cases:

- the company may be divided or absorbed by another company as a way of restructuring;
- the sale to a third party of the whole business or of an independent business unit, after consultation with the unions; and
- a payment in kind with a particular asset or assets that are not necessary to the activity, so long as certain restrictions on the asset's valuation are complied with.

Where a disposal of an asset affected by a security interest is to happen in the context of a composition of creditors, the approval of this composition shall require the consent of the affected class of secured creditors, as described in section 2.9 above.

In case the asset is part of a business unit, the special rules mentioned below (see 'In the sale of the business as a going concern to an entrepreneur...') apply, particularly when analysing the sale of business units.

In any event, a disposal programme as a possible content of a composition may be supervised by a board to be created by creditors and will be supervised in all cases by the court in charge of approving the fulfilment of the composition. In case the composition is breached, the normal effect will be the opening of the winding up, as examined above.

Regarding the sale of assets – other than business units – securing a claim other than in the context of a composition of creditors, particularly a part of the winding up of the debtor, such liquidation normally takes place by means of a public auction (Article 155 IA). Nevertheless:

- the insolvency judge, at the request of the receiver or of the secured creditor, may also authorise a direct sale or the appropriation of the asset by the secured creditor (or a third party appointed by the secured creditor), provided that by means of such sale the whole secured claim is satisfied or the shortfall is recognised as an insolvency claim; and
- other than the above, the bidder shall be required to offer a price (to be paid immediately) in excess of the minimum agreed in the security arrangements unless the debtor and the secured creditor accept a lower

bid – always provided that market prices are used in the realisation process as determined by official appraisers.

In the realisation process, the proceeds paid by the successful bidder shall be used to repay the secured claim and therefore cancel the security arrangement. Any surplus shall be used to pay other claims in the order of preference determined by the IA. Nevertheless, the judge may authorise that the security be preserved and the successful bidder surrogated in the indebtedness with the secured creditor, which shall be removed from the liabilities of the estate.

However, in the case of a sale of a business unit comprising assets given as security of creditors, within the framework of a winding-up process, when it comprises any asset subject to a security interest, some additional rules apply (Article 149.1.3ª IA), namely:

- if the security arrangement is not to follow the asset in the sale (ie the security is to be cancelled), secured lenders shall be entitled to receive the part of the proceeds of the sale equivalent to the part of the price that the specific asset given to them as security represents on the total value of the business unit; or
- if the price does not cover the value of the security, secured lenders with right of separate enforcement representing at least 75 per cent of the class affected by the transfer will have to consent to it.

The consent of secured lenders shall not be required if the asset is transferred with subsistence of the security arrangement and subrogation of the purchaser in the secured debt, but the judge will have to ensure that the purchaser has the financial means and creditworthiness to assume the indebtedness.

The above are principles that would only apply in the absence of other specific winding-up arrangements contained in the winding-up plan, but will certainly inspire the content of said plan.

Can it be postponed and be part of the plan? Will sanctions be imposed if not completed? Is it possible for creditors to monitor the process?

Creditors affected by a composition may appoint a steering committee to supervise compliance with the agreed terms. In any event, any breach of the composition will entail sanctions to the debtor, mainly the opening of the winding up and the liability assessment described in section 3 below.

In the case of debt conversion(s), what approvals are necessary? Is it possible to force shareholders' consent?

See section 2.10 in respect of approvals required for debt conversion.

Shareholders' consent cannot be forced but, pursuant to the amendments to the IA by Royal Decree Act 4/2014 a, negative incentive addressed to shareholders and directors to agree on a debt for equity swap has been created. Shareholders that, absent reasonable grounds, in the context of an out-of-court RA or under AP 4 IA, decline to accept a debt for equity swap or the issue of convertible debt instruments may be held accountable in at-fault insolvency (see section 3.1 below in this respect).

In the sale of the business as a going concern to an entrepreneur, do creditors have the right to make their own proposal?

As examined above, the sale of a business unit is a possibility that is foreseen in the IA not only as a way of liquidation, but also as part of the composition of creditors or as an extraordinary sale authorised by the court during the common phase (ie as set forth in Article 43 IA; see section 2.7 above). In particular, a proposal of composition may also include the disposal of all the assets devoted to the economic activity of the debtor to a particular legal person or individual. All creditors of the company are entitled to bid for the assets of the business unit. For the time being, this possibility is only clear as part of an alternative proposal.

For the sale of a business unit, Article 146 bis IA sets forth that contracts attached to the continuation of the activity of such unit shall be transferred to the purchaser, provided that no termination event had been previously called. The purchaser shall step into the contractual position of the insolvent debtor under such contracts without the need of consent by the counterparty. The assignment of administrative contracts shall take place as per Article 226 of the Public Procurement Act.

Also, licences and public law authorisations attached to the continuation of the activity of such unit shall be transferred to the purchaser, provided that the purchaser carries on with the activities in the same premises.

Is credit-bidding possible?

The IA foresees public auction as the ordinary way of realisation of assets at any stage of the insolvency proceedings. In such public auctions creditors as well as third parties may post bids. The IA forbids the possibility of creditors paying in this auction by setting off their claims except in the case of secured creditors (Article 155 IA), who may post bids by way of offsetting their secured claim (see section 2.15 above).

Automatic release/survival of existing pledges and charges

See 'Term out + asset disposal programme' above.

2.16 Are 'prepackaged' plans, arrangements or agreements permissible?

The IA does not regulate prepackaged plans, though the debtor may file an advanced composition proposal, as referred to in section 2.6 above.

2.17 Is a public authority involved?

Does a public authority have powers?

A public authority only has powers in case of certain special insolvency regimes, such as the one applicable to financial institutions (even when filing for insolvency proceedings, especially under the special resolution regimes examined in section 2.2 above). Furthermore, in case of insolvencies with a duly justified public interest and at the request of a public law creditor, an additional receiver shall be appointed from amongst the public law creditors (see section 2.7 above).

Does it have to rule on the debtor's eligibility to the court protection?
No.

Does it have to approve/opine upon the feasibility/sustainability of the plan?
Not really; it will have to provide the court with a general opinion upon the terms of any composition proposal.

2.18 What is the treatment of claims arising after filing/admission?

As described in section 2.10 above, in principle, those claims will be held 'claims against the asset pool' and paid at their maturity date.

2.19 Are there ongoing contracts?

As discussed in section 2.4 above, Article 61(3) IA contains a general rule setting forth that, in respect of contracts with pending obligations at the time of the initiation of insolvency proceedings, termination events consisting exclusively of the onset of insolvency proceedings shall be ineffective and therefore these contracts shall remain in force, except in case of breach by any of the parties, which is validly declared by the commercial court in charge of the proceedings.

2.20 Are consolidated proceedings for members of a corporate family/group possible?

Articles 25 *et seq* IA establish several circumstances in which a group may be collectively declared insolvent, such as, in particular, groups of companies and directors, shareholders or other members of a legal entity which are personally liable for its debts. Also note that there are special rules regarding insolvency proceedings of concessionaires of public works and services and public procurement contractors which allow the public administration to make proposals for a composition in the context of insolvency proceedings onset on any of those. These insolvency proceedings shall be accumulated in cases where a composition proposal affecting more than one of these entities has been proposed. Each of these proposals may be made conditional on the approval of the other ones accumulated with this.

The court to hear the collective insolvency is the one that was hearing the insolvency of the debtor of the group with the biggest aggregated liabilities or, if applicable, the insolvency of the parent company. In any other case, the preference is to the court that had first heard of the insolvency of any of the group companies.

What are the consequences with regard to the pooling of assets and liabilities? Do creditors have a right to challenge such pooling?
Collective insolvencies will be processed in a coordinated way, but without consolidation or pooling of the debtor's estates. Exceptionally, the court may decide to consolidate all inventories and lists of creditors when there is commingling of assets and liabilities the segregation of which is not feasible without incurring extraordinary expenses or an unjustified delay.

2.21 What are the charges, fees and other costs?
In addition to the court agent's and the qualified lawyer's fees, and some necessary registration costs, the main cost to be borne will be the receiver's fees as set forth in Royal Decree 1860/2004 of 6 September 2004. This decree establishes the different percentages that can be modulated by the judge in order to adapt it to the particularities of the proceedings.

Furthermore, this remuneration will depend on the phase of insolvency that is effectively opened:

- when a composition is negotiated as a solution to the insolvency, the remuneration shall be equal to 10 per cent of the remuneration approved at the common phase, per month of duration of the composition proposal phase; or
- if the winding-up phase is opened, the remuneration shall be equal to 10 per cent of the remuneration approved at the common phase, during each of the first six months of the winding-up phase. See Tables 1 and 2.

Table 1. Percentages applicable to the assets

Assets (up to, in euros)	Amount of the remuneration	Remaining assets (up to, in euros)	Percentage applicable to the remaining assets
0	0	500,000	0.600
500,000	3,000	500,000	0.500
1,000,000	5,500	9,000,000	0.400
10,000,000	41,500	40,000,000	0.300
50,000,000	161,500	50,000,000	0.200
100,000,000	261,500	400,000,000	0.100
500,000,000	661,500	500,000,000	0.050
1,000,000,000	911,500	Onwards	0.025

Table 2. Percentages applicable to the liabilities

Liabilities (up to, in euros)	Amount of the remuneration	Remaining liabilities (up to, in euros)	Percentage applicable to the remaining liabilities
0	0	500,000	0.300
500,000	1,500	500,000	0.200
1,000,000	2,500	9,000,000	0.100
10,000,000	11,500	40,000,000	0.050
50,000,000	31,500	50,000,000	0.025
100,000,000	44,000	400,000,000	0.012
500,000,000	92,000	500,000,000	0.006
1,000,000,000	122,000	Onwards	0.003

3. LIABILITY ISSUES

3.1 What is the liability of managers/directors vis-à-vis creditors?

The judge dealing with the insolvency process shall open a special section of the proceedings (*Sección de Calificación de la Insolvencia*) to address liability issues:

- in case of winding up;
- in cases where the composition agreed by creditors involves write-offs exceeding 33.3 per cent or a payment deferral beyond three years; or
- in cases of breach of the terms of the composition agreed with creditors.

The aim of these procedural pleas is for the court to decide whether the insolvency was a no-fault (a consequence of the course of business) or an at-fault insolvency, and in the latter case to find evidence against some or all of the directors or individuals or entities defined below as 'affected parties'.

Affected parties could potentially be the directors, legal representatives, receivers, liquidators (both *de jure* and *de facto*), holders of general powers of attorney and those holding such office during the two-year period preceding the onset of insolvency proceedings.

Also, shareholders that in the context of RA pursuant to Article 71 or under AP 4 IA declined to accept a debt for equity swap or the issue of convertible debt instruments (but in this case only to the extent that they contributed with their vote to the rejection of the resolution at the relevant corporate body) may be affected parties unless they had reasonable grounds for objecting to such swap or debt instrument issuance.

Pursuant to existing case law, including the judgments of the Supreme Court dated 6 October 2011, 17 November 2011, 26 April 2012 and 21 May 2012, the judge shall rule on the opening of the liability section of the insolvency section depending on whether general, objective or specific grounds of liability apply to the particular case.

- Generally speaking, the judge shall carry out an analysis as to whether an affected party could have generated or aggravated the financial distress of the company (general grounds of liability).
- Despite the general analysis mentioned above, the insolvency shall in any case be held at-fault in any of the following circumstances, which may determine objective grounds of liability on the affected parties (objective grounds of liability):
  - for a severe breach of the legal duties in connection with financial record keeping, including double accounting;
  - for severe misrepresentations or falsehood in any of the documents attached to the petition of insolvency or in the documents submitted during such proceedings;
  - in case of winding-up proceedings instigated by the insolvency judge due to a breach of the composition with creditors for reasons attributable to the debtor;
  - in cases of fraudulent conveyance by the debtor of all or part of its assets to the detriment of its creditors, or of actions that delay, hinder or jeopardise the effectiveness of a seizure of any kind as a result of enforcements commenced or foreseeable;
  - in cases of fraudulent conveyance of the assets of the debtor in general during the two-year period preceding the onset of insolvency proceedings; or
  - for actions aiming at simulating a fictitious financial situation of the debtor before the onset of insolvency proceedings.
- Finally, Article 165 IA sets forth some presumptions in the presence of which the affected parties shall be deemed to have acted with gross negligence or wilful misconduct (specific grounds of liability):
  - breach of the duty to make an insolvency filing within the deadlines referred to in section 2.2 above;
  - failure to comply with the duty to (i) cooperate with the insolvency court and the insolvency receiver, (ii) deliver the information necessary or convenient in the interest of the insolvency proceedings or (iii) attend the creditors' meeting, personally or by proxy;
  - if applicable, failure to comply with the legal duty to (i) keep financial records and accounts, (ii) draw annual accounts, (iii) submit annual accounts to audit or (iv) file the annual accounts with Companies House in any of the three fiscal years preceding the onset of insolvency proceedings; or
  - other than based on reasonable grounds, rejection of (i) a debt for equity swap or (ii) the issue of a convertible debt instrument which jeopardises the achievement of a RA.

In the absence of objective or specific grounds of liability (ie where general grounds of liability apply), the judge will need to justify that the actions of the affected party at stake actually contributed to the generation or aggravation of the insolvency and the specific impact of the action or omission on the insolvency.

In contrast with the above, the judge shall hold the insolvency to be at-fault and henceforth shall be allowed to predicate the liability of the affected parties regardless of whether or not the court justifies they indeed aggravated or generated the insolvency of the debtor in the circumstances defined as objective grounds of liability.

Finally, where specific grounds of liability apply, the burden of proof that their actions did not contribute to the generation or aggravation of the insolvency is shifted to the affected parties.

The consequences for affected parties pursuant to the IA in the event of actually being found liable for the aggravation or generation of the insolvency of the debtor would be the following:

- barring of the affected persons to manage third party's assets for a period ranging from two to fifteen years, and to represent any person during that same period;
- the loss of any rights or claims in the insolvency proceedings and, if any, the restitution to the insolvent's assets of any property or rights unduly received from the insolvency assets and compensatory damages; or
- if the assessment of liability had been triggered by the opening of the winding-up stage, to the satisfaction of the recovery shortfall of creditors under the insolvency proceedings.

In respect of the liability of shadow or *de facto* directors, among others, and for its clarity and relevance for lenders in general, it is worth briefly referring to the judgment of the Commercial Court of Madrid dated 3 June 2014 handed down in the *MAG IMPORT* case. The court clarifies (in line with others of the Spanish Supreme Court, such as those dated 22 March 2004 and 26 January 2007) that '*de facto* directors' are those that, regardless of not being formally instituted as directors of a company (ie they were never formally appointed as such or their term in office lapsed), meet the following requirements:

- they take part in the management of the company in connection with matters pertaining to either the internal management (calling for shareholders' meetings, drawing accounts, etc) or the business activities of the company (the entrepreneurial activity of the company);
- they carry out the aforementioned activities with complete autonomy in the decision-making process (holding a mere power of attorney does not suffice for this purpose); and
- they engage in the said activities on a continuous basis as opposed to sporadically.

What is relevant is the carrying out of activities that pertain to the role of a general manager with a continuous participation in said management role and an effective and constant control of the activities of the company (judgment of the Provincial Commercial Court of Madrid dated 25 February 2013).

In the *MAG IMPORT* case, the judge had to determine whether the lenders in a particular refinancing deal could be considered as *de facto* directors on the grounds that

- they were entitled to appoint legal counsel for themselves, the cost of which would be paid by the company;
- they controlled the movements to be made in the accounts of the company; and
- they also controlled the payments that were to be made against the same accounts.

The judge understood that these activities do not imply the effective management of the company but, rather, were simply aimed at making sure that the terms of the (re)financing arrangements entered into with MAG IMPORT were complied with and therefore declined to consider the lenders as *de facto* directors of the company.

3.2 What is the liability of the lender?

Other than the specific application to banks of the generally applicable IA provisions (see sections 2.10, 2.13 and 3.1 above), Spanish law does not set forth any specific liability regime for lenders.

Sweden

Setterwalls
Odd Swarting, Mathias Winge & Nina Baecklund

1. WHAT COURT-MONITORED RESTRUCTURING PRE-INSOLVENCY PROCEEDINGS OR SCHEMES HAVE BEEN DEVISED BY THE LAW OF YOUR COUNTRY TO LIMIT VALUE DESTRUCTION FOR FAILING BUSINESS ENTITIES?

In Sweden, a company with financial difficulties can be restructured through a court-monitored proceedings under the Swedish Company Reorganisation Act (Company Reorganisation Act) – a so-called 'company reorganisation'.

1.1 What is the objective of the proceedings?

Company reorganisation provides a company with financial difficulties to reorganise its business with the protection of the court. This is to prevent companies with financial difficulties, but with potentially viable businesses, from being put into bankruptcy unnecessarily. With a well-planned reorganisation plan, often combined with a public composition, a company reorganisation may avert a financial crisis and prevent the deterioration of asset value.

1.2 Do all kinds of businesses qualify?

In order to obtain a court order granting the petition for company reorganisation, must be deemed that the debtor is unable to make payment of its debts as they become due or that such an inability will exist within a short time. Furthermore, it is required that there is a reasonable cause to assume that the purpose of company reorganisation can be achieved.

The Company Reorganisation Act does not apply to some debtors, eg banks, insurance companies and securities companies; nor does it apply to such debtors over whose business the state, a municipality, a county council or a municipal association has a controlling influence.

Upon the approval of an application for company reorganisation, the court shall appoint the administrator proposed in the application. The administrator is normally a lawyer specialising in restructuring and insolvency who is used to administering reorganisations and insolvencies.

1.3 What are the necessary approvals?

An application for company reorganisation may be submitted by the debtor or a creditor. An application submitted by a creditor may, however, only be granted if the debtor consents thereto, which is rare with such applications. (The situation with a creditor as applicant will therefore not be commented on below.) A debtor's application must be personally signed by the board of directors or the debtor's representative. The company reorganisation proceedings do not start until the court has approved the application.

1.4 What is the procedure?

Normally, the debtor files an application with the court. The application shall contain a brief account of the debtor's finances and the reasons for the payment difficulties, a schedule of creditors, a statement regarding the manner in which the debtor believes the business should be operated and how an agreement can be reached with the creditors, and a nomination of an administrator together with any necessary information regarding such person's suitability for the position. A complete application can be examined immediately by the court.

An application for company reorganisation filed with the court is considered a public document and can be handed out to any person requesting it. However, the court does not normally inform the creditors of the application until the application has been approved. Upon approval, the court determines the time for a meeting of the creditors before the court, at which the creditors will have the opportunity to comment on the continuation of the proceedings.

Within one week following the order regarding company reorganisation, the administrator shall notify all known creditors in respect of the order.

1.5 Is there recourse against the opening judgment?

Orders regarding company reorganisations shall apply with immediate effect, unless otherwise determined by the court. Such decisions by the court may be appealed by an affected party within three weeks from the day the decision was announced. Leave to appeal is required. An appeal of the company reorganisation normally occurs when the court has rejected the application. In recent years, a couple of applications for companies within the car industry have been rejected in first instance but later been approved by the appeal court. An appeal is a matter to be dealt with expeditiously by the court, but there is no formal time limit for the decision.

1.6 What are the substantive tests/definitions?

In order to obtain a court order granting the application for company reorganisation, the debtor must be deemed to be unable to make payment of its debts as they become due or that such inability will exist within a short time. It is also required that there is a reasonable cause to assume that the purpose of company reorganisation can be achieved.

Thus the debtor must show either insolvency or that such inability to pay its debts as they fall due will exist within a short time.

1.7 What is the role of a court-appointed agent?

An administrator shall investigate if and how the business of the debtor can be continued and whether a financial settlement, or composition, with the creditors can be reached. The debtor shall disclose all information of importance regarding the company's financial situation and comply with the instructions of the administrator in managing the business. The administrator shall, in cooperation with the debtor, prepare a restructuring plan showing how the purpose of the reorganisation will be achieved. The plan shall be submitted to the court and the creditors.

An administrator, in the execution of his assignment, shall not act in a way so that the interests of the creditors are set aside. The administrator shall inform the creditors of the company's situation and send them updated information on the financial situation, the reorganisation plan and the time of the creditors' meeting. A voluntary arrangement with the creditors is often preferable; however, if no such settlement is reached, the debtor may apply for a public composition (more about public composition is presented in section 1.8 below).

The mandate of the administrator in a company reorganisation is limited, in that the debtor retains the right of disposition of the business and assets. However, the debtor is not allowed to pay debts, take on new commitments or transfer ownership of assets of substantial importance without the administrator's consent. That said, if the debtor fails to comply with these rules, this does not affect the validity of such actions.

1.8 What protection is there from creditors?

The Company Reorganisation Act prohibits creditors from levying execution or taking other enforcement measures pursuant to the Enforcement of Judgments Code in respect of the debtor. Nor may orders be entered regarding attachment or other debt enforcement measures during the company reorganisation. However, enforcement of claims for which the creditor possesses a general or particular lien is excluded from this prohibition. Furthermore, upon the request of the debtor, a petition of bankruptcy shall be stayed, pending the termination of the reorganisation.

If there are special reasons to believe that the debtor is executing or failing to execute a particular measure and is thereby jeopardising a creditor's rights, the court may, upon request by the creditor, make appropriate orders in order to secure such rights by lifting the protection against creditors.

In order to prevent suppliers and others from undermining the reorganisation by cancelling their contracts with the debtor, the Company Reorganisation Act contains special provisions regarding contractual relationships. These provisions can prevent a creditor/supplier from terminating an agreement with the debtor (even though the creditor is entitled to termination) if the debtor, with the consent of the administrator, demands that the agreement shall be performed. Where an agreement is to be performed, the debtor shall, upon request by the other party, perform its corresponding obligations or provide the creditor/supplier with a security for future performance. If the debtor fails to provide notice or fails to perform its obligations according to the above, the counterparty is entitled to cancel the agreement.

There is no formal procedure for lodging proof of claims in company reorganisations. However, in a public composition, a creditor does need to lodge a proof of claims to be able to vote and thereby influence the outcome of the composition.

1.9 What is the usual duration of the restructuring process?

The reorganisation procedure shall last no longer than three months, but the court may extend the period by a further three months if special cause exists. However, company reorganisation may not proceed any longer than one year in the absence of composition proceedings. Most company reorganisations need to be continued for more than three months to be able to reach the goals of the proceedings. Before a decision on an extension is made, the debtor, administrator and creditors present at the creditors' meeting should be given the opportunity to submit their approach for the extension.

1.10 Who prepares the restructuring agreement and what are the available tools?

As mentioned in section 1.7 above, the administrator shall prepare, in cooperation with the debtor, a restructuring plan showing how the purpose of the reorganisation will be achieved. The administrator will negotiate with the creditors in order to reach a voluntary financial settlement. If no such settlement is reached, the debtor may apply for a public composition where the debtor with consent from the required majority of creditors can cram down the descendent creditors.

Upon the request of the debtor, the court may decide on the commencement of proceedings for composition. The Company Reorganisation Act contains detailed provisions regulating the public composition proceedings. Only creditors whose claims arose prior to an application for company reorganisation may participate in composition proceedings. A creditor whose claim may be satisfied through set-off or whose claim is subject to rights of priority may not participate in the proceedings. Nor may a creditor who, in the event of bankruptcy or insolvent liquidation, would only be entitled to payment after other creditors participate in the proceedings, unless the other creditors who are participating in the proceedings so consent.

The composition shall normally provide all similarly entitled creditors with at least 25 per cent of the amount of the claims.

Following the court's decision for composition proceedings, the court shall summon the debtor, the administrator and the creditors to the creditors' meeting, where the creditors' voting procedure will take place.

A composition proposal giving a dividend of at least 50 per cent of the claims shall be deemed to be accepted by the creditors where 60 per cent of the creditors voting have accepted the proposal and their claims amount to 60 per cent of the total amount of claims held by creditors entitled to vote. Where the composition percentage is lower, the composition proposal shall be deemed to be accepted by the majority of 75 per cent of the respective creditors and claims. Once the composition is approved, it is binding on all creditors who were entitled to take part in the composition.

Upon request by a creditor whose claim is subject to the composition, the court may, where cause exists, appoint the administrator or some other suitable person to supervise a debtor's performance of its obligations pursuant to the composition. However, there is no formal right for creditors, without security, to influence the sale of assets or which investors should invest in the business. In order to receive the creditors' approval of the composition, the debtor must, however, consider the creditors' views and come up with a serious proposal on how to refinance its business.

1.11 Are subordination agreements necessarily given full effect?

The starting point is that no discrimination between creditors is valid. The administrator is, however, free to negotiate with the creditors. A deviation which results in a disadvantage for a particular creditor may be valid provided such creditor consents thereto. However, discrimination of creditors through subordination agreements concluded before the reorganisation was initiated will still be valid during the company reorganisation procedure.

1.12 How is exit managed?

The court does not have to approve any restructuring agreement reached by settlements out of court. A formal composition must, however, be established by the court.

When it comes to ending formal reorganisation proceedings, the court shall terminate the proceedings after three months, provided that the proceedings is not extended. The company reorganisation shall also be terminated where, for example, the purpose of the reorganisation has been achieved, where the debtor or the administrator so requests and the purpose of the company reorganisation has not been achieved, or if the debtor has been declared bankrupt.

1.13 Who are the necessary parties?

As follows from section 1.12 above, the court shall terminate the company reorganisation when the purpose of the reorganisation may be deemed to have been achieved or upon the request of the debtor, creditor or administrator.

Orders regarding the termination of company reorganisations shall normally apply with immediate effect. Decisions by the court pursuant to the Company Reorganisation Act may be appealed individually by affected parties, which usually means within three weeks from the court order.

2. POST-INSOLVENCY PROCEEDINGS

In Sweden, there are two formal proceedings applicable to a company in financial distress:

- company reorganisation, mentioned above in section 1; and
- bankruptcy proceedings, which are mainly governed by the Swedish Bankruptcy Act (Bankruptcy Act).

The latter proceedings will be commented on below. Company reorganisation proceedings will only be described if not already commented on under a corresponding question in section 1.

2.1 What is the objective of the proceedings?

The primary objectives of the bankruptcy proceedings is to liquidate the assets of the debtor for the benefit of the creditors. Debtors/creditors sometimes, however, choose bankruptcy proceedings in order to receive a quick reorganisation of the debtor's business under a new legal entity and perhaps with new owners.

2.2 Do all kinds of business entities qualify?

A Swedish bankruptcy proceedings constitutes a proceedings where the combined assets of a debtor are taken charge of collectively and compulsory, on behalf of the creditors by the bankruptcy estate, for payment of debts. A debtor who is insolvent shall, following his own or a creditor's petition, be declared insolvent. Insolvency means that the debtor cannot pay his debts when due and this incapacity is not merely temporary.

The Bankruptcy Act does not exclude any entities but, according to case law, the Bankruptcy Act does not apply to such debtors as a municipality. Special regulations also apply to some legal entities, such as banks.

The main rule is that all creditors can file for bankruptcy. The creditor must prove the existence of the claim and the company's insolvency. Any claim entitles a creditor to file a bankruptcy petition. The Bankruptcy Act stipulates some situations in which the debtor is presumed insolvent: for example, when an attempt by the Swedish Enforcement Authority to enforce a writ of execution has been carried out during the past six months, revealing that the debtor did not have enough assets to cover the claim, or the debtor has suspended payments and has informed a substantial number of creditors of such suspension.

However, a creditor is not entitled to have a debtor declared bankrupt if, for example, the creditor's claim is not due and the creditor has a secure charge or collateral equivalent thereto in property belonging to the debtor.

2.3 What are the necessary approvals?

A debtor's petition must be personally signed by the debtor's directors. Information from the debtor that he is insolvent shall be accepted unless there is special reason not to do so.

As mentioned above in section 2.2, the main rule is that all creditors can file for bankruptcy.

The court decides on whether to approve or disapprove the bankruptcy application and appoints at the same time an official receiver. Before a decision is made on an application from the creditor, the debtor should be given the opportunity to submit his approach to the petition in a court hearing.

2.4 Is it valid and binding to agree that such proceedings be a default/termination event?

The opening of bankruptcy proceedings does not automatically affect the debtor's contractual relationships concluded before the opening of the proceedings, but such proceedings are usually a reason for termination. However, there are some certain contracts, such as employment contracts and rental contracts, that are governed by special provisions concerning the right of the estate and the counterparty after the opening of the procedure. There is also a general compulsory right for the bankruptcy estate to enter into contracts of its choosing which may result in agreements regarding default/termination not be binding.

2.5 What is the procedure?

The procedure for filing a petition for insolvency is described above in section 2.2.

When the court decides to approve the bankruptcy, it will appoint a receiver at the same time. The debtor is then no longer free to dispose of its property. Instead, the receiver assumes full authority of the property. However, the debtor in bankruptcy is still represented in its capacity as debtor by the board of directors. The receiver shall take control of the debtor's assets as soon as possible, together with the accounting material and other documents relevant for the liquidation. The main task for the receiver is to liquidate the assets in a way that provides the best dividend for the creditors. This can be done by selling the debtor's business either as a whole or in part or by selling the assets separately. In order to get the best result, the receiver may have to continue the debtor's business for some time (usually one month).

2.6 Please provide information about voluntary filings

As described above in section 2.2, the board of directors or a general meeting of shareholders of an insolvent corporation may pass a resolution to file a petition for bankruptcy. The petition must be personally signed by the debtor's directors and filed with the district court. The petition should be supported by a signed statement of the company's assets and debts accompanied by a specification of every creditor's name and postal address, the accounting material and other documents affecting the estate. The court shall examine the debtor's petition immediately. The debtor's statement of insolvency will normally be accepted by the court without any further examination and the company will be declared bankrupt. In practice, this is normally done the same day on a rather short application.

The bankruptcy decision will be published in the Official Swedish Gazette and in one or more newspapers in the applicable geographical area. Once the decision has been published, the creditors are deemed aware of the proceedings.

Voluntary filings for reorganisations have been described above in section 1.4.

2.7 How are creditors' representatives chosen?

In bankruptcy proceedings, no formal creditors' committees will be appointed and no formal creditors' meetings are held. Instead, the appointed receiver, in his administration of the estate, is obliged to look after the rights and interests of the creditors and to provide the creditors with the best possible dividend. Furthermore, the receiver shall take all measures necessary to achieve an expedient winding up of the estate. The receiver has a passive information duty to provide information about the estate and its administration upon the request of the creditors. The receiver is also obliged to hear the creditors specially affected on important issues, provided that there is no impediment to doing so.

A creditor can influence the choice of receiver by suggesting a receiver for the court to appoint. If the debtor and the Supervisory Authority approve the suggested receiver, he will normally be appointed by the court. A creditor that is dissatisfied with the receiver's administration has the right to request the appointment of an examiner for the supervision of the receiver's administration or petition the court with a request for removal of the receiver.

In company reorganisation, the creditors normally have a limited influence on the choice of the administrator since he has often already been chosen by the debtor in the application. However, it is possible in company reorganisation to appoint a creditors' committee. The court shall, upon the request of a creditor, appoint such a committee at the creditors' meeting. The members of the committee are chosen from amongst the creditors and normally consist of three persons.

2.8 Is there recourse against the opening judgment?

Provided that all formal requirements were met, a bankruptcy petition may not be withdrawn after a decision of bankruptcy has been made by the court. However, such decisions may be appealed. Normally, it is the creditors' applications that are appealed. But even if the debtor himself has applied for bankruptcy or consented to the bankruptcy petition of a creditor, a superior court can revoke the decision if the debtor on his appeal shows that he is solvent.

2.9 What are the roles and powers of committees?

In bankruptcy proceedings, there are no formal committees.

In company reorganisation, the creditors' committee has the tasks of monitoring the reorganisation process and looking after the creditors' collective interests, and the administrator shall consult with the creditors' committee on material issues.

2.10 What are the consequences of opening judgments for creditors?

Following the issue of a bankruptcy decision, the debtor may not control property belonging to the bankruptcy estate. Instead, the appointed receiver assumes full authority over the property. Nor can the debtor enter into obligations which could be claimed in the bankruptcy. Any transactions made later than the day following that on which the public notice of the bankruptcy decision was inserted in the Official Gazette are thus void unless it is shown that the other person did not know of the decision nor had a reasonable cause to assume that the debtor was declared bankrupt.

During bankruptcy proceedings, only creditors holding a pledge (including mortgages) are allowed to continue execution procedures through the Enforcement Authority. Sales of pledged assets other than through the Enforcement Authority are restricted in several ways and may need the consent of the receiver. Property that is not pledged or mortgaged, including assets to which a creditor has a security interest by way of a floating charge, is to be sold by the receiver.

Opening of bankruptcy proceedings is normally a draw stop for undrawn facilities. The receiver is, however, free to raise new loans. Such loans will be loans of the estate and preferential to the company's debts.

A creditor's pecuniary claim should be filed and tested in the bankruptcy proceedings. A creditor who has started legal proceedings before the declaration of bankruptcy may, however, continue the proceedings. The court's decision in the case of a pecuniary claim is not necessarily binding for the bankruptcy estate and the pecuniary claim can therefore be tried again in the bankruptcy proceedings. During bankruptcy proceedings, legal actions related to property that belongs to the bankruptcy estate generally cannot be brought against or by the debtor. Should legal proceedings regarding ownership of assets be pending at the time when the debtor is declared bankrupt, the proceedings may continue and the bankruptcy receiver will have a right to intervene in the proceedings.

Only claims arising before commencements of bankruptcy proceedings are recognised. If only preferential creditors are assumed to obtain a distribution in the bankruptcy, the creditors need only to notify the receiver of their claim and do not have to file proof of debt. However, in more complicated bankruptcies and in bankruptcies where non-preferential creditors may receive a dividend, the receiver may decide that a lodging of proofs procedure shall take place. If the court approves such a procedure, the court shall decide the period within which the lodging of proof shall take place and also notify known creditors of the time period in which proofs must be filed with the court. The period for lodging of proofs shall be at least four and at most 10 weeks. After that period and until the bankruptcy is concluded, a creditor may still, upon payment of a small charge, file proofs of debt. Foreign creditors are not treated differently and the same rules apply for them.

Interest accrued after the opening of an insolvency case may be claimed, but only in cases where all debts are paid in full.

The debtor does not obtain a discharge from any claim duly lodged in the bankruptcy proceedings unless such claim is paid in full. Therefore, the debtor's liabilities for full settlement of all claims lodged in accordance with the provisions of the Bankruptcy Act can be satisfied also from any assets the debtor may acquire in the future. For legal entities, such liabilities rarely arise in practice, since they more or less cease to exist after the bankruptcy is completed.

These matters have been discussed with regard to company reorganisation in section 1.8 above.

2.11 What is the duration of the restructuring process?

There is no statutory maximum for how long a bankruptcy can proceed. In practice, it differs for each bankruptcy proceedings. In large and more complex bankruptcy proceedings with, for example, cross-border elements, the proceedings can take up to around 10 years. However, most bankruptcy proceedings last for about six months up to one or two years.

2.12 How do creditors vote?

There are no formal voting rights for creditors in bankruptcy proceedings. Upon request of the debtor, the court may order the commencement of proceedings for composition in such proceedings. Basically, the rules regarding composition in bankruptcy proceedings are materially equivalent to the rules applicable in company reorganisation, with the exception that the receiver holds the role of the administrator. These rules are almost never used in practice.

As described in section 1.10, the creditors in company reorganisation will vote on the composition in company reorganisations if the court has initiated such composition proceedings.

2.13 What are the rules on clawback/voidability?

The Bankruptcy Act has several clawback rules, dealing with different types of improper transactions. There are both a number of objective rules which apply to certain types of legal transactions and a subjective general clause which, if the conditions are met, allows for the recovery of various types of legal transactions.

According to the main objective rule, any payment of debts made within three months prior to the 'limitation date', ie the date when the petition for bankruptcy was filed, shall be recovered, if made by non-customary means, prematurely or in an amount causing a substantial deterioration of the financial position of the debtor, unless considered ordinary having regard to the circumstances. This provision also applies when set-off has taken place if the creditor was not entitled to a set-off in the bankruptcy.

A similar provision is applicable to delivery of security less than three months prior to the limitation date. Such security shall be recovered unless it was agreed at the time when the debt arose or has been delivered without delay if the security nevertheless cannot, with regard to the circumstances, be considered as ordinary. There are also objective rules stating that gifts and unreasonably high salary payments made less than six months prior to the limitation date can be recovered.

Generally, all the objective rules have extended recovery periods for close relatives and such transactions shall be annulled unless the relative shows that the debtor neither was, nor by the transaction became, insolvent. Close relatives to legal entities are typically affiliated companies, shareholders and persons in a management position.

The general subjective recovery provision states that an act which took place less than five years before the limitation date shall be recovered if:

- it has in an unfair manner favoured one creditor over other creditors, concealed property from creditors or increased the debtor's debts; and
- the debtor was or became insolvent by the procedure and the other party knew or ought to have known of the insolvency of the debtor and the circumstances making the legal act improper.

A close relative of the debtor shall be considered to have such knowledge unless it is shown that he probably neither knew nor ought to have had such knowledge. There is no stated time limit for such a relative.

A recovery action in a general court may be instituted within one year of the day of the bankruptcy decision. An action may also be instituted within six months of when grounds for doing so became known to the bankruptcy estate. The receiver has the primary right to demand recovery. With the receiver's acceptance, a creditor can challenge avoidable transactions. Assets recovered by the creditor have to be handed over to the bankruptcy estate.

The recovery provisions in the Bankruptcy Act also apply when the court has decided that company reorganisation is to take place and a public composition has been established.

2.14 What are the rules on set-off/netting?

A claim against a debtor which may be recognised in the bankruptcy may be used by the creditor to set off a claim that the debtor had against the creditor when the bankruptcy decision was issued. This does not apply if set-off was not allowed by reason of the nature of the claims. For example, the opposing claims normally have to be of the same type of assets (eg money against money and not coffee beans against wheat) and basically originate from the same contractual relationship.

A claim against the debtor acquired by a transfer from a third party less than three months prior to the limitation date may not be used in set-off against a claim which the debtor had when the creditor acquired his claim. This also applies if a claim against the debtor has been transferred previously by such transfer and the creditor then had reasonable reason to assume that the debtor was insolvent. Further, a creditor who has placed himself in debt to the debtor in circumstances equivalent to payment by means other than customary means of payment may not set off to the extent that such payment could have been the subject of recovery.

During company reorganisation, any person who possessed a claim against the debtor at the time the application for reorganisation was filed may, notwithstanding that the claim is not due and payable, offset such claim against claims which the debtor possessed at such time against such person. This shall not, however, apply where set-off is not possible as a consequence of the nature of any of the claims as mentioned above (cp above). In company reorganisation, there are also similar limitations to the possibilities to set off with regard to transactions to acquire set-off possibilities and incurring liabilities which may be equated with payments with other than customary means, as in the bankruptcy situation.

2.15 How is exit managed?

As mentioned above, the main task for the receiver is to liquidate the assets in a way that provides the best dividend for the creditors, and there is no statutory maximum for how long a bankruptcy can proceed. Liquidation can be done either by selling the debtor's business as a whole or in part, or by selling the assets separately. During the administration, the receiver is obliged to hear creditors who are particularly affected on important issues, and to obtain the consent of creditors holding security in real property and personal property before selling such property. When the receiver is selling the debtor's business as a whole, the creditors are free to make their own proposals for buyers. Those are, however, not binding for the receiver.

As mentioned in section 2.10 above, only creditors holding a pledge (including mortgages) are allowed to continue execution procedures through the Enforcement Authority during bankruptcy proceedings. Sales of pledged assets other than through the Enforcement Authority are restricted in several ways and may need the consent of the receiver. Property that is not pledged or mortgaged, including assets to which a creditor has a security interest by way of a floating charge, is to be sold by the receiver.

Once the assets have been sold, the balance must be distributed. If the assets of the bankruptcy estate are not sufficient to pay for the bankruptcy expenses incurred and the expected and other debts that the estate has incurred, the court shall decide to write off the bankruptcy.

If assets remain in the estate when the receiver has paid the expenses in the bankruptcy and other debts that the estate has incurred, the receiver shall draw up a dividend proposal, which will be announced and then confirmed by the court. A creditor can make an objection to the proposal if he finds it incorrect. The insolvency proceedings is concluded once the dividend proposal has been approved by the court and the order has gained legal force. The creditors are then entitled to what is due to them.

If there are no known creditors, the receiver shall restore the property to the debtor.

As described in section 1.12 above regarding company reorganisation, there is a possibility of cramming down dissenters through a public composition procedure since a composition is binding on all creditors who were entitled to take part in the composition, even on those creditors voting against the proposal.

2.16 Are 'prepackaged' plans, arrangements or agreements permissible?

In Sweden, there is no special codified regime for 'prepackaged' restructuring plans negotiated in advance between stakeholders. Instead, it is the ordinary statutory rules regarding bankruptcy and company reorganisation that will be applicable, depending on which proceedings is initiated.

Before initiating company reorganisation, a solid preparation is almost a necessity for an advantageous outcome. A debtor can always negotiate with its creditors to seek acceptance for the restructuring plan and/or improve its finances through a loan or a shareholder's contribution before initiating the reorganisation proceedings in order to try to speed up the formal proceedings.

In bankruptcy proceedings, it is perhaps less common to find such a 'prepackaged' plan, but it is nonetheless not disadvantageous. Before the bankruptcy proceedings was initiated, the debtor may already have consulted a prospective receiver, searched for and negotiated with prospective buyers for its business, etc in order to speed up the proceedings once the bankruptcy decision has been made.

2.17 Is a public authority involved?

The court of first instance in both bankruptcy and reorganisation proceedings is the district court, the decisions of which may be appealed to the court of appeal and ultimately to the Supreme Court.

The court has no direct jurisdiction over the assets of the debtor. Instead, the receiver has full authority over the property in bankruptcy proceedings. In bankruptcies, the court's jurisdiction is basically confined to appointing a receiver and initiating the lodging of proofs procedures upon the request of the receiver. Other duties for the court are trying disputed claims and approving the receiver's dividend proposal. The fees for the administrator are also decided by the court. Other disputed questions (such as recovery of disputed debts that the debtor may have) must be initiated in separate proceedings.

The receiver's administration is supervised by the Supervisory Authority, which is a government authority. The receiver has a passive duty to provide information about the estate and its administration upon the request of the court and the Supervisory Authority. The receiver is also obliged to hear the Supervisory Authority on important issues, provided that there is no impediment to doing so.

In business reorganisations, the district court appoints an administrator and also administers public composition proceedings upon request from the administrator (or the receiver if a composition procedure is initiated in a bankruptcy proceedings). The court does not have to approve upon the sustainability of the reorganisation plan or rule on the debtor's eligibility to the court protection. However, as mentioned above in section 1.8, the court may, upon request by a creditor, make appropriate orders in order to secure a creditor's rights by lifting the protection against creditors.

2.18 What is the treatment of claims arising after filing/ admission?

In bankruptcy proceedings, the main rule is that only claims arising before the issue of the bankruptcy decision may be recognised. If, however, the receiver chooses to continue the debtor's business for a certain period, the debts arising during this period are treated as debts of the bankruptcy estate.

In company reorganisation, old debts shall normally not be paid during the reorganisation but be a part of the composition. New debts shall be paid accordingly during the proceedings. If, however, a new agreement or debt (incurred with the consent of the administrator) were not to be paid by the debtor and the debtor were to be declared bankrupt, the creditor may have a high privileged claim.

2.19 Are there ongoing contracts?

As mentioned above in section 2.4, an opening of bankruptcy proceedings does not automatically affect the debtor's contractual relationships concluded before the opening of the proceedings, though such proceedings are usually a reason for termination. However, there are certain contracts, such as employment contracts and lease contracts, that are governed by special provisions concerning the right of the estate and the counterparty after the opening of the procedure. As a result, agreements regarding default/termination may not be binding. The receiver can also choose to enter into an agreement concluded by the debtor before the bankruptcy in order to liquidate the assets in the best possible way.

Ongoing contracts in company reorganisations have been described above in section 1.8. As stated in that section, special rules have been created for contractual relationships in order to prevent suppliers and others from undermining the entire reorganisation by cancelling contracts due to the debtor's difficulties in paying its debt. These rules give the debtor the opportunity, with the consent of the administrator, to demand fulfilment. Where an agreement is to be performed, the debtor shall perform its corresponding obligations or provide the creditor/supplier with a security for future performance. Under certain conditions, the other party is entitled to some sort of security. Thus, a credit agreement can continue provided that the creditor has a valid security or receives a new security. If the debtor fails to provide acceptable security, the creditor/lender is normally entitled to cancel the agreement.

To facilitate a financing of the company reorganisation, new loans raised with the consent of the administrator are preferential in a future bankruptcy (liquidation) situation. This is also applicable in company reorganisation on claims based on contracts entered into by the debtor during the reorganisation, provided that the administrator consented to the contract being entered into.

2.20 Are consolidated proceedings for members of a corporate family/group possible?

Insolvency proceedings involving a corporate group are not formally combined in Sweden. Instead, each legal entity is treated separately. However, depending on the circumstances, the same person can be (and often is) appointed as receiver for all members in a corporate group. This is mainly done to cut costs and to render a more effective liquidation of the assets.

2.21 What are the charges, fees and other costs?

If a creditor is filing a petition for bankruptcy, the district court charges a small application fee. Other fees and costs include:

- fees and payment of expenses to the receiver;
- payment to the state for supervision of the administration;
- remuneration for any expert assistants engaged by the receiver;
- the cost of public notices of decisions or measures concerning the bankruptcy; and
- the cost of written summonses and notifications to the debtors issued in the bankruptcy.

The bankruptcy expenses shall be paid out of the bankruptcy estate before other debts that the estate has incurred. To the extent that the bankruptcy expenses cannot be taken out of the estate, they should be paid by the state.

In company reorganisation, there is initially a small fee for filing an application to the court for starting the proceedings. The administrator shall be reimbursed for expenses, and his fees are normally prepaid or paid on current account in accordance with an individual agreement between the debtor and the administrator.

3. LIABILITY ISSUES

3.1 What is the liability of managers/directors *vis-à-vis* creditors?

The Swedish Companies Act contains detailed rules to safeguard that a company has sufficient equity at all times and, if insufficiency occurs, to force primarily the directors of the company to take action. The board must specifically take action if there are reasons to believe that the company's shareholders' equity is less than one-half of the registered share capital.

In such situation, the directors are obliged to immediately prepare, and engage the company's auditors to examine, a balance sheet for liquidation purposes. Where the balance sheet shows that the company's shareholders' equity is less than one-half of the registered share capital, the board of directors shall summon a shareholders' meeting as soon as possible. If the directors fail to comply with the capitalisation rules and fulfil the duties provided in the Swedish Companies Act, they can face personal liability for debts arising after a balance sheet for liquidation purposes ought to have been drawn up. Thereafter there are also several specific duties to observe in restoring the share capital.

Claims against a director for not fulfilling his liabilities under the equity rules may be brought by any creditor whose debt arose after a balance sheet for liquidation purposes ought to have been drawn up. Such claims are not normally brought by the receiver.

The directors may also be held liable for unpaid taxes and duties if they have failed to pay in due time. This probably should not apply if the company has effectively suspended payments before the taxes became due for payment. Such claim against a director is brought by the Tax Authority alone and not by the receiver.

The directors and the managing directors can also be personally liable if, in the performance of their duties, they intentionally or negligently cause damage to the company. In such case they shall compensate the damage. The damages could be a consequence of a violation of, for example the Swedish Companies Act, the applicable annual reports legislation or the articles of association. One example of this is participation in unlawful dividends.

Claims regarding damage to the company may be brought where the majority or a minority consisting of owners of not less than one-tenth of all shares in the company have, at a general meeting, supported a resolution to bring such a claim in damages or, with respect to a member of the board of directors or the managing director, have voted against a resolution regarding discharge from liability.

Where the company has been placed into bankruptcy, the bankruptcy estate shall bring the proceedings instead. If the proceedings was initiated before the bankruptcy, the receiver can intervene in the process.

It should also be noted that company directors may face criminal liability for continuing to trade while a company is insolvent or potentially insolvent, and under certain conditions can be subject to an injunction against trading.

3.2 What is the liability of the lender?

Generally, there is no specific provision in the Bankruptcy Act or in the Swedish Company Act aimed directly at the liability of lenders. Such liability has been discussed from time to time between academics, but in practice should be determined on the basis of general contract law and tort law (with some exceptions for insolvency of individuals) on a case-by-case basis.

However, a lender could be liable to return what he received as loan repayment if the repayment was a value transfer in violation of the Swedish Companies Act and the company proves that the lender knew or should have realised that the value transfer was in violation of that act.

Further, a lender could be liable if, in the performance of his duties, he intentionally or by gross negligence caused damage to the company by participating in unlawful dividends to other parties. The lender could, for example, have participated indirectly in the execution of the decision or in the preparation or adoption of an incorrect balance sheet which constituted the basis for the decision regarding a value transfer. If the recipient in such case fails to return what he or she has received, the lender could be liable for the deficiency.

There is also a risk that, according to the rules regarding clawback mentioned in section 2.13 above, a lender could be liable to return received loan repayments.

Claims regarding transfer of value, damage and recovery may be initiated by the company or in bankruptcy by the receiver.

Turkey

Pekin & Pekin Gokben Erdem Dirican & Erdem Atilla

1. WHAT COURT-MONITORED RESTRUCTURING PRE-INSOLVENCY PROCEEDINGS OR SCHEMES HAVE BEEN DEVISED BY THE LAW OF YOUR COUNTRY TO LIMIT VALUE DESTRUCTION FOR FAILING BUSINESS ENTITIES?

Concerning pre-insolvency stage, there are two main court-monitored restructuring proceedings types regulated under the Execution and Bankruptcy Law (Law No. 2004) (published in the Official Gazette dated 19 June 1932 and numbered 2128; the EBL): amicable restructuring and concord restructuring.

1.1 What is the objective of the proceedings?

The objective of both amicable restructuring and concord restructuring is to protect debtors the financial situations of which have been negatively affected due to reasons such as economic crisis, unfavourable market/business conditions and inaccurate business forecasts.

1.2 Do all kinds of businesses qualify?

Banks and insurance companies are not entitled to propose amicable restructuring as a debtor (Article 309(t) of the EBL). For amicable restructuring, the debtor, which must be an equity company or a cooperative, must have failed to pay its debts or the debtor's assets must be insufficient to recover its debts, or there must be a situation where it is highly likely that the debtor is under the threat of facing these situations (Article 309(m) of the EBL).

However, all debtors can be subject to concord restructuring (Article 285 of the EBL). Concord restructuring allows the debtor to restructure certain liabilities in accordance with a plan. There is no threshold related to indebtedness, turnover or asset value.

1.3 What are the necessary approvals?

There is no specific provision in the law as to the requirement of a resolution by the corporate body of the debtor in order to propose amicable restructuring or concord restructuring; however, if such requirement is included in the articles of association of the debtor, for limited liability companies, a resolution must be granted unanimously by all shareholders of the debtor for proposing the restructuring; for joint stock companies, a decision of the board of directors shall be passed for proposing the restructuring. The request for concord restructuring can also be made by a creditor of the debtor.

1.4 What is the procedure?

The application for amicable restructuring is made by the debtor together with the following documents (Article 309(o) of the EBL):

- the restructuring plan;
- balance sheets and commercial books of the debtor and other information and documents demonstrating the financial status of the debtor;
- documents indicating the cash flow of the debtor;
- a list of all creditors of the debtor and the creditors of the creditors of the debtor;
- documents explaining the negotiation period between the debtor and the creditors prior to the application and indicating that the affected creditors have been sufficiently informed of the plan;
- documents approved by a notary public indicating the declarations of approval of the affected creditors;
- a table demonstrating the approximate amount that the creditors will receive after the plan and the approximate amount the creditors will receive in case of bankruptcy of the debtor;
- documentation demonstrating that the majority quorum has been reached; and
- a financial analysis report prepared by an independent auditing firm indicating that the debtor will return to a state of solvency and it is possible to comply with the terms of the plan.

The creditors affected by the restructuring plan shall be invited for restructuring project negotiations through a notification sent by registered mail or through notary public, containing the required information regarding the project (Article 309(o)/5 of the EBL). This notification will enable the affected creditors to decide on the project and must be sent in a reasonable period prior to the voting date.

The application for concord restructuring is made by the debtor together with the following documents (Article 285 of the EBL):

- the concord restructuring plan;
- balance sheets and statement of income; and
- commercial books of the debtor (if any).

The concord request made to the execution court is announced by the execution court within a national newspaper the circulation of which is more than 50,000. The creditors may apply to the execution court if they have any objections within 10 days from the announcement date. The creditors objecting to the concord request and the debtor shall be heard in a hearing the date and time of which shall be determined by the execution court.

1.5 Is there recourse against the opening judgment?

Concerning amicable restructuring, the approval decision to be granted by the court can be appealed by objecting creditors affected by the project. If the court rejects the restructuring plan, the rejection judgment can be appealed by the debtor or the creditors affected by the plan that approved the plan. Correction of the judgment after review by the court of appeals as a result of the initial appeal examination is not possible.

Concerning concord restructuring, the approval decision of the court can be appealed by the objecting creditors. If the court rejects the concord, the rejection judgment can be appealed only by the debtor. Parties may apply for correction of the judgment to be granted as a result of the appeal examination.

The appeal period is 10 days, starting from the service of the reasoned judgment to the relevant party, for an amicable restructuring and 10 days, starting from the hearing date when the decision is granted for approval/rejection, for a concord restructuring.

1.6 What are the substantive tests/definitions?

Concerning amicable restructuring, an amicable restructuring plan must be ratified by a court in a hearing, in which it will hear submissions from the mid-term auditor (if any), the debtor's representatives and the creditors attending the hearing.

Courts will ratify the application if satisfied that the debtor has filed the application in good faith, provisions of the EBL have been fulfilled and the amount to be received by each creditor that rejected the plan will be at least equal to the amount to be received at the end of the bankruptcy liquidation. Otherwise, the court will reject the application (Article 309(p) of the EBL).

Concerning concord restructuring, the execution court either grants the concord period for a maximum term of three months or rejects the application made by the debtor (Article 287 of the EBL).

In a case where the execution court grants the concord period, the concord officer conducts a creditors meeting, after which the concord officer delivers all documents submitted in the meeting to the commercial court. The commercial court decides on approving the concord plan by examining whether:

- the proposed amount is proportional to the sources of the debtor;
- the concord plan is duly accepted by the creditors; and
- the amount of money or guarantee letter required by law is deposited by the debtor (Article 298 of the EBL).

If not, the concord plan is rejected by the commercial court.

1.7 What is the role of a court-appointed agent?

Concerning amicable restructuring, if the court takes measures to protect the debtor's assets until its decision on ratification or rejection of the amicable restructuring plan, the creditors and debtor – or, if the same fail to agree on one, the court – can appoint one or more mid-term auditors who have the necessary knowledge, experience and characteristics agreed by the creditors and debtor to assume responsibility for directing, managing and supervising the debtor's activities from the date of appointment until the court's ratification or rejection of the plan (Article 309(ö) of the EBL).

In the event that the plan is ratified by the court, it may in its ratification decision appoint one or more plan supervisors, who will have authority to supervise and monitor whether the plan is being fulfilled and to report on the situation to the creditors (Article 309(p) of the EBL).

Concerning concord restructuring, the concord officer is liable to supervise the acts of the debtor, report to the execution court and inform the creditors regarding the concord period (Article 290 of the EBL).

Also, one or more concord liquidators shall be appointed by the creditors. The concord officer may be appointed as concord liquidator (Article 309(a) of the EBL). The concord liquidators conduct all actions regarding the protection, liquidation and, in some cases, the transfer of the assets of the debtor (Article 309(c) of the EBL).

1.8 What protection is there from creditors?

Concerning amicable restructuring, the commercial court of first instance is competent to take the necessary protective measures with regards to debtor's assets and activities. In this respect, the court may appoint a mid-term auditor(s).

Concerning concord restructuring, creditors are entitled to file their objections within 10 days from the announcement date of the concord request. If the concord request is accepted, a concord period, which cannot be more than three months, shall be granted to the debtor and a concord officer(s) will be appointed. The concord officer is liable to supervise the acts of the debtor, to report to the execution court and inform the creditors regarding the concord period (Article 290 of the EBL).

Also, one or more concord liquidators shall be appointed by the creditors. The concord officer is eligible for such appointment (Article 309(a) of the EBL). The concord liquidators conduct all actions regarding the protection, liquidation and, in some cases, the transfer of the assets of the debtor (Article 309(c) of the EBL).

1.9 What is the usual duration of the restructuring process?

Concerning amicable restructuring, there is no statutory period set by the EBL.

Concerning concord restructuring, if the execution court approves the concord request, it shall grant to the debtor a concord period of no more than three months (Article 287/2 of the EBL). If the three-month period is not sufficient, the execution court may extend this period for an additional period of two months (Article 287/6 of the EBL).

1.10 Who prepares the restructuring agreement and what are the available tools?

Concerning amicable restructuring, the debtor and the creditors may agree on restructuring of indebtedness and reorganisation of the debtor in the amicable restructuring plan to be submitted to the court. Such plan must be accepted by at least a qualified majority of the creditors affected by the plan participating in the negotiations representing at least two-thirds of the receivables of the creditors who vote (Article 309(m) of the EBL). If the project in question contains more than one group of creditors, the project must be internally accepted in each group based on the majority requirements explained above.

The amicable restructuring plan shall explain in detail the matters which ensure that the plan is applicable, such as:

- the conditions which the affected creditors will be subject to;
- how the equality between the creditors will be reached;
- the effect of the plan on the agreements that the debtor is a party to;
- the effect of the plan on the power of possession of the debtor on its assets;
- whether the debtor will be able to apply for financial resources such as loans;
- whether the debtor can be transferred;
- amendment of the article of associations of the debtor;
- the persons who will act in the management of the debtor;
- the extension of the term of maturity of the debtor's debts; and
- the change in the interest rates (Article 309(n) of the EBL).

Concerning concord restructuring, the concord plan is a formal plan regarding the liquidation of debts, prepared and presented by the debtor to the execution court for its approval, under which the debtor is released from his or her debts once the partial payments have been paid in full. Since the concord request is made through a petition addressed by the debtor to the execution court, a detailed balance sheet, an income statement and a chart indicating the status of the commercial books of the debtor must also be attached to the petition (Article 285/1 of the EBL). The creditors who can request bankruptcy of the debtor may also file a concord request for the debtor. Upon the concord restructuring request, in order to protect the assets of the debtor, the execution court may take some protective measures set forth in the EBL limiting the power of disposal of the debtor.

1.11 Are subordination agreements necessarily given full effect?

Concerning amicable restructuring, it is not mandatory for the debtor to group the creditors. However, if a grouping is made, it must be in accordance with Article 6 of the Amicable Restructuring Regulation. In the event that there is discrimination between categories of creditors, approval of other creditors within the same group must be obtained.

Concerning concord restructuring, the debtor must apply the conditions of the concord plan, and any other undertakings of the debtor towards the creditors shall be deemed null and void. The debtor must treat all the creditors equally. In the event that it is determined that the debtor did not act honestly by discriminating between certain creditors, a criminal sanction may be applied as per Article 333 of the EBL.

1.12 How is exit managed?

Following approval of the concord, each creditor may initiate an execution proceedings against the debtor if its receivables are not paid to the said creditor in line with the concord conditions or may request that the concord be terminated only for itself (Article 307 of the EBL).

However, if it is determined afterwards that the debtor has acted in contradiction to *bona fides* rules (eg the debtor executes an agreement with some debtors to provide them with greater amounts or securities, just in order for the concord to be approved) during the approval process of the concord, each creditor may request termination of the concord. In that case, the concord shall be terminated for all of the creditors (Article 308 of the EBL).

The competent court for this termination lawsuit is the commercial court that approved the concord.

The above-mentioned provisions shall also be applicable for amicable restructuring by analogy.

1.13 Who are the necessary parties?

Concerning amicable restructuring, the approval decision to be granted by the court can be appealed by the objecting creditors affected by the project. If the court rejects the restructuring plan, the rejection judgment can be appealed by the debtor or the creditors affected by the plan who approved the plan. Correction of the judgment to be granted by the Court of Appeals as a result of the appeal examination is not possible.

Concerning concord restructuring, the approval decision of the court can be appealed by the objecting creditors. If the court rejects the concord, the rejection judgment can be appealed only by the debtor. Parties may apply for correction of the judgment to be granted as a result of the appeal examination.

The appeal period is 10 days, starting from the service of the reasoned judgment to the relevant party, for amicable restructuring and 10 days, starting from the hearing date when the decision is granted for approval/rejection, for the concord restructuring.

2. POST-INSOLVENCY PROCEEDINGS

2.1 What is the objective of the proceedings?

The objective of post-insolvency concord restructuring is to protect the debtors who were already declared bankrupt by the commercial court.

2.2 Do all kinds of business entities qualify?

A debtor who has already been declared bankrupt by the commercial court may apply for post-insolvency concord restructuring even though it requested direct bankruptcy at the bankruptcy lawsuit.

2.3 What are the necessary approvals?

The bankrupt debtor must prepare a concord request (project) and submit the same to the Bankruptcy Administration. If the Bankruptcy Administration has not been constituted yet, such request shall be given to Bankruptcy Office (Article 223 of the EBL). The Bankruptcy Office prepares a report regarding the bankrupt debtor and submits the same, together with the concord request, to the second creditors' meeting (Article 237/3 of the EBL), where the post-insolvency concord request shall be evaluated.

2.4 Is it valid and binding to agree that such proceedings be a default/termination event?

It can be agreed by the parties of a contract that, if a party requests concord, such shall cause default/termination of the contract.

2.5 What is the procedure?

See section 2.3 above. In addition, evaluation of this concord request is similar to the procedure explained in section 1 above.

2.6 Please provide information about voluntary filings

As mentioned above, the concord request is filed with the Bankruptcy Administration. The concord request does not have to include a detailed balance sheet or a chart including the status of commercial books. Likewise, no concord officer needs to be appointed since the power of disposal of the debtor's assets is exercised by the Bankruptcy Administration. In other words, the duties of the concord officer are performed by the Bankruptcy Administration concerning post-insolvency concord restructuring.

The concord request shall be evaluated at the second creditors' meeting. Within the announcement for the second creditors' meeting, it shall be indicated that the debtor requested concord and that this request shall be negotiated in the meeting. In principle, the evaluation of this concord request is the same as the pre-insolvency concord restructuring process. At the end of the meeting, those who accept the concord request are listed in the minutes and the concord is open for participation for 10 days.

Upon expiry of this 10-day participation period, the Bankruptcy Administration grants the bankruptcy and passes the concord file, along with the reasoned report, to the commercial court that declared the debtor bankrupt. Until a decision is granted by the commercial court as to whether the concord request shall be approved or not, sale of the bankrupt's assets shall be postponed.

2.7 How are creditors' representatives chosen?

Concerning post-insolvency concord restructuring, no concord officer is appointed. The creditors may participate in the second creditors' meeting either themselves or through an attorney who has been granted the required power of attorney.

2.8 Is there recourse against the opening judgment?

In the event that the commercial court decides to approve/reject the concord, the appeal process is the same as mentioned above for pre-insolvency concord restructuring. However, by the time the decision of the court as to approval of concord becomes final following the appeal and correction of judgment procedure, the Bankruptcy Administration shall be notified regarding this issue. The Bankruptcy Administration shall then request from the commercial court that the bankruptcy judgment be removed (Article 309 of the EBL). Once the removal judgment has been issued, it can also be appealed. In the event that the removal judgment becomes final, the assets entered into the bankrupt's estate shall be given back to the debtor.

2.9 What are the roles and powers of committees?

Concerning the role of the Bankruptcy Administration and Bankruptcy Office, see section 2.3 above; for the creditors' meeting, see section 2.6 above.

2.10 What are the consequences of opening judgments for creditors?

In the event that the bankruptcy judgment is removed, the debtor can no longer be deemed 'bankrupt' and it shall be deemed as never having been declared bankrupt. Accordingly, the normal course of business of the debtor shall continue as it was prior to bankruptcy.

2.11 What is the duration of the restructuring process?

Concerning the post-insolvency concord restructuring, there is no concord period/duration granted by the court to the debtor due to the fact that, upon declaration of the bankruptcy, all of the attachable assets of the debtor constitute the bankrupt's estate and the power of disposal of the debtor on those assets is limited. Moreover, upon this declaration of bankruptcy, it is prohibited to initiate execution proceedings or to continue the existing execution proceedings against the debtor (Articles 184–94 of the EBL).

2.12 How do creditors vote?

Even though there is no 'voting', at the end of the second creditors' meeting, those who accept the concord request are listed in the minutes and the concord can be participated in for 10 days.

2.13 What are the rules on clawback/voidability?

Under Turkish law, the hardening period is a key concept in insolvency and bankruptcy proceedings. It provides that new collateral granted by a debtor during a hardening period to secure a pre-existing claim may be deemed invalid by a court upon the application and request of the creditors and/or the liquidation/bankruptcy officer of the debtor.

During the debt collection and liquidation process, the transactions of the insolvent/bankrupt company completed prior to its insolvency/bankruptcy – particularly transactions within the hardening period – shall also be considered and reviewed. This may result in the cancellation of such transactions provided that such fall within the scope of Articles 278, 279 and 280 of the EBL, which state three different hardening periods, of one, two and five years.

The one-year hardening period applies to:

- security interests, if such security interest is created to secure an existing debt and the security collateral provider has not committed to providing security interest at the time of incurring a debt;

- payments made via instruments other than cash or ordinary payment instruments;
- payments made before their due date; and
- certain annotations to the title deed registries.

In order for the above-mentioned transactions to be annulled, such transactions should have been made within a one year prior to the bankruptcy of the debtor or attachment of its assets.

The two-year hardening period applies to donations and gifts.

The five-year hardening period applies to transactions made by the debtor with one of its creditors with the aim of harming its other creditors, provided that the creditor with whom the transactions are made is aware of the insolvency and the aim of the debtor at the time of the transaction. In order for the aforementioned transactions to be annulled, they should have been made within five years prior to the initiation of bankruptcy or execution proceedings.

2.14 What are the rules on set-off/netting?

Concord is, in principle, mandatory for all bankruptcy receivables. However, concerning preferred receivables (registered to the bankrupt's estate), public receivables arising from an asset and receivables secured by a pledge, it is not mandatory (Articles 298/3, 303/1 and 309/2 of the EBL). Therefore, the mentioned receivables must be paid immediately upon removal of the bankruptcy. Concerning the other receivables subject to concord restructuring, the debtor must pay the same within the period and proportion accepted in the concord.

2.15 How is exit managed?

See section 1.12 above. The provisions mentioned therein apply to post-insolvency restructuring by analogy.

2.16 Are 'prepackaged' plans, arrangements or agreements permissible?

Concerning post-insolvency concord restructuring, the relevant provisions applicable for pre-insolvency concord restructuring are applicable by analogy. The debtor must apply the conditions of the concord plan, and any other undertakings of the debtor towards the creditors shall be deemed null and void. The debtor must treat all the creditors equally. In the event that it is determined that the debtor did not act honestly by discriminating between certain creditors, a criminal sanction may be applied as per Article 333 of the EBL.

2.17 Is a public authority involved?

Concerning post-insolvency, no public authority is involved other than the commercial court and the Bankruptcy Office.

2.18 What is the treatment of claims arising after filing/admission?

As mentioned above, the concord request shall be evaluated in the second creditors' meeting, moderated by the bankruptcy office director. The Bankruptcy Administration shall present the status of the bankrupt's estate (active and passive assets) within this meeting and shall declare whether continuation of bankruptcy liquidation or acceptance of concord shall be more beneficial for the creditors.

2.19 Are there ongoing contracts?

Upon removal of the bankruptcy judgment, since the debtor can no longer be deemed 'bankrupt' and as it shall be deemed as never having been declared bankrupt, the normal course of business of the debtor shall continue as it was prior to bankruptcy, also covering existing contracts. Therefore, the contracts executed by the debtor prior to the bankruptcy judgment shall be ongoing due to the removal of the bankruptcy.

2.20 Are consolidated proceedings for members of a corporate family/group possible?

Pursuant to sample judgments of the 19th Civil Law Chamber of the Court of Appeals, even though it is theoretically possible for the debtors to file consolidated proceedings, the approval conditions for the concord restructuring must be met for each of the debtors separately. Therefore, evaluation as to whether required conditions for approval of the concord request were met shall be performed for each debtor as a separate legal entity.

2.21 What are the charges, fees and other costs?

Pursuant to the Annex of the Law of Charges, a fixed charge amounting to TRY 41.50 (for 2014) shall be paid while applying for a concord request. Moreover, 1.138 per cent of the amount determined to be distributed among the creditors shall also be paid as a pro rata charge. In addition, expert examination, announcement expenses, concord officer expenses (not applicable for post-insolvency concord) and other service expenses shall also be paid by the debtor in advance.

3. LIABILITY ISSUES

3.1 What is the liability of managers/directors vis-à-vis creditors?

Concerning criminal sanctions, pursuant to Article 331 of the EBL, those who, in order to cause damage to the creditors, dispose of, destroy or devalue a part or all of their assets, or transfer such by simulation to another party, in order to reduce its activities within a period of two years prior to a concord request shall be sentenced to imprisonment and face a judicial fine in the event that the creditor can prove with concrete evidence that it could not collect its receivable.

Pursuant to Article 332 of the EBL, those who cause their insolvency or aggravate their financial situation by their own operations within a period of two years prior to a concord request shall be sentenced to imprisonment and face a judicial fine in the event that the creditor can prove with concrete evidence that it could not collect its receivable.

Pursuant to Article 333 of the EBL, those who provide or undertake to provide a particular interest for a creditor, the Bankruptcy Office or the Bankruptcy Administration in order to obtain its approval for the concord process shall be sentenced to imprisonment.

Pursuant to Article 333/a of the EBL, persons who are *de jure* or *de facto* empowered for management and who wilfully cause damage to creditors by not paying the commercial enterprise's debts partially or entirely shall be sentenced to imprisonment and face a judicial fine upon complaint of the creditor unless the mentioned action constitutes another crime.

Pursuant to Article 334 of the EBL, those who wilfully cause damage by manipulating the creditors, concord officers, mid-term auditor or authorised officer, or those who act in contradiction of the restructuring plan in order to obtain a concord period or to obtain approval for a concord or an amicable restructuring plan, shall be sentenced to imprisonment.

Concerning civil law sanctions, in the event that the creditors cannot collect their receivables due to the fact that the debtor did not act in compliance with the concord plan, such creditors are entitled to file an execution proceedings or a lawsuit for collection of their receivable. Moreover, in those cases, pursuant to Article 307 of the EBL, they can also request termination of the concord for their part. In terms of Article 308 of the EBL, if the debtor has acted contrary to *bona fides* rules (ie has acted in bad faith), the creditors can also request termination of the concord for all of the creditors.

With regards to amicable restructuring, Articles 307 and 308 shall be applicable by analogy. Furthermore, in terms of Article 309(t) of the EBL, in the event that the debtor fails to fulfil (partially or entirely) its obligations arising from the restructuring plan, this shall be notified to the court. In the event that the court determines that the debtor failed to perform its obligations or acted contrary to the restructuring plan, or that the creditors could not collect their receivables, it shall rule for bankruptcy of the debtor.

3.2 What is the liability of the lender?

Pursuant to Article 333 of the EBL, those who provide or undertake to provide a particular interest for a creditor, the Bankruptcy Office or the Bankruptcy Administration in order to obtain its approval for the concord process shall be sentenced to imprisonment. The creditors who obtained this interest shall also be sentenced to imprisonment.

UK

Macfarlanes Jatinder Bains, Paul Keddie & Simon Beale

1. WHAT COURT-MONITORED RESTRUCTURING PRE-INSOLVENCY PROCEEDINGS OR SCHEMES HAVE BEEN DEVISED BY THE LAW OF YOUR COUNTRY TO LIMIT VALUE DESTRUCTION FOR FAILING BUSINESS ENTITIES?

There are two types of pre-insolvency proceedings available to companies under English law; a company voluntary arrangement, or CVA, and a scheme of arrangement, or Scheme.

CVAs were introduced by the Insolvency Act 1986 (the Act), which is the main piece of primary insolvency legislation in England and Wales, as an alternative to liquidation for companies experiencing financial difficulties. A CVA must involve either a *'composition in satisfaction of a company's debt'* (ie that creditors will receive a payment of a sum of money in place of the entirety of an existing debt) or a *'scheme of arrangement'* (not to be confused with a Scheme), which involves some form of arrangement of the company's affairs but does not necessarily need to involve a compromise of claims (although usually will).

A Scheme involves a compromise or arrangement between a company and its creditors (or any class of them) and/or its members (or any class of them). Unlike a CVA, when voting on a Scheme, creditors must be divided into different classes, with each class comprising creditors whose *'rights are not so dissimilar for it to be impossible for them to consult together with a view to their common interest'* (*Sovereign Life Assurance Co v Dodd* [1892] 2 QB 753). Further, a CVA can only affect the right of a secured creditor to enforce its security with its consent, whereas a Scheme may bind secured creditors provided that the requisite number of creditors (75 per cent or more, together with a majority in number) vote in favour of the Scheme (and secured creditors are likely to form a separate class for voting purposes).

CVAs are usually initiated by the company's directors, but can also be used as a way of agreeing creditors' claims as part of an administration or liquidation (described in more detail below). A Scheme may also be proposed by a creditor or shareholder of a company, although, in practice, it will usually be the directors who propose the Scheme.

1.1 What is the objective of the proceedings?

In both cases, the company proposing the CVA/Scheme is usually able to pay its debts in the short term, but is facing financial difficulties which have got to the stage where a compromise with creditors is needed to ensure that the company avoids a formal insolvency process in future. For example, in recent years CVAs have been used as a means for companies in England and Wales to exit over-rented premises or come to a binding compromise regarding rental payments with landlords (even where those landlords do not vote in favour of the CVA, they can still be bound if the requisite majority of creditors – 75 per cent or more in value and more than 50 per cent of 'unconnected' creditors – vote in favour). Consequently, the overriding objective of a Scheme or CVA is usually to reduce a company's debt burden to a level which will allow it to avoid a formal insolvency process, but not by so much that creditors are unlikely to vote in favour of the CVA or Scheme.

1.2 Do all kinds of businesses qualify?

Yes – there are no thresholds in relation to a company's assets or turnover in a CVA or Scheme.

Recent years have also seen a number of overseas companies using English law Schemes as a means to come to a compromise with creditors. This is on the basis that a Scheme does not fall within the remit of Council Regulation (EC) 1346/2000 on insolvency proceedings (EC Regulation), so even where a company does not have its centre of main interests (COMI) in England or Wales, it may still utilise a Scheme where the requirements under section 221 of the Act, which governs the winding up of unregistered companies, are met. A foreign company can be deemed to be an unregistered company for these purposes (and, therefore, be subject to a Scheme) if:

- it has a sufficient connection to England and Wales;
- there is a reasonable possibility of benefit to the company applying for the Scheme; and
- one or more persons interested in the distribution of the company's assets (ie creditors) are persons over whom the court can exercise jurisdiction (*Real Estate Development Co* [1991] BCLC 210, applied in *Stocznia Gdanska SA v Latreefers Inc (No 2)* [2000] EWCA Civ 36).

A 'sufficient connection' for these purposes has included the company's finance documents being governed by English law and, recently, a Scheme was sanctioned in respect of a company which had amended the governing law clause of its documentation to English law, with the requisite lender consent, in order to propose a Scheme.

CVAs, on the other hand, fall within the procedures which are covered by the EC Regulation so, in order to propose a CVA, a company's COMI must be in England or Wales.

1.3 What are the necessary approvals?

The company's board will have to resolve that the company proposes a Scheme or CVA (other than where proposed by an administrator or liquidator).

A Scheme requires that 75 per cent in value and a majority in number of each class of creditor votes in favour of the Scheme. Unlike a CVA, the court will also have to sanction the Scheme at a hearing specifically for that purpose, and will do so provided that the Scheme satisfies three requirements as to fairness, which are discussed in more detail below.

In respect of a CVA, 75 per cent in value of the company's unsecured creditors, and at least 50 per cent of unconnected creditors who are present (in person or by proxy) and voting at a meeting of creditors held to vote on the CVA, will need to vote in favour for it to be approved (as well as any secured creditors whose rights of enforcement are affected by the CVA). Whilst the CVA proposal (and a report on the outcome of the meetings to approve the CVA) will be filed at court, the court does not sanction a CVA as it does a Scheme, although any creditors who wish to challenge the CVA must do so at court.

1.4 What is the procedure?

In respect of a CVA, the directors of the company prepare a proposal for the CVA, which will include certain information prescribed by the Insolvency Rules 1986. The directors will also provide a statement of the company's assets and liabilities, known as a statement of affairs, and file such statement along with the CVA proposal at court. In practice the proposal and the statement of affairs will be prepared with the assistance of a licensed insolvency practitioner, termed, at this stage, the nominee, who will act as the supervisor of the CVA and administer its implementation if it is successfully voted through.

Once the CVA proposal is filed, the nominee must lodge a report on the contents of the CVA proposal at court and then call a meeting of creditors to vote on the proposal on 14 days' notice. Provided the requisite number of creditors vote in favour of the proposal, the nominee becomes the supervisor of the CVA and will file a report of the outcome of the creditors meeting at court within four business days.

A CVA proposed by an administrator or liquidator differs in that the liquidator/administrator will normally act as nominee and will file the proposal at court, but will not be required to report on it.

A Scheme will involve the proposer preparing the proposal for the Scheme and then making an application to court to obtain two hearing dates for the Scheme. At the first hearing the court will make orders requiring that the proposer convenes meetings of the requisite classes of creditors/shareholders to vote on the Scheme and will provide directions as to how the proposer should give notice of the meetings to creditors/shareholders. The proposer will then give notice of the meetings and advertise the meetings in the manner directed by the court, together with an explanatory statement concerning the contents of the Scheme. The meetings are held and, if the requisite voting majorities are obtained, the proposer reapplies to court for a hearing, at which the Scheme is sanctioned.

1.5 Is there recourse against the opening judgment?

A CVA may be challenged by a creditor making an application to court on one of two grounds: that the CVA unfairly prejudices the interests of that creditor or that there was some form of material irregularity during the CVA process. An unfair prejudice challenge will only succeed where the prejudice arises from the unfairness of the proposal itself – for instance, by treating different types of creditors differently as regards distributions.

Material irregularity involves a challenge based on procedural matters, eg a valid vote being rejected at the creditor's meeting.

As above, a creditor may challenge the fairness of a Scheme at the second, sanction hearing on the basis that:

- the meetings of creditors/shareholders were not properly convened and held (ie that the procedural requirements in respect of the Scheme were not complied with);
- each class was not fairly represented (ie that a majority of each class was not acting bona fide when voting on the Scheme); or
- the proposal for the Scheme is, itself, unfair and unfairly prejudices any creditor or class of creditors.

1.6 What are the substantive tests/definitions?

Insolvency is not a pre-requisite to a Scheme or CVA, although may well be the outcome if the Scheme or CVA is not voted through. There is no concept of insolvency in the Act – instead, the Act introduces a concept of a company being *'unable to pay its debts'* in section 123. The two most prominent definitions of a company being unable to pay its debts are where it is *'deemed to the satisfaction of the court that the company is unable to pay its debts as they fall due'* in section 123(e) (generally known as the cash-flow test) and where it is proved to the satisfaction of the court that *'the value of the company's assets is less than the value of its liabilities, including contingent and prospective liabilities'* in section 123(2) (generally known as the balance sheet test).

1.7 What is the role of a court-appointed agent?

In a CVA, the nominee will assist the company's directors in preparing the CVA proposal and statement of affairs, and will then file a report on the proposal at court. Once the CVA has been approved at the meetings called to vote on the CVA, the nominee will act as supervisor and administer the CVA in accordance with the terms of the CVA proposal. This will usually include putting the company into liquidation or administration if the CVA fails (ie the company breaches the terms of the CVA), and the supervisor may then act as administrator or liquidator if creditors approve.

There is no supervisor or court-appointed agent in a Scheme, which will be administered by the company itself (even though, as stated above, the court is involved).

1.8 What protection is there from creditors?

Once a CVA is approved (and the proposal will usually contain restrictions on enforcement by those bound by the CVA), it will bind every person who had notice of and was entitled to vote at the meeting to approve the CVA and every person who would have been had he had notice of it (section 5(2) of the Act). However, there is no protection from creditor enforcement before the CVA is approved. Certain companies may apply for protection if they meet the criteria for a 'small company' set out in section 382(3) of the Companies Act 2006 by way of a 'small company moratorium' but, in practice, this is rarely used due to the criteria for obtaining such a moratorium being quite strict.

A Scheme will also bind all persons who were entitled to vote on it, including creditors who did not vote or voted against. Again, the Scheme will usually restrict creditor enforcement once approved, and it is common for the proposer of the Scheme to seek contractual protection under 'lock-up' agreements from creditors to ensure that they vote in favour of the Scheme, and to refrain from enforcement action until the Scheme is approved.

1.9 What is the usual duration of the restructuring process?

Assuming that no application for a small company moratorium is involved, a CVA will usually take around two to three months to implement. The proposal will need to be drawn up and then, once filed at court, the nominee has 28 days to file his report. The nominee will call meetings of creditors at the date and time specified in his report (usually on 14 days' notice), and a creditor may challenge the decision of the meeting within 28 days of it. The CVA itself will vary in duration depending on the number of distributions to creditors, complexity, type of assets which may be sold to realise funds for creditors and so on, but will usually last for anything up to five years.

A Scheme will usually take longer than a CVA to implement due to the increased involvement of the court. The proposer will need to draw up the Scheme proposal, determine the composition of each class of creditor, apply to court, hold meetings as prescribed by the court to vote on the Scheme and attend the two court hearings. Consequently, the Scheme could take as long as six months to implement.

1.10 Who prepares the restructuring agreement and what are the available tools?

Absent a company fulfilling the conditions for a small company moratorium in a CVA, lock-up agreements may be used to bind creditors to vote in favour of the CVA or Scheme proposal and to refrain from selling their debt in the period covered by the lock-up agreement. In larger cases, creditors may also appoint a committee of three to five members to represent them at meetings held during the term of the CVA or Scheme to vote on certain matters.

1.11 Are subordination agreements necessarily given full effect?

Generally yes. Because the CVA or Scheme is essentially a contractual arrangement between a company and its creditors, distributions will follow the order of priorities set out in any subordination agreements. It is also likely that any CVA or Scheme proposal which sought to reorder priorities amongst creditors could be challenged on unfair prejudice grounds if any affected creditor did not consent.

1.12 How is exit managed?

If a CVA comes to an end in accordance with the terms of its proposal, the supervisor will send notice to creditors that the CVA has terminated. This includes if the CVA has failed, whereby the supervisor is usually authorised by the proposal to put the company into administration or liquidation. A Scheme would usually involve the same process and, normally, where the CVA or Scheme has been a success, the company will return to solvent trading.

1.13 Who are the necessary parties?

The proposer of the CVA or Scheme and, in the case of a CVA, the nominee/supervisor will need to ensure that the requisite number of creditors will vote in favour of the CVA or Scheme. Consequently, it is unlikely that a proposal will be made absent the proposer being assured that sufficient creditors will vote in favour. The proposer will also want to ensure that the proposal itself is not unfair to avoid any creditor challenge.

2. POST-INSOLVENCY PROCEEDINGS

2.1 What is the objective of the proceedings?

There are, effectively, two types of insolvency proceedings in England and Wales: administration and liquidation. In administration, a company is placed under the control of a licensed insolvency practitioner, known as an administrator, who must pursue one of three statutory objectives, in a hierarchical order:

1. the rescue of the company as a going concern;
2. failing which, achieving a better result for creditors than would be likely if the company were to enter liquidation; and
3. failing which, realising the company's property to make a distribution to one or more secured or preferential (essentially the claims of company's employees, up to certain prescribed limits) creditors.

In contrast, in liquidation, the objective of an insolvency practitioner appointed to the company (in this case termed the liquidator) is to collect in the company's assets, realise those assets and distribute the proceeds to the company's creditors in accordance with their claims.

2.2 Do all kinds of business entities qualify?

Generally yes, subject to certain prescribed exceptions where some types of company are made subject to their own slightly different form of administration process (such as investment banks).

2.3 What are the necessary approvals?

There are three routes into administration for a company:

- an appointment made under paragraph 14 of Schedule B1 to the Act by the holder of security over all or substantially all of a company's assets, known as a 'qualifying floating charge' or QFC (which can be made out of court by a simple filing of forms at the court office, without the need for a court hearing);

- an appointment by the company's directors or members pursuant to paragraph 22 of Schedule B1 to the Act, which can also be made out of court subject to notice of the directors'/members' intention to appoint an administrator being first served on the holder of any QFC; and
- an appointment made by certain other prescribed persons, including an unsecured creditor, by way of a court application and hearing pursuant to paragraph 12 of Schedule B1 to the Act.

In respect of an appointment by the company's directors or members out of court, or any person via a court application, certain qualifications apply. These include that the company must be unable to pay its debts within the meaning of section 123 of the Act and is not already in liquidation. An appointment by the holder of a QFC requires that the QFC has become enforceable in accordance with its terms and the company is not already in liquidation.

There are two types of liquidation; voluntary liquidation and compulsory liquidation. Voluntary liquidation can be broken down further into two types: members' voluntary liquidation (MVL) and creditors' voluntary liquidation (CVL). MVL differs from CVL in that it requires that the company's directors swear a declaration that, having made a full enquiry into the company's affairs, they believe that the company will be able to discharge all of its liabilities (including contingent and prospective liabilities) in full within the following 12 months. Knowingly swearing such a statement where there are no reasonable grounds to do so can lead to civil or even criminal penalties.

Both CVL and MVL are initiated by the company's shareholders passing a special resolution (ie a resolution of the holders of 75 per cent or more of its shares) to initiate the process. CVL differs from MVL in that a separate meeting of the company's creditors will be held to vote on the identity of the liquidator.

Compulsory liquidation results from the court making an order, known as a winding up order, upon the presentation of a petition by one or more prescribed persons, including a creditor owed more than £750. Section 122 of the Act sets out the grounds on which the court can wind up a company, and include that the company is unable to pay its debts or that it is just and equitable to do so.

2.4 Is it valid and binding to agree that such proceedings be a default/termination event?

Broadly, yes: financing documents, as well as other contracts such as leases and commercial agreements will usually contain a provision whereby a borrower or guarantor under the agreement, or another company in the same group, going into administration or liquidation triggers a default or termination right (which English law will give effect to). Further, several 'pre-insolvency' events may also be included as defaults, including the company becoming insolvent on either a cash-flow or balance sheet basis, even where a liquidator or administrator is yet to be appointed. However, in respect of defaults caused by balance-sheet insolvency, recent case law, including, most notably, the decision in *BNY Corporate Trustee Services Limited v Eurosail 2007 3BL plc (Eurosail)*, requires that the party relying upon a default caused by balance-sheet insolvency first performs a commercial assessment of a company's situation, taking into account its prospective future liabilities and assets. Consequently, it is not merely enough that a company's liabilities exceed its assets at any given time, but an assessment must be made of the company's future liabilities and assets to determine whether it will be able to meet those liabilities when they fall due before a default can be called. This, in practice, makes relying upon defaults caused by balance-sheet insolvency incredibly uncertain.

2.5 What is the procedure?

Administration, if by way of the out-of-court route, simply requires a filing of forms at court. For a directors' appointment, notice of intention to appoint administrators must be filed at court before the appointment is made and served on any holders of a QFC. The holder of the QFC is then given five business days to agree to the appointment or appoint its own choice of administrator. Where a QFC holder is making the appointment, it must serve notice on any holder of a prior-ranking QFC, which then has two business days to consent or seek to appoint its own choice of administrator.

A court application for an administration requires that the applicant files notice, together with a witness statement and other documents in support at court, and then serves at least five business days' notice on certain prescribed persons, including the holder of any QFC. The court will then make an administration order if it is satisfied that the company is, or is likely to become, unable to pay its debts and the administration would be likely to achieve one of the statutory purposes described above. As above, voluntary liquidation is commenced by the company's shareholders, who must resolve to put the company into liquidation. In a CVL, a creditors' meeting is then called within 14 days of the shareholder resolution being passed (on at least seven days' notice) to vote upon the identity of the liquidator.

A compulsory liquidation commences when the petitioner files a winding up petition at court and serves it on the company. The court will set a date for the hearing of the petition (usually within six weeks of filing) and the petitioner will be required to advertise the petition no less than seven business days before the hearing.

2.6 Please provide information about voluntary filings

In an out-of-court administration appointment, the filings required are, if notice is to be served on any QFC holder, a 'notice of intention to appoint administrators', which is filed at court, and, once the relevant notice period expires or consent is obtained, a further notice, known as a 'notice to appoint administrators'. If there is no QFC holder in a directors/members appointment or no prior-ranking QFC in a QFC appointment, then there is no need to file a notice of intention to appoint administrators prior to filing the notice to appoint administrators. The proposed administrators are also required to file a statement confirming that, amongst other things, they accept the appointment and reasonably believe that the purpose of the administration can be achieved.

A voluntary liquidation will require that the relevant shareholder resolutions (and the statutory declaration of solvency in respect of an MVL) are all subsequently filed at the company registry and that the liquidation is advertised in the London Gazette.

Only compulsory liquidation and a court application to appoint an administrator require a court hearing. Notice of the hearing will be served on a number of prescribed parties, including the holder of any QFC, the company itself and certain types of creditor. Whilst those parties may attend the hearing (and make submissions), if the applicant can satisfy the conditions for an administration/winding up order contained in the Act (and described above), the court is unlikely to refuse to make the order sought.

2.7 How are creditors' representatives chosen?

In an administration, creditors may appoint a committee of between three and five members. This will usually be at the first meeting of creditors, which will be held by the administrator within 10 weeks of his appointment, where the administrator's proposals for the conduct of the administration will be considered for approval by creditors. Any creditor of the company can sit on the committee (and whilst it is normal that different types of creditor will be present on the committee, there is no legal requirement for any given class to be represented), provided that their claim has not been rejected by the administrator and is not fully secured. A committee may also be appointed in a CVL and compulsory liquidation, either at the creditors' meeting held to vote for the appointment of the liquidator in respect of a CVL or at the first meeting of creditors in a compulsory liquidation.

Once the requisite number of creditors agree to act on the committee, the administrator or liquidator will issue a 'certificate of due constitution', at which point the committee comes into effect.

2.8 Is there recourse against the opening judgment?

In an out-of-court administration, the holder of a QFC in a directors' appointment or a prior-ranking QFC in a QFC appointment may appoint their own choice of administrator during the notice periods described above. An interested party (most feasibly the company's directors or shareholders) may also apply to court to challenge the appointment of the administrator if it can prove that the conditions for the appointment were not met (ie that the company was not unable to pay its debts in respect of a directors' appointment or that the QFC had not become enforceable in respect of a QFC appointment or on COMI grounds). In a court-appointed administration, the court hearing to appoint the administrator would be the most appropriate forum to challenge the need for the appointment (and, on the basis that the application will be before a considered hearing, the courts are generally reluctant to allow appeals at a later date).

An MVL (provided that all procedural formalities have been complied with) will not be open to challenge but, if it turns out that the company will not be able to pay its creditors in full, the liquidator will need to convert the MVL into a CVL. There may also be civil and criminal consequences for the directors who swore the false declaration. In a CVL, any creditor's concerns as to the appointment may be voiced at the meeting to appoint the liquidator and, in a compulsory liquidation, at the hearing of the winding up petition.

2.9 What are the roles and powers of committees?

Generally, the committee will act as a sounding board for the administrator/liquidator, vote upon certain issues, approve the administrators'/liquidators' remuneration and call upon the administrator/liquidator to answer questions raised about the conduct of the process. A liquidation committee has an additional role in sanctioning or approving powers of the liquidator (certain powers can only be exercised by a liquidator if he has obtained sanction), which is not required in respect of an administrator (whose powers are freely exercisable).

In terms of voting, each committee member has one vote and any resolution put to the meeting, provided that it is quorate (ie at least three members are in attendance and able to vote, either in person or remotely), will be voted through upon a simple majority. In certain cases individual members may be prohibited from voting on matters put to the committee, such as where there is a conflict of interest or the committee member concerned will obtain a personal benefit from the transaction or matter being voted upon. Creditors may also be disqualified from acting on the committee in certain scenarios.

2.10 What are the consequences of opening judgments for creditors?

An administration causes an automatic stay on creditor action, known as a moratorium, which prevents court proceedings against the company or enforcement action without the consent of the administrator or an order of the court. A similar moratorium does not apply to secured creditor enforcement in liquidation, whereby a secured creditor may enforce its security freely (although there is still a moratorium on court proceedings).

An unsecured creditor is required to file a written notice of its claim, known as a proof, in order to have a valid claim in the administration or liquidation. The ultimate responsibility regarding whether the proof should be admitted, and in what amount, lies with the administrator/liquidator, and there are guidelines regarding how to treat, for example, claims in a foreign currency or claims for future debts.

2.11 What is the duration of the restructuring process?

An administration automatically ends after 12 months unless extended. An extension can be obtained either from creditors (which may be given once, and for a maximum period of six months) or by way of a court application (which usually extends the administration for individual periods of up to 12 months, provided that there is good reason for the extension).

There is no set -time limit for liquidation – the liquidation will end when the liquidator has dealt with all of the company's assets and claims.

2.12 How do creditors vote?

At the initial meetings of creditors described above (ie the meeting to consider the administrator's proposals – although such meeting can be bypassed where the administrator needs to act quickly – or the meeting to vote upon the choice of a liquidator), or where no creditors' committee has been appointed, votes are based upon the value of each creditor's claim. As above, where a committee has been appointed, its members vote by simple majority.

2.13 What are the rules on clawback/voidability?

There are three main types of voidable transaction that can be attacked by an administrator or liquidator if certain conditions are met. These are:

- **Transaction at undervalue:** pursuant to section 238 of the Act, where the company enters into a transaction for a consideration at a value which is significantly less in money or money's worth than the consideration provided by the company, or makes a gift for no consideration at a relevant time, the transaction may be challenged. The 'relevant time' for these purposes is during the period of up to two years prior to the administration or liquidation, and the company must be insolvent at the time of, or become insolvent as a result of, the transaction which is being challenged. Where the companies which are party to the transaction are connected, insolvency is presumed (ie it must be rebutted by the company rather than proved by the administrator or liquidator).
- **Preference:** pursuant to section 239 of the Act, where during the relevant time the company does anything or suffers anything to be done that has the effect of putting a creditor or guarantor in a better position upon the company entering administration/liquidation than it would have been, the transaction can be challenged. The relevant time for these purposes is up to six months prior to the company entering administration/liquidation or two years if the party to the relevant transaction was connected with the company, and the company must be insolvent at the time or as a result of it. There is an additional condition that the company must be 'influenced by the desire to prefer' the recipient of the preference, although such desire is presumed where the companies are connected.
- **Invalid floating charges:** pursuant to section 245 of the Act, where a company grants a floating charge during the relevant time, the charge shall be invalid to the extent that no 'new value' was received by the company. Essentially, this prevents companies from securing pre-existing debts with a floating charge.

The relevant period is 12 months prior to the company entering administration or liquidation as regards unconnected companies, and the company granting the charge must be insolvent at the time, or as a result of, the transaction. In respect of connected companies, the period is extended to two years, and insolvency need not be proven.

It should, however, be noted that the charge will only be invalid as regards the 'old' consideration it secures. Consequently, to the extent that the charge is granted to secure a pre-existing debt as well as new debt advanced after the charge was granted, it will still validly secure the new debt.

2.14 What are the rules on set-off/netting?

Where a contract between a creditor and the company in liquidation or administration contains contractual provisions as to set off, the administrator or liquidator will honour these provisions when making distributions to creditors who are also debtors of the company (or collecting amounts due from them).

There is also a form of statutory set-off applicable in liquidations and administrations where the administrator has declared his intention to make a distribution to unsecured creditors (which, in an administration, requires a court order; liquidators can make a distribution without court consent). This allows the administrator or liquidator to set-off amounts due from the creditor to the company against amounts due to that creditor before making a distribution to it.

2.15 How is exit managed?

An administration must be brought to an end by way of a method of exit prescribed by the Act. In rare cases, the company will be restored to trading on a solvent basis and the administrator can simply file a notice to bring the administration to an end. Otherwise, an administrator may put the company into liquidation as a means to wind down the company's affairs and make a distribution to unsecured creditors.

A CVA or scheme may also be used as a means to agree claims with creditors and make distributions to them. However, this form of exit is fairly rare.

The company will simply be struck off the register of companies and dissolved once the liquidation comes to an end. This can be achieved by a simple filing of forms by the liquidator.

2.16 Are 'prepackaged' plans, arrangements or agreements permissible?

Yes – prepackaged administrations are a common restructuring tool in the English market and involve an administrator negotiating a sale of a company or its assets and then executing the sale immediately upon his appointment. The fact that an out-of-court appointment can be made without the need for a court hearing further streamlines the process, and has the benefit of avoiding value erosion due to creditors and other stakeholders only becoming aware that the company entered administration after the sale has completed.

2.17 Is a public authority involved?

As above, the court will be involved in compulsory liquidations or court-appointed administrations. Other than that, certain government departments will be involved in respect of certain aspects of the administration or liquidation (for example, a government-established insurance fund is available to meet certain claims of former employees of the company), but there is no public authority whose responsibility is to oversee either process.

2.18 What is the treatment of claims arising after filing/ admission?

Distributions to unsecured creditors are based upon the amounts due at the date on which the company entered administration/liquidation. If the administrator or liquidator incurs liabilities during their appointment (such as liabilities to suppliers, or rental payments for properties occupied during the administration or liquidation), then such liabilities are payable as 'expenses' of the administration or liquidation and rank ahead of normal, unsecured, claims and certain claims of secured creditors.

2.19 Are there ongoing contracts?

There is no provision under English law whereby a contract will automatically terminate due to insolvency. An administrator or liquidator will, generally, continue to perform any contracts to which the company is a party, although certain of those contracts may enable the counter-party to terminate the contract upon the company entering an insolvency process. A liquidator, but not an administrator, also has the power to 'disclaim' any onerous contract (essentially, a contract which is costing the company money to maintain), which has the effect of determining the rights of the parties to the contract at the date of the disclaimer.

2.20 Are consolidated proceedings for members of a corporate family/group possible?

No, each company must be put into a separate process and the duties of the administrator or liquidator will be owed to that company's creditors, rather than the creditors of the group as a whole (although creditors may include other group companies as regards inter-company debts).

2.21 What are the charges, fees and other costs?

As above, the general costs of an administration or liquidation will be paid as expenses, including the administrator/liquidators remuneration (which are usually charged on a time-costs basis). The costs of the petitioning creditor in a compulsory liquidation are also generally recoverable as expenses of the liquidation, although the costs of shareholders meetings/ creditors meetings and court filings in voluntary liquidations or out-of-court administration appointments are generally borne by the applicant/company (although the court costs are generally quite low).

3. LIABILITY ISSUES

3.1 What is the liability of managers/directors *vis-à-vis* creditors?

There are three key areas where directors can be held liable to contribute to the assets of a company in liquidation. Each of these apply to directors who have been appointed and act as directors of the company, as well as directors who have been appointed but the appointment has not formalised and those acting as 'shadow directors' (ie persons in respect of whose instructions the board is accustomed to act).

Wrongful trading

Pursuant to section 214 of the Act, a director can be required to make such contribution as the court thinks proper (usually determined by the amount by which assets have been depleted by their conduct) if the liquidator can show that, before the commencement of the winding up, that person knew or ought to have known that there was no reasonable prospect of the company avoiding insolvent liquidation.

This does not merely cover 'trading' activity: any act, or failure to act, unless it minimises losses to creditors, may attract personal liability. There is no requirement to prove intent or dishonesty.

The only defence open to a director is that he took every step that he ought to have taken with a view to minimising the potential loss. This assumes knowledge that insolvent liquidation was unavoidable, and a director is deemed to know facts which ought to have been known or ascertained by a reasonably diligent person having:

- the knowledge, skill and experience reasonably expected of a company director; and
- the knowledge, skill and experience that he in fact possesses.

To that end, the courts will often impose a higher standard of care upon a finance director or managing director than upon a non-executive or part-time director.

Misfeasance

Pursuant to section 212 of the Act, if any of the directors (or other persons involved in the promotion, formation or management of a company) has misapplied, retained or become liable or accountable for any money or property of the company, or has been guilty of a misfeasance, a breach of fiduciary duty or any other duty in relation to the company, the liquidator is able to recover money or damages for the benefit of the company in question.

Such conduct will cover, amongst other things, improper payments of dividends, application of monies for unauthorised purposes and any unauthorised loans or remuneration to directors.

A court may grant relief from liability if the director acted honestly and reasonably and, if having regard to all the circumstances, he ought fairly to be excused. Relief from liability for misfeasance is a discretionary remedy.

Fraudulent trading

Pursuant to section 213 of the Act, if the business of a company is carried on with the intent to defraud creditors or for any other fraudulent purpose prior to its winding up, the liquidator can apply to the court for a contribution from any person who was knowingly a party to the carrying on of the fraud.

This provision is rarely invoked since it requires evidence of actual dishonesty. However, where the directors allow a company to continue to trade and incur liabilities when they know there is no real prospect that these will be repaid, they risk personal liability under this provision. Fraudulent trading has wider application than wrongful trading in that:

- it applies to any persons (not just directors) who were knowingly parties to the carrying on of the business in question;
- it attracts a criminal penalty of up to 10 years' imprisonment or an unlimited fine, or both, as well as civil liability; and
- there is no defence of taking steps to minimise loss to creditors.

3.2 What is the liability of the lender?

Lenders are largely free from risk, other than in certain circumstances. First, lenders could be deemed as shadow directors if they provide instructions to the board of the borrower and upon which the board acts. This would mean that they could be liable for, for example, wrongful trading. Lenders are, however, alert to this and will take steps to avoid giving specific instructions to a borrower's directors (and will instead phrase any requests as conditions to continued funding).

Secondly, lenders who enforce security as 'mortgagee' (which, effectively, means the lender takes possession of the relevant secured assets and sell them itself) run the risk of being liable for liabilities and outgoings which attach to the assets during the period in which they are in possession. These can include environmental liabilities and unfunded pension liabilities (which can be extensive) and, consequently, lenders are generally reluctant to enforce security in this manner.

Lastly, lenders who enforce security or accelerate a loan where they are not entitled to do so under the terms of the underlying loan or security documentation can be liable for 'wrongful acceleration'. This is, essentially, a claim for breach of contract, so if the borrower suffers loss as a result of the wrongful acceleration it will be entitled to pursue a damages claim against the lender.

United States

James-Bates-Brannan-Groover-LLP
J William Boone, Michael A Dunn & Doroteya N Wozniak

1. WHAT COURT-MONITORED RESTRUCTURING PRE-INSOLVENCY PROCEEDINGS OR SCHEMES HAVE BEEN DEVISED BY THE LAW OF YOUR COUNTRY TO LIMIT VALUE DESTRUCTION FOR FAILING BUSINESS ENTITIES?

The court-monitored restructuring pre-insolvency proceedings or schemes devised within the United States for purposes of limiting value destruction for failing business entities are the following:

- A bankruptcy proceeding under:
  - Chapter 11 of the Bankruptcy Code (restructuring for individuals and businesses whereby the entity is empowered to retain control of the assets and no trustee is initially appointed) (Chapter 11);
  - Chapter 12 of the Bankruptcy Code (restructuring for family farmers and fishermen) (Chapter 9 (restructuring proceedings for municipalities and other government agencies), 12 and 13 (individual debtor) filings will not be discussed in this chapter as these filings are rarely used; furthermore, Chapter 13 filing is reserved solely for individuals) or
  - Chapter 15 of the Bankruptcy Code (ancillary and other international cases which initiate bankruptcy proceedings in the United States based upon the Model Law on Cross Border Insolvency prepared by the United National Commission on International Trade Law).
- A receivership action under:
  - applicable state law; or
  - federal law; and

Generally, in the United States, the main avenue for limiting value destruction and addressing creditor's rights in connection with a failing business entity is through the filing of bankruptcy proceedings by a company under one of the aforementioned chapters of the Bankruptcy Code. The reason for this is that 'insolvency' is not a requirement for commencing restructuring bankruptcy proceedings under any of the above-mentioned chapters. See *In re Integrated Telecom Express, Inc.*, 384 F.3d 108, 121 (3rd Cir. 2004) (citing *In re SGL Carbon Corp.*, 200 F.3d 154, 163–64 (3rd Cir. 1999)); *In re Stolrow's, Inc.*, 84 B.R. 167 (Bankr. 9th Cir. 1988) (*'Neither insolvency nor inability to pay debts is a prerequisite to seeking voluntary relief under the Bankruptcy Code'*); *In re Local Union 722 Int'l Bhd. of Teamsters*, 414 B.R. 443, 450 (Bankr. N.D. Ill. 2009); *In re Int'l Oriental Rug Ctr.*, 165 B.R. 436, 442 (Bankr.N.D.Ill.1994); *In re Hulse*, 66 B.R. 681 (Bankr. M.D. Fla. 1986).

Access to Chapter 11 for solvent debtors is designed to avoid *'a hopeless situation'* later. *SGL Carbon*, 163. Ultimately, *'[i]t is not uncommon for debtors to be solvent under the balance sheet test, and yet to have severe financial problems ... The United States bankruptcy law is designed to provide relief from creditor pressures for debtors with cash flow difficulties, even where they are clearly solvent under a balance sheet test.' Integrated Telecom*, 122 (quoting *In re Marshall*, 300 B.R. 507, 513 (Bankr. C.D. Cal. 2003)). In other words, a business entity which is still solvent but experiencing financial troubles can proceed directly with the filing of bankruptcy proceedings instead of having to resort to other restructuring options. As a result, the likelihood of a successful restructuring is increased immeasurably since the company does not have to wait until it is actually insolvent to take advantage of the many tools available to a Chapter 11 debtor. Furthermore, the Bankruptcy Code allows for creditors to initiate involuntary bankruptcy proceedings if the requirements of section 303(b) of the Bankruptcy Code are met.

The only other court-monitored restructuring pre-insolvency framework for preserving a failing business's assets is a receivership initiated under either state or federal law. Unlike a filing typically initiated by the company itself under the Bankruptcy Code, a receivership is usually initiated by one or more of the company's creditors. However, the use of a receivership for restructuring purposes is not very common in the United States for various reasons. Unlike the vast body of law in the area of bankruptcy which applies throughout the United States and its territories, the law with respect to receiverships, whether sought under state or federal law, is not very well developed, is far from uniform and, in the case of state receiverships, is controlled by the specific laws of the applicable state. This lack of uniformity may sometimes lead to inconsistent results and a climate of uncertainty. Moreover, unlike the nationwide jurisdiction bankruptcy courts have, a receivership's authority may be limited to a failing business's assets located within the particular state's jurisdiction authorising the receivership. This can result in complications if the failing business's assets are located in multiple jurisdictions. Another important point to consider is that receivership cases are usually heard by state, superior or federal district court judges, whose responsibilities cover many areas of civil and criminal law, whose calendars are very busy and who thus may not have significant experience in dealing with pre-insolvency restructuring of entities and administration of their assets to creditors.

At the same time, there may be benefits to the use of a receivership action. For example, a receivership action allows for greater flexibility in terms of a secured creditor's ability to shape the scope and influence the course of the receivership. Moreover, a receivership action can be commenced by a single interest holder or creditor, whereas an involuntary bankruptcy proceeding has to be commenced by at least three unsecured creditors. Finally, although a receivership can be less expensive than a Chapter 11 bankruptcy filing, it does not include all the tools available to a debtor in a Chapter 11 filing (eg ability to select contracts for assumption or rejection).

Some of the answers to the questions below will apply equally to a pre- and post-insolvency restructuring. To be concise, where applicable, the chapter may refer back to previous sections.

1.1 What is the objective of the proceedings?

The objective of any bankruptcy proceeding, in general, is to give a distressed entity a fresh start. See *Local Loan Co. v Hunt*, 292 U.S. 234, 244 (1934). The specific objective of a Chapter 11 proceeding is the orderly, court-supervised restructuring through a court-approved plan of reorganisation without the necessity for the appointment of a bankruptcy trustee. The underlying theme is to maximise value for the creditors. Meanwhile, the objective of a receivership is to appoint a neutral non-party who can receive, preserve, protect and/or manage specific assets of a distressed business pursuant to a court order. The objective and scope of a receivership are entirely defined by the terms of the appointing order.

1.2 Do all kinds of businesses qualify?

Bankruptcy proceedings

Most any types of businesses can initiate a Chapter 11 bankruptcy proceeding with the exception of a stockbroker, a domestic insurance company, an insured bank or similar institution as defined in section 3(h) of the Federal Deposit Insurance Act, or a commodity broker. 11 U.S.C. § 109(d); see *In re Morris Plan Co. of Iowa*, 62 B.R. 348, 356 (1986). A railroad and an uninsured state member bank are allowed to file a Chapter 11. *Id.* There is no minimum debt requirement that must be met before a proceedings is filed.

When a distressed business files for a Chapter 11 bankruptcy, it is allowed to remain in control of its assets and continue operating its business as a debtor-in-possession. 11 U.S.C. §§ 1101 and 1104. The case is overseen by the United States Trustee, a division of the United States Department of Justice whose task is to ensure parties' compliance with applicable bankruptcy processes. A Chapter 11 trustee is rarely appointed – typically, only where the debtor has proven to be untrustworthy or has violated the law. 11 U.S.C. § 1104. The Chapter 11 trustee is chosen by the local United States Trustee's Office and is usually a bankruptcy professional, such as an attorney, consultant or accountant.

State and federal court receivership actions

Generally, a receivership action, under both state and federal law, can be commenced against any type of business without regard for the value of assets or the level of indebtedness involved. However, some states may have special rules with respect to the appointment of receivers over certain types of businesses, such as insurance companies, railroads, nursing facilities, cemeteries, public utilities and financial institutions. See Alaska Stat. §§ 6.55.601 and 18.20.370; Colo. Rev. Stat. Ann. §§ 10-3-501 *et seq.* and 25-3-108; Fla. Stat. Ann. §§ 429.22, 400.126, 497.160, 718.501(1)(c), 516.23, 394.903, 501.207(3) and 617.191; O.C.G.A. §§ 14-2-1431 and 7-1-150; 210

ILCS 45/3-501; 220 ILCS 5/4-501; 215 ILCS 5/188; 205 ILCS 5/53; N.Y. Not-for-Profit Corp. Law §§ 1201–08; N.Y. R.R. Law § 146; N.Y. Gen. Bus. Law § 353-a. As such, a careful review of the governing state law must be done prior to the filing of any state receivership action.

1.3 What are the necessary approvals?

Bankruptcy proceedings

There is no pre-filing approval to commence a bankruptcy proceeding other than to obtain an applicable corporate resolution of the company authorising the filing of a proceeding. The internal approval process for filing for bankruptcy protection is dependent upon the guidelines set forth in each distressed entity's governing documents, whether they are by-laws, an operating agreement, a partnership agreement or a shareholder's agreement. As such, a distressed business can file its Chapter 11 petition for relief without obtaining any outside prior approvals.

State and federal court receivership action

The court before which the petition for appointment of a receiver is pending must approve the appointment before the receiver is granted any powers over the receivership assets. In the case of a federal court receivership, the receiver is also required to take an oath and post a bond. Some states may require the same as well.

1.4 What is the procedure?

Bankruptcy proceedings

To commence a voluntary Chapter 11 bankruptcy proceeding, a debtor must file a bankruptcy petition (Official Form B1) and pay the respective Chapter 11 filing fee (the majority of the bankruptcy forms needed to initiate a bankruptcy case can be found at: *http://www.uscourts.gov/FormsAndFees/Forms/BankruptcyForms.aspx*; the filing fees for each chapter under the Bankruptcy Code can be found at: *http://www.uscourts.gov/FederalCourts/Bankruptcy/BankruptcyResources/BankruptcyFilingFees.aspx*). 11 U.S.C. § 301(a). An involuntary Chapter 11 bankruptcy action begins with the filing of an involuntary bankruptcy petition (Official Form B5) and the payment of the respective Chapter 11 filing fee. 11 U.S.C. 303(b). The debtor is also required to file schedules containing all secured and unsecured creditors, all assets and liabilities, current income and expenses, a statement of debtor's financial affairs, etc. 11 U.S.C. § 521. All pleadings filed with the bankruptcy courts become a public record available to the general public. 11 U.S.C. § 107(a). Thus, the general requirement is that the debtor must be transparent with its creditors in connection with its financial and operating information. In certain circumstances, a party can petition the court to allow it to file a pleading under seal. 11 U.S.C. § 107(b).

Immediately upon the filing of the Chapter 11 petition, any and all activities to collect debt from the debtor are suspended under the *'automatic stay'* provided for in 11 U.S.C. § 362(a). The primary purpose of the automatic stay is to afford debtors seeking reorganisation the opportunity to *'continue their businesses with their available assets'. In re National Cattle Congress, Inc.*, 179 B.R. 588, 592 (N.D. Iowa 1995) (citing *Small Business Admin. v Rinehart*, 887 F.2d 165, 168 (8th Cir. 1989)).

In a bankruptcy case, the court asserts jurisdiction over all of the debtor's property no matter where it is located on the globe. The debtor must list each creditor in its schedules, and each creditor must receive notice of the filing of the petition under 11 U.S.C. § 342. Under 11 U.S.C. § 341, the United States Trustee will conduct a meeting of the creditors within a reasonable time after the filing of the petition. The creditors identified by the debtor are mailed a notice of the Chapter 11 bankruptcy filing notifying them of the date and time for the meeting of the creditors. The meeting of the creditors is the creditors' and the United States Trustee's opportunity to examine the debtor under oath. Typically, the United States Trustee will question the debtor regarding the contents of the petition and corresponding schedules (to identify creditors and other relevant information) and the statement of financial affairs. Depending on the specific jurisdiction, the notice of bankruptcy filing may also contain a set date (a 'bar date') within which creditors must file a 'proof of claim' to substantiate both the nature (secured, unsecured, etc) and the amount of their claim. In certain cases, the notice of bankruptcy filing would not set the bar date; rather, later on in the case, the debtor-in-possession or Chapter 11 trustee would petition the court to set such a date. A proof of claim is a document which a creditor needs to file in order to participate in the distribution of the debtor's estate. Failure to timely file a claim may bar the creditor from entitlement to participate in the case or to receive any distribution.

The next steps in the Chapter 11 case are the filing and confirmation of a plan of reorganisation. For a detailed discussion on this issue, see 'Bankruptcy proceedings' in sections 1.9 and 1.12 below.

State court receivership action

Generally, the parties who have standing to seek the appointment of a receiver are those with a protectable interest in the receivership assets, such as secured creditors and equity holders. As a result, an unsecured creditor may not be able to initiate a receivership action as it usually does not have any protectable interest in specific property of the distressed business. Qualified parties can initiate a receivership action as an independent action seeking the appointment of a receiver as either the sole remedy or an ancillary remedy to a related lawsuit. In some states, such as Alabama, Connecticut, Delaware, Florida and Illinois, the appointment of a receiver can be sought only as an ancillary remedy to a related lawsuit, and not as an independent remedy. See *C. E. Development Co. v Kitchens*, 288 Ala. 660 (1972); *Hartford Federal Sav. and Loan Ass'n v Tucker*, 196 Conn. 172, 491 A.2d 1084 (1985); *Keystone Fuel Oil, Inc. v Del-Way Petroleum, Co*, 3 Del. J. Corp. L. 575, 1977 WL 2572 (Del. Ch. 1977); *Akers v Corbett*, 138 Fla. 730 (1939); *PSL Realty Co. v Granite Inv. Co.*, 42 Ill. App. 3d 697 (5th Dist. 1976); *First Federal Sav. and Loan Ass'n of Chicago v National Boulevard Bank of*

Chicago, 104 Ill. App. 3d 1061, 1063–64 (1st Dist. 1982). As such, in these states, the appointment of a receiver is only allowable in connection with an action filed for some other purpose containing a prayer for other relief.

Typically, if the party petitioning the court for the appointment of a receiver is seeking the appointment of a receiver as an ancillary remedy to the main claims brought in a lawsuit, then the movant should file:

- a separate motion to that effect;
- an affidavit establishing the controlling facts set out in the motion;
- an affidavit from the proposed receiver establishing the receiver's qualifications;
- a legal memorandum establishing the basis for the relief sought; and
- a proposed order.

On the other hand, if the appointment of a receiver is sought as a main remedy, then the movant should file:

- a complaint seeking appointment of a receiver;
- an affidavit establishing the controlling facts set out in the motion;
- an affidavit from the proposed receiver establishing the receiver's qualifications;
- a legal memorandum establishing the basis for the relief sought; and
- a proposed order.

All pleadings filed with the state courts in connection with the appointment of a receiver become public records available to the general public. Each state may have different variations as to the type of documents which may need to be filed to initiate a receivership action. Accordingly, the respective state law must be consulted prior to initiating any receivership actions or filing receivership motions. After the filing, the defendant party will be allowed time to respond to the motion or complaint and the court will likely schedule a hearing on the issue. Some states allow the *ex parte* appointment of a receiver if certain requirements are met. Once the order appointing the receiver has been entered, depending on the particular state's law, a notice of such order may have to be mailed to all creditors and interested parties.

Upon the appointment of a receiver, the receiver obtains jurisdiction only over the assets identified in the appointment order within the state in which the receiver has been appointed. *Booth v Clark*, 58 U.S. 322, 328 (1854). As such, if the receivership assets are located outside of the state in which the receiver has been appointed, then the receiver does not have control over those out-of-state receivership assets. To obtain control over such assets, either the receiver or the petitioning party must file a lawsuit in the other state where the out-of-state receivership assets are located.

Federal court receivership action

The appointment of a receiver in federal court is governed by Federal Rule of Civil Procedure 66. See Fed. R. Civ. P. 66. However, this rule is a procedural rule and does not create a substantive right to a receiver. As such, under federal law, a receivership action can be initiated only as an ancillary remedy to a lawsuit seeking some other primary relief. *National Partnership Inv. Corp.*

v National Housing Development Corp., 153 F.3d 1289 (11th Cir. 1998); see also 12 Fed. Prac. & Proc. Civ. § 2983 (2d ed.).

To request the appointment of a federal court receiver, a secured creditor can file a motion to that effect at the same time that it files its complaint seeking the primary relief. The secured creditor will have to serve a copy of the complaint and the motion on the defendant and any other necessary parties. The defendant is usually allowed time to respond to these pleadings. The court usually conducts a hearing prior to determining whether to grant the request to appoint a receiver. *Ex parte* relief with regards to the appointment of a receiver is allowed; however, special circumstances must exist to render the necessity immediate. All pleadings filed with the federal court in connection with the appointment of a receiver become public record, and as such are available to the general public. When seeking the appointment of a federal receiver, it is important to remember that a receiver cannot be a clerk or deputy of the court, a federal employee or person employed by the appointing judge, or a person related to the judge by consanguinity within the fourth degree. 28 U.S.C. §§ 458, 957, 958. Furthermore, a proposed receiver is required to post a bond and take an oath. Once the order appointing the receiver has been entered, local rules may require the mailing of a notice of such order to all creditors and interested parties within 30 days of such appointment. For example, a copy of the order appointing the receiver must be mailed to the Secretary of the Internal Revenue Service. 26 U.S.C. § 6036.

Generally, upon appointment and posting of the requisite bond, a receiver has complete jurisdiction over the receivership assets in the respective judicial district in which the receiver was appointed. 28 U.S.C. § 754. As such, to obtain control over receivership assets outside the jurisdiction of the appointing court, the receiver must file, within 10 days of the appointment, a copy of the complaint and order of appointment in the district court for each district in which receivership assets are located. *Id.* The failure to file a copy of the complaint and order of appointment in a specific district in which there are receivership assets can possibly result in divesting the receiver of jurisdiction and control over all such assets in that district. 28 U.S.C. § 754; *S.E.C. v Vision Communications, Inc.*, 74 F.3d 287 (D.C. Cir. 1996); but see *S.E.C. v Equity Service Corp.*, 632 F. 2d 1092, 1095 (3d Cir. 1980); *FTC v NHS Systems, Inc.*, 708 F.Supp.2d 456, 463 (E.D. Pa. 2009) (allowing a receiver to have jurisdiction over property in a district in which the receiver did not file timely notice, because no prejudice was caused by the delay). Once the receivership has been approved, some local court rules will require the receiver to mail creditors notices of the need to file claims against the receivership estate. This procedure is similar to the notice of bankruptcy filing provided for in the Bankruptcy Code.

1.5 Is there recourse against the opening judgment?

The equivalent of the opening judgment in the United States is the 'order for relief', also known as the 'bankruptcy petition'. As mentioned above, the filing of a bankruptcy petition triggers the automatic stay, which in essence prohibits any creditors from taking any actions against the debtor or property of the debtor. 11 U.S.C. § 362. The only way a creditor can proceed with any collection efforts or enforcing judgments against a debtor is by asking the court for relief from the automatic stay under 11 U.S.C. § 362(d). Usually, the creditor needs to file a motion asking the court to lift the automatic stay with respect to the proposed activity along with a memorandum of law explaining the legal justification for such request. The Bankruptcy Code requires the creditor to provide a notice of such filing to the debtor and to the committee of unsecured creditors, if one has been appointed, or, if one has not been appointed, then to the 20 largest unsecured creditors and on such other entities as the court may direct. Fed. R. Bankr. P. 4001(a)(1) and 9014. The court usually holds a hearing on the matter within 30 days unless specifically waived by the movant. 11 U.S.C. § 362(e)(1). In some circumstances, a relief from the automatic stay may be granted *ex parte*, but the requirements of Federal Rule of Bankruptcy Procedure 4001(a)(2) must be satisfied. Fed. R. Bankr. P. 4001(a)(2).

Generally, the creditor most establish 'cause' for lifting the stay; cause is very fact intensive, thus great discretion is granted to the court to determine if sufficient cause has been granted in any given situation. Creditors holding claims secured by real or personal property often avail themselves to 11 U.S.C. § 362(d)(2)(A) & (B) and argue that the debtor does not have equity in the collateral property and the collateral property is not necessary for an effective reorganisation. For example, to determine if cause exists in cases where a creditor commenced its collection activities before the filing of the bankruptcy petitions, courts will ask whether:

- any 'great prejudice' to either the bankrupt estate or the debtor will result from lifting the automatic stay;
- the hardship to the creditor by maintenance of the stay considerably outweighs the hardship to the debtor; or
- the creditor has a probability of prevailing on the merits of its case.

In re South Oakes Furniture, Inc., 167 B.R. 307, 308 (1994).

If the creditor is successful in lifting the automatic stay, the creditor can proceed with the respective collection activity it sought in its motion. However, creditors' collection activities must be confined to the ones specifically allowed in the order entered by the court.

The creditor may seek to have the bankruptcy case dismissed as having been filed in bad faith. Although a fact-intensive inquiry, the grounds may generally include the allegation that the case is merely a two-party dispute (between the debtor and its lender) or filed purely to avoid a tax.

1.6 What are the substantive tests/definitions?

Bankruptcy proceedings

Generally, to obtain the protections of the Bankruptcy Code, a distressed entity must be a qualified debtor under 11 U.S.C. § 109 and file a voluntary petition with the accompanying schedules and statement of financial affairs. There are no substantive tests which a Chapter 11 debtor must satisfy.

However, if creditors wish to begin involuntary bankruptcy proceedings, they must satisfy the requirements of section 303(b) of the Bankruptcy Code. Specifically, the involuntary petition must be filed by three or more creditors of a business under Chapter 7 or Chapter 11. Each of these creditors must be *'either a holder of a claim against [the company] that is not contingent as to liability or the subject of a bona fide dispute as to liability or amount, or an indenture trustee representing such holder, if such noncontingent, undisputed claims aggregate at least $15,325 more than the value of any lien on property of [the company] securing such claims held by the holders of such claims'.* 11 U.S.C. § 303(b)(2). If, however, the total number of creditors is fewer than 12 (excluding any employee, insider or transferee disallowed under section 544, 545, 547, 548, 549 or 724(a) of Title 11), one creditor may bring an involuntary bankruptcy petition against the company if that creditor holds in the aggregate at least $15,325 of all claims against the company. See 11 U.S.C. § 303(b)(2). The requirements for bringing an involuntary bankruptcy petition against a partnership are set out in 11 U.S.C. § 303(b)(3).

Federal and state court receiverships

Every state has a different test or different requirements for allowing the appointment of a receiver. As such, the controlling state law must be consulted prior to requesting the appointment of a receiver under state law.

In the case of federal receiverships, the appointment of a receiver is an equitable remedy and the court has full discretion on whether to grant a request to appoint a receiver. Federal courts have generally held that the appointment of a receiver is an *'extraordinary'* remedy which must be *'employed with the utmost caution'* and *'granted only in cases of clear necessity'*. See eg *Solis v Matheson*, 563 F.3d 425, 437 (9th Cir. 2009); *Rosen v Siegel*, 106 F.3d 28, 34 (2d Cir. 1997); *Aviation Supply Corp. v R.S.B.I. Aerospace, Inc.*, 999 F.2d 314, 316 (8th Cir. 1993). Federal courts consider the following factors when determining whether the appointment of a receiver is necessary:

- whether there is a valid claim by the party seeking the appointment;
- the probability that fraudulent conduct has occurred or will occur to frustrate that claim;
- whether there is imminent danger that property will be concealed, lost or diminished in value;
- the adequacy of the legal remedies available;
- whether there is the lack of a less drastic equitable remedy; and
- the likelihood that appointing the receiver will do more good than harm.

Aviation Supply Corp., 316–17.

1.7 What is the role of a court-appointed agent?

Bankruptcy proceedings

The primary role of a Chapter 11 bankruptcy trustee is to represent a debtor's estate. 11 U.S.C. § 323. A Chapter 11 trustee must, among other things, also be accountable for all property received, examine proofs of claim and object if necessary, file the requisite Chapter 11 schedules if they have not been already filed by the debtor, investigate the financial condition of the business and make a determination as to the desirability of the continuance of such business, and investigate any other matter relevant to the confirmation of a plan. *Id.* However, typically the debtor itself remains in control and has the same duties to its creditors as the Chapter 11 trustee. 11 U.S.C. § 1107.

State and federal court receivership actions

The role of a state court receiver is *'to act as a fiduciary representing the court and all parties in interest, and the purpose and scope of a receivership is defined by court order'*. *Equity Trust Co. Custodian ex rel. Eisenmenger IRA v Cole*, 766 N.W.2d 334, 341 (Minn. Ct. App. 2009). The role of a federal court receiver is similar, but is mandated by a federal statute. See 28 U.S.C. § 959(b). Once appointed, a federal receiver *'shall manage and operate the property in his possession as such ... receiver ... according to the requirements of the valid laws of the state in which such property is situated, in the same manner that the owner or possessor thereof would be bound to do if in possession thereof'*. *Id.* The receiver has no independent powers as his or her powers stem only from the respective authorising statute, if applicable, and/or the appointment order. *Hosford v Henry*, 107 Cal. App. 2d 765 (3d Dist. 1951); *Stowell v Arizona Sav. & Loan Ass'n*, 93 Ariz. 310 (1983). The receiver is also a neutral who, upon being appointed, takes control of the debtor's assets for the purposes of preserving, managing and/or liquidating the property interests under court supervision. See *Wuliger v Christie*, 310 F. Supp. 2d 897, 908 (N.D. Ohio 2004); *Lowder v All Star Millks, Inc.*, 309 N.C. 695, 701 (1983). As such, upon appointment, the receiver becomes a provisional officer of the court. *Booth v Clark*, 58 U.S. 322, 331 (1854). A receiver acquires no greater rights in property than the received entity had and stands in the shoes of the entity in receivership. *Eberhard v Marcu*, 530 F.3d 122, 132 (2d Cir. 2008) (citing *Fleming v Lind–Waldock & Co.*, 922 F.2d 20, 25 (1st Cir. 1990)); *Armstrong v McAlpin*, 699 F.2d 79, 89 (2d Cir. 1983); *Javitch v First Union Sec., Inc.*, 315 F.3d 619, 625 (6th Cir. 2003); *Wuliger v Christie*, 310 F. Supp. 2d 897 (N.D. Ohio 2004); *Good Shepherd Health Facilities of Colorado, Inc. v Department of Health*, 789 P.2d 423 (Colo. App. 1989).

1.8 What protection is there from creditors?

Bankruptcy proceedings

The Bankruptcy Code provides debtors with numerous protections from creditors. Some of the most notable ones are:

- the automatic stay pursuant to section 362 of the Bankruptcy Code;
- the avoidance powers under sections 544–49 of the Bankruptcy Code (typically preference or fraudulent transfer actions);
- the ability to use, sell or lease the estate assets free and clear of all liens, interests and claims under section 363 of the Bankruptcy Code;
- the ability to obtain a discharge from debts under section 1141 of the Bankruptcy Code;

- the ability to reject or reaffirm executory contracts under section 365 of the Bankruptcy Code; and
- the ability to restructure a creditor's claim through a Chapter 11 repayment plan over a creditor's objections as a 'cram down' under section 1129 of the Bankruptcy Code.

The automatic stay is an automatic injunction against the continuance or initiation of any action by a creditor against the debtor or debtor's property. 11 U.S.C. § 362(a). The automatic stay in a Chapter 11 bankruptcy extends only to the debtor and does not cover any co-debtors. The automatic stay generally remains in effect until:

- the subject property is no longer property of the estate;
- the court grants a creditor or an interested party's motion to lift the automatic stay;
- the case is dismissed or closed; and
- the court grants or denies the debtor a discharge.

11 U.S.C. § 362(c).

The automatic stay may be terminated earlier if the Chapter 11 petition is a refiling of a previous bankruptcy case. 11 U.S.C. § 362(c)(3) and (4). The automatic stay has certain exceptions, such as the interception of a tax refund, an act to perfect or maintain or continue the perfection of, an interest in property to the extent that the debtor-in-possession rights and powers are subject to such perfection, or an audit by a governmental unit to determine tax liability. 11 U.S.C.§ 362(b). A party in interest can seek permission from the court to lift the automatic stay for cause if certain conditions are met, such as lack of adequate protection of an interest in property of such party in interest or if the debtor does not have any equity in the subject property and the property is not necessary for an effective reorganisation of the debtor. See 11 U.S.C. § 362(d).

The avoidance powers granted to a debtor-in-possession and a Chapter 11 trustee are very powerful. These powers are codified in 11 U.S.C. §§ 544–49. They are as follows:

- the authority to file adversary proceedings to recover property that was transferred by the debtor to other entities prior to the filing of the bankruptcy petition;
- the authority and power to avoid liens that were not properly perfected or to avoid other undisclosed claims that existed before the bankruptcy petition was filed;
- the authority to file fraudulent transfer actions (based upon either actual or constructive fraud); and
- the authority and power to avoid certain transfers of property of the bankruptcy estate that occur after the commencement of the bankruptcy case (preference actions).

Furthermore, under the Bankruptcy Code, a Chapter 11 debtor-in-possession can use, sell or lease property of the estate free and clear of all liens, interests and claims. 11 U.S.C. § 363. The debtor has to obtain the court's permission prior to effectuating the sale. The ability to sell assets free and clear of all liens, interests and claims allows the debtor-in-possession to sell its assets in a quick manner as buyers do not have to worry about establishing whether the assets are subject to any liens and, if so, whether such lienholders consent to the sale. The liens attach to the proceeds of the sale in the same priority as they had to the collateral sold. Buyers also obtain certain protections under the Bankruptcy Code, such as protections against successor liability (with certain limitations) and protections against setting aside of the order authorising the sale.

Another powerful tool for a debtor-in-possession is the ability to obtain a discharge of its debts. Upon confirmation of debtor's proposed restructuring plan, the debtor obtains a discharge from any debt that arose before the date of such confirmation regardless of whether a proof of claim based on such debt has been filed, whether such claim is allowed or whether the holder of such claim has accepted the proposed restructuring plan. 11 U.S.C. § 1141(d). There are exceptions to discharge, but they are very limited. 11 U.S.C. § 1141(d) (3) (prohibiting the discharge of a debtor upon confirmation of a proposed plan if the debtor does not engage in business after consummation of the plan, the plan provides for the liquidation of all or substantially all of the property of the estate, and the debtor concealed property or made misrepresentations about its assets). Another protection against creditors granted to debtors under the Bankruptcy Code is the ability to cram down a proposed chapter 11 plan over a creditor's objections. In a Chapter 11 bankruptcy, a debtor is required to propose a restructuring plan which needs to be approved by the court. Generally, a proposed plan separates similar creditors into different classes. Some of the classes will be impaired and some will not. To obtain court approval, the plan must be approved by at least one class of impaired claims. If a class or classes of creditors reject the proposed restructuring plan, the court can still confirm the plan over the objection as long as the plan:

- does not unfairly discriminate against the rejecting class or classes of creditors;
- is fair and equitable with respect to a rejecting class or classes of creditors; and
- satisfies all the requirements set out in 11 U.S.C. § 1129(a).

This is a powerful tool that can compel a rejecting creditor to accept a treatment proposed under a restructuring plan.

State and federal court receivership actions

A receivership does not offer nearly as many protections from creditors as the filing of proceedings under Chapter 11 of the Bankruptcy Code. For example, a receivership does not impose an automatic stay on creditors' collection activities against the debtor and does not discharge the debtor from its debts. As such, the approval of a receivership does not prevent collection actions against or prosecution of lawsuits against the distressed entity that has been placed in receivership.

In some cases, a federal receiver may be able to achieve some protection from creditors by the entry of orders in the beginning of the receivership. See *S.E.C. v Wencke*, 622 F.2d 1363, 1369–70 (9th Cir. 1980). A federal receiver can seek an order imposing an equitable stay prohibiting third parties from instituting or continuing the prosecution of lawsuits which may interfere with the receiver's control of the receivership assets. However, such order can bind only third parties over which the issuing court has jurisdiction. Another order which can be entered early in the receivership case is an order requiring creditors and interested parties to file a proof of claim. The order is similar to a bar date notice under the Bankruptcy Code. In limited circumstances, a federal and some state receivers can also sell the receivership assets free and clear of liens, though there must be a reasonable likelihood that the sale will generate enough to pay off holders of the encumbrances and a surplus for distribution to the general creditors. *Novor v Fourth St. Bargain Store Co.*, 16 Del. Ch. 259 (1929); *Melrose v Industrial Associates*, 136 Conn. 518 (1950); *Bogosian v Foerdered Tract Committee*, 264 Pa. Super. 84 (1979). In some cases, a receiver may not be bound by a distressed entity's existing contracts, including leases, unless the receiver affirmatively indicates his or her election to be responsible for the prior obligations of the distressed business. *Citibank, N.A. v Nyland (CF8) Ltd.*, 839 F.2d 93, 98 (2d Cir. 1988).

1.9 What is the usual duration of the restructuring process?

Bankruptcy proceedings

The duration of a Chapter 11 bankruptcy filing is not set either by statute or by the court. Rather, the duration of each filing depends on the circumstances of that case.

Generally, the restructuring process under Chapter 11 can vary in length. The main reason for this is that, in a Chapter 11 case, a debtor-in-possession is required to propose a repayment plan as part of the restructuring process. There are some deadlines within which only the debtor may exclusively propose a reorganisation plan (see 'Bankruptcy proceedings' in section 1.4 above). Because the debtor wants to retain control of the plan process or because the debtor cannot survive indefinitely without restructuring once a case is filed, it is common to have a restructuring plan proposed within 180 days of the filing of the case. The Bankruptcy Code contains no time limit for the length of such repayment plan. As a result, the duration of Chapter 11 repayment plans can vary. The average Chapter 11 plan usually lasts anywhere from two to six years. The Chapter 11 case may remain open for as long as the repayment plan is open.

State and federal court receivership actions

The duration of a receivership depends on the facts and circumstances of each case, but must be temporary. *Bethlehem Steel Corp. v Williams Indus., Inc.*, 245 Va. 38, 42 (1993). *'In general, a receiver should be discharged and the receivership terminated when the initial reasons for the receivership cease to exist.'* *Ypsilanti Fire Marshal v Kircher*, 273 Mich. App. 496, 540 (2007). However, unless expressly limited when established, a receivership stays in place until the court orders its termination. *Milo v Curtis*, 100 Ohio App. 3d 1 (1994) (citing *Hoover-Bond Co. v Sun-Glow Indus., Inc.*, 57 Ohio App. 246, 10 O.O.

424 (1936)). Some states, such as Texas, also impose limits on the length of time an entity can be in receivership. See Tex. Civ. Prac. & Rem. Code Ann. § 64.072; *Chandler v Jorge A. Gutierrez, P.C.*, 906 S.W.2d 195, 202 (Tex. App. – Austin 1995, writ denied).

1.10 Who prepares the restructuring agreement and what are the available tools?

Bankruptcy proceedings

In Chapter 11 bankruptcy proceedings, the restructuring agreement, ie the repayment plan, is usually prepared by the debtor. 11 U.S.C. § 1121. However, other interested parties, such as creditors, may propose competing plans as well. *Id.* A competing plan cannot be proposed until after 120 days have passed since the filing of the Chapter 11 bankruptcy (although it can be extended, but not beyond 300 days). *Id.* The reason for the delay is that, in that so-called 'exclusivity period', the only party who can propose a plan is the debtor. This initial period allows the debtor to retain control of the restructuring effort and prevents aggressive creditors from taking control of the process. After the expiration of that period, other interested parties can propose competing repayment plans.

State and federal court receivership actions

In a state or federal receivership action, there is no restructuring agreement *per se*. The party petitioning for the appointment of a receiver proposes the order which grants and describes the receiver's powers, duties and receivership assets. Of course, this order can be modified by the court. This order is the controlling document for the receivership.

1.11 Are subordination agreements necessarily given full effect?

Bankruptcy proceedings

A subordination agreement is enforceable in bankruptcy proceedings to the same extent that such agreement is enforceable under applicable nonbankruptcy law. 11 U.S.C. § 510(a). In some instances, rights granted pursuant to a subordination agreement can be waived by a beneficiary if such beneficiary accepts a proposed restructuring plan which modifies or nullifies such rights. See *In re American White Cross, Inc.*, 269 B.R. 555 (D. Del. 2001). While the Bankruptcy Code allows the enforcement of subordination agreements, a subordination agreement cannot override contrary provisions of the Bankruptcy Code. *In re 203 N. LaSalle St. P'ship*, 246 B.R. 325, 331 (Bankr. N.D. Ill. 2000). As such, subordination agreement clauses which address substantive bankruptcy law rights and procedures may be held to be unenforceable. *Id.* (a subordination agreement provision granting a senior creditor the right to vote a subordinated claim could not provide a basis for disregarding Bankruptcy Code § 1126(a)). Furthermore, it should be noted that the automatic stay does not toll the running of a specific time period in a subordination agreement such as the expiration date, if one has been specified. *Hazen First State Bank v Speight*, 888 F.2d 574, 576 (8th Cir. 1989) (*'The automatic stay provided for by section 362(a) does not enlarge the rights of individuals under a contract nor does it toll the running of time under a contract. It will not prevent the automatic termination of a contract by its own terms'*).

State and federal court receivership actions

The issue will be determined under applicable state law which can vary widely among the 50 states; consequently, it is not feasible to provide a general answer other than that most states recognise subordination agreements.

1.12 How is exit managed?

Bankruptcy proceedings

For a Chapter 11 case to be finalised, the court must confirm a plan of reorganisation. Generally, such plan can either be proposed by the debtor-in-possession or by any party-in-interest such as a creditor or a Chapter 11 trustee, if one has been appointed. 11 U.S.C. § 1121. Only the debtor-in-possession can file a restructuring plan for the first 120 days after the date of the order for relief, ie the date the bankruptcy petition was filed. *Id.* The 120-day period can be reduced or extended by the court, but cannot exceed 180 days. *Id.* Once this exclusivity period has expired, any party in interest can propose a reorganisation plan. *Id.* The Bankruptcy Code requires the plan to provide specific information, such as the classes of claims, adequate means for implementation of the plan and the treatment of any class of claims or interests that is impaired under the plan. 11 U.S.C. § 1123.

The plan proponent must file a disclosure statement along with its proposed plan. 11 U.S.C. § 1125. The general purpose of a disclosure statement is to provide the creditors with information which is sufficient to allow the creditor to make a meaningful decision as to whether to support or resist the proposed plan. Before the plan proponent can solicit votes with regard to the approval of a proposed restructuring plan, the court must conduct a hearing on the disclosure statement. *Id.* (The one exception is the Chapter 11 prepackaged bankruptcy plans, ie a Chapter 11 bankruptcy plan where the plan has been negotiated prior to the filing of the bankruptcy petition. In such cases, the debtor-in-possession would have been allowed to solicit approval of the plan prior to the court approving the disclosure statement.) Once the disclosure statement has been approved, the debtor-in-possession must provide all creditors, the United States Trustee and all equity security holders with copies of:

- the plan;
- the disclosure statement
- a notice of the time within which acceptances and rejections of the proposed plan may be filed; and
- notice of the time fixed for filing objections and the hearing on the confirmation of the proposed plan.

Fed. R. Bankr. P. 3017(d).

The court may require the debtor-in-possession to serve additional information. *Id.* The debtor-in-possession must also provide creditors and equity security holders entitled to vote on the proposed plan a ballot conforming to the appropriate official form. *Id.*

Any party in interest may object to the confirmation of a proposed plan. 11 U.S.C. § 1128(b). The Bankruptcy Code requires the court, after notice, to hold a hearing on confirmation of a plan. 11 U.S.C. § 1128(a). At the confirmation hearing, regardless of whether an objection has been filed to the proposed plan, the court must determine whether it complies with the requirements of 11 U.S.C. § 1129(a) (plan approval with each class of creditors' consent) or 11 U.S.C. § 1129(b) (plan approval with at least one impaired class of creditors' consent).

If a class of impaired creditors rejects the plan, it may be possible to cram down the plan over their objection if the debtor can demonstrate to the court that the plan is fair and equitable with respect to the proposed treatment of their class of claims and will provide the indubitable equivalent of their claims. See 11 U.S.C. § 1129(b)(2). Examples of allowable cram down include:

- stretching out a secured creditor's loan beyond its original term and changing the interest rate to the current market rate;
- providing a secured creditor with substitute collateral as long as the debtor can establish that the value of the substitute collateral is the indubitable equivalent of the collateral being released; and
- giving back some, but not all, of the collateral (eg real estate or other collateral) to the secured creditor, crediting the value of such against the entire debt and restructuring the balance (this often prompts a valuation battle between the parties which the court will have to determine).

In addition to plans that provide for a restructuring of the debts, plans could alternatively provide for (i) a sale of the assets to a third party who is free and clear of existing liens, claims and encumbrances with the liens and claims to attach to the sale proceeds or (ii) an orderly liquidation, which may include the appointment of a liquidation trustee whose job is to administer the liquidation of available assets, pursue claims of the debtor which might result in monetary recovery for the creditors, and ultimately make pro rata distributions to the creditors. If the debtor can satisfy the court that speed is of the essence in order to preserve the value of assets and maximise the recovery for creditors, a sale of the assets very early in the case through section 363 of the Bankruptcy Code may be authorised. This process often includes an auction process designed to maximise the ultimate sale price. The Bankruptcy Code allows secured creditors to credit bid their claim at the auction.

Upon confirmation of a reorganisation plan, a business debtor obtains a discharge of most debts incurred prior to the confirmation of the reorganisation plan. 11 U.S.C. §1141(d)(1). Once the reorganisation plan has been confirmed, the business debtor is required to make the requisite payments to creditors and comply with the terms of the plan. The court retains the power to issue any other order necessary to administer the estate. Fed. R. Bankr. P. 3020(d). Furthermore, the debtor-in-possession and the Chapter 11 trustee are required to report the status of the plan consummation and apply for the entry of a final decree. 11 U.S.C. §§ 1106 and 1107. After the Chapter 11 bankruptcy estate has been fully administered, the court on its own motion or on the motion of an interested party must enter a final decree closing the case. 11 U.S.C. § 350; Fed. R. Bankr. P. 3022. However, there are times when the Chapter 11 case remains open for the duration of the proposed plan.

State and federal court receivership actions
The receivership generally continues until the court orders its termination. *Milo v Curtis*, 100 Ohio App. 3d 1 (1994). Some states, such as Texas, also impose limits on the length of time an entity can be in receivership. See Tex. Civ. Prac. & Rem. Code Ann. § 64.072. Usually, the receiver must submit an accounting to the court describing his or her activities as a receiver and any disposition of property. The court has full discretion to decide whether the receiver should be discharged.

1.13 Who are the necessary parties?

Bankruptcy proceedings
The only necessary party to voluntary bankruptcy proceedings is the debtor. In a case of involuntary bankruptcy proceedings, the necessary parties are three or more unsecured creditors or, if there are fewer than 12 unsecured creditors, one or more unsecured creditors. 11 U.S.C. §303. Once the bankruptcy petition has been filed, the debtor or the unsecured creditors must file a list of all creditors. 11 U.S.C. § 521.

State and federal court receivership actions
The necessary parties to a receivership action vary. If the receivership is sought as an ancillary remedy, then the necessary parties will be the parties named in the accompanying complaint. If the receivership is sought as a sole remedy, then the necessary parties will generally be the party seeking the appointment of a receiver and the party over whose assets a receivership is sought. A notice in this case may have to also be provided to all interested parties and creditors. Each state has different rules for the parties that must be included in a receivership action. As such, the respective state's law must be consulted prior to the filing of the petition or motion for appointment of a receiver.

2. POST-INSOLVENCY PROCEEDINGS

2.1 What is the objective of the proceedings?

See the answer to question 1.1 above.

2.2 Do all kinds of business entities qualify?

See 'Bankruptcy proceedings' in section 1.2 above.

2.3 What are the necessary approvals?

See 'Bankruptcy proceedings' in section 1.3 above.

2.4 Is it valid and binding to agree that such proceedings be a default/termination event?

Generally, courts will uphold a 'bankruptcy default clause' unless the contract at issue is an executory contract or an unexpired lease. See *In re General Growth Properties, Inc.*, 451 B.R. 323, 329 (S.D. NY 2011) (citing 11 U.S.C. § 365(e)(1)). Situations do exist, however, in which courts may decline to enforce such a clause, *'such as where the clause may impede a debtor's ability to enjoy a "fresh start"'*. *Id.* (citing *Riggs Nat'l Bank v Perry*, 729 F.2d 982, 984 (4th Cir. 1984)). Furthermore, and importantly, upon the filing of bankruptcy proceedings, an automatic stay is imposed which prevents creditors from taking any action to seize or otherwise impact the debtor's assets, thereby negating to a large degree any substantial benefit of the bankruptcy default clause.

2.5 What is the procedure?

See 'Bankruptcy proceedings' in section 1.4 above.

2.6 Please provide information about voluntary filings

See 'Bankruptcy proceedings' in section 1.4 above.

2.7 How are creditors' representatives chosen?

In a Chapter 7 proceeding, there is no creditors' committee. The initial Chapter 7 trustee is appointed through a random process from an approved list of qualified trustees. However, at the initial meeting of creditors, the creditors may elect a trustee of their choosing. In contrast, in Chapter 11 proceedings, where the debtor retains control of its operations, the US Trustee will appoint an unsecured creditors' committee, typically chosen from the creditors with the seven largest claims, who can fairly represent the different types of unsecured creditors in the case. See 11 U.S.C. § 1102(a)(b)(1). The committee is entitled to hire its own counsel, which is paid by the Chapter 11 debtor. See 11 U.S.C. 1103. The committee has the duty to fairly represent all the unsecured creditors in the case to ensure their rights and interests are being protected and to help maximise the distribution to be made to the unsecured creditors. In doing so, the committee, among other things, may:

(1) consult with the trustee or debtor in possession concerning the administration of the case;
(2) investigate the acts, conduct, assets, liabilities, and financial condition of the debtor, the operation of the debtor's business and the desirability of the continuance of such business, and any other matter relevant to the case or to the formulation of a plan;
(3) participate in the formulation of a plan, advise those represented by such committee of such committee's determinations as to any plan formulated, and collect and file with the court acceptances or rejections of a plan;
(4) request appointment of a trustee or examiner under section 1104 of [the Bankruptcy Code]; and

(5) perform such other services as are in the interest of those represented. 11 U.S.C. § 1103(a) & (c)(1)–(5).

2.8 Is there recourse against the opening judgment?

See the answer to question 1.5.

2.9 What are the roles and powers of committees?

See the answer to question 2.7. Also, the US Trustee has broad discretion on who is appointed to the creditors' committee in a Chapter 11 proceedings. The make-up of the committee is also dependent upon whether a given creditor is willing to serve on it; they are not required to do so. In certain circumstances, a committee may pursue claims of the debtor which the debtor refuses to pursue directly (often because the claim may be against an insider of the debtor). In addition, the committee can participate in all major aspects of the case and is often the direct reason for the treatment ultimately provided on unsecured creditors' claims.

2.10 What are the consequences of opening judgments for creditors?

See the answer to question 1.5.

2.11 What is the duration of the restructuring process?

See 'Bankruptcy proceedings' in section 1.9 above.

2.12 How do creditors vote?

As part of the plan process, the Bankruptcy Code sets out the particular details on plan voting. In general, if a creditor is not to receive any distribution under a plan, it will be automatically deemed to reject the plan and thus does not get to vote. Similarly situated creditors are classified in the same class. Each class gets to vote for or against the plan within its class. A class is deemed to accept the plan if two-thirds in amount and one-half in number vote to accept the plan. The debtor determines what classes are to be included in its plan, but the court will ultimately determine if the classification is fair and treats similarly situated creditors the same.

2.13 What are the rules on clawback/voidability?

In the United States, clawback claims are typically referred to as avoidance claims. These can include fraudulent transfer claims (for both actual and constructive fraud), preference claims (an objective test to recover payments made on antecedent debt within 90 days (one year for insiders) prior to the filing of the bankruptcy petition, subject to certain defences) and unauthorised payments made post-petition. The Bankruptcy Code includes its own fraudulent transfer rule, which has a two-year lookback from the date of the filing of the petition, but the Bankruptcy Code also incorporates applicable state law fraudulent transfer statutes, which may have varying statutes of limitation of four to six years after the transfer.

2.14 What are the rules on set-off/netting?

Under section 553 of the Bankruptcy Code, state law and contractual rights of set-off are preserved; however, the party seeking to effectuate the set-off must seek permission from the bankruptcy court or risk being held in contempt for violating the automatic stay. In addition, set-off is only allowed if both claims are either pre-petition or post-petition. In other words, the Bankruptcy Code does not allow a creditor to set-off a post-petition claim against a pre-petition claim. A typical example would be a bank which has secured loans to the debtor and also holds the debtor's operating accounts. Under its contracts, it would typically have the right to seize the funds in the account to set off against the debt owed. In order to do so, it must quickly seek bankruptcy court approval after the filing or risk the debtor either depleting the account or being held in contempt if the bank attempts to freeze the account to prevent the debtor from having access to the funds. With respect to financial swap-type agreements, there is a special carve-out which exempts these types of set-off from application of the automatic stay. The rules require more description than allowed here so we highly recommend you consult counsel before acting if this issue arises.

2.15 How is exit managed?

See 'Bankruptcy proceedings' in section 1.12 above.

2.16 Are 'prepackaged' plans, arrangements or agreements permissible?

Yes, although it is more typical for plans to be pre-negotiated when a Chapter 11 case is filed so as to expedite the process through the plan of reorganisation. A true 'prepackaged plan' is more difficult to obtain approval for because many actions are taken before the actual case is filed and it is not done under Bankruptcy Court supervision. It thus gives opponents more opportunity to raise objections to the process, thereby delaying or even defeating the prepackaged plan. For example, 11 U.S.C. § 1126 (b)(1)–(2) provides that a debtor may solicit and obtain pre-petition acceptance of a Chapter 11 plan of reorganisation as long as the solicitation of such acceptance complied with the controlling state law or, in the absence of such law, after the disclosure of adequate information as defined in 11 U.S.C. 1125(a). Obviously, the questions of compliance with the controlling state law and the disclosure of adequate information lend themselves to factual disputes with opponents of the prepackaged plan.

In contrast, a pre-negotiated plan will typically have the agreement of the major creditors as to the treatment to be provided to their claims and will require the debtor to file a plan that is consistent with the agreement. The advantage is that all of the actual plan process is under court supervision and thus, as a practical matter, it generally proceeds to approval much quicker than a pure pre-negotiated plan.

2.17 Is a public authority involved?

No public authority is involved in the sense that a specific agency of the government must approve the plan. If a government agency has a claim against the debtor, such as the taxing authorities, they can participate in the case much like other creditors who seek to protect their claims. However, there is no requirement that any government agency grant its approval as a precondition to a debtor filing for protection in a Chapter 11 or 7 proceedings.

There are some limitations on who can file for protection in bankruptcy. For example, generally financial institutions that come under the jurisdiction of the Federal Deposit Insurance Corporation are precluded from filing bankruptcy. Similarly, insurance companies cannot file for bankruptcy.

2.18 What is the treatment of claims arising after filing/admission?

As noted above, typically a bar date is set by which creditors must file their claim unless the debtor has scheduled the same as non-disputed, non-contingent and liquidated. If timely filed, the debtor may challenge the allowance or nature of the claim and the court will decide the merits of the objection. Similarly situated claims must be given similar treatment under the plan.

2.19 Are there ongoing contracts?

In the US, financial agreements are distinguished from executory contracts such as leases, supply agreements, or service agreements. As to financial agreements, the lender, if secured, has certain rights, such as the right to require adequate protection of its cash collateral (a typical example would be the proceeds generated from the collection of accounts receivable) before the debtor will be allowed to use such cash to pay for post-petition operating expenses. Adequate protection can come in many different forms, including monthly cash payments, granting of a super priority administrative claim or replacement secured liens, or any combination of these.

In contrast, a debtor may decide which executory contract is beneficial or harmful to its ongoing business operations and accordingly can either accept or reject the same. On real estate leases, the Bankruptcy Code provides a maximum cap on claims that can be asserted. This provides the debtor with an important tool to help it in the restructuring process so that it is not burdened with uneconomic contracts post-restructuring.

2.20 Are consolidated proceedings for members of a corporate family/group possible?

As an initial point, it is quite common for members of a corporate group to file separate bankruptcy actions but to obtain court permissions to 'jointly administer' the same under the main case, typically the parent's. This action retains the recognition of corporate separateness but provides substantial savings to the debtors, and indirectly to the creditors, in managing the restructuring, as often the family members all constitute various parts of an overall connected and intertwined business operation. There is no statutory right to consolidate the assets and liabilities of the family members, though there is a court-created principal of 'substantive consolidation' whereby the pooling of assets and liabilities could be allowed. However, the recent trend in cases indicates that it is becoming more difficult to meet the various tests that the courts have established as preconditions to allowing such pooling. It is still allowable to submit one plan for multiple debtors as long as the corporate separateness and corresponding treatment of creditors by debtor is retained.

2.21 What are the charges, fees and other costs?

There are filing fees imposed by statute for the filing of different types of bankruptcy cases, but these are generally not so oppressive as to prevent debtors from taking advantage of the bankruptcy process. For example, in 2014, the fee to file a Chapter 7 bankruptcy petition is $335.00 and the fee to file a Chapter 11 bankruptcy petition is $1,717.00.

3. LIABILITY ISSUES

3.1 What is the liability of managers/directors *vis-à-vis* creditors?

Typically, the officers and directors of a solvent corporation only owe duties to the company's shareholders. These duties typically include the duties of care, loyalty and good faith. See *Cede & Co. v Technicolor, Inc.*, 634 A.2d 345, 361 (Del. 1993). However, recent trends indicate that, when a company becomes insolvent, the company's officers and directors may owe these same fiduciary duties to the company's creditors. See *N. Am. Catholic Educ. Programming Found., Inc. v Gheewalla*, 930 A.2d 92, 99 (Del. 2007). In most states, officers and directors may seek protection under the 'business judgment rule', which presumes that officers or directors are attempting to act in the company's best interest unless a rational business purpose may not be attributed to the officer's or director's actions. See *In re Walt Disney Co. Derivative Litigation*, 907 A.2d 693, 747 (Del. Ch. 1963).

3.2 What is the liability of the lender?

If the bankruptcy debtor believes it possesses a claim against its lender for pre-bankruptcy actions of the lender, the debtor may list the claim as an asset on its initial bankruptcy schedules and pursue the claim against the lender in the bankruptcy action as 'core proceedings' under 28 U.S.C. § 157(b)(2).

Contact details

FOREWORD

Alessandro Varrenti
CBA Studio Legale e Tributario
Galleria San Carlo 6
20122 Milan
Via Flaminia 135
00196 Rome
Italy
T: +39 02 778061
F: +39 02 76002790
E: alessandro.varrenti@cbalex.com
W: www.cbalex.com

Lars Lindencrone Petersen & Ole Borch
Bech-Bruun
Langelinie Allé 35
2100 Copenhagen
Denmark
T: +45 72270000
F: +45 72270027
E: llp@bechbruun.com
obo@bechbruun.com
W: www.bechbruun.com

BELGIUM

Glenn Hansen
Laga
Berkenlaan 8A, 1831
Brussels Diegem
Belgium
T: +32 2 800 70 00
+32 2 800 70 22
F: +32 2 800 70 01
E: glhansen@laga.be
W: www.laga.be

CANADA

Justin R Fogarty, Jason Dutrizac & Pavle Masic
Justin R Fogarty Barrister & Solicitors
180 Bloor Street West, Suite 1000
Toronto, ON M5S 2V6
T: +1 416 840 8992
F: +1 416 369 7610
E: justin@fogartyllc.ca
jd@fogartyllc.ca
pavle.masic@fogartyllc.ca
W: www.justinrfogarty.com

CHINA

Victor Wang
AllBright Law Offices
28th Floor, Hong Kong Plaza
No. 283 Huai Hai Road (Mid)
Huangpu District
Shanghai 200021
P. R. China
T: +86 21 2326 1888
F: +86 21 2326 1999
E: victorwang@allbrightlaw.com
W: www.allbrightlaw.com

DENMARK

Lars Lindencrone Petersen & Ole Borch
Bech-Bruun
Langelinie Allé 35
2100 Copenhagen
Denmark
T: +45 72270000
F: +45 72270027
E: llp@bechbruun.com
obo@bechbruun.com
W: www.bechbruun.com

FINLAND

Pekka Jaatinen, Salla Suominen & Anna-Kaisa Remes
Castrén & Snellman Attorneys Ltd
Finland
T: +358 20 7765 765
F: +358 20 7765 001
E: pekka.jaatinen@castren.fi
salla.suominen@castren.fi
anna-kaisa.remes@castren.fi

W: www.castren.fi

FRANCE

Joanna Gumpelson
De Pardieu Brocas Maffei A.A.R.P.I.
57 Avenue d'Iéna – CS 11610
F-75773 Paris Cedex 16
France
T: +33 1 53 57 61 96
+33 1 53 57 71 71
F: +33 1 53 57 71 70
E: gumpelson@de-pardieu.com
W: www.de-pardieu.com

GERMANY

Florian Gantenberg, LLM
LADM Liesegang Aymans Decker
Mittelstaedt & Partner Rechtsanwälte
Wirtschaftsprüfer Steuerberater
Germany
T: +49 211 300490-25
F: +49 211 300490-22
E: f.gantenberg@ladm.com
W: www.ladm.com

HONG KONG

Philip Gilligan, Richard Hudson
& Tiffany Cheung
Deacons
5th Floor, Alexandra House, 18
Chater Road
Central
Hong Kong
T: +852 2825 9211
F: +852 2810 0431
E: philip.gilligan@deacons.com.hk
richard.hudson@deacons.com.hk
tiffany.cheung@deacons.com.hk
W: www.deacons.com.hk

ITALY

Alessandro Varrenti
CBA Studio Legale e Tributario
Galleria San Carlo 6
20122 Milan
Via Flaminia 135
00196 Rome
Italy
T: +39 02 778061
F: +39 02 76002790
E: alessandro.varrenti@cbalex.com
W: www.cbalex.com

MALTA

Nicolai Vella Falzon
Fenech & Fenech Advocates
198, Old Bakery Street
Valletta VLT1455
Malta
T: +356 21241232
F: +356 25990641
E: nicolai.vellafalzon@fenlex.com
W: www.fenechlaw.com

THE NETHERLANDS

Lucas Kortmann & Niels Pannevis
RESOR NV
Symphony Offices
Gustav Mahlerplein 27
1082 MS Amsterdam
The Netherlands
T: +31 20 570 9020
F: +31 20 570 9021
E: niels.pannevis@resor.nl
lucas.kortmann@resor.nl
W: www.resor.nl

NORWAY

Jon Skjørshammer
Advokatfirmaet Selmer DA
Tjuvholmen allé 1 N-0252
Oslo
Norway
T: +47 23 11 65 00
F: +47 23 11 65 01
E: j.skjorshammer@selmer.no
W: www.selmer.no

POLAND

Dr Marcin Olechowski &
Borys D Sawicki
Sołtysiński Kawecki & Szlęzak
ul. Jasna 26
00-054 Warsaw

Poland
T: +48 22 608 7062
+48 22 608 7369
F: +48 22 608 7070
E: marcin.olechowski@skslegal.pl
borys.sawicki@skslegal.pl
W: www.skslegal.pl

PORTUGAL

Mafalda Barreto & Carlos Soares
Gómez-Acebo & Pombo
Avenida Duque d'Avila
nº 6, 6º
Lisbon
Portugal
T: +351 213 408 600
F: +351 213 408 608
E: mbarreto@gomezacebo-pombo.com
csoares@gomezacebo-pombo.com
W: www.gomezacebo-pombo.com

ROMANIA

Bogdan Bibicu
Kinstellar
8 – 10 Nicolae Iorga
010434 Bucharest
Romania
T: +40 21 307 1664
E: bogdan.bibicu@kinstellar.com
W: www.kinstellar.com

SINGAPORE

Sim Kwan Kiat
Rajah & Tann Singapore LLP
9 Battery Road
#25-01 Straits Trading Building
Singapore 049910
Republic of Singapore
T: +65 6535 3600
F: +65 6225 9630
E: kwan.kiat.sim@rajahtann.com
W: www.rajahtannasia.com

SPAIN

Fermín Garbayo Renouard & Julio Pernas Ramírez
Gómez-Acebo & Pombo
Abogados, S. L. P.
Castellana, 216
28046 Madrid
Spain
T: +34 91 582 91 00
F: +34 91 582 91 14
E: fgarbayo@gomezacebo-pombo.com
jpernas@gomezacebo-pombo.com
W: www.gomezacebo-pombo.com

SWEDEN

Odd Swarting, Mathias Winge & Nina Baecklund
Setterwalls
Arsenalsgatan 6
Stockholm
Sweden
T: +46 8 598 890 00
F: +46 8 598 890 90
E: odd.swarting@setterwalls.se
mathias.winge@setterwalls.se
nina.baecklund@setterwalls.se
W: www.setterwalls.se

TURKEY

Gokben Erdem Dirican & Erdem Atilla
Pekin & Pekin
Lamartine Cad. No:10, Taksim
Beyoglu, Istanbul
Turkey 34437
T: +90 212 313 35 00
F: +90 212 313 35 35
E: gerdem@pekin-pekin.com
eatilla@pekin-pekin.com
W: www.pekin-pekin.com

UNITED KINGDOM

Jat Bains, Simon Beale & Paul Keddie
Macfarlanes LLP
20 Cursitor Street
London EC4A 1LT
UK
T: +442078319222

F: +442078319607
E: jatinder.bains@macfarlanes.com
simon.beale@macfarlanes.com
paul.keddie@macfarlanes.com
W: www.macfarlanes.com

UNITED STATES

J William Boone, Michael A Dunn &
Doroteya N Wozniak
James-Bates-Brannan-Groover-LLP
3399 Peachtree Rd NE, Suite 1700
Atlanta, GA 30326
USA
T: +4048442766
F: +4049976021
E: bboone@jamesbatesllp.com
mdunn@jamesbatesllp.com
dwozniak@jamesbatesllp.com
W: www.jamesbatesllp.com